THE

William Saroyan

READER

PREFACE BY *Aram Saroyan*

BARRICADE BOOKS INC.

FORT LEE, NEW JERSEY

Published by Barricade Books Inc.
185 Bridge Plaza North
Suite 308A
Fort Lee, New Jersey 07024
www.barricadebooks.com

Printed in Canada.

Library of Congress Cataloging-in-Publication Data

Saroyan, William, 1908-1981
  [Selections. 1994]
  The William Saroyan reader / preface by Aram Saroyan.
      p.   cm.
  ISBN 1-56980-019-7: $15.95
PS3537.A826A6 1994
818'.5209—dc20   94-25439
                                          CIP

10 9 8 7 6 5 4 3 2

could no more live without hope than he could without the earth underfoot.

Life rules the world, impersonal and free life. The anonymous living tell their story every day, with the help of professional or amateur writers, but the greatest story-teller of all is time and change, or death. But death is not our doom and not our enemy. Next to birth it is our best gift, and next to truth it is our best friend.

I am back in San Francisco on the occasion of the twentieth anniversary of the publication of my first book—the beginning of my life as a writer, as a force in the life of my time, as a voting representative of my anonymous self and of any and all others whose aspirations parallel my own—to live creatively, to live honorably, to hurt no one insofar as possible, to enjoy mortality, to fear neither death nor immortality, to cherish fools and failures even more than wise men and saints since there are more of them, to believe, to hope, to work, and to do these things with humor.

To say yes, and not to say no.

What advice have I for the potential writer?

I have none, for anybody is a potential writer, and the writer who *is* a writer needs no advice and seeks none.

What about courses in writing in colleges and universities?

Useless, they are entirely useless.

The writer is a spiritual anarchist, as in the depth of his soul every man is. He is discontented with everything and everybody. The writer is everybody's best friend and only true enemy—the good and great enemy. He neither walks with the multitude nor cheers with them. The writer who is a writer is a rebel who never stops. He does not conform for the simple reason that there is nothing yet worth conforming to. When there is something half worth conforming to he will not conform to that, either, or half conform to it. He won't even rest or sleep as other people rest and sleep. When he's dead he'll probably be dead as others are dead, but while he is alive he is alive as no one else is, not even another writer. The writer who is a writer is also a fool. He is the easiest man in the world to belittle, ridicule, dismiss, and scorn: and that also is precisely as it should be. He is also mad, measurably so, but saner than all others, with the best sanity, the only sanity worth bothering about—the living, creative, vulnerable, valorous, unintimidated, and arrogant sanity of a free man.

I am a writer who is a writer, as I have been for twenty years, and expect to be for twenty more.

I am here to stay, and so is everybody else. No explosive is going to be employed by anybody on anybody. Knowing this, believing this, the writer who is a writer makes plans to watch his health casually, and to write his writing with more and more purposeful intelligence, humor, and love.

I am proud of my twenty years, undecorated as they may be. I am proud to be a writer, the writer I am, and I don't care what anybody else is proud of.

CONTENTS

CONTENTS

CONTENTS

PREFACE

ALL my life I've been mistakenly identified with the eponymous central character of my father's *My Name Is Aram*, which was recently reissued in a Modern Classics edition commemorating the fiftieth anniversary of the book's publication. To begin with, I'm four years younger than the original edition. Then too, it's a book in which the writer looks back at a child still earlier in time, recalling in an elegiac mood the Armenian immigrant community in Fresno circa World War I.

As I explain to readers who believe they've happened on the real life model for Aram, the book is about my *father's* childhood. And yet that's not quite the case either. Here is the opening of the celebrated first story, "The Summer of the Beautiful White Horse":

> *One day back there in the good old days when I was nine and the world was full of every imaginable kind of magnificence, and life was still a delightful and mysterious dream, my cousin Mourad, who was considered crazy by everybody who knew him except me, came to my house at four in the morning and woke me up by tapping on the window of my room.*
>
> *Aram, he said.*
>
> *I jumped out of bed and looked out the window.*
>
> *I couldn't believe what I saw.*
>
> *It wasn't morning yet, but it was summer and with daybreak not many minutes around the corner of the world it was light enough for me to know I wasn't dreaming.*
>
> *My cousin Mourad was sitting on a beautiful white horse.*

If there is another single page of prose that better evokes the wonder and mystery of childhood, I would love to know about it. What makes the book even more remarkable—and *My Name Is Aram* lives up to the promise of its opening—is the fact that its author spent the years from before he was three until after his eighth birthday in the Fred Finch Orphanage in Oakland, California.

This was a consequence of the death of my father's Armenian immigrant father, Armenak Saroyan, at 37 in 1911. A gentle, handsome man who wrote poetry, Armenak was an ordained minister in the Armenian church. But he found no parish in Fresno that would sustain him and his family, and discovering himself a cast-off in the new world, he became a chicken farmer—and not long afterwards, evidently broken in spirit, died of peritonitis.

He left his wife, Takoohi, with four children—the youngest, my father, was the only one who had been born in America—and no means of support. She put her children into the orphanage and took work as a domestic. Five years later, with the help of her younger brother, she was able to take her children back from the orphanage and bring them to a little home in Fresno.

The name of Takoohi's younger brother was Aram. Uncle Aram, as he was widely known, was for my father a source of endless delight and inspiration, and, equally, exasperation. A loud, importunate, powerful man, he had arrived in the new world at twelve, young enough to learn the ropes without an already developed "old world" sensibility to hamper him, as it would seem to have hampered Armenak. Uncle Aram became a criminal lawyer, famous in Fresno for emotional courtroom summaries that sometimes won cases for the guilty.

When Aram's nephew Willie, back from the orphanage and selling papers after school to help out at home, expressed at a relatively early age an interest in writing, the lawyer was loudly disdainful. When at twenty my father quit his job as the youngest manager of a Postal Telegraph office in the country to devote his full time to writing, Uncle Aram tried to throw him bodily out of his own house until Takoohi stopped him.

In 1934, when the publication of his first book, *The Daring Young Man on the Flying Trapeze and Other Stories*, made the twenty-six year old William Saroyan an international literary sensation, very likely no one was more astonished than Uncle Aram, suddenly eclipsed by his lowly nephew, who overnight had become the pride not only of his immediate family, but of the entire Armenian race. Interviewed at the time about his newly famous relative, Aram remarked impatiently: "Willie? Willie was *nervous*"—a response my father would remember with amusement years afterward.

How had the young writer, who had dropped out of school before finishing the eighth grade, achieved so swift and unlikely an ascent? In these first stories he found in the national disaster of the Depression a dark cheer and camaraderie, a bittersweet poetry that seemed to catch the national psyche by surprise.

By making light of what had up to then held everyone in gloomy thrall, my father became for the 1930s a figure comparable to what F. Scott Fitzgerald had been for the 1920s, the literary equivalent of a movie star. "I hadn't had a haircut in forty days and forty nights, and I was beginning to look like several violinists out of work," begins one story with characteristic panache. Six years and six more story collections later came *My Name Is Aram* in which he did more or less the same thing for the childhood of a poor immigrant Armenian boy in Fresno. He made a prose bouquet of youth and comedy and sweet melancholy out of what had been more grim and desolate than any reader might have guessed.

And the name on the cover of the book was Aram, a foreign name that now became famous and beloved in America not because of Uncle Aram, whose celebrity was a local thing, but because of the once-disdained literary gift of his nephew Willie. Indeed, the year *My Name Is Aram* was published, 1940, was also the year my father at thirty-two won a Pulitzer Prize for his play "The Time of Your Life"—and turned town the award along with its $1,000 honorarium. "Commerce has no business patronizing art," his wire to the award committee stated with chilly economy.

For me, it's hard not to see in this celebrated act a symbolic nose-thumbing by the young artist at the whole American officialdom that hadn't cared whether he was alive several years earlier, and more personally at his surrogate father, Uncle Aram. The orphaned son of the failed poet-preacher had made good on a bet Armenak had lost, and when his chips came in he didn't need the establishment's pat on the back or the cheek that came with it. In turning down the Pulitzer Prize he made evidence in life of what he seemed at the time determined not to show in his art, his darker side.

In 1943 came "The Human Comedy," his most popular book, which in now identifiably "Saroyanesque" fashion rendered the home-front experience during World War II more heart-warming than the writer himself would later feel entirely comfortable with. The same year Saroyan married a beautiful and witty eighteen-year-old New York debutante named Carol Marcus. At the time of their marriage he was unaware his bride's early background was similar to his own, if not quite a bit worse. An illegitimate child who had never known her father, Carol was boarded in a series of foster homes until her young and beautiful mother made a fortunate marriage and brought her daughter—now eight years old, the same age Saroyan got out of the orphanage—home to Park Avenue.

The marriage of Bill and Carol was a disaster. It was almost as if Saroyan married a human incarnation of one of his own stories in which enchantment held sway over unspoken tragedy. The two married and divorced each other twice in eight years, after which Saroyan, embittered and with the years of his greatest fame behind him, went on for the rest of his days alone. He died of cancer in 1981 at 72.

As I grew up with the name in the title of his famous story collection, I grappled with a complex legacy of poetry and bitter personal failure, of public legend and private reality not easy to sort out. Although he was known for his celebrations of close-knit family life, these had been written before his own efforts at marriage had failed. The man I came to know could be both forceful and warm, but also cutting and insistently remote. When he died he left a will that effectively disinherited both my sister Lucy and me, as well as his three grandchildren, in its own terms perpetuating the cycle, orphaning two succeeding generations as he had been orphaned. Even so in his hospital room not long before he died, my seven-year-old daughter Cream and I had a more healing visit with him than I would have dared to imagine.

At the end, the room at the Veterans Administration hospital in Fresno, the poet marked irrevocably by the death of his father was alive and well. In his final days, confined to his bed, my father seemed very nearly to be *playing* with the biggest of all the riddles. "I'm letting go," he said at one point during our visit. "Well, somebody said, maybe that's not the right thing to do. And I said—maybe it isn't. I don't know. I'm grappling with the mystery of . . .what . . . *is*." His eyes that day were the large, wide-open eyes of a child, a boy like Aram who after a whole lifetime was still looking with wonder at something as profound and astonishing as a white horse.

—Aram Saroyan

WHY I WRITE

IT is a quarter of a century, almost, since my first book was published, but as I began to write when I was nine, I have been writing for forty years: that is to say, I have lived in a special way for forty years—the way that takes hold of a man who is determined to understand the meaning of his own life, and to be prepared to write about it.

But I think it goes even farther back than forty years. I think I began to live in my own special way when I became aware that I had memory. That happened before I was three. I also had a memory that went back to a time before I was *two*, but it was an isolated one. At that age I wasn't given to remembering *everything*, or rather I hadn't yet noticed that it had come to pass that I remembered.

In the past were some of the best things I had, several of them gone: my father, for instance, who had died before I was three.

My first memory, the one that went back to a time when I was not yet two, was of my father getting up onto a wagon, sitting beside my mother, and making a sound that told the horse to go. My two sisters and my brother and I sat in the back of the wagon as it moved slowly down a dusty road between vineyards on a hot afternoon in the summertime. I remembered sensing sorrow and feeling *with*— with mine, my people—a father, a mother, two sisters, a brother, our horse, our wagon, our pots and pans and books. The rest is lost in the sleep that soon carried me away. The next thing I knew my father was gone, which I didn't understand.

I was fascinated by having memory, and troubled by the sorrow of it. I refused to accept the theory that things end, including people, including my father. I refused to believe that my father was dead. (In the sense that every man *is* his father, I wasn't much mistaken.)

All the same, I felt impelled from the time I knew I had memory to do something about the past, about endings, about human death.

My first impulse was simple. I wanted to cause the impossible to happen, because if I was able to do that, I knew I would be able to cause *anything* to happen. Thus, death would not be death, if anybody wanted it not to be.

I found two large empty cans. One I filled with water. The empty can I placed two feet from the full can. I asked myself to cause the water in the full can to pass into the empty can, by itself, because I wanted it to.

The experiment failed. I had begun with the maximum, I had failed, and so I began to consider what might be the next best.

For a long time there didn't appear to be *any* next best at all. It was a matter of all or nothing, or at any rate the equivalent of nothing: continuous *gradual* loss, and finally total loss, or death.

What could a man do about this? Wait? That didn't seem to be enough.

Why should I be troubled by memory at all if all memory told me was that things change, fail, decline, end, and die? I didn't want good things to do that, and I didn't think they should. How could I seize a good thing when I saw it and halt its decline and death? As far as people were concerned, there just didn't seem to be *any* way.

And so I came to accept the theory that as far as I knew, as far as *anybody* knew, as far as there appeared to be any order to the action of things at all, the end of the order was invariably and inevitably decline, disappearance, and death.

And yet the world was full of people all the time. And the earth, the sea, and the sky were full of all manner of other living things: plants, animals, fish, birds.

Thus, something *did* stay, something *was* constant, or appeared to be. It was the *kind* that stayed. *One* of a kind couldn't stay, and couldn't apparently be made to. I myself was one of a kind, and everybody I knew and loved was one of a kind, and so what about us? What could I do about our impermanence?

How could I halt this action? How had other men halted it?

I learned that they never had halted it. They had only pretended to.

They had done this by means of art, or the putting of limits upon the limitless, and thereby holding something fast and making it seem constant, indestructible, unstoppable, unkillable, deathless.

A great painter painted his wife, his son, his daughter, and himself, and then one by one they all moved along and died. But the painting remained. A sculptor did the same thing with stone, a composer with musical sounds, and a writer with words.

Therefore, as the next best thing, art in one form or another would have to be the way of my life, but which form of art?

Before I was eight I didn't think it could possibly be writing, for the simple reason that I couldn't read, let alone write, and everybody else I knew could do both. At last, though, I got the hang of reading and writing, and I felt (if I didn't think), "This is for me."

It had taken me so long to learn to write that I considered being able to write the greatest thing that could happen to anybody.

If I wrote something, it *was* written, it was itself, and it might continue to be itself forever, or for what passes as forever.

Thus, I could halt the action of things, after all, and at the same time be prepared to learn new things, to achieve new forms of halting, or art.

That is roughly how and why I became a writer.

In short, I began to write in order to get even on death.

I have continued to write for many reasons.

A long time ago I said I write because it is the only way I am willing to survive.

Mainly, though, I write because I want to.

William Saroyan

MALIBU, CALIFORNIA
January 11, 1958

To the writers who impelled me to write: Jack London, Guy de Maupassant, Charles Dickens, Anton Tchekhov, Mark Twain, August Strindberg, Maxim Gorky, Ambrose Bierce, Leo Tolstoy, Molière, George Bernard Shaw, Walt Whitman, Henri Fréderic Amiel, Henrik Ibsen, Sherwood Anderson, and Solomon, the son of David, who wrote *The Book of Ecclesiastes.*

THE *William Saroyan* READER

TRACY'S TIGER

CHAPTER 1

Thomas Tracy had a tiger.

It was actually a black panther, but that's no matter, because he *thought* of it as a tiger.

It had white teeth.

This is how he came to get his tiger:

When he was three and went by the sound of things somebody said *tiger!* Whatever a *tiger!* was, Tracy wanted his own.

One day he was walking in town with his father when he saw something in the window of a fish restaurant.

"Buy me that tiger," he said.

"That's a lobster," his father said.

"I don't want it, then," Tracy said.

Several years later Tracy visited the zoo with his mother and saw a real tiger in a cage. It was something like the tiger of the word, but it wasn't *his* tiger.

For years Tracy saw pictures of all kinds of animals in dictionaries, paintings, encyclopaedias, and movies. Among these animals stalked many black panthers, but not once did Tracy think of one of them as his own tiger.

One day, however, Tracy was at the zoo alone, fifteen years of age, smoking a cigarette and leering at girls, when all of a sudden he came face to face with his tiger.

It was a sleeping black panther that instantly awoke, raised its head, stared straight at Tracy, got to its feet, hummed the way black panthers do, saying something that sounded like *Eyeej*, walked to the edge of the cage, stood for a moment looking at Tracy, then wandered back to the platform on which it had been sleeping. There it plopped down again and began to stare far out into space, as many miles and years out into space as there are miles and years in space.

Tracy in turn stood staring at the black panther. He stared five

3

minutes, chucked away his cigarette, cleared his throat, spat, and walked out of the zoo.

"That's my tiger," he said.

He never went back to the zoo to have another look at his tiger because he didn't need to. He'd got it. He'd got it whole in the five minutes he'd watched it staring into infinity with a tiger's terrible resignation and pride.

CHAPTER 2

When he was twenty-one Tracy and his tiger went to New York, where Tracy took a job at Otto Seyfang's, a coffee importer's on Warren Street in Washington Market. Most of the other businesses of that area were produce houses, so that besides having free coffee to drink—in the Tasting Department—Tracy had free fruit and vegetables to eat.

The pay for the unskilled work Tracy did was poor, but the work was good and hard. It was not easy at first for Tracy to throw a sack of coffee beans weighing a hundred pounds over his shoulder and walk fifty yards with it, but after a week it was nothing at all, and even the tiger marvelled at the ease with which Tracy threw the stuff around.

One day Tracy went to his immediate superior, a man named Valora, to discuss his future.

"I want to be a taster," Tracy said.

"Who ast you?" Valora said.

"Who ast me *what?*"

"Who ast you to be a taster?"

"Nobody."

"What do you know about tasting?" Valora said.

"I *like* coffee," Tracy said.

"What do you know about tasting?" Valora said again.

"I've done a little in the Tasting Department."

"You had coffee and doughnuts in the Tasting Department, the same as all the others who ain't professional tasters," Valora said.

"When the coffee was good I knew it," Tracy said. "When it was bad I knew it."

"How did you know?"

"By tasting."

"We got three tasters—Nimmo, Peberdy, and Ringert," Valora said. "They been with Otto Seyfang's twenty-five, thirty-five, forty-one years. How long you been with the firm?"

"Two weeks."

"You want to be a taster?"

"Yes, sir."

"You want to get to the top of the ladder in two weeks?"

"Yes, sir."

"You don't want to wait your turn?"

"No, sir."

At this moment Otto Seyfang himself came into Valora's office. Valora jumped up from his chair, but Otto Seyfang, a man of seventy, wouldn't have it—the jumping up, that is—and he said, "Sit down, Valora! Go ahead!"

"Go ahead?" Valora said.

"Now, go ahead where I interrupted and don't act dumb," Otto Seyfang said.

"We was talking about this new man applying for a job as taster."

"Go ahead."

"He's been here two weeks, and he wants to be a taster."

"Go ahead and talk about it," Otto Seyfang said.

"Yes, sir," Valora said. He turned to Tracy. "After only two weeks," he said, "you want a job that Nimmo, Peberdy, and Ringert didn't get until they was with the firm twenty, twenty-five, thirty years? Is that right?"

"Yes, sir," Tracy said.

"You want to come in here to Otto Seyfang's just like that and get the best job?"

"Yes, sir."

"You know all about coffee tasting?"

"Yes, sir."

"What's good coffee taste like?"

"Coffee."

"What's the *best* coffee taste like?"

"Good coffee."

"What's the difference between *good* coffee and the *best* coffee?"

"Advertising," Tracy said.

Valora turned to Otto Seyfang as much as to say, "What are you

going to do with a wise guy like this from out of town?" But Otto
Seyfang didn't encourage Valora's attitude. He just waited for Valora
to go on.

"They ain't no opening in the Tasting Department," Valora said.

"When *will* there be an opening?" Tracy said.

"Just as soon as Nimmo dies," Valora said. "But there are thirty-
nine others at Otto Seyfang's who are ahead of you for the job."

"Nimmo won't die for some time," Tracy said.

"I'll tell him to hurry," Valora said.

"I don't want Nimmo to hurry."

"But you want his job?"

"No, sir," Tracy said. "I want *four* tasters in the Tasting Department."

"*You* want to be the fourth?" Valora said. "Not Shively, who's
next in line?"

"What line?"

"The coffee tasters' line," Valora said. "You want to step in ahead
of Shively?"

"I don't want to step in ahead of him," Tracy said. "I want to step
over to the side into the Tasting Department, because I *can* taste
coffee, and I know when it's good."

"You do?"

"Yes, sir."

"Where you from?" Valora said.

"San Francisco," Tracy said.

"Why don't you go back to San Francisco?"

Valora turned to Otto Seyfang.

"That's about it, isn't it, sir?" he said.

Valora didn't know, and neither did Otto Seyfang, that it was
Tracy's tiger that had done the talking. They thought it had been
Tracy himself.

At first Otto Seyfang believed he might do something surprising
that he had seen happen in a stage play once. Surprising, that is, to
Valora, and perhaps even to Tracy. But after a while he decided he
wasn't in any stage play, he was in his coffee importing house and
open for business, not art. He had believed he would hire a fourth
coffee taster at that, Tracy himself, because Tracy had had guts
enough to go up to Valora and tell him the truth: that he, Tracy,
knew good coffee when he, Tracy, tasted it, and on top of that to
make known that he, Tracy, had ideas in his head. Advertising, for

instance. (What a joke art is when you get right down to it, Otto Seyfang thought. Just because a boy from California comes back with quick answers to an imbecile's questions, in art you're supposed to give the boy what he asks for, and make something of him. But what was the boy *actually?* Was he a coffee man? Did he live and breathe coffee? No. He was a smart aleck.)

Thus, Otto Seyfang decided against doing anything surprising.

"What's your work?" Otto Seyfang said to Tracy.

"I'm a song writer," Tracy said.

"Ah! What's your work at *Otto Seyfang's?*" the old man said. "Do you know who I am?"

"No, sir," Tracy said. "Who are you?"

"Otto Seyfang."

"Do you know who I am?" Tracy said.

"Who are you?"

"Thomas Tracy."

(*I've got this company,* Otto Seyfang thought. *I've had it forty-five years. What have you got?*)

(*I've got a tiger,* Tracy thought in reply to Otto Seyfang's thought.)

They went on talking, but first these thoughts were neatly exchanged.

"What's your work at Otto Seyfang's?" the old man said.

"I throw and carry the sacks," Tracy said.

"Do you want to keep your job?" Otto Seyfang said.

Tracy knew what the tiger was going to say and he was eagerly waiting for the tiger to say it when he discovered that the tiger had fallen asleep from boredom.

Tracy soon heard himself say, "Yes, sir, I want to keep my job."

"Then get the hell back to your work," Otto Seyfang said. "And if you ever waste Valora's time again by coming in here to talk nonsense, I'll fire you. Valora knows how to waste his own time without any help from you. Don't you, Valora?"

"Yes, sir," Valora said.

Tracy went back to his work, leaving the tiger fast asleep under Valora's desk.

When the tiger woke up and went back to Tracy, Tracy wouldn't speak to it.

"Eyeej," the tiger said in the hope of breaking the ice.

"Eyeej my foot," Tracy said. "That was a nice trick to play on a pal. I thought you were going to kick it around. I didn't think you were going to fall asleep. When he said do you want to keep your job, I thought you were going to say something sensible. You call yourself a tiger?"

"Moyl," the tiger murmured.

"Moyl," Tracy said. "Go away."

Tracy threw the sacks in angry silence the rest of the day, for never before had the tiger fallen asleep at a time so appropriate for bad manners, and Tracy didn't like it. He was deeply troubled about the probability of a dubious strain in the tiger's lineage.

After work that day Tracy walked with Nimmo to the subway. Nimmo was nervous all the way there from having tasted coffee all day. Nimmo was almost as old as Otto Seyfang himself and Nimmo had no tiger, had in fact no idea there *were* tigers to be had. All Nimmo was doing was standing in Shively's way. And Shively was standing in the way of the thirty-eight others at Otto Seyfang's.

Well, Tracy had gone to work, but at the same time he had also written three lines to a song. He would go on working at Otto Seyfang's for a while, waiting for the tiger to snap out of it, but he would stand in nobody's way and in nobody's line.

When Tracy got off the subway and went up to Broadway he decided to have a cup of coffee, and he *had* a cup. He was an expert taster, and knew it. He just didn't want to wait any thirty-five years to prove it. He drank a second cup, then a third, tasting expertly.

CHAPTER 3

The eye of Tracy's tiger now and then wandered on the chance that it might behold a young lady tiger with appropriate manners for whatever might come of their seeing of one another, but almost never, when the tiger looked, did it see a young lady tiger. It was young lady alley cats. On the few occasions when it did see a young lady tiger Tracy's tiger was going somewhere in a hurry and had time enough only to turn, still moving ahead, to look again. This seemed a sad state of affairs, so the tiger said so.

"Lune," it said.

"What do you mean?" Tracy said.

"Alune."

"I don't get it."

"Ah lune."

"What's that?"

"Lunalune."

"Doesn't mean anything."

"Ah lunalune," the tiger said patiently.

"Speak English if you want to say something," Tracy said.

"La," the tiger said.

"That's almost French," Tracy said. "Speak English. You know I don't know French."

"Sola."

"Solar?"

"So," the tiger said.

"Don't *shorten* the words," Tracy said, "lengthen them, so I can figure out what you're trying to say."

"S," the tiger said.

"You can talk better than that," Tracy said. "Talk or shut up."

The tiger shut up.

Tracy considered what the tiger *had* said, and then suddenly it came to him.

This happened during the lunch hour. Tracy was standing in the sunlight on the steps of the entrance to Otto Seyfang's listening to Nimmo, Peberdy, and Ringert talking about the eminence they had achieved in the coffee world through faithful tasting. Every now and then Tracy tried to get a word in edgewise about the song he was writing, but he never quite made it.

He was trying to figure out what the tiger had said when a girl in a tight-fitting yellow knit dress came walking down Warren Street. She had a great deal of black hair combed straight down. There was so much of it that it seemed to be a mane. It shined with life and crackled with electricity. The muscles of Tracy's tiger became taut, its slim head pushed forward toward the girl, its tail shot straight out, rigid except for the almost imperceptible vibrating of it, and the tiger hummed low and violently, saying, "Eyeej."

The professional coffee tasters hearing the hum turned to Tracy in astonishment, for never before had they heard such an extraordinary sound.

"Oh," Tracy said to the tiger. "I get it."

"Eyeej," the tiger replied, as if in pain, its head moving out still farther, while Tracy's own eyes *dived* into the young lady's. The hum and the diving happened at the same time. The girl heard the hum, received the dive, almost stopped, almost smiled, pushed herself tighter against the yellow knit dress, and then danced on, the tiger moaning softly.

"Is that what they say in California?" Nimmo said.

"Eyeej," Tracy said.

"Say it again," Peberdy said.

Tracy, watching the girl go, watching the tiger lope after her, said it again.

"Hear that, Ringert?" Peberdy said. "That's what they say in California when they see a beauty."

"Don't worry," Ringert said. "I heard it."

"You *heard* it," Nimmo said, "but can you *do* it?"

"Of course I can't do it," Ringert said, "but neither can either of you old coffee tasters."

The coffee tasters agreed with regret that they could not do it, and then everybody went back to work, Tracy's tiger loping after Tracy to the piled sacks of coffee at the far end of the store room overlooking the alley. Tracy threw the sacks around all afternoon as if they were bean bags.

"Whoever she is," he said to the tiger, "she works around here somewhere. I'll see her tomorrow during the lunch hour, and the next day, too. The day after that I'll ask her to lunch."

Tracy talked to the tiger all afternoon, but all the tiger did was hum. Every now and then the other sack-throwers heard the hum. They were all young men, and they wanted to imitate the hum, but it was inimitable. You had to have a tiger. One of them, a man named Kalany, came near doing it, and boldly remarked to Tracy that anything anybody from California could do, *he* could do, being from Texas.

"Tomorrow, the next day, the day after," Tracy said to the tiger. "Then I'll ask her to lunch."

Sure enough, the schedule was met.

There she was across the table from Tracy at the O.K. Café, both of them eating, the tiger stalking around the table, trying not to hum or gulp.

"My name's Tom Tracy," Tracy said.

"I know," the girl said. "You told me."

"I forgot."

"I know. You told me three times. You mean Thomas of course, not Tom, don't you?"

"Yes," Tracy said. "Thomas Tracy. That's my name. That's all it is. I mean, that's just my name. A man's name isn't all there is to a man."

"Any middle name?" the girl said.

"No," Tracy said. "Just Thomas Tracy. Tom for short, if you want to shorten it."

"I don't want to," the girl said.

"No?" Tracy said, for this remark had great meaning for him. He was thrilled by the hope of the wonderful nature of this meaning. He was too thrilled to notice that the tiger was staring at something with so much excitement that its whole body was vibrating. He looked to see what it was that the tiger was staring at, and he saw that it was a young lady tiger.

"No?" Tracy said again.

"Yes," the girl said. "I like the name Thomas Tracy just as it is. Aren't you going to ask me *my* name?"

"What is it?" Tracy asked in a hushed voice.

"Laura Luthy," the girl said.

"Oh," Tracy moaned. "Oh, Laura Luthy."

"Do you like it?" Laura Luthy said.

"Do I *like* it?" Tracy said. "Oh, Laura, Laura Luthy."

The tigers chased around Laura Luthy and Thomas Tracy while they had lunch and they chased around them when they got up after lunch and walked to the cashier's where Tracy plunked down eighty-five cents for both lunches.

What did he care about money?

In the street Tracy took Laura's arm and walked past Otto Seyfang's, past Nimmo, Peberdy, and Ringert, standing out front. The two tigers walked sedately side by side. Tracy walked Laura to the office where she worked as a stenographer, two blocks down Warren Street near the docks.

"Tomorrow?" he said, not knowing what he meant but hoping *she* did.

"Yes," Laura said.

Tracy's tiger hummed. Laura's tiger half-smiled, hung its head, then turned away.

Tracy walked back to Otto Seyfang's, to the coffee tasters standing out front.

"Tracy," Nimmo said. "I hope I live long enough to see how this is going to turn out."

"You will," Tracy said. He spoke with anger and sincerity. "You'll live, Nimmo, because you've *got* to."

The tiger was now standing in the middle of the sidewalk staring into space.

On his way home after work that day Tracy found the tiger still standing in the middle of the sidewalk, and stood there himself, getting in the way of the after-work human traffic. He stood there beside the tiger a long time, then turned and began to walk to the subway, the tiger reluctantly following him.

CHAPTER 4

Laura Luthy lived in Far Rockaway. Saturdays and Sundays she stayed home with her mother.

Laura's mother, if anything, was more beautiful than Laura herself, so that there was a continuous if delicate rivalry in them in the mirrors around the house, and in their remarks about moving-picture actors, stage actors, men of the neighbourhood, and men of the church. (The church was across the street, so that they were able to *see* who the men were. Saturdays and Sundays they watched together, but the rest of the time Laura's mother watched alone, or, being *free* to do so, didn't bother to do so. Now and then, though, it just happened that she saw a fine upright man enter the church late in the afternoon to confess, or collect a bill.)

This rivalry between mother and daughter enjoyed vigorous life in spite of the fact that Oliver Luthy, Laura's father, came home every night from work in Manhattan, and for twenty-four years had slept in the same bed with Mrs. Luthy, whose first name was Viola.

Mr. Luthy was in accounting. He had been in accounting as long as he'd been in the same bed, so to say, with Mrs. Luthy. It was she who had put him into it, expressing the opinion that it would be nicer if he were in something like accounting instead of in something like shipping, which was what he had been in when he had married her.

What he'd actually been was a shipping clerk, but Viola's way of putting it had always been that he was in shipping, for in putting it that way she often permitted herself to believe that it was cattle or tractors that he shipped, or perhaps *ships* themselves. She frequently believed that others got this fleeting impression, too, which she did not hasten to dispel. The impression seemed to dispel itself soon enough, anyway, but there was always that fleeting instant of daring if dubious glory.

Fine folk from nowhere in particular visited the Luthys quite frequently. There was something attractive about these visitors. They seemed to be, unlike the people one reads about in the society pages of newspapers, dirt. And yet, as their true selves became revealed—through the answering of kind questions asked by Viola—they seemed less and less to be dirt, and more and more as if, except for bad luck, they might have gone on the stage.

These visits were carefully planned, and generally fell on a Saturday afternoon. Once—no one knew but Viola herself—a man named Glear, stepping out of the bathroom into the hall and finding himself face to face with Viola, on her way back to the parlor from her bedroom with an old copy of the *Reader's Digest* in which she wished to show Mr. Glear an article about transportation, took her swiftly into his arms and did something to her face that was approximately a kiss. He smelled of Sen-Sen, she remembered, and had he gone into pictures would have been given office work to do—that is, in the pictures themselves. Knowing what she knew, knowing the effect she'd had on a dynamic man who might have been a film actor, she was rather difficult for Mr. Luthy for two years. By that time she had forgotten Mr. Glear's appearance and thought of him, not as Glear, but as Sherman, though God knows why.

"Whatever happened to that interesting man Sherman?" she once asked her husband, who replied that he had been made into a statue and placed in a park in Savannah.

Thomas Tracy himself visited the Luthys in Far Rockaway one Sunday afternoon.

The tiger had been tense during the entire journey to the Luthy house, impatient to see Laura's tiger again, and once Tracy and the tiger were inside the house extraordinary things began to happen.

Tracy noticed Laura's mother Viola, and Viola noticed Tracy. This noticing was not casual. It was understandable perhaps that Tracy *would* notice Viola, for there was a good deal about her that would have been impossible *not* to notice. She was all of Laura herself, not made larger by time, but more wicked by tiresome innocence.

Laura noticed this noticing that took place between Tracy and her mother, then noticed her father. *He* noticed that there was a great deal of action at the church across the street. Viola sent him for ice cream, which he was glad to fetch, for the church was on the way to the store, and he wanted to step in there to see what was going on.

When he was out of the house Viola brought a box of chocolates to Tracy and offered them to him with a considerable amount of implication. Laura, pretending to be glad that Tracy and her mother were getting on so well, asked to be excused a moment in order to see if she could find her penmanship certificate in which her name had been spelled Luty instead of Luthy.

Laura went off gaily, and there was Tracy and the tiger alone with Mrs. Luthy and the chocolates.

Tracy accepted a chocolate each time one was offered to him until he'd had six, whereupon, unable to account for it, he got up suddenly and accepted everything.

He was surprised to find that his acceptance was not unexpected, but rather anticipated. He, too, like Glear before him, grabbed the innocent woman and did something to her face that approximated a kiss. *His* breath smelled of teeth, Mrs. Luthy observed instantly. Tracy stepped aside just in time to let the tiger go by, and then stepped aside again as the tiger came back, moving with fury. He then gave the theory of the kiss another go.

He was in the midst of this second effort when Laura Luthy returned to the room.

Tracy tried to pretend that what he was actually doing was *not* what it appeared to be, although he could not imagine anything like it at all that he could pretend it was instead.

He saw Laura's tiger standing beside Laura, glaring at him with astonishment and hate. He then looked for the other tiger, but it was gone.

Tracy took his hat and left the house.

He saw Mr. Luthy coming around the church with the ice cream, but he hurried away in the opposite direction.

It was not until he was back on Broadway, among the Sunday evening multitudes, that the tiger found its way through the people to walk beside him again.

"Don't ever do that again," Tracy said.

The next day during the lunch hour Tracy stood in front of Otto Seyfang's in the hope of seeing Laura Luthy, but she didn't come down the street.

It was the same every day of that week.

CHAPTER 5

"How's it turning out?" Nimmo asked Tracy on Friday at noon.

"The song?" Tracy said.

"No," Nimmo said. "Who cares about the song? How's it turning out with you and the black-haired beauty in the bright yellow dress?"

"Eyeej," Tracy said mournfully.

"What do you mean?" Nimmo said.

"I went to her house in Far Rockaway last Sunday and met her mother," Tracy said. "She brought out a box of chocolates, and I ate six of them. I hate chocolates, but she kept pushing the box in front of my face and I kept taking them and eating them. I'm afraid it's not turning out very well."

"Why?" Nimmo said.

"Well," Tracy said, "I'd had all those chocolates, the father had gone for ice cream, the daughter had gone for the penmanship certificate, I grabbed the mother and kissed her."

"No?" Nimmo said.

"Yes," Tracy said.

The coffee taster began to hiccup violently.

"What's the matter?" Tracy said.

"I don't know," Nimmo said.

"Maybe you'd better go home and lie down," Tracy said.

"No, I'm all right," Nimmo said. "Just tell me exactly what happened. I've got to know."

"Well," Tracy said. "It's like I said. I guess the chocolates made me crazy."

"What are you going to do?" Nimmo said.

"I'll make it turn out all right some way or another," Tracy said.

"How?"

"I'll be standing out here in front of Otto Seyfang's someday during my lunch hour," Tracy said, "and another girl something like Laura

Luthy will come down Warren Street, and this time when I go out to her house and meet her mother I won't eat any chocolates, that's all."

"There isn't another girl *like* Laura Luthy, though," Nimmo said. "I guess I'll go in and taste some coffee."

"You've got twenty minutes more on your lunch hour," Tracy said.

"No, I'll go in now," Nimmo said. "What's the use standing out here? What's the use waiting any more?"

Nimmo was on his way in when he heard Tracy moan. He turned, and saw the black-haired beauty passing. But with her walked an unknown young man, obviously not from California, by appearance a bookkeeper.

Nimmo turned away in disgust, while Tracy stared in disbelief.

Tracy tried to smile but couldn't.

Laura Luthy passed by without even looking at him.

Nimmo couldn't stop hiccuping and was finally given the afternoon off. The following day he did not come to work. Monday morning Shively was in the Tasting Department at last, coming to work in his blue serge Sunday suit, for Nimmo was dead.

Some people say he died of the hiccups, but they are the kind of people who say Camille died of catarrh.

CHAPTER 6

What hearts have broken in times gone by, what hearts break now in our own times, what hearts shall break in times to come, Nimmo gone, Laura Luthy lost, Shively in the Tasting Department at last, Peberdy and Ringert treating him like a dog, frequently questioning his taste, looking at one another knowingly.

The three lines of Tracy's song turned out to be, as so many other things turn out to be, dirt. The song faded away, the very scrap of paper on which Tracy had so carefully written the words was lost, the melody was forgotten.

Tracy and the tiger walked one Sunday to Saint Patrick's on Fifth Avenue, burning with the fervor of an old and undefined religion that somehow seemed new, each of them walking in man's or animal's loneliness.

They went in and looked at everything.

The following Saturday Tracy quit his job at Otto Seyfang's and went back to San Francisco.

A number of years went by.

Then one day Tracy was twenty-seven, and he was back in New York, and he was walking there as he'd walked six years ago.

He turned off Broadway when he came to Warren Street and went down the street to Otto Seyfang's, which now bore the name of Keeney's Warehouse.

Did that mean coffee had failed, too? Nimmo, Peberdy, Ringert, Shively, Seyfang—had they all failed?

The tiger stiffened when it saw the entrance of the building, for it was there the tiger had stood one whole afternoon staring the way Laura Luthy had gone.

Tracy hurried away from Keeney's Warehouse, stopped a taxi, got in, and got out at the Public Library.

From there Tracy and the tiger began to walk up Fifth Avenue again. The street was full of Sunday people, men and women and their children.

Tracy had not yet found the one to take the place of Laura Luthy. Nimmo had predicted that Tracy would *never* find her, and perhaps Nimmo had been right, after all.

Tracy stood on a corner, a block from Saint Patrick's, and watched a small boy and the boy's sister cross the street. The tiger came up beside him. Tracy rested his hand on the tiger's head.

"They might have been mine," Tracy said.

"Eyeej," the tiger said.

Tracy strolled on, the tiger beside him. He was astonished to find that all of the people on his side of the street were moving swiftly to the other side of the street. He glanced at the other side of the street and saw people standing there, crowds of them, looking at him, some of them through cameras.

In all innocence Tracy decided to go across the street to find out what all the excitement was about, but when he stepped down from the curb to go, the people across the street began to run, some of them shouting, and a number of women screaming.

Tracy turned and looked at the tiger again.

Well, he'd had the tiger beside him most of his life, but never before had anything like this happened.

Never before had anybody else seen the tiger.

Was it possible now that the tiger was actually being *seen* by others, by everybody?

A number of dogs on leashes began to yap and bark and carry on. This also was something new. Tracy stopped in the middle of Fifth Avenue to let a bus go by, and was astonished once again, this time by the face of the driver of the bus, and by the faces of the passengers.

"Well, what do you know?" Tracy said to the tiger. "I believe they can see you. I believe they can actually see you, just as I've seen you most of my life, but look at them, they're terrified, they're scared to death. Good God, they ought to know there's nothing to be afraid of."

"Eyeej," the tiger said.

"Yes," Tracy said. "I haven't heard you speak so well since we were at Otto Seyfang's and Laura Luthy came dancing down Warren Street."

Tracy and the tiger moved up Fifth Avenue until they were across the street from Saint Patrick's. Tracy had planned to go into the church, as he and the tiger had done six years ago, and so he began to cross the street, to get to the church, but as he did so the few people in front of the church broke and ran. And then everybody in the church came out. Tracy and the tiger were late for church, but even so, they would go in, and Tracy would walk all the way down the centre aisle with the tiger and look again at all the fine things there, the wonderful height and light, the stained-glass windows, the fine pillars, the burning candles.

The people who came out of the church seemed at peace, and then suddenly they deteriorated, some of them running down side streets, some up and down Fifth Avenue, and some back into the church, to hide there.

"I'm awful sorry about this," Tracy said. "It's never happened before, as you know."

"Eyeej," the tiger said.

"We're going to church anyway," Tracy said.

He rested his hand on the tiger's head, and thus they went together to the steps of the church, up the steps, and then on to the handsome area that was inside.

But if the *area* was handsome, the people still in the area were not, including several men in robes. Their going was swift and untidy.

Tracy and the tiger walked slowly down the centre aisle. He noticed shut doors here and there opening a little, frightened eyes staring out at him, and he saw the doors shut again, heard them being locked or bolted.

"Well, it *is* a beautiful place," Tracy said, "but you remember how different it was when we came here six years ago. The place was full of people then, men, women, and children, and they were all glad about something, not the way they are now, scared to death, gone running, or hiding behind doors. What are they afraid of? What's happened to them?"

"Eyeej," the tiger said.

Tracy and the tiger left the church by a side door that opened on 50th Street, but when they came to the street Tracy saw an armoured car standing there, with gun barrels pointed at him and the tiger. He looked down the street, and there near Madison Avenue he saw another armoured car. He looked up to Fifth Avenue, and there on the corner he saw two more of them. Beyond the armoured cars was a multitude of people, all terrified, waiting for a fight of some kind, and an outcome.

The man who sat in the driver's seat of the armoured car directly in front of Tracy quickly raised the window of the car, to be better protected against the tiger.

"What's the matter?" Tracy said.

"For God's sake man," the driver replied, "don't you see the animal beside you?"

"Of course I see it," Tracy said.

"It's a panther escaped from the circus," the driver said.

"Don't be silly," Tracy said. "It's never been *near* the circus. And it's *not* a panther, it's a tiger."

"Stand aside, man," the driver said, "so one of the men can shoot the animal."

"Shoot it?" Tracy said. "Are you crazy?"

He began to walk down 50th Street toward Madison Avenue. The driver of the armoured car started the motor, and the car moved slowly beside Tracy, the driver trying to argue him into stepping away from the tiger.

"Stand aside, man," the driver said.

"Go on," Tracy said. "Take your armoured car back to the bank or the garage or wherever it is you keep it."

"Stand back or we'll shoot anyway," the driver said.

"You wouldn't dare," Tracy said.

"O.K., boy," the driver said. "You asked for it."

Tracy heard the shot. He looked to see if the tiger had been hit. It hadn't, but it *was* off for Madison Avenue.

The tiger was swift, swifter than Tracy had ever before known it to be. When it reached the second armoured car on 50th Street another shot was fired, the tiger leaped, fell, and when it began to run again Tracy noticed that it did so with the right front foot held up. When the tiger reached Madison Avenue, it turned uptown, and disappeared, the nearest armoured car going after it with all of its slow might.

Tracy broke into a trot, chasing after the tiger.

He was stopped at the corner by three officers. They pushed him into the second armoured car and drove off with him.

"What do you want to kill my tiger for?" Tracy said to the driver.

"That animal escaped from the circus last night, after mauling a keeper," the driver said.

"What are you talking about?" Tracy said.

"You heard me," the man said.

"I've had that tiger most of my life," Tracy said.

"You haven't had *any* tiger most of your life," the driver said, "but you've had *something*, and we'll soon find out what it is."

CHAPTER 7

Tracy sat in a Bank of England chair at the center of an enormous room in which newspapermen, photographers, police officers, animal trainers, and a good many others milled about.

If the tiger had actually not been his own tiger, as they said, his own tiger was certainly not with Tracy now.

He sat alone.

The tiger did not sit on the floor at his feet.

Tracy had been in the chair more than an hour.

Somebody new came into the room suddenly.

"Dr. Pingitzer," Tracy heard somebody say.

This was a small, smiling man of seventy or so.

"Now," the man said quickly to the crowd. "What is it?"

The doctor was drawn to one side and surrounded by a group of experts, several of whom told him what it was.

"Ah ha," Tracy heard the doctor say. The doctor went quickly to Tracy.

"My boy," he said. "I am Rudolph Pingitzer."

Tracy got up and shook Rudolph Pingitzer's hand.

"Thomas Tracy," he said.

"Ah ha, Thomas Tracy," Dr. Pingitzer turned to the others. "Perhaps a chair like this for *me*, too?"

Another Bank of England chair was quickly fetched for the doctor. He sat down and said pleasantly, "I am seventy-two years old."

"I am twenty-seven," Tracy said.

Dr. Pingitzer filled a pipe, spilled a good deal of tobacco over his clothing which he did not bother to brush off, used seven matches to get the pipe lighted, puffed at it a dozen times, then said with the pipe in his mouth, "I have wife, sixty-nine years old, boy forty-fife years old, psychiatrist, boy forty-two years old, psychiatrist, boy thirty-nine years old, psychiatrist, girl thirty-six years old, says *thirty-one* years old, psychiatrist, girl thirty-one years old, says *twenty-six* years old, psychiatrist, furnished apartment, phonograph, piano, television, typewriter, but with typewriter I have mechanical disorder."

"Why don't you get it fixed?" Tracy said.

"Ah, yes," Dr. Pingitzer said. "Never use typewriter. Is for grandchildren. Junk. I have these things, mostly psychiatrist."

"Do you have any money?" Tracy said.

"No," Dr. Pingitzer said. "Is expensive so many psychiatrists. Have books. Have also, ah, yes, bed. For sleep. At night. I lie down. Sleep. Is change."

"Do you have any friends?" Tracy said.

"Many friends," Dr. Pingitzer said. "Of course when I say friends" —Dr. Pingitzer's hands moved quickly, he made odd little noises— "you understand I mean"—more noises—"naturally. Who knows?"

"Do you go to church?" Tracy said.

"Ah," Dr. Pingitzer said. "Yes. Sentiment. I like it. It is nice."

A newspaperman stepped forward, and said "How about *you* asking the questions, doctor?"

"Ah ha?" the doctor said quickly. "If to be interview with Dr. Pingitzer room to be empty."

A police captain who was in charge, a man named Huzinga, said quickly, "O.K., you heard the doctor. Everybody out."

There was a good deal of protesting on the part of the newspapermen, but Huzinga and his men got everybody out into the hall. When the room was empty, the doctor, puffing on his pipe peacefully, smiled at Tracy, then began to doze. Tracy himself was tired by now, so he began to doze, too. The old man snored, but Tracy didn't.

After a moment the door was pushed open, and a photographer quickly took a picture of the men asleep in the Bank of England chairs.

Huzinga then came in and woke the doctor up.

"Ah ha," the doctor said.

Huzinga was about to wake Tracy up, too, but the doctor said, "No. Important."

"Yes, doctor," Huzinga said.

He tiptoed out of the room.

The little man sat and watched Tracy's face. After a moment Tracy opened his eyes.

"I dream I was in Vienna," the doctor said.

"When were you there last?" Tracy said.

"Twenty years ago," Dr. Pingitzer said. "Long, long ago. I like very much ice cream. Vanilla."

"Do you like coffee?" Tracy said.

"Coffee?" Dr. Pingitzer said. "I am from Vienna. I *live* on coffee. Ah ha." He shouted, so that they would hear him beyond the door. "Coffee, please!"

Outside, Huzinga sent an officer for a pot of coffee and two cups.

"He knows," Huzinga said to the officer. "He knows what he's doing."

"We will have coffee," the little man said. "Is happened something. I don't know."

"They shot my tiger," Tracy said.

"I am sorry," Dr. Pingitzer said.

"We went into Saint Patrick's," Tracy said, "just as we did six years ago, but when we came out they were waiting there in an armoured car, and another one farther down on 50th Street. The first shot went wild, but it frightened the tiger, and it began to run. When it reached the second armoured car the tiger was shot in the foot."

"This tiger, it is *your* tiger?"

"Yes."

"Why?"

"It's been with me most of my life."

"Ah," the little man said. "It is tiger, like dog is dog?"

"Do you mean," Tracy said, "is it a *real* tiger, as a tiger in the jungle is, or in the circus?"

"Precise," Dr. Pingitzer said.

"No, it is not," Tracy said. "It wasn't until today, at any rate, but it *was* real today. It was still *my* tiger, though."

"Why do they say tiger is escape from circus?"

"I don't know."

"Is possible?"

"I suppose so. A caged animal of any kind might escape from a circus, if possible."

"You are not afraid of this tiger?" Dr. Pingitzer said. "We have here someplace photographs taken by newspaper photographers. My young daughter have hobby of photography one time. Pictures, pictures—all pictures of Papa. *Me!*" He turned to the door and spoke loudly. "Photographs, please."

Huzinga came in, and off the top of a desk picked up a dozen photographs, handed them to the doctor, who quickly ran through them, with scarcely time enough to look at any of them, his hands and eyes moving extraordinarily swiftly.

"You are not afraid of this animal," he said again quickly, "this tiger. This is *black panther*."

"Yes, I know," Tracy said, "but it's my tiger just the same."

"You have this name *tiger* for this animal?"

"Yes, I know it's a black panther," Tracy said, "but I've always thought of it as a tiger."

"*Your* tiger?"

"Yes."

"You are not afraid of this tiger?"

"No."

"Everybody is afraid of tiger."

"Everybody is afraid of many things," Tracy said.

"I am afraid of night," Dr. Pingitzer said. "In Vienna at night I go as a young man where are many lights, much brightness. That way I am not afraid of night."

The coffee was brought in and poured by Huzinga, who seemed, for some reason, worshipful of Dr. Pingitzer.

"Now, we taste coffee," the doctor said.

"I wanted to be a coffee taster once," Tracy said.

"Ah, yes?" Dr. Pingitzer said. "Let us drink coffee now. Enjoy coffee. Life is too short." He waved at the door. "Much—much—

much——" He made a face, and was unable to finish the thought.
"Yes," Tracy said.

They drank coffee in silence, Tracy tasting it carefully, as he had
done six years ago at Otto Seyfang's, sitting with Nimmo, Peberdy,
and Ringert.

CHAPTER 8

After they had tasted three cups each Dr. Pingitzer said, "Ah ha.
Work. I hate work. I hate psychiatry. I *always* hate work. I like fun,
play, imagination, magic."

"Why do you work, then?" Tracy said.

"Why?" Dr. Pingitzer said. "Confusion." The doctor reflected a
moment. "In Vienna I see this girl. Elsa. This is Elsa Varshock.
Ah ha. Elsa is wife, is mother, is say, "Where's for food, money?
So? I work.""

"You understand psychiatry?" Tracy said.

"Psychiatry, no," Dr. Pingitzer said. "People—little bit. Little,
little, little bit. Every year, every day—less, less, less. Why? People
is difficult. People is people. People is fun, play, imagination, magic.
Ah ha. People is pain, people is sick, people is mad, people is hurt,
people is hurt *people*, is kill, is kill self. Where is fun, where is
play, where is imagination, where is magic? Psychiatry I hate. People
I love. Mad people, beautiful people, hurt people, sick people, broke
people, in pieces people, I love, I love. Why? Why is lost from
people fun, play, imagination, magic? What for? Ah ha. Money?"
He smiled. "I think so. Money. Is love, this money. Is beauty, this
money. Is fun, this money. Where is money? I do not know. No
more fun. Work, now. Work. Tiger. Tiger."

"Do you know the poem?" Tracy said.

"*Is poem?*" Dr. Pingitzer said.

"Of course."

"What is this poem?" Dr. Pingitzer said.

> "*Tiger! Tiger! burning bright,*" Tracy said.
> "*In the forests of the night,*
> *What immortal hand or eye*
> *Could frame thy fearful symmetry?*"

"Ah ha. Is more?" Dr. Pingitzer said.

"Yes, quite a bit," Tracy said, "if I haven't forgotten it."

"Please," Dr. Pingitzer said.

> *"In what distant deeps or skies,"* Tracy went on.
> *"Burnt the fire of thine eyes?*
> *On what wings dare he aspire?*
> *What the hand dare seize the fire?"*

"Ho ho," Dr. Pingitzer said. "Is poem like *this* I do not hear seventy-two years! Who do this poem?"

"William Blake," Tracy said.

"Bravo, William Blake!" Dr. Pingitzer said. "Is more?"

"Yes," Tracy said. "Let me see. Oh yes,

> *"And what shoulder, and what art,*
> *Could twist the sinews of thy heart?*
> *And when thy heart began to beat,*
> *What dread hand? and what dread feet?"*

"More?" the doctor said.

"I think I've got it all now," Tracy said.

> *"What the hammer? What the chain?*
> *In what furnace was thy brain?*
> *What the anvil? What dread grasp*
> *Dare its deadly terrors clasp?*
>
> *"When the stars threw down their spears,*
> *And watered heaven wth their tears,*
> *Did He smile His work to see?*
> *Did He who made the Lamb make thee?*
>
> *"Tiger! Tiger! burning bright*
> *In the forests of the night,*
> *What immortal hand or eye,*
> *Dare frame thy fearful symmetry?"*

Tracy stopped.

"That's the whole poem," he said.

"Ah, ha," Dr. Pingitzer said. "Thank you. Now, you have this poem since childhood. Yes?"

"Yes," Tracy said. "I began to recite it when I was three."

"You *understand* this poem?" Dr. Pingitzer said.

"I don't *understand* anything," Tracy said. "I *like* this poem."

"Ah ha. True."

The old man turned to the door.

"Much—much—much—" he said. "Now. Two questions. One. Your tiger, is *what?*"

"Mine," Tracy said.

"Two," Dr. Pingitzer said. "Tiger in street, is *what?*"

"Well," Tracy said, "I suppose a black panther mauled a keeper and escaped from the circus last night. Such things happen. I suppose a wounded black panther is now loose in New York. I suppose it will, out of fear, kill somebody if it thinks it must. But the black panther that is loose in the city is *also* my tiger."

"So?"

"Yes."

"Why?" Dr. Pingitzer said.

"I don't know," Tracy said, "but it walked up Fifth Avenue with me and into Saint Patrick's. It didn't attack anybody. It stayed beside me. It didn't run until it was shot at. Wouldn't *you* run if you were shot at?"

"Very fast," Dr. Pingitzer said. "Seventy-two, but very fast." He paused a moment, to imagine himself running very fast at seventy-two.

"The police, they will kill this animal," Dr. Pingitzer said.

"They'll *try* to," Tracy said.

"They *will.*"

"They'll *try*," Tracy said, "but they won't, because they can't."

"Why? They can't?" Dr. Pingitzer said.

"The tiger can't be killed."

"One tiger? Can't be killed? Why not?"

"It can't, that's all," Tracy said.

"But *tiger* will kill?" Dr. Pingitzer said.

"If it must," Tracy said.

"Is this right?"

"I don't know. Is it?"

"I also don't know," the doctor said. "I know very little. Very, very, very little. Ah ha. Question of psychiatry. You are mad?"

"Yes, of course," Tracy said.

The old man looked toward the door. He put a finger to his lips. "Soft," he whispered.

"I'm mad because they wounded the tiger," Tracy said. "I'm mad because they put the tiger in the cage in the first place. I'm mad because they put it in the circus. But I am also mad, from birth."

"I, also, but this is information *not* to say," Dr. Pingitzer said. He looked at the door again. He got up suddenly. "I speak so. *This man is sane.* This they understand. Ah ha! Work finish." He called out loudly. "O.K., please."

Huzinga was the first to enter the room, but soon everybody was back in.

Dr. Pingitzer surveyed the faces, waited a long time for silence, then said, "Ah ha! This man is sane."

A man altogether unlike Dr. Pingitzer stepped forward and said, "Dr. Pingitzer, I am Dr. Scatter, in charge of Neuro, Borough of Manhattan. May I ask the psychiatric course by which you have reached your conclusion?"

"No," Dr. Pingitzer said. He turned to Tracy. "Good-bye, my boy," he said.

"Good-bye," Tracy said.

Dr. Pingitzer glanced at everyone in the room, then went to the door.

On his way he was photographed by a number of newspaper photographers, one of whom said, "Dr. Pingitzer, how about the black panther? Is it *his*, as he said it is?"

"I have examine *him*, not black panther," the doctor said.

A reporter stepped up to Dr. Pingitzer.

"How did it happen that the black panther didn't harm him, doctor?" the reporter said.

"I don't know," Dr. Pingitzer said.

"Well, what have you found out about it, after talking to him?" the reporter said.

"Nothing," the doctor said.

"What about a black panther being loose in the city?" the reporter said.

"This is not psychiatry problem," the doctor said.

"What kind of a problem is it?" the reporter said.

"Where from is this black panther?"

"From the circus."

"Circus problem," Dr. Pingitzer said.

He walked out of the room.

Everybody gathered around Dr. Scatter, who was not at all satisfied with Dr. Pingitzer's conclusion, or manners.

CHAPTER 9

Tracy, in walking with the tiger, had broken no law.

Still, what he *had* done seemed so enormous and unbelievable as to *seem* illegal, or at any rate arrogant, thoughtless, and rude.

At the very least, it was felt, he must be insane. A man just naturally doesn't walk with a black panther escaped from the circus as if the animal and he were on terms of perfect understanding.

Therefore, after the departure of Dr. Pingitzer, Tracy was examined by Dr. Scatter, who found it irresistible to interpret Tracy's replies in a manner convenient to his education and prejudices.

Dr. Scatter had no difficulty in proving, step by step, that Tracy was in fact mad. This is easy to do. It can be done with anybody.

"Futhermore," Dr. Scatter said to the others involved, including Police Captain Earl Huzinga, who was the only one in the group who maintained disbelief in Dr. Scatter's findings and persisted in being respectful of Dr. Pingitzer's, "when the subject was asked what his reaction would be to an indefinite visit at Bellevue for the purpose of more prolonged and thorough psychiatric investigation, he replied that he would rather go home but that if forced to go to Bellevue he would make the most of his visit and feel just as much at home there as anywhere else, if not more at home. This attitude suggests that, in addition to all the other symptoms already identified, the subject has a martyr complex. It also reveals psychotic arrogance, and contempt for the collective intelligence. The subject is obviously deluded, believing that he is personally exempted from the laws which guide and control the rest of society. This belief is based upon, and has been strengthened by, a prolonged association with a fantasy tiger, which he declares is his, and his alone; which he has confessed is capable of speech—that is, communication by speech with *himself alone*. I am sure there is no doubt in anyone's mind that he must be placed in Bellevue for observation and treatment."

Thus, Thomas Tracy, on a pleasant Sunday afternoon in October, was placed in Bellevue.

He found the people there quite mad. He also found that each of them had a tiger: a very troubled one, a very angry one, a most deeply wounded one, a tiger deprived of humour, and love of freedom and fun, imagination, and hope.

Nimmo's son was there with a depressed and dying tiger. Peberdy's daughter was there with a terrified tiger that paced back and forth. Ringert himself was there with a tiger that resembled a weary old dog.

And Laura Luthy was there, her once magnificent tiger now thin, starved, and pathetic. . . .

Only Tracy was without a tiger.

Tracy's tiger was hiding under the establishment of Roush, Rubeling and Ryan on Madison Avenue between 55th and 56th. The place was dark, secret, and deathly. The tiger was in hiding under the room in which Roush, Rubeling, and Ryan decorated the dead with powder, rouge, and smiles.

The tiger lay there in terror and loneliness, bereaved, heartsick, and eager itself to be dead.

CHAPTER 10

What's the use trying to describe the effect upon the people of New York of the story of Tracy and the tiger, as reported on the front pages of every newspaper, as told by anonymous and famous newscasters of radio and television, as embellished by newsreels of Tracy and the tiger walking up Fifth Avenue, entering Saint Patrick's, coming out of Saint Patrick's? As further embellished by photographs of Tracy drinking coffee with Dr. Pingitzer, surrounded by police, newspaper reporters, psychiatrists, others?

The effect was the usual one.

Innocent dogs, on their way to relief, came upon men who dropped dead, women screamed at shadows, then slapped their children for wanting to go out and play.

Everybody stayed home Sunday night, and quite a few Monday morning, for the tiger was still at large, and Tracy was in Bellevue.

He was examined a good deal of the time.

He in turn found his examiners interesting.

In his spare time Tracy visited Laura Luthy, who could not remember him. He brought up the matter of the Sunday visit in Far Rockaway, but Laura, pale and wan now, did not remember.

"I ate six soft chocolates," Tracy said.

"You should have had seven," Laura said.

"Why?"

"Then you would have had one extra," Laura said. "One extra is always nice. I have always believed that. One extra for everybody."

"Chocolates?" Tracy said.

"Anything," Laura said. "Mother, father, life, chance. Six is fine, but one extra makes it finer. Another and another, you should have had another."

"Don't you remember?" Tracy said. "Your father went for ice cream."

"Ice cream melts," Laura said. "That is the secret of ice cream. It melts."

"Laura," Tracy said. "Look at me. Listen to me."

"Nothing is so sad as ice cream melting," Laura said.

"It's *not* sad, Laura," Tracy said. "Ice cream's *supposed* to melt."

"It is?"

"Of course."

"I didn't know," Laura said. "I cried so hard when I saw the ice cream melt."

"What ice cream, Laura?"

"The ice cream girl, the ice cream boy," Laura said. "I didn't know. All those tears for nothing. I cried until I melted, too. Are you sure?"

"No," Tracy said. "No, I'm not sure. I don't know what happened, but whatever it was, listen to me, Laura. Six years ago I was standing in front of Otto Seyfang's."

"Why were you standing *there*?" Laura said.

"I *worked* there," Tracy said. "I was standing there talking to the coffee tasters, Nimmo, Peberdy, and Ringert."

"Where are they now?" Laura said.

"Nimmo's dead," Tracy said. "Ringert's here, and I don't know where Peberdy is. While I was standing there a beautiful girl came down Warren Street."

"*Was* she beautiful?" Laura said.

"The most beautiful girl in the world."

"Who was she?"

"You, Laura," Tracy said.

"Me?" Laura said. "The most beautiful girl in the world? You must be mistaken."

"No. It *was* you, Laura."

"Well, I'm certainly not the most beautiful girl in the world any more," Laura said.

"That's what I want to talk about," Tracy said.

"All right," Laura said. "Talk about it."

"I want *you* to come down Warren Street again."

"You do?"

"Yes."

"Why?"

"Well, I don't know how else to put it," Tracy said. "I love you."

"What do you mean?" Laura said.

"I don't know," Tracy said. "I suppose I mean—you're still the most beautiful girl in the world."

"I'm not," Laura said.

"Yes, you are," Tracy said. "You are to *me*."

"No," Laura said. "It's so arrogant to be beautiful. It's such bad taste. It's so pathetic, too. So much more pathetic than just lying still and knowing you're dead."

"You're not dead, Laura."

"Oh, I am."

"Laura!" Tracy said. "For God's sake, Laura, I love you."

"I'm sorry," Laura said. "I'm terribly sorry. I think I prefer to be dead."

Tracy didn't know what to think. Was she *actually* mad?

Like Dr. Pingitzer, he didn't know.

She was at Bellevue, at any rate.

She'd had a high fever for months. The opinion of the experts was that she would soon be dead.

Later on, they knew, they too would be dead, but this did not trouble them because they believed they might die sane.

CHAPTER 11

A hectic week for New York went by.

The tiger was still at large. That is to say, it was dying of starvation and fear under the embalming room of Roush, Rubeling and Ryan.

According to the newspapers, however, on Monday morning the tiger was seen in three different places in Harlem, two in Greenwich

Village, six in Brooklyn, and a boy in Fresno, California, killed a black cat with a .22 rifle because it looked enough like Tracy's tiger to make it worth his while. A photograph of the boy, proudly holding the cat by the tail, appeared in newspapers all over the country.

His name was Benintendi, first name Salvatore.

By sundown Tuesday Tracy's Tiger, as it was now called, was seen by miscellaneous people all over the country.

A man in London saw it in Soho and explained in a letter to *The Times* how the creature, as he called it, had reached there. His explanation was quite interesting, and his sympathies were entirely with the creature, as British sympathies sometimes are, at least among her gentle eccentrics.

A bookie in Seattle who had been beaten by a rival bookie's thugs informed the police that he had been attacked by Tracy's Tiger.

A saloon-keeper in Chicago advertised a new drink called Tracy's Tiger, twenty-five cents a shot.

A toy manufacturer in Toledo called in his designers and salesmen, and by Saturday morning had a black velvet Tracy's Tiger for children to take to bed. He also had a sweater on which was stamped a picture of the animal and its name, all sizes of Tracy's Tiger made of inflated rubber, and a jack-in-the-box out of which Tracy's Tiger sprang at one's loved ones.

The animal itself had a cold that was quickly turning to pleurisy. Its eyes were lustreless. They were giving off a good deal of yellow mucus. Its nose was clogged. Its white teeth had become coated with something that tasted like the end.

The observing of Tracy continued, and was dutifully reported to the nation and the world every day, along with other, equally peculiar, news.

A dozen or more reputations were made by psychiatrists and newspapermen on Tracy and his Tiger.

Tracy's devotion to Laura Luthy was discovered by an astute newspaperman who scooped the world wth a story captioned

TRACY LOVES LAURA

TIGER BOY WOOS BELLEVUE BELLE

The *Mirror*, however, having had poor luck in its photographs and stories about Tracy and the tiger, got even with the other newspapers by demanding an instantaneous investigation of the city's police, and if need be the dismissal of Chief August Bly, for if he could not kill or capture a lame tiger, how would he take care of the citizens of New York in the event a bomb was dropped on the city?

This theme was taken up by a number of people who readily take up miscellaneous themes.

Chief Bly was asked point-blank by the *Mirror*, "When can you assure the people of the greatest city in the world that Tracy's Tiger will be killed or captured, and permit the people to sleep peacefully again?"

The question was asked by telegram.

Chief Bly called in his brightest men and asked them to answer the telegram. There were a dozen different answers, all unsatisfactory, because nobody *knew* when the tiger would be killed or captured.

"I don't know," the Chief wanted to say but didn't dare.

Instead, a 500-word reply was written and dispatched by telegram to the *Mirror*. The reply was run on the front page of the *Mirror* under the heading of *Shame on the New York Police*. The *Mirror* demanded that Chief Bly resign. It also offered a reward of $5,000 to any man, woman, or child, regardless of race, color, creed, or religion, who brought Tracy's Tiger to the *Mirror*, dead or alive.

The following day a man went to the *Mirror* with a black panther shot through the head, and the *Mirror* had the scoop it wanted at last.

The stories and photographs of the killing of Tracy's Tiger were sent all over the country and all over the world.

The man, Art Pliley, in a matter of hours received hundreds of 'phone calls at the *Mirror*, mostly from women, several of whom offered to be his bride. Negotiations were under way for him to buy a clean suit and appear in a Men of Distinction advertisement when the police escorted Tracy to the *Mirror* to have a look at the tiger.

Each of the other papers had a reporter and a photographer on hand, just in case. It seemed a wild and pathetic chance for the Chief of Police to be taking, but it was worth looking into just the same.

The *Mirror*, however, refused to permit Tracy to examine the tiger.

Art Pliley was asked to shake hands with Tracy for a photograph, but by now he knew the ropes, and said, "I couldn't do that for less than five."

"Five what?" he was asked.

"Hundred," Art Pliley said. "The *Mirror* can photograph me for nothing. That's in my contract. Any other paper, though, five."

"This is a high school paper," the photographer said as a joke, and Art Pliley, never having attended high school and believing it was his duty, shook hands with Tracy free of charge.

He was given a severe bawling out by the managing editor of the *Mirror*, however.

As for Tracy, he shook hands with everybody. He believed they were sincere. Either that, or helpless.

The *News* charged that the *Mirror* had perpetrated a hoax on the citizens of New York, and that the dead tiger in their possession was not Tracy's Tiger.

The upshot of this rivalry and jealousy resulted after two days in a formal and ceremonious examination of the *Mirror's* tiger by Tracy, by the animal's trainer at the circus, and by a half-dozen people who wanted any kind of publicity they could possibly get.

The ceremony was swift. Tracy looked at the poor dead black panther lying beside the specially built casket in which the *Mirror* planned to bury it. He looked, that is, from across the room. He spoke altogether out of turn, too, making a shambles of the whole ceremony.

"That's not my tiger," he said. "That's not even a black panther. That's a mountain lion that's had its fur dyed black."

Art Pliley, to sum up the hoax, was arrested, his bank account confiscated by the *Mirror*, and he was put in jail. There he was visited by the managing editor of the *News*, however, and a new deal was made. If Pliley would confess exclusively to the *News*, the *News* would give him *six* thousand dollars. Pliley confessed every day for three days, whereupon he was sent to the penitentiary, for in confessing, he was thorough, and revealed that he had a good many other clever things. He said he'd always wanted to be famous mainly, and since he *was* famous at last, he didn't want to stop half-way.

It would be tedious to go into the nature of his confessions. He wanted to be famous, that's all.

Tracy's Tiger grew very ill on the ninth day of hiding under the embalming room of Roush, Rubeling and Ryan. That night, in trembling desperation, it crawled out from its hiding place to an open garbage can in which it found meat scraps, bones, and outer leaves of miscellaneous vegetables. Much of this scrap it carried to its hiding place, making one trip after another.

A small boy, awake at two in the morning, coughing and waiting for his mother to bring him the cough medicine, said to her when she came with it, "Look at the big cat in the garbage can, Mama."

Mama looked and woke up Papa. Papa had no gun, but he *was* an amateur photographer, and he *did* have a flash camera.

Papa sat at the window three minutes, waiting for the tiger to come back to the garbage can. When the tiger came back Papa got something like buck fever, and found that he couldn't snap the picture.

Mama took the camera angrily out of his hands and handed it to the boy, eight years old. The boy focused as well as he was able to, the tiger saw the flash, leaped, and went back to its hiding place.

The man put on his clothes and developed the picture in his own dark-room. The picture showed the rear half of the tiger.

The man went to the police with the picture of the rear half of Tracy's Tiger. The police questioned the man an hour, and at four that morning the sick tiger heard voices and saw lights. It watched and listened a long time.

When things quieted down, the tiger came out, and began to move downtown.

The photograph, and the story of its achievement, was duly published in the newspapers, along with photographs of the sick boy, who immediately grew sicker.

The area of New York in which the boy lived was drawn by special map-makers, and speculations were made as to where the tiger was now hiding.

CHAPTER 19

Police Captain Earl Huzinga, after many quiet chats with Tracy at Bellevue, made up his mind to go directly to Chief Bly and say his piece, even if it cost him his job.

"He can get us the tiger," Captain Huzinga said.

"How?" Chief Bly said.

"Well, it *sounds* complicated," Huzinga said, "but I've had a lot of talks with him, and it's *not* complicated. I know he can do it."

"*How?*" Bly said again.

"First," Huzinga said, "he doesn't want anybody to know about it. No publicity at all."

"We can keep it quiet," the Chief said. He was sick and tired of the whole thing and beginning to feel older than his sixty-six years.

"There's a place on Warren Street that used to be Otto Seyfang's, a coffee importing house," Huzinga said. "It's out of business now, but the building's still there. It's a warehouse now. Tracy wants a sign made like the old sign, *Otto Seyfang's*, and he wants the sign put up where it was. He wants the Tasting Department restored, and he wants a man named Peberdy, a man named Ringert, and a man named Shively to sit there and taste coffee. Peberdy's living in a furnished room. Ringert's at Bellevue. Shively's living with his daughter in the Bronx."

"What's he want all this nonsense for?" Bly said.

"I know it doesn't sound reasonable," Huzinga said, "but I know he'll get us the tiger. He needs only one day. It's got to be a Sunday. That suits us fine because there won't be anybody but one or two drunks on Warren Street at noon on a Sunday."

"You've been at Bellevue so long," Chief Bly said, "you've gone a little bats yourself, but go on, let's hear the whole thing."

"He wants at least a hundred sacks of coffee in the storeroom," Huzinga said.

"What for?"

"He used to work there," Huzinga said. "On this Sunday he's going to get there at eight in the morning. He's going to lift and carry the sacks. Peberdy, Ringert, and Shively will be in the Tasting Department tasting coffee. Every now and then Tracy will stop carrying sacks, and go in there and taste some coffee with them. At noon he'll stop work, go out front, and stand there in the sun. At half-past twelve a girl named Laura Luthy will come walking down Warren Street. She'll stop in front of Otto Seyfang's."

"She will?" Bly said.

"Yes," Huzinga said.

"So what?" Bly said.

"In a moment Tracy's Tiger will be there, too," Huzinga said. "He'll take the girl by the arm and walk down Warren Street with her. There's an empty store three doors down from Otto Seyfang's—it used to be a produce house. He'll walk into this store with the girl and the tiger. In the store will be a cage. The tiger will go into the cage. Tracy will lock the cage. Then, he and the girl will walk out of the store."

"He will?"

"Yes."

"Go ahead," the Chief said. "Tell me more."

"Two things we've got to promise him," Huzinga said. "*One.* Absolutely no publicity. No photographs, not even for our own records. You and I can watch from the building across the street. *Two.* We can *have* the tiger in the cage, but we have got to promise that we do not announce to anybody that we've got it. If the tiger's ill, we've got to give it expert care, especially the injured foot. It's the right front one."

"You believe this nut, don't you?" Chief Bly said.

"Yes, sir."

"Why?"

"You put me on the case ten days ago," Huzinga said. "I've been with him the entire time. That was no bull in the papers about Laura Luthy. The doctors said she was dying, and all you had to do was see her to *know* she was. Well, she's not dying any more. Pingitzer's in there every day talking with both of them, trying to figure it out. He says everybody at Bellevue is somebody who lost love somewhere along the line. The ones that love means the most to get sick, a lot of them die. It doesn't take very long, either. Tracy's not crazy."

"What about Dr. Scatter and all the other experts who say he *is* crazy?" the Chief said.

"I don't know," Huzinga said. "Their reports seem to stack up all right. I guess there are a couple of ways of looking at things like that, though. Pingitzer's studying Tracy's way. He says it's a way he's always *believed* might work, especially if it's started early enough, but he's never seen it work in an advanced case like Laura Luthy's. He says when it comes to human beings, you've got to be patient, you've got to be willing to learn, because anything can happen, especially if love's involved. You wouldn't think there'd be laughter in Bellevue, would you?"

"No, I wouldn't, not decent laughter anyway," Bly said.

"Well, there is, and it's *damned* decent," Huzinga said. "Scatter and all the others are getting annoyed by it, too. They're trying to stop it. They're bringing out new regulations every day, but they can't stop it. They're sore because the patients aren't acting the way they're *supposed* to act. They get up, visit one another, help one another, tell stories, dance, sing—and I don't mean in a crazy way, either. I mean in a natural, decent, kind way. Most of them are sad, of course, but not much sadder than people anywhere else." Huzinga stopped a moment. "He'll get the tiger for us all right. When that happens we'll know where we stand, at any rate, even if we won't be able to tell anybody about it. Everybody will forget the whole thing after a couple of weeks anyway. How about it?"

"No," the Chief said. "It's silly. It would get around. I'd be the laughing stock of New York."

"Today's Wednesday," Huzinga said. "We'd know in four days. Will you give *me* permission to do it? If it flops, I'll take the rap. I'll say it was my idea. I did it on my own. Pingitzer's with me. He wants to watch."

The Chief thought about all this a long time.

"O.K.," he said at last. "O.K., I'll watch, too."

"We've got to keep our promise, though," Huzinga said.

"O.K.," the Chief said. "Get going."

The Captain, glad and confident but at the same time deeply frightened, got going.

CHAPTER 13

One bright Sunday morning Tracy came up out of the earth, climbing the subway steps.

He stood in the light, looking around as he had done six years ago. The scene was not greatly changed.

He walked across Bowling Green Park to Warren Street, glanced at his watch, then hurried, as he'd always done, for the time was five minutes to eight.

Warren Street was empty. Like most Sunday streets, it seemed to be a street that was being dreamed.

Tracy saw that the place was again Otto Seyfang's. He hurried to the entrance and went in, and from the building across the street Captain Huzinga and Chief Bly saw him do so.

They had already seen Peberdy, Ringert, and Shively go in.

"Well," Chief Bly said, "I don't know how you feel, but I feel Tracy's crazier than *anybody* knows, or ever will know. How do *you* feel?"

"It's a little early," Huzinga said. "At half-past twelve, I know

Laura Luthy is going to come down Warren Street, as she did six years ago."

"Well, that's nice," Chief Bly said. "Now, this work that he's going to be doing in there—it's going to *draw* the tiger away from wherever it's hiding to Otto Seyfang's, is that right?"

"Yes."

They were interrupted by the police radio, the speaker reporting all quiet.

"Now, let me go over everything again," Chief Bly said. "She'll be wearing a yellow knit dress, is that right?"

"Yes," Huzinga said.

"She'll come by around half-past twelve, is that right?"

"Yes."

"Tracy will be standing in front there, on the steps, is that right?"

"Yes."

"The girl will stop when she sees Tracy, is that right?"

"Yes."

"At that moment the tiger will appear, is that right?"

"Yes."

"Tracy will take the girl by the arm and walk down Warren Street, the tiger walking beside him, is that right?"

"Yes."

"Three doors down the block, in that empty store there that is now full of paintings of animals hanging on the walls, will be a cage, is that right?"

"Yes."

"Where'd you get the paintings?" Bly said.

"Raymond & Raymond," Huzinga said. "They're reproductions of the most famous animal paintings in the world."

"The tiger will walk into the cage, and Tracy will shut the cage, is that right?" the Chief said.

"Yes," Huzinga said.

"On the mezzanine of the store, unnoticed, are two of our younger men, Splicer and Slew, to report what they see to us later on, is that right?"

"Yes. They're there now."

"Call them."

Huzinga called, and Slew came to the 'phone. Huzinga and Slew spoke a moment.

"They're all set," Huzinga said.

"What was it you told him not to do?" the Chief said.

"He asked if he could take some photographs," Huzinga said. "He doesn't know what he's going to be observing, but he's got his camera."

"Don't you think it might be a good idea to have him take some pictures?" the Chief said.

"We promised we wouldn't," Huzinga said.

"This is the Police Department," the Chief said. "What do we care what we promised?"

"Even so, I don't think we'd better take any pictures," Huzinga said.

"O.K.," the Chief said. "If we've not all of us gone mad, and he does get the tiger in the cage, he's going to leave the store and go on down Warren Street with the girl, is that right?"

"Yes."

"Where's he going?" Bly said.

"None of our business," Huzinga said. "For a walk, I suppose."

"We're to go to the store the minute he leaves, for the reports of Splicer and Slew, is that right?"

"Yes."

"In back of the store is a moving van," the Chief said. "The tiger in the cage will be placed in the van. As soon as possible the tiger will be examined, given any care it may need, and then turned loose where it can harm no one, is that right?"

"Yes."

"Where would that be?" Bly said.

"The animal's trainer has stated that the animal was born in captivity," Huzinga said. "The place was Madison Square Garden. Tracy has asked that the tiger be turned loose in the mountains nearest New York."

"Who says it will be safe there?" the Chief said.

"The nearest mountains that are wild," Huzinga said. "Where people do not live."

"I'm not thinking of people," Bly said. "I'm thinking of the tiger. How's it going to live? It's liable to run into a hunter, and be shot."

"Those are decent chances," Huzinga said.

"That's if everything goes the way Tracy and you like to believe they're going to go," the Chief said. "What do we do if the tiger doesn't appear?"

The younger man looked at the older one.

"You'll *have* to fire me," Huzinga said, "so I'll resign."

"No one else knows, is that right?" Bly said.

"Just you and I," Huzinga said, "but if it flops, I resign."

"What about Tracy and the girl—if it flops?"

"I've given Dr. Scatter my word to take them both back to Bellevue," Huzinga said.

"Does Dr. Scatter know about all this?"

"No, I cooked up another story," Huzinga said. "Pingitzer knows. I mean, he knows Laura Luthy's going to meet Tracy at half-past twelve in front of Otto Seyfang's. He doesn't know anything else, though."

"Where's *he?*" Bly said.

"Tracy asked Dr. Pingitzer to sit in the Tasting Department," Huzinga said. "I saw him go in a few minutes before you arrived."

"What's he doing in there?" Bly said.

"Tracy wanted him in there."

"Does Tracy know that if the thing flops he and the girl go back to Bellevue?"

"No," Huzinga said. "That's the thing that bothers me. I *did* keep that from him. I thought I'd better. I don't feel easy about it, though."

The radio reported again at half-past eight. Again it was all quiet. The Chief telephoned his secretary.

"We've had two all quiets," he said. "I want to know exactly what's happened, *whatever* it is. Call me back."

The secretary called back and said, "All precincts report no events of any kind."

"Are you sure?"

"Yes, sir."

"Has this ever happened before?" the Chief said. "A whole New York hour with no events at all?"

"Not as far as I know," the secretary said.

"Well," Bly said to Huzinga, "*something's* happened. No episodes of any kind, not even drunks, not even a family fight, not even a petty theft, not even a disturbance of the peace in a whole New York hour."

CHAPTER 14

Back at his old job, Tracy lifted a coffee sack to his shoulder, carried it fifty yards, and set it down, but it was not easy to do.

Tracy walked with another sack from the far end of the storage room to the wall of the Tasting Department, and then another. Each time he set a sack down he wanted to go in and taste some coffee with Peberty, Ringert, Shively, and Pingitzer because he could hear them talking, although he could not make out what they were saying. But he knew it would not do to go in until he had achieved again the knack of doing the work easily, until he had begun to enjoy doing it.

He was tired after each trip. The weight of each sack on his shoulder was enormous. Several times his knees almost gave way. He couldn't understand. It was only six years ago that the work had been so easy for him. His breathing was difficult and his heart pounded each time he lifted a sack and walked with it.

He stopped at the rear window at last, to rest, to think about the problem, to look down at the alley and the things there.

Well, it was still the same: asphalt, old brick and stone, discoloured wood, garbage cans, miscellaneous junk and rubbish strewn about, a stubborn old tree, a few weeds, a low arch in the brick of the building across the alley, a number of bricks having fallen loose, two of them still lying in the alley.

He needed to rest a long time, staring down at the miserable scene. It was all new once, hopeful, bright and clean, but now it was pathetic.

And yet on the next trip he longed to see it again, as a lover longs to see his beloved, lying sick in bed.

When he came back from the fifth trip and looked at the scene, he began to see beauty in it, and the next sack he lifted was the first not to make him groan.

He walked with it easier, too, and when he set it down he heard Pingitzer and the others laugh.

The next time he looked at the scene the tree was beautiful. He smiled, thinking of the years it had been there—certainly more than six, for he had seen it then, too. Its leaves weren't green, but only because the city had covered them with its dirt. It wasn't big because there wasn't earth enough for its roots to spread out in, or space enough for its branches. But what there *was* of it was there, and it *was* a tree. In all probability its patience had been rewarded from time to time by the arrival of a bird, to greet it and go, or even to stay, to build a nest in it. The tree *was* there, there was no question about that. It had been there for a long time, and was still there. Its trunk was hard and tough, bruised here and there, but for all that still strong.

Each sack Tracy lifted and carried to the wall of the Tasting Department was easier to lift and carry. The lifting and carrying of the ninth sack wasn't work at all.

It was almost nine o'clock then, there was still a great deal to be done before twelve, but Tracy stepped into the Tasting Department.

The men sat around the round table, each of them with a silver coffee-pot beside him, Pingitzer's pot percolating.

"Ah ha," Pingitzer said. "Just in time. Here is coffee, my own idea, from Vienna, long ago." He poured a cup for Tracy, lifted it, Tracy took the cup, then tasted the coffee in it. He took his time tasting it, then tasted it again.

"Good," he said.

"My own idea," Pingitzer said. "Vienna."

Tracy walked around the room, listening to the others, as he had done six years ago. When his cup was empty, he took it to Shively, who filled it for him out of *his* pot. Shively's coffee was good, too.

"Well, I've got to get back to work," Tracy said. "I've got a lot to do."

"Ah ha," Pingitzer said. "This is way of youth. This is illusion of youth. This is *fine* illusion. Was time in Vienna when Pingitzer have this way and this illusion. This was fine time, fine way, fine illusion. Ah ha. Here is Pingitzer, seventy-two, wishing no more to work, to have fine illusion."

"I'll be back after a while," Tracy said.

He went straight to the window to have another look at the alley. There was much for him to think about that he wanted to get to as slowly as possible, but at the same time get to in the next hour or two. Time had always fascinated him. He knew he didn't understand it, but he also knew that anything you ever got—anything that ever mattered—any thought—any truth—you got *instantly*. You could wait forever if you wanted to, and let it go at that, or you could get moving—moving *into* time and *with* time—working at the thought to be received, and then suddenly, from having moved into time and with time, and from having worked at the thought, get it, get it whole, get it clean, get it instantly.

But you had to stay slow somewhere inside of yourself, too, to give the arrival a place to stop. You had to be going swiftly and you had to be almost not moving at all at the same time.

There was much for Tracy to think about, much to do, and the doing of what needed to be done had to begin with Tracy working. All that needed to be done—and it was a great deal—had to begin with the doing of a simple work, had to do with the lifting and carrying of the coffee sacks.

Tracy stood a moment, smiling at the miserable scene that was also beautiful, at the enormity of the work to be done, remembering each of the matters involved but trying not to hurry them, his eyes wandering to the low arch in the old building across the alley.

He carried a half-dozen more sacks before he stopped to glance at the scene again, and this time he only *glanced*, for the work had become exhilarating and he wanted to get on with it. But during the glance it seemed to him that he had seen something. He was carrying another sack when he wondered what it had been that he'd seen, or if he'd imagined it, from having been at a time so intense with possibilities.

He decided to carry at least a half-dozen more sacks before stopping a moment again. This time he would go to the back door, open it, and go out on the steps and look from there.

When he was on the steps, not looking anywhere in particular, he thought he saw it again, and there was a deep gladness in him. It was there, whatever it was. It was there somewhere. There was no doubt about that.

He went back to work, carried three more sacks, then stepped into the Tasting Department to spend another moment with the coffee tasters.

"How does it feel after six years?" Ringert said.

"It's beginning to feel all right again," Tracy said. "How about you, Ringert?"

"Oh," Ringert said. "Can't kick, Tracy."

"Ah ha," Pingitzer said. "This kick. This is two? One. To move foot? Two. To make complaint? Can't move with foot? Can't make complaint?"

"I don't know," Ringert said. "I can move with foot all right, but not the way I *could*. And I can complain, too, but not the way I could. I used to be able to complain about anything, and it was a lot of fun. Now, I have only one thing to complain about, and I don't even want to complain about *that*."

"Is what, this thing?" Pingitzer said.

"Ringert's end."

"Ah ha. What is taste of Ringert's coffee?"

"Good," Tracy said.

"Please," Pingitzer said, holding his cup across the table to Ringert, who poured it full. Dr. Pingitzer tasted the coffee, then said, "Ah ha. Good."

Tracy carried three more sacks, then stood at the window, with his back turned to the scene, listening. He stood a long time, perhaps three minutes. There was silence in the alley. When he was not sure he had heard something, he decided he was not sure, and went back to work. Each time he came for a new sack he paused for a moment to listen again. When he'd carried six more sacks and had listened six more times, he sat on a sack, not to rest, but to be thankful, to be near things, near the inside of things, and to smile at anything that might be near.

When he was finally sure he had heard the word, he was not surprised. He did not leap to his feet. He did not turn. He said the word back very softly. After a moment he heard it again, and then very slowly he got up and lifted a sack to his shoulder and walked with it.

When he put the sack down and turned he saw the tiger.

Its appearance was pitiful, even from so far away. It was starved, sick, weak, and wounded. He went back to the pile of sacks, scarcely looking at the tiger, lifted another sack and walked off with it. On this third trip the tiger climbed to the top of the pile of sacks, spread itself flat, to rest there and watch.

Tracy and the tiger talked, but this time not with words, not even with sounds, and each of them understood.

The swift thought had arrived to stay.

When all the sacks had been moved, it was a quarter after twelve. The coffee tasters had left the Tasting Department to go to lunch. The tiger stood beside Tracy, and then together they went down two flights of stairs to the entrance of the building. The tiger was frightened by the door to the street, and hung back. Tracy stayed near the tiger a moment, saying nothing, then went out alone, to stand on the steps, the door swinging shut behind him.

CHAPTER 15

In the second-floor room across the street Captain Huzinga and Chief Bly watched.

There, on schedule, was Thomas Tracy standing in front of Otto Seyfang's.

"What time is it?" Bly said.

"Half-past twelve," Huzinga said. "Don't you think it'll happen?"

"Something's *already* happened," Bly said. "You heard the reports on the radio every half-hour."

"Yes."

"All quiet for four full hours."

"Yes. Do you think it'll happen?"

"I don't care if it doesn't," the Chief said. "Look at him. He's no madman."

"He's mad all right," Huzinga said suddenly. "This whole thing is. I got it wrong. I misunderstood. We've got that sign up there. *Otto Seyfang's.* Otto Seyfang's been dead three years. The place is a warehouse. It's not a coffee importing house. This is *now.* It's not six years ago. He's mad all right, but not as mad as I am to have believed any of us could do the one thing that's broken the human heart since the beginning of time. It can't be done. It can't be done, that's all. I feel sorry for him. He's crazy. He doesn't know it, but he's got to go back to Bellevue, and the girl with him. Nothing's going to happen, Chief. I'm sorry. I'll resign. I believed with all my heart he could do it. It's madness to believe *that.* Nothing's going to happen."

"What about the stuff that's *already* happened?" Bly said.

"An accident," Huzinga said. "Besides, it's happened before. I happen to have studied the old records. In December, 1882, there were *seven* hours in which nothing was reported. In March of 1896 there were *eleven* hours, in July of 1901 *five*, in August of 1908 *nine*. It's happened before."

"Yes," the Chief said. "Well, how do you know something *else* didn't happen at the same time that nobody knows about? Something else happened secretly?"

"You mean, you think something's *still* going to happen?" Huzinga said.

"I say it's *already* happened," the Chief said. "And I say don't take them back to Bellevue."

"I gave Dr. Scatter my word," Huzinga said. "In a few minutes I'll take them back and resign."

"You don't have to resign," Bly said. "We can go out on a limb, can't we? We've done it before—many times. You haven't lost your job. There's nothing at stake for you here. So the thing flops. Who cares?"

"I care," Huzinga said.

Suddenly they saw Laura Luthy walking down Warren Street.

They saw Tracy and Laura meet. They saw them smile. They saw their lips move in speech. They saw Laura go up the three steps to Tracy. They saw him put his arms around her. They saw her arms tighten around him. They saw Peberdy, Ringert, Shively, and Ping-itzer standing together, watching. They saw Tracy take Laura by the arm to go, but just before going they saw Tracy reach over to the door, and open it.

He didn't open it very much, just enough.

Then they saw Tracy's tiger come out and stand beside Laura Luthy.

It was a black panther that limped on its right front foot. Except for the limp, it was the handsomest black panther anybody ever saw.

They saw Tracy and Laura Luthy and Tracy's tiger walk together down Warren Street. They saw them go into the store with the pictures of the animals hanging on the walls of it.

After a while they saw Tracy and Laura come out and walk away, toward the docks at the end of Warren Street.

And they saw that there was no longer a tiger with them.

Bly and Huzinga ran downstairs, out of the building to the street, across the street, and into the store. They found Splicer and Slew standing together, waiting for them.

"Which one of you is Slew?" Bly said.

"I am, sir," one of the men said.

"All right," Bly said. "Tell me *exactly* what you just saw."

"I saw a young man and a young woman come in here and look

at every picture hanging on the walls of this store," Slew said. "I saw them go out."

"Anything else?" Bly said.

"No, sir."

"You, Splicer," Bly said. "Tell me exactly what *you* saw."

"I saw the same, sir," Splicer said.

"Are you sure?"

"Yes, sir."

"Return to your stations, please," Bly said.

The two young officers left the store.

"Well?" Bly said to Huzinga. "How about it?"

"I don't know," Huzinga said. "You *did* see the tiger, didn't you?"

"I saw the tiger," Bly said.

"You're not just saying that, are you?" Huzinga said. " You *did* see him open the door? You did *see* the tiger come out and stand beside her, didn't you?"

"Yes, I saw it all," Bly said.

"Splicer and Slew *didn't* see the tiger," Huzinga said.

"No, they didn't," Bly said.

"And the tiger's gone," Huzinga said.

"Yes, it is," Bly said.

"What happened to the tiger?" Huzinga said.

"I don't know," the Chief said.

"Well," Huzinga said. "I'd like the rest of the day off, if it's all right with you."

"Your work's done," Bly said. "What are you going to do? Go to a ball game?"

"No," Huzinga said. "I think I'd like to go up to St. Patrick's for a while. Then I think I'd like to go home. I can't wait to see my wife and kids again."

"Yes," the Chief said. "Well, get going."

Huzinga went from one painting in the room to the other, and then left the store and went to Saint Patrick's. Bly now looked at each of the pictures. He went back for one last look at the picture of the Arab asleep in the desert, with the lion standing over him.

Then he too left the store and went to Saint Patrick's.

That is the story of Thomas Tracy, Laura Luthy, and the tiger, which is love.

THE SAROYAN PRIZES,
1908–1939

HAVING been awarded prizes,
Ribbons, money, honors, invitations,
And other things,
I, William Saroyan,
Born August 31, 1908,
In Fresno, California;
Student at Emerson Public School
On L Street, between San Benito and Santa Clara;
Holder of the First Prize for Street Sales,
The Fresno *Evening Herald*, 1917;
Twice Winner of the Around-the-Block Race, 1918;
Founder, Manager, and Boss of Henry-and-
Willie's Empty Lot for Sons of Armenians,
Assyrians, and Other Immigrants;
Winner of Highest Third-Grade Binet-Simon Intelligence Rating,
"Far Above Average, Although Poor at Arithmetic";
Official Letter-Writer to Mayor Toomey
For the Fifth Grade;
Speaker at the First Meeting
Of the Parent-Teachers' Association;
Singer of "The River Shannon";
Author of "How I Earned My First Dollar";
First to Dive from the Oak Tree
Into Thompson Ditch at Malaga;
First to Climb Geggenheim's Water Tank
And Drop a Cat;
Most Frequent Visitor of the Public Library;
Borrower of the Most and Best Books;
First Reader of the Autobiography of Benjamin Franklin;
First to Subscribe to Lionel Strongfort's
Body-Building Course;

Holder of the Certificate for Freehand Penmanship;
Fastest Postal Telegraph Messenger
In the San Joaquin Valley, 1921,
And Other Things Too Recent
Or Too Numerous to Mention,
Award:

To the leaders of the English, French,
German, Italian, Spanish, Russian,
Jewish, Japanese, Chinese, Balinese,
Arab, Afghan, African, American,
And all other peoples,

For their superhuman acceptance
And extension of stupidity,
Lying, and conniving
As a basis for correct human behavior—

11¢.

To all soldiers, excepting professionals,

For their skill at marching,
And for their pathetic faith
In killing and dying for nonsense,
Or at least for nothing they can understand—

One cancelled air-mail stamp.

To all intellectuals,

For the effectiveness with which
They have introduced the truths and beauties
Of art into life
And saved the living from disgrace—

One plugged nickel.

To the Church, in all its variations,

For its noble influence everywhere—

One oyster-shell button.

To you, for being fond of me—

Any prize you like,
Any colored ribbon,
Any amount of money,
Whatever honor you please,
An open invitation,
My typewriter, my cornet, my bicycle,
All my letters from important people,
All my prizes, ribbons, medals, honors, awards,
As well as the things you care about.

THE DARING YOUNG MAN
ON THE FLYING TRAPEZE

CHAPTER 1 *Sleep*

Horizontally wakeful amid universal widths, practising laughter and mirth, satire, the end of all, Rome and yes of Babylon, clenched teeth, remembrance, much warmth volcanic, the streets of Paris, the plains of Jericho, much gliding as of reptile in abstraction, a gallery of water-colours, the sea and the fish with eyes, symphony, a table in the corner of the Eiffel Tower, jazz at the opera house, alarm clock and the tap-dancing of doom, conversation with a tree, the river Nile, the roar of Dostoyevsky, and the dark sun.

This earth, the face of one who lived, the form without the weight, weeping upon snow, white music, the magnified flower twice the size of the universe, black clouds, the caged panther staring, deathless space, Mr. Eliot with rolled sleeves baking bread, Flaubert and Guy de Maupassant, a wordless rhyme of early meaning, Finlandia, mathematics highly polished and slick as a green onion to the teeth, Jerusalem, the path to paradox.

The deep song of man, the sly whisper of someone unseen but vaguely known, hurricane in the cornfield, a game of chess, hush the queen, the king, Karl Franz, black Titanic, Mr. Chaplin weeping, Stalin, Hitler, a multitude of Jews, tomorrow is Monday, no dancing in the streets.

O swift moment of life: it is ended, again the earth is now.

CHAPTER 2 *Wakefulness*

He (the living) dressed and shaved, grinning at himself in the mirror. Very unhandsome, he said; where is my tie? (He had but one.) Coffee and a grey sky, Pacific Ocean fog, the drone of a passing street car, people going to the city, time again, the day, prose and poetry. He moved swiftly down the stairs to the street and began to walk, thinking suddenly. *It is only in sleep that we may know we live. There only, in that living death, do we meet ourselves and the far earth, God and the saints, the names of our fathers, the substance of remote moments: it is there that the centuries merge in the moment, that the vast becomes the tiny, tangible atom of eternity.*

He walked into the day as alertly as might be, making a definite noise with his heels, perceiving with his eyes the superficial truth of streets and structures, the trivial truth of reality. Helplessly his mind sang, *He flies through the air with the greatest of ease, the daring young man on the flying trapeze,* then laughed with all the might of his being. It was really a splendid morning: grey, cold, and cheerless, a morning for inward vigour; ah, Edgar Guest, he said, how I long for your music.

In the gutter he saw a coin which proved to be a penny dated 1923, and placing it in the palm of his hand he examined it closely, remembering that year and thinking of Lincoln, whose profile was stamped upon the coin. There was almost nothing a man could do with a penny. I will purchase a motor-car, he thought. I will dress myself in the fashion of a fop, visit the hotel strumpets, drink and dine, and then return to the quiet. Or I will drop the coin into a slot and weigh myself.

It was good to be poor, and the Communists—but it was dreadful to be hungry. What appetites they had, how fond they were of food! Empty stomachs. He remembered how greatly he needed food. Every meal was bread and coffee and cigarettes, and now he had no more bread. Coffee without bread could never honestly serve as supper, and there were no weeds in the park that could be cooked as spinach is cooked.

If the truth were known, he was half starved, and there was still no end of books he ought to read before he died. He remembered the young Italian in a Brooklyn hospital, a small sick clerk named Mollica, who had said desperately, I would like to see California once before I die. And he thought earnestly, I ought at least to read *Hamlet* once again; or perhaps *Huckleberry Finn*.

It was then that he became thoroughly awake: at the thought of dying. Now wakefulness was a state in the nature of a sustained shock. A young man could perish rather unostentatiously, he thought; and already he was very nearly starved. Water and prose were fine, they

filled much inorganic space, but they were inadequate. If there were
only some work he might do for money, some trivial labour in the
name of commerce. If they would only allow him to sit at a desk
all day and add trade figures, subtract and multiply and divide, then
perhaps he would not die. He would buy food, all sorts of it: un-
tasted delicacies from Norway, Italy, and France; all manner of
beef, lamb, fish, cheese; grapes, figs, pears, apples, melons, which he
would worship when he had satisfied his hunger. He would place a
bunch of red grapes on a dish beside two black figs, a large yellow
pear, and a green apple. He would hold a cut melon to his nostrils
for hours. He would buy great brown loaves of French bread, vegetables of all sorts, meat, life.

From a hill he saw the city standing majestically in the east, great
towers, dense with his kind, and there he was suddenly outside of it
all, almost definitely certain that he should never gain admittance,
almost positive that somehow he had ventured upon the wrong
earth, or perhaps into the wrong age, and now a young man of
twenty-two was to be permanently ejected from it. This thought was
not saddening. He said to himself, sometime soon I must write *An
Application for Permission to Live.* He accepted the thought of dying
without pity for himself or for man, believing that he would at least
sleep another night. His rent for another day was paid; there was
yet another tomorrow. And after that he might go where other homeless men went. He might even visit the Salvation Army—sing to
God and Jesus (unlover of my soul), be saved, eat and sleep. But
he knew that he would not. His life was a private life. He did not
wish to destroy this fact. Any other alternative would be better.

Through the air on the flying trapeze, his mind hummed. Amusing it was, astoundingly funny. A trapeze to God, or to nothing, a
flying trapeze to some sort of eternity; he prayed objectively for
strength to make the flight with grace.

I have one cent, he said. It is an American coin. In the evening
I shall polish it until it glows like a sun and I shall study the words.

He was now walking in the city itself, among living men. There
were one or two places to go. He saw his reflection in plate-glass windows of stores and was disappointed with his appearance. He seemed
not at all as strong as he felt; he seemed, in fact, a trifle infirm in
every part of his body, in his neck, his shoulders, arms, trunk, and
knees. This will never do, he said, and with an effort he assembled
all his disjointed parts and became tensely, artificially erect and solid.

He passed numerous restaurants with magnificent discipline, refusing even to glance into them, and at last reached a building which he entered. He rose in an elevator to the seventh floor, moved down a hall, and, opening a door, walked into the office of an employment agency. Already there were two dozen young men in the place; he found a corner where he stood waiting his turn to be interviewed. At length he was granted this great privilege and was questioned by a thin, scatter-brained miss of fifty.

Now tell me, she said; what can you do?

He was embarrassed. I can write, he said pathetically.

You mean your penmanship is good? Is that it? said the elderly maiden.

Well, yes, he replied. But I mean that I can write.

Write what? said the miss, almost with anger.

Prose, he said simply.

There was a pause. At last the lady said:

Can you use a typewriter?

Of course, said the young man.

All right, went on the miss, we have your address; we will get in touch with you. There is nothing this morning, nothing at all.

It was much the same at the other agency, except that he was questioned by a conceited young man who closely resembled a pig. From the agencies he went to the large department stores: there was a good deal of pomposity, some humiliation on his part, and finally the report that work was not available. He did not feel displeased, and strangely did not even feel that he was personally involved in all the foolishness. He was a living young man who was in need of money with which to go on being one, and there was no way of getting it except by working for it; and there was no work. It was purely an abstract problem which he wished for the last time to attempt to solve. Now he was pleased that the matter was closed.

He began to perceive the definiteness of the course of his life. Except for moments, it had been largely artless, but now at the last minute he was determined that there should be as little imprecision as possible.

He passed countless stores and restaurants on his way to the Y.M.C.A., where he helped himself to paper and ink and began to compose his *Application*. For an hour he worked on this document, then suddenly, owing to the bad air in the place and to hunger, he became faint. He seemed to be swimming away from himself with great strokes, and hurriedly left the building. In the Civic Centre Park, across from the Public Library Building, he drank almost a quart of water and felt himself refreshed. An old man was standing in the centre of the brick boulevard surrounded by sea-gulls, pigeons, and robins. He was taking handfuls of bread crumbs from a large paper sack and tossing them to the birds with a gallant gesture.

Dimly he felt impelled to ask the old man for a portion of the crumbs, but would not allow the thought even nearly to reach consciousness; he entered the Public Library and for an hour read Proust, then, feeling himself to be swimming away again, he rushed outdoors. He drank more water at the fountain in the park and began the long walk to his room.

I'll go and sleep some more, he said; there is nothing else to do. He knew now that he was much too tired and weak to deceive himself about being all right, and yet his mind seemed somehow still lithe and alert. It, as if it were a separate entity, persisted in articulating impertinent pleasantries about his very real physical suffering. He reached his room early in the afternoon and immediately prepared coffee on the small gas range. There was no milk in the can, and the half pound of sugar he had purchased a week before was all gone; he drank a cup of the hot black fluid, sitting on his bed and smiling.

From the Y.M.C.A. he had stolen a dozen sheets of letter paper upon which he hoped to complete his document, but now the very notion of writing was unpleasant to him. There was nothing to say. He began to polish the penny he had found in the morning, and this absurd act somehow afforded him great enjoyment. No American coin can be made to shine so brilliantly as a penny. How many pennies would he need to go on living? Wasn't there something more he might sell? He looked about the bare room. No. His watch was gone; also his books. All those fine books; nine of them for eighty-five cents. He felt ill and ashamed for having parted with his books. His best suit he had sold for two dollars, but that was all right. He didn't mind at all about clothes. But the books. That was different. It made him very angry to think that there was no respect for men who wrote.

He placed the shining penny on the table, looking upon it with the delight of a miser. How prettily it smiles, he said. Without reading them he looked at the words, *E Pluribus Unum One Cent United States of America*, and turning the penny over, he saw Lincoln and the words, *In God We Trust Liberty* 1923. How beautiful it is, he said.

He became drowsy and felt a ghastly illness coming over his blood, a feeling of nausea and disintegration. Bewildered, he stood beside his bed, thinking there *is nothing to do but sleep.* Already he felt himself making great strides through the fluid of the earth, swimming away to the beginning. He fell face down upon the bed, saying, I ought first at least to give the coin to some child. A child could buy any number of things with a penny.

Then swiftly, neatly, with the grace of the young man on the trapeze, he was gone from his body. For an eternal moment he was all things at once: the bird, the fish, the rodent, the reptile, and man. An ocean of print undulated endlessly and darkly before him. The city burned. The herded crowd rioted. The earth circled away, and knowing that he did so, he turned his lost face to the empty sky and became dreamless, unalive, perfect.

THE PARSLEY GARDEN

ONE day in August Al Condraj was wandering through Woolworth's without a penny to spend when he saw a small hammer that was not a toy but a real hammer and he was possessed with a longing to have it. He believed it was just what he needed by which to break the monotony and with which to make something. He had gathered some firstclass nails from Foley's Packing House where the boxmakers worked and where they had carelessly dropped at least fifteen cents' worth. He had gladly gone to the trouble of gathering them together because it had seemed to him that a nail, as such, was not something to be wasted. He had the nails, perhaps a half pound of them, at least two hundred of them, in a paper bag in the apple box in which he kept his junk at home.

Now, with the ten-cent hammer he believed he could make something out of box wood and the nails, although he had no idea what. Some sort of a table perhaps, or a small bench.

At any rate he took the hammer and slipped it into the pocket of his overalls, but just as he did so a man took him firmly by the arm without a word and pushed him to the back of the store into a small office. Another man, an older one, was seated behind a desk in the office, working with papers. The younger man, the one who had captured him, was excited and his forehead was covered with sweat.

"Well," he said, "here's one more of them."

The man behind the desk got to his feet and looked Al Condraj up and down.

"What's *he* swiped?"

"A hammer." The young man looked at Al with hatred. "Hand it over," he said.

The boy brought the hammer out of his pocket and handed it to the young man, who said, "I ought to hit you over the head with it, that's what I ought to do."

He turned to the older man, the boss, the manager of the store, and he said, "What do you want me to do with him?"

58

"Leave him with me," the older man said.

The younger man stepped out of the office, and the older man sat down and went back to work. Al Condraj stood in the office fifteen minutes before the older man looked at him again.

"Well," he said.

Al didn't know what to say. The man wasn't looking at him, he was looking at the door.

Finally Al said, "I didn't mean to steal it. I just need it and I haven't got any money."

"Just because you haven't got any money doesn't mean you've got a right to steal things," the man said. "Now, does it?"

"No, sir."

"Well, what am I going to do with you? Turn you over to the police?"

Al didn't say anything, but he certainly didn't want to be turned over to the police. He hated the man, but at the same time he realized somebody else could be a lot tougher than he was being.

"If I let you go, will you promise never to steal from this store again?"

"Yes, sir."

"All right," the man said. "Go out this way and don't come back to this store until you've got some money to spend."

He opened a door to the hall that led to the alley, and Al Condraj hurried down the hall and out into the alley.

The first thing he did when he was free was laugh, but he knew he had been humiliated and he was deeply ashamed. It was not in his nature to take things that did not belong to him. He hated the young man who had caught him and he hated the manager of the store who had made him stand in silence in the office so long. He hadn't liked it at all when the young man had said he ought to hit him over the head with the hammer.

He should have had the courage to look him straight in the eye and say, "You and who else?"

Of course he *had* stolen the hammer and he had been caught, but it seemed to him he oughtn't to have been so humiliated.

After he had walked three blocks he decided he didn't want to go home just yet, so he turned around and started walking back to town. He almost believed he meant to go back and say something to the young man who had caught him. And then he wasn't sure he didn't mean to go back and steal the hammer again, and this time *not* get caught. As long as he had been made to feel like a thief anyway, the least he ought to get out of it was the hammer.

Outside the store he lost his nerve, though. He stood in the street, looking in, for at least ten minutes.

Then, crushed and confused and now bitterly ashamed of himself, first for having stolen something, then for having been caught, then for having been humiliated, then for not having guts enough to go back and do the job right, he began walking home again, his mind so troubled that he didn't greet his pal Pete Wawchek when they came face to face outside Graf's Hardware.

When he got home he was too ashamed to go inside and examine his junk, so he had a long drink of water from the faucet in the back yard. The faucet was used by his mother to water the stuff she planted every year: okra, bell peppers, tomatoes, cucumbers, onions, garlic, mint, eggplants and parsley.

His mother called the whole business the parsley garden, and every night in the summer she would bring chairs out of the house and put them around the table she had had Ondro, the neighborhood handyman, make for her for fifteen cents, and she would sit at the table and enjoy the cool of the garden and the smell of the things she had planted and tended.

Sometimes she would even make a salad and moisten the flat old-country bread and slice some white cheese, and she and he would have supper in the parsley garden. After supper she would attach the water hose to the faucet and water her plants and the place would be cooler than ever and it would smell real good, real fresh and cool and green, all the different growing things making a green-garden smell out of themselves and the air and the water.

After the long drink of water he sat down where the parsley itself was growing and he pulled a handful of it out and slowly ate it. Then he went inside and told his mother what had happened. He even told her what he had *thought* of doing after he had been turned loose: to go back and steal the hammer again.

"I don't want you to steal," his mother said in broken English. "Here is ten cents. You go back to that man and you give him this money and you bring it home, that hammer."

"No," Al Condraj said. "I won't take your money for something I don't really need. I just thought I ought to have a hammer, so I could make something if I felt like it. I've got a lot of nails and some box wood, but I haven't a hammer."

"Go buy it, that hammer," his mother said.

"No," Al said.

"All right," his mother said. "Shut up."

That's what she always said when she didn't know what else to say.

Al went out and sat on the steps. His humiliation was beginning to really hurt now. He decided to wander off along the railroad tracks to Foley's because he needed to think about it some more. At Foley's he watched Johnny Gale nailing boxes for ten minutes, but Johnny was too busy to notice him or talk to him, although one day at Sunday school, two or three years ago, Johnny had greeted him and said, "How's the boy?" Johnny worked with a boxmaker's hatchet and everybody in Fresno said he was the fastest boxmaker in town. He was the closest thing to a machine any packing house ever saw. Foley himself was proud of Johnny Gale.

Al Condraj finally set out for home because he didn't want to get in the way. He didn't want somebody working hard to notice that he was being watched and maybe say to him, "Go on, beat it." He didn't want Johnny Gale to do something like that. He didn't want to invite another humiliation.

On the way home he looked for money but all he found was the usual pieces of broken glass and rusty nails, the things that were always cutting his bare feet every summer.

When he got home his mother had made a salad and set the table, so he sat down to eat, but when he put the food in his mouth he just didn't care for it. He got up and went into the three-room house and got his apple box out of the corner of his room and went through his junk. It was all there, the same as yesterday.

He wandered off back to town and stood in front of the closed store, hating the young man who had caught him, and then he went along to the Hippodrome and looked at the display photographs from the two movies that were being shown that day.

Then he went along to the public library to have a look at all the books again, but he didn't like any of them, so he wandered around town some more, and then around half-past eight he went home and went to bed.

His mother had already gone to bed because she had to be up at five to go to work at Inderrieden's, packing figs. Some days there would be work all day, some days there would be only half a day of it, but whatever his mother earned during the summer had to keep them the whole year.

He didn't sleep much that night because he couldn't get over what had happened, and he went over six or seven ways by which to adjust the matter. He went so far as to believe it would be necessary to kill the young man who had caught him. He also believed it would be necessary for him to steal systematically and successfully the rest of his life. It was a hot night and he couldn't sleep.

Finally, his mother got up and walked barefooted to the kitchen for a drink of water and on the way back she said to him softly, "Shut up."

When she got up at five in the morning he was out of the house, but that had happened many times before. He was a restless boy, and he kept moving all the time every summer. He was making mistakes and paying for them, and he had just tried stealing and had been caught at it and he was troubled. She fixed her breakfast, packed her lunch and hurried off to work, hoping it would be a full day.

It was a full day, and then there was overtime, and although she had no more lunch she decided to work on for the extra money, anyway. Almost all the other packers were staying on, too, and her neighbor across the alley, Leeza Ahboot, who worked beside her, said, "Let us work until the work stops, then we'll go home and fix a supper between us and eat it in your parsley garden where it's so cool. It's a hot day and there's no sense not making an extra fifty or sixty cents."

When the two women reached the garden it was almost nine o'clock, but still daylight, and she saw her son nailing pieces of box wood together, making something with a hammer. It looked like a bench. He had already watered the garden and tidied up the rest of the yard, and the place seemed very nice, and her son seemed very serious and busy. She and Leeza went straight to work for their supper, picking bell peppers and tomatoes and cucumbers and a great deal of parsley for the salad.

Then Leeza went to her house for some bread which she had baked the night before, and some white cheese, and in a few minutes they were having supper together and talking pleasantly about the successful day they had had. After supper, they made Turkish coffee over an open fire in the yard. They drank the coffee and smoked a cigarette apiece, and told one another stories about their experiences in the old country and here in Fresno, and then they looked into their cups at the grounds to see if any good fortune was indicated, and there was: health and work and supper out of doors in the summer and enough money for the rest of the year.

Al Condraj worked and overheard some of the things they said, and then Leeza went home to go to bed, and his mother said, "Where you get it, that hammer, Al?"

"I got it at the store."

"How you get it? You steal it?"

Al Condraj finished the bench and sat on it. "No," he said. "I didn't steal it."

"How you get it?"

"I worked at the store for it," Al said.

"The store where you steal it yesterday?"

"Yes."

"Who give you job?"

"The boss."

"What you do?"

"I carried different stuff to the different counters."

"Well, that's good," the woman said. "How long you work for that little hammer?"

"I worked all day," Al said. "Mr. Clemmer gave me the hammer after I'd worked one hour, but I went right on working. The fellow who caught me yesterday showed me what to do, and we worked together. We didn't talk, but at the end of the day he took me to Mr. Clemmer's office and he told Mr. Clemmer that I'd worked hard all day and ought to be paid at least a dollar."

"That's good," the woman said.

"So Mr. Clemmer put a silver dollar on his desk for me, and then the fellow who caught me yesterday told him the store needed a boy like me every day, for a dollar a day, and Mr. Clemmer said I could have the job."

"That's good," the woman said. "You can make it a little money for yourself."

"I left the dollar on Mr. Clemmer's desk," Al Condraj said, "and I told them both I didn't want the job."

"Why you say that?" the woman said. "Dollar a day for eleven-year-old boy good money. Why you not take job?"

"Because I hate the both of them," the boy said. "I would never work for people like that. I just looked at them and picked up my hammer and walked out. I came home and I made this bench."

"All right," his mother said. "Shut up."

His mother went inside and went to bed, but Al Condraj sat on the bench he had made and smelled the parsley garden and didn't feel humiliated any more.

But nothing could stop him from hating the two men, even though he knew they hadn't done anything they shouldn't have done.

THE HUMMINGBIRD THAT
LIVED THROUGH WINTER

SOMETIMES even instinct is overpowered by individuality—in creatures other than men, I mean. In men instinct is supposed to be controlled, but whether or not it ever actually is I leave to others. At any rate, the fundamental instinct of most—or all—creatures is to live. Each form of life has an instinctive technique of defense against other forms of life, as well as against the elements. What happens to hummingbirds is something I have never found out— from actual observation or from reading. They die, that's true. And they're born somehow or other, although I have never seen a hummingbird's egg, or a young hummingbird.

The mature hummingbird itself is so small that the egg must be magnificent, probably one of the most smiling little things in the world. Now, if hummingbirds come into the world through some other means than eggs, I ask the reader to forgive me. The only thing I know about Agass Agasig Agassig Agazig (well, the great American naturalist) is that he once studied turtle eggs, and in order to get the information he was seeking, had to find fresh ones. This caused an exciting adventure in Boston to a young fellow who wrote about it six or seven years before I read it, when I was fourteen. I was fourteen in 1922, which goes to show you how unimportant the years are when you're dealing with eggs of any kind. I envy the people who study birds, and some day I hope to find out everything that's known about hummingbirds.

I've gathered from rumor that the hummingbird travels incredible distances on incredibly little energy—what carries him, then? Spirit? But the best things I know about hummingbirds are the things I've noticed about them myself: that they are on hand when the sun is out in earnest, when the blossoms are with us, and the smell of them everywhere. You can hardly go through the best kind of day without seeing a hummingbird suspended like a little miracle in a

shaft of light or over a big flower or a cluster of little ones. Or turning like gay insanity and shooting straight as an arrow toward
practically nothing, for no reason, or for the reason that it's alive.
Now, how can creatures such as that—so delicately magnificent
and mad—possibly find time for the routine business of begetting
young? Or for the exercise of instinct in self-defense? Well, however
it may be, let a good day come by the grace of God, and with it
will come the hummingbirds.

As I started to say, however, it appears that sometimes even
instinct fails to operate in a specie. Or species. Or whatever it is.
Anyhow, when all of a kind of living thing turn and go somewhere,
in order to stay alive, in order to escape cold or whatever it might
be, sometimes, it appears, one of them does not go. Why he does
not go I cannot say. He may be eccentric, or there may be exalted
reasons—specific instead of abstract passion for another of its kind—
perhaps dead—or for a place. Or it may be stupidity, or stubborn-
ness. Who can ever know?

There was a hummingbird once which in the wintertime did not
leave our neighborhood in Fresno, California.

I'll tell you about it.

Across the street lived old Dikran, who was almost blind. He
was past eighty and his wife was only a few years younger. They
had a little house that was as neat inside as it was ordinary outside
—except for old Dikran's garden, which was the best thing of its
kind in the world. Plants, bushes, trees—all strong, in sweet black
moist earth whose guardian was old Dikran. All things from the
sky loved this spot in our poor neighborhood, and old Dikran loved
them.

One freezing Sunday, in the dead of winter, as I came home from
Sunday School I saw old Dikran standing in the middle of the street
trying to distinguish what was in his hand. Instead of going into our
house to the fire, as I had wanted to do, I stood on the steps of the
front porch and watched the old man. He would turn around and
look upward at his trees and then back to the palm of his hand.
He stood in the street at least two minutes and then at last he
came to me. He held his hand out, and in Armenian he said, "What
is this in my hand?"

I looked.

"It is a hummingbird," I said half in English and half in Armenian.

Hummingbird I said in English because I didn't know its name in Armenian.

"What is that?" old Dikran asked.

"The little bird," I said. "You know. The one that comes in the summer and stands in the air and then shoots away. The one with the wings that beat so fast you can't see them. It's in your hand. It's dying."

"Come with me," the old man said. "I can't see, and the old lady's at church. I can feel its heart beating. Is it in a bad way? Look again, once."

I looked again. It was a sad thing to behold. This wonderful little creature of summertime in the big rough hand of the old peasant. Here it was in the cold of winter, absolutely helpless and pathetic, not suspended in a shaft of summer light, not the most alive thing in the world, but the most helpless and heartbreaking.

"It's dying," I said.

The old man lifted his hand to his mouth and blew warm breath on the little thing in his hand which he could not even see. "Stay now," he said in Armenian. "It is not long till summer. Stay, swift and lovely."

We went into the kitchen of his little house, and while he blew warm breath on the bird he told me what to do.

"Put a tablespoonful of honey over the gas fire and pour it into my hand, but be sure it is not too hot."

This was done.

After a moment the hummingbird began to show signs of fresh life. The warmth of the room, the vapor of the warm honey—and, well, the will and love of the old man. Soon the old man could feel the change in his hand, and after a moment or two the hummingbird began to take little dabs of the honey.

"It will live," the old man announced. "Stay and watch."

The transformation was incredible. The old man kept his hand generously open, and I expected the helpless bird to shoot upward out of his hand, suspend itself in space, and scare the life out of me—which is exactly what happened. The new life of the little bird was magnificent. It spun about in the little kitchen, going to the window, coming back to the heat, suspending, circling as if it were summertime and it had never felt better in its whole life.

The old man sat on the plain chair, blind but attentive. He listened carefully and tried to see, but of course he couldn't. He kept asking about the bird, how it seemed to be, whether it showed signs of weakening again, what its spirit was, and whether or not it appeared to be restless; and I kept describing the bird to him.

When the bird was restless and wanted to go, the old man said, "Open the window and let it go."

"Will it live?" I asked.

"It is alive now and wants to go," he said. "Open the window."

I opened the window, the hummingbird stirred about here and there, feeling the cold from the outside, suspended itself in the area of the open window, stirring this way and that, and then it was gone.

"Close the window," the old man said.

We talked a minute or two and then I went home.

The old man claimed the hummingbird lived through that winter, but I never knew for sure. I saw hummingbirds again when summer came, but I couldn't tell one from the other.

One day in the summer I asked the old man.

"Did it live?"

"The little bird?" he said.

"Yes," I said. "That we gave the honey to. You remember. The little bird that was dying in the winter. Did it live?"

"Look about you," the old man said. "Do you see the bird?"

"I see humming*birds*," I said.

"Each of them is our bird," the old man said. "Each of them, each of them," he said swiftly and gently.

FABLE IX

The Tribulations of the Simple Husband Who Wanted Nothing More than to Eat Goose but was Denied this Delight by His Unfaithful Wife and Her Arrogant but Probably Handsome Lover.

A simple husband one morning took his wife a goose and said, Cook this bird for me; when I come home in the evening I shall eat it.

The wife plucked the bird, cleaned it, and cooked it. In the afternoon her lover came. Before going away he asked what food he could take with him to his friends. He looked into the oven and saw the roasted goose.

That is for my husband, the wife said.

I want it, the lover said. If you do not let me take it, I shall never love you again.

The lover went off with the goose.

In the evening the husband sat at the table and said, Bring me the goose.

What goose? the wife said.

The goose I brought you this morning, the husband said. Bring it to me.

Are you serious? the wife said. You brought me no goose. Perhaps you dreamed it.

Bring me the goose, the husband shouted.

The wife began to scream, saying, My poor husband has lost his mind. My poor husband is crazy. What he has dreamed he imagines has happened.

The neighbors came and believed the wife, so the husband said nothing and went hungry, except for bread and cheese and water.

The following morning the husband brought his wife another goose and said, Is this a goose?

Yes, the wife said.

Am I dreaming?—No.

Is this the goose's head?—Yes.

Wings?—Yes.

Feathers?—Yes.

All right, the husband said, cook it. When I come home tonight I'll eat it.

The wife cooked the goose. The lover came.

There is another goose today, he said. I can smell it.

You cannot take it, the wife said. I had a terrible scene with my husband last night, and again this morning. It is too much, I love you but you cannot have the goose.

Either you love me or you don't love me, the lover said. Either I take the goose or not.

So he took the goose.

Bring the goose, the husband said.

My poor husband, the wife screamed. He's stark raving mad. Goose, goose, goose. What goose? There is no goose. My poor, poor husband.

The neighbors came and again believed the wife.

The husband went hungry.

The following morning he bought another goose in the city. He hired a tall man to carry the goose on a platter on his head. He hired an orchestra of six pieces, and with the musicians in a circle around the tall man carrying the goose, he walked with them through the streets to his house, calling to his neighbors.

When he reached his house there were many people following him.

He turned to the people and said, Mohammedans, neighbors, the world, heaven above, fish in the sea, soldiers, and all others, behold, a goose.

He lifted the bird off the platter.

A goose, he cried.

He handed the bird to his wife.

Now cook the God Damned thing, he said, and when I come home in the evening I will eat it.

The wife cleaned the bird and cooked it. The lover came. There was a tender scene, tears, kisses, running, wrestling, more tears, more kisses, and the lover went off with the goose.

In the city the husband saw an old friend and said, Come out to the house with me tonight; the wife's roasting a goose; we'll take a couple of bottles of *rakki* and have a hell of a time.

So the husband and his friend went out to the house and the husband said, Have you cooked the goose?

Yes, the wife said. It's in the oven.

Good, the husband said. You were never really a bad wife. First, my friend and I will have a few drinks: then we will eat the goose.

The husband and his friend had four or five drinks and then the husband said, All right, bring the goose.

The wife said, There is no bread; go to your cousin's for bread; goose is no good without bread.

All right, the husband said.

He left the house.

The wife said to the husband's friend, My husband is crazy. There is no goose. He has brought you here to kill you with this enormous carving knife and this fork. You had better go.

The man went. The husband came home and asked about his friend and the goose.

Your *friend* has run off with the goose, the wife said. What kind of a friend do you call that, after I slave all day to cook you a decent meal?

The husband took the carving knife and the fork and began running down the street. At length in the distance he saw his friend running and he called out, Just a leg, my friend, that's all.

My God, the other said, he is truly crazy.

The friend began to run faster than ever. Soon the husband could run no more. He returned wearily to his home and wife. Once again he ate his bread and cheese. After this plain food he began to drink *rakki* again.

As he drank, the truth began to come to him little by little, as it does through alcohol.

When he was very drunk he knew all about everything. He got up and quietly whacked his wife across the room.

If your lover's got to have a goose every day, he said, you could have told me. Tomorrow I will bring *two* of them. I get hungry once in a while myself, you know.

THE STORY OF THE YOUNG
MAN AND THE MOUSE

A WEEK of drinking turned the young man's fancy to mice, *the* mouse, the one and only, the mouse of all mice, the city mouse, the brilliant mouse, the genius of mice, the Great Northern Hotel mouse.

He, or it, arrived one night prancing in the manner of an over-joyed retriever. The mouse came fearlessly to the young man and dropped the money at his feet. The money was four ten-dollar bills which the mouse carried in its mouth. The mouse carried the money so dexterously, or rather so magnificently, so thoughtfully, so deli-cately that not even slight teeth marks impaired the beauty of the money. The young man picked up the money casually, examined it, and studied the mouse, which stood by in perfect harmony with everything.

The young man moved two paces and also stood by in perfect harmony with everything.

"Well," he said. "This *is* delightful."

He looked at the mouse thoughtfully.

"Stealing, hey?" he said.

The mouse nodded the way a clown nods when he acknowledges the commission of some petty but delightful crime.

"All right," the young man said. "I believe in live and let live. You bring me money this way so I can live and I'll try not to improve your morals. If you want to steal, that's all right with me."

This arrangement appeared to be all right with the mouse, which continued exploring the rooms of the hotel, going to those places where traveling people or retired army officers or people taking a shower like to leave their folding money. Almost every day the mouse returned to the room of the young man to deposit various foldings of American currency: sometimes tens, sometimes fives, sometimes a five and a couple of ones, and one day four ones, which was a crisis and a bitter disappointment to the young man, who was drinking a great deal.

"Live and let live of course," he said to the mouse, "but you can do better than that. Now, let me explain. This number. That's ten. That's good. Get that kind when you can. This is five. Half as good. If you can't get tens, get fives. This is a two. Bad luck. Don't leave them, but they aren't so good. This is one. Awful. Try for tens."

The mouse accepted this simple instruction and was lucky enough to enter rooms where guests who were having showers had left big folding money lying around here and there, so that for many days the young man lived pretty much like a king. He bought clothes. Odds and ends. Ate well. And drank exceptionally well.

The mouse, however, lived on very feeble fare. Old stockings.

"Now," the young man said one day to the mouse, "this may get around. Folks may begin to get suspicious. There is no law against a mouse stealing money, and you'll always be innocent according to the statutes. There isn't a jury in the country that would convict you. But some busybody somewhere may take a long-shot chance and set a trap. They're horrible things, but very attractive outwardly. Cheese is involved. With only one of these pieces of paper which you have just fetched I could buy, I believe, close to twenty pounds of the finest cheese imaginable—which, I daresay, you wouldn't like. They'll try to attract you with cheap cheese. Ten cents a pound. Something like that. Something I haven't eaten in months. Don't be a fool. Don't get taken in. Don't swoon and move into the trap because the smell of the cheese is so wonderful. I'm counting on you to stay in good health."

The mouse had never heard.

Cheese?

Traps?

He didn't know. It was all very exciting.

Money, for some reason, he *did* know. It didn't smell good. It was tasteless and official, but even so.

The young man might have furnished the mouse a little cheese, but he was afraid that if he did the mouse would cease to appreciate anything but food. That, he didn't want. It would be better for the mouse to fend for itself.

"But," he said clearly, "stay away from little pieces of cheese artfully attached to gadgets which appear to be perfectly static and harmless. Once you swoon, you're a goner. It may mean death."

Death?

The mouse hadn't heard.

The drinking continued. Many times the mouse went away and returned with money, but one day the mouse didn't return. Soon the young man began to be poor again. He began to be a little worried, too. First he worried about how he was ever going to be able to keep up appearances without money, but little by little he began to worry about the mouse. In a psychic or alcoholic way, he was able to trace the mouse's course from his room two days ago to where it had fallen into a trap.

This was room 517, one floor down, two doors to the left. The room was inhabited by an old woman whose children sometimes took her to Larchmont for week-ends.

It was a little difficult getting in through the window, but he made it, and sure enough in the corner of the room was the mouse. The old woman was in Larchmont.

The young man burst into tears.

"I told you," he wept. "You see what happens? Now look at you. Here. Let me get you out of this God-damned gadget."

He got the mouse out of the trap and carried it carefully in the palm of his left hand to his room, taking the elevator and weeping.

The elevator boy burst into tears with the young man, but suggested heat and quiet.

Heat and quiet were provided the mouse, and five cents' worth of cheese, which the mouse did not wish to eat.

This frightened the young man.

"Those ungodly people," he said again and again.

The mouse watched the young man quietly for five days and five nights, and then it died.

The young man wrapped it carefully in hotel stationery, appropriately white, and carried it to Central Park where he dug a small grave with the toe of his right shoe, and buried it.

He returned to the hotel and checked out, complaining bitterly about the type of people inhabiting the world.

THE GREAT
LEAPFROG CONTEST

ROSIE MAHONEY was a tough little Irish kid whose folks, through some miscalculation in directions, or out of an innate spirit of anarchy, had moved into the Russian-Italian-and-Greek neighbourhood of my home town, across the Southern Pacific tracks, around G Street.

She wore a turtle-neck sweater, usually red. Her father was a bricklayer named Cull and a heavy drinker. Her mother's name was Mary. Mary Mahoney used to go to the Greek Orthodox Catholic Church on Kearny Boulevard every Sunday, because there was no Irish Church to go to anywhere in the neighbourhood. The family seemed to be a happy one.

Rosie's three brothers had all grown up and gone to sea. Her two sisters had married. Rosie was the last of the clan. She had entered the world when her father had been close to sixty and her mother in her early fifties. For all that, she was hardly the studious or scholarly type.

Rosie had little use for girls, and as far as possible avoided them. She had less use for boys, but found it undesirable to avoid them. That is to say, she made it a point to take part in everything the boys did. She was always on hand, and always the first to take up any daring or crazy idea. Everybody felt awkward about her continuous presence, but it was no use trying to chase her away, because that meant a fight in which she asked no quarter, and gave none.

If she didn't whip every boy she fought, every fight was at least an honest draw, with a slight edge in Rosie's favour. She didn't fight girl-style, or cry if hurt. She fought the regular style and took advantage of every opening. It was very humiliating to be hurt by Rosie, so after a while any boy who thought of trying to chase her away, decided not to.

It was no use. She just wouldn't go. She didn't seem to like any

of the boys especially, but she liked being in on any mischief they
might have in mind, and she wanted to play on any teams they
organized. She was an excellent baseball player, being as good as anybody else in the neighbourhood at any position, and for her age an
expert pitcher. She had a wicked wing, too, and could throw a ball
in from left field so that when it hit the catcher's mitt it made a
nice sound.

She was extraordinarily swift on her feet and played a beautiful
game of tin-can hockey.

At pee-wee, she seemed to have the most disgusting luck in the
world.

At the game we invented and used to call *Horse* she was as good
at *horse* as at *rider*, and she insisted on following the rules of the
game. She insisted on being horse when it was her turn to be horse.
This always embarrassed her partner, whoever he happened to be,
because it didn't seem right for a boy to be getting up on the back
of a girl.

She was an excellent football player too.

As a matter of fact, she was just naturally the equal of any boy
in the neighbourhood, and much the superior of many of them.
Especially after she had lived in the neighbourhood three years. It
took her that long to make everybody understand that she had come
to stay and that she was *going* to stay.

She did, too; even after the arrival of a boy named Rex Folger,
who was from somewhere in the south of Texas. This boy Rex was
a natural-born leader. Two months after his arrival in the neighbourhood, it was understood by everyone that if Rex wasn't the leader
of the gang, he was very nearly the leader. He had fought and licked
every boy in the neighbourhood who at one time or another had
fancied himself leader. And he had done so without any noticeable
ill-feeling, pride, or ambition.

As a matter of fact, no-one could possibly have been more good-
natured than Rex. Everybody resented him, just the same.

One winter, the whole neighbourhood took to playing a game
that had become popular on the other side of the tracks, in another
slum neighbourhood of the town: *Leapfrog.* The idea was for as many
boys as cared to participate, to bend down and be leaped over by
every other boy in the game, and then himself to get up and begin
leaping over all the other boys, and then bend down again until all
the boys had leaped over him again, and keep this up until all the

other players had become exhausted. This didn't happen, sometimes, until the last two players had travelled a distance of three or four miles while the other players walked along, watching and making bets.

Rosie, of course, was always in on the game. She was always one of the last to drop out, too. And she was the only person in the neighbourhood Rex Folger hadn't fought and beaten.

He felt that that was much too humiliating even to think about. But inasmuch as she seemed to be a member of the gang, he felt that in some way or another he ought to prove his superiority.

One summer day during vacation, an argument between Rex and Rosie developed and Rosie pulled off her turtle-neck sweater and challenged him to a fight. Rex took a cigarette from his pocket, lighted it, inhaled, and told Rosie he wasn't in the habit of hitting women—where he came from that amounted to boxing your mother. On the other hand, he said, if Rosie cared to compete with him in any other sport, he would be glad to oblige her. Rex was a very calm and courteous conversationalist. He had poise. It was unconscious, of course, but he had it just the same. He was just naturally a man who couldn't be hurried, flustered, or excited.

So Rex and Rosie fought it out in this game Leapfrog. They got to leaping over one another, quickly, too, until the first thing we knew the whole gang of us was out on the State Highway going south towards Fowler. It was a very hot day. Rosie and Rex were in great shape, and it looked like one was tougher than the other and more stubborn. They talked a good deal, especially Rosie, who insisted that she would have to fall down unconscious before she'd give up to a guy like Rex.

He said he was sorry his opponent was a girl. It grieved him deeply to have to make a girl exert herself to the point of death, but it was just too bad. He had to, so he had to. They leaped and squatted, leaped and squatted, and we got out to Sam Day's vineyard. That was half-way to Fowler. It didn't seem like either Rosie or Rex were ever going to get tired. They hadn't even begun to show signs of growing tired, although each of them was sweating a great deal.

Naturally, we were sure Rex would win the contest. But that was because we hadn't taken into account the fact that he was a simple person, whereas Rosie was crafty and shrewd. Rosie knew how to figure angles. She had discovered how to jump over Rex Folger in a way that weakened him. And after a while, about three miles out of Fowler, we noticed that she was coming down on Rex's *neck*, instead of on his back. Naturally, this was hurting him and making the blood rush to his head. Rosie herself squatted in such a way that it was impossible, almost, for Rex to get anywhere near her neck with his hands.

Before long, we noticed that Rex was weakening. His head was getting closer and closer to the ground. About a half mile out of Fowler, we heard Rex's head bumping the ground every time Rosie leaped over him. They were good loud bumps that we knew were painful, but Rex wasn't complaining. He was too proud to complain.

Rosie, on the other hand, knew she had her man, and she was giving him all she had. She was bumping his head on the ground as solidly as she could, because she knew she didn't have much more fight in her, and if she didn't lay him out cold, in the hot sun, in the next ten minutes or so, she would fall down exhausted herself, and lose the contest.

Suddenly Rosie bumped Rex's head a real powerful one. He got up very dazed and very angry. It was the first time we had ever seen him fuming. By God, the girl was taking advantage of him, if he wasn't mistaken, and he didn't like it. Rosie was squatted in front of him. He came up groggy and paused a moment. Then he gave Rosie a very effective kick that sent her sprawling. Rosie jumped up and smacked Rex in the mouth. The gang jumped in and tried to establish order.

It was agreed that the Leapfrog contest must not change into a fight. Not any more. Not with Fowler only five or ten minutes away. The gang ruled further that Rex had had no right to kick Rosie and that in smacking him in the mouth Rosie had squared the matter, and the contest was to continue.

Rosie was very tired and sore; and so was Rex. They began leaping and squatting again; and again we saw Rosie coming down on Rex's neck so that his head was bumping the ground.

It looked pretty bad for the boy from Texas. We couldn't understand how he could take so much punishment. We all felt that Rex was getting what he had coming to him, but at the same time everybody seemed to feel badly about Rosie, a girl, doing the job instead of one of us. Of course, that was where we were wrong. Nobody but Rosie could have figured out that smart way of humiliating a very powerful and superior boy. It was probably the woman in her, which, less than five years later, came out to such an extent that she became one of the most beautiful girls in town, gave up tomboy activities, and married one of the wealthiest young men in Kings County, a college man named, if memory serves, Wallace Hadington Finlay VI.

Less than a hundred yards from the heart of Fowler, Rosie, with great and admirable artistry, finished the job.

That was where the dirt of the highway siding ended and the paved main street of Fowler began. This street was paved with cement, not asphalt. Asphalt, in that heat, would have been too soft to serve, but cement had exactly the right degree of brittleness. I think Rex, when he squatted over the hard cement, knew the game was up. But he was brave to the end. He squatted over the hard cement and waited for the worst. Behind him, Rosie Mahoney prepared to make the supreme effort. In this next leap, she intended to give her all, which she did.

She came down on Rex Folger's neck like a ton of bricks. His head banged against the hard cement, his body straightened out, and his arms and legs twitched.

He was out like a light.

Six paces in front of him, Rosie Mahoney squatted and waited. Jim Telesco counted twenty, which was the time allowed for each leap. Rex didn't get up during the count.

The contest was over. The winner of the contest was Rosie Mahoney.

Rex didn't get up by himself at all. He just stayed where he was until a half-dozen of us lifted him and carried him to a horse trough, where we splashed water on his face.

Rex was a confused young man all the way back. He was also a deeply humiliated one. He couldn't understand anything about anything. He just looked dazed and speechless. Every now and then we imagined he wanted to talk, and I guess he did, but after we'd all gotten ready to hear what he had to say, he couldn't speak. He made a gesture so tragic that tears came to the eyes of eleven members of the gang.

Rosie Mahoney, on the other hand, talked all the way home. She said everything.

I think it made a better man of Rex. More human. After that he was a gentler sort of soul. It may have been because he couldn't see very well for some time. At any rate, for weeks he seemed to be going around in a dream. His gaze would freeze on some insignificant object far away on the landscape, and half the time it seemed as if he didn't know where he was going, or why. He took little part in the activities of the gang, and the following winter he stayed away altogether. He came to school one day wearing glasses. He looked broken and pathetic.

That winter Rosie Mahoney stopped hanging around with the gang, too. She had a flair for making an exit at the right time.

THE DECLARATION OF WAR

ON September the third, 1939, a boy by the name of John came running into the barber shop on Moraga Avenue where I was getting a haircut.

"War's been declared in Europe," he said.

Mr. Tagalavia dropped the comb from one hand and the scissors from the other.

"You get out of this shop," he said. "I told you before."

"What's your name?" I said to the young man.

"John," he said.

"How old are you?" I said.

"Eleven," John said.

"You get out of this shop," Mr. Tagalavia said.

I was under the impression that Mr. Tagalavia was talking to John, but apparently he wasn't. He was talking to me. He wasn't talking to *himself*.

John had left the shop.

The barber untied his apron and threw it aside.

"Who?" I said.

"You," Mr. Tagalavia said.

"Why?"

"I try to run a respectable barber shop."

"I'm respectable."

"You talked to that foolish boy," the barber said. "I don't want people like you to come to my shop."

"He didn't *seem* foolish," I said.

"He is a foolish, foolish boy," the barber said. "I don't want foolish people to come here."

"I suppose it *was* a little foolish of me to ask the boy his name," I said. "I'm sorry about that. I'm a writer, you see, and I'm *always* asking people questions. I apologize. Please finish my haircut."

"No," the barber said. "That's all."

I got out of the chair and examined my head. My haircut was less than half finished. The shape of my head wasn't exactly what it might be, but I could always walk three or four blocks and have the job finished by an ordinary barber. I put on my tie and coat.

"Excuse me," I said. "How much do I owe you?"

"Nothing," the barber said. "I don't want money from people like you. If I starve—if my family starves—all right. No money from foolish people."

"I'm sorry," I said, "but I believe I owe you *something*. How about thirty-five cents?"

"Not a penny," the barber said. "Please go away. I will make a present of the haircut to you. I *give* to people. I do not take. I am a man, not a fool."

I suppose I should have left the shop at this point, but I felt quite sure that what he *really* wanted to do was talk.

I have a power of understanding which is greater than the average, and at times uncanny. I sense certain things which other people, for one reason or another, are unable to sense.

(Sometimes what I sense is wrong and gets me in trouble, but I usually manage to get out of it. A kind word. A friendly tone of voice. A worldly attitude about such things. We are all brothers. The end is death for each of us. Let us love one another and try not to get excited.)

I sensed now that the barber was troubled or irritated; that he wished to speak and be heard; that, in fact, unless I missed my guess, his message was for *the world*. Traveling thousands of miles he could not have found anyone more prepared to listen to the message or to relay it to the world.

"Cigarette?" I said.

"I don't want anything," the barber said.

"Can I help you with the towels?"

"You get out of my shop."

Here, obviously, was an equal if I had ever encountered one. I have at times been spoken of by certain women who follow the course of contemporary literature as enigmatic and unpredictable, but after all I am a writer. One expects a writer to be impressive along the lines of enigma and so on, but with barbers one usually expects a haircut or a shave or both, along with a little polite conversation, and nothing more. Women who have time to read are likely to believe that it is natural for a writer to have certain little idiosyncrasies, but perhaps the only man in the world who can allow a *barber* similar privileges is a writer.

There is little pride in writers. They know they are human and shall some day die and be forgotten. We come, we go, and we are forgotten. Knowing all this a writer is gentle and kindly where another man is severe and unkind.

I decided to offer the barber the *full* cost of a haircut. Sixty-five cents, instead of thirty-five. A man can always get a haircut. There are more important things than making sure one has not been swindled.

"Excuse me," I said. "I don't think it's fair to you for me not to pay. It's true that you haven't finished my haircut, but perhaps some other day. I live near by. We shall be seeing more of one another."

"You get out of my shop," the barber said. "I don't want people like you to come here. Don't come back. I have no time."

"What do you mean, people like me? I am a writer."

"I don't care what you are," Mr. Tagalavia said. "You talked to that foolish boy."

"A few words," I said. "I had no idea it would displease you. He seemed excited and eager to be recognized by someone."

"He is a foolish, foolish boy," the barber said.

"Why do you say that?" I said. "He seemed sincere enough."

"Why do I say that!" the barber said. "Because he *is* foolish. Every day now for six days he has been running into my shop and shouting, War! War! War!"

"I don't understand," I said.

"You don't understand!" the barber said. "War! I don't know who you are, but let me tell you something."

"My name is Donald Kennebec," I said. "You may have heard of me."

"My name is Nick Tagalavia," the barber said. "I have never heard of you."

He paused and looked me in the eye.

"War?" he said.

"Yes," I said.

"You are a fool," the barber said. "Let me tell you something," he went on. "There is no war! I am a barber. I do not like people who are foolish. The whole thing is a trick. They want to see if the people are still foolish. They *are*. The people are more foolish now than ever. The boy comes running in here and says, 'War's been declared in Europe,' and you talk to him. You encourage him. Pretty soon he believes everything, like you."

The barber paused and looked at me very closely again. I took off my hat, so he could see how far he had gone with the haircut, and how much he had left unfinished.

"What do you write?" he said.

"Memoirs," I said.

"You are a fool," the barber said. "Why do you encourage the boy? He's going to have trouble enough without wars. Why do you say, 'How old are you'?"

"I thought he was rather bright," I said. "I just wanted him to know I was aware of it."

"I don't want people like you to come to my shop," the barber said.

"People like me?" I said. "I *hate* war."

"Shut up," the barber said. "The world is full of fools like you. You hate war, but in Europe there *is* a war?"

The implication here was a little too fantastic.

"Excuse me," I said. "*I* didn't start the war."

"You hate war," the barber said again. "They tell you there's a war in Europe, so you believe there's a war in Europe."

"I have no reason to believe there's peace in Europe," I said.

"You hate war," he said. "The paper comes out with the headline War. The boy comes running into the shop. War. You come in for a haircut. War. Everybody believes. The world is full of fools. How did you lose your hair?"

"Fever," I said.

"Fever!" the barber said. "You lost your hair because you're a fool. Electric clippers. Comb. Scissors. You've got no hair to cut. The whole thing is a trick. I don't want any more fools to come here and make me nervous. There is no war."

I had been right in sensing that the barber had had something to say and had wanted someone to say it to. I was quite pleased.

"You are a remarkable man," I said.

"Don't talk," the barber shouted. "I'm no foolish boy of eleven. I'm fifty-nine years old. I am a remarkable man! Newspapers. Maps. You've got no hair on your head. What am I supposed to cut? The boy comes running in. You can't sit still. 'War is declared in Europe,' he says. 'What's your name? How old are you?' What's the matter? Are you crazy?"

"I didn't mean to upset you," I said. "Let me pay you."

"Never," the barber said. "I don't want anything. That's no haircut. Not a penny. If a man with a head of hair comes in here and sits down, I will take the electric clippers and give him a haircut. The hair falls down on the floor. No trouble. No excitement. No foolishness. He gets out of the chair. His head is in good shape. Ears feel fine. Sixty-five cents. Thank you. Good-bye. The boy comes running in. I say, 'Get out of my shop.' The boy runs out. No trouble."

"*Other* barbers give me haircuts," I said.

"All right," he said. "Go to other barbers. Please go to other barbers. Remember one thing. There is no war. Don't go around spreading propaganda."

I was now satisfied that I had successfully gotten to the bottom of the man's irritation, and had obtained fresh and original material for a new memoir, so without another word, I sauntered out of the shop and down the street.

I feel that I have effectively utilized the material; that I have shaped it into a work which, if anything, will enhance my already considerable fame.

THE STOLEN BICYCLE

THIS movie of 1919 was full of high spirits, recklessness, and excellent timing, so that when Ike George left the theater he himself was like a man in a movie: full of energy, afraid of nothing, and eager to get on with his life.

As if it were not himself, as if it were not wrong to do so, he took the brand-new bike out of the bicycle rack in front of the theater, and, in full view of the whole world, rode away on it.

Johnny Faragoh, who sold bicycles for Kebo the Jap, was standing in front of his house on L Street.

As the boy rode by, Johnny noticed the new bike.

"Hey, kid!" he called out.

The boy turned in the street and coasted up. He knew Johnny. If he called you, you had to stop. It was a pleasure for the boy, though: he had always admired Johnny, who was like somebody in a movie himself.

"That's a swell bike," Johnny said. "Where'd you get it?"

"Mr. York gave it to me for my birthday," the boy said.

"You mean the guy who's in charge of street sales for *The Herald*?"

"Yeah."

The boy got off the bike and let the older one take the handlebars. Johnny lifted the bike, bounced it, sat on it, and very easily began riding around in a small circle.

"He gave you a good one, boy. What's your name?"

"Ike."

"Ike what?"

"Ike George," the boy said.

"You anything to *Cookie* George?"

"He's my cousin."

"First or second?"

"First."

"Cookie's a good friend of mine," Johnny said.

"He's always in trouble," Ike said.

86

"Where'd you steal it?" Johnny said. "You can tell *me*."

"I didn't steal it," Ike said. "Mr. York gave it to me for my birthday."

"Cookie's my pal," Johnny said. "Somebody else gave it to you. That guy York wouldn't give you a bike if you saved his life."

"He gave me *this* bike," the boy said.

"Tell them Cookie gave it to you," Johnny said. "Somebody'll go and ask York and you'll get in trouble."

"Cookie's got no money," the boy said.

"Sometimes he has and sometimes he hasn't," Johnny said. "I'm going to see him tonight," Johnny said. "I'll tell him about it. Go on home now."

The boy got on the bicycle and rode home.

When his father saw the bicycle he said, "Haig, where did you get that bicycle?"

"Cookie gave it to me," the boy said.

"You mean your cousin Gourken?"

"Yes," the boy said.

"Gourken has no money," the boy's father said. "You've borrowed it, haven't you?"

"No," the boy said. "It's mine."

"Go inside and eat your supper," the father said.

The boy went inside and ate his supper. It took him less than five minutes. When he came out of the house his father was riding the bike in the yard.

"Haig," the father said, "take the bicycle back where you got it. You're no thief."

"Cookie gave it to me," the boy said.

The next day he rode the bicycle to school, just the way it was. He didn't turn it over and hammer out the numbers the way you were supposed to do. The numbers were 137620R. After school he rode the bicycle to *The Evening Herald*, and told everybody his cousin Cookie had given it to him for a birthday present.

"What's your birthday?" his friend Nick Roma asked him.

"September 7, 1909," the boy said.

"This is May," Nick said. "You'll get in trouble, Ike."

He rode the bicycle to his corner, Mariposa and Eye, and sold papers all afternoon. Cookie came to the corner in the evening. "Is this the bike?" he said.

"Yeah," the boy said.

"I sure gave you a good one, didn't I?"

"Yeah. Thanks."

By October he had almost forgotten how the bicycle had come into his possession. In November the chain broke while he was sprinting. The rim of the front wheel broke and the fork buckled. It cost him a dollar-and-a-quarter for a new rim. Another dollar to have the buckled fork replaced by a straight secondhand one, and fifty cents for labor.

After that the bike was his, out and out.

One day a year after he had taken the bike from the rack in front of the Liberty Theatre, he put it back into the rack, and went on in and saw the show.

When he came out, the bike was gone. He walked home, and when he saw his father he said, "They stole my bike."

"That's all right," his father said. "Go inside and eat your supper."

"I'm not hungry," the boy said. "If I catch the fellow who stole it, I'll give him the worst beating he ever got."

"Go inside and eat," the boy's father said.

"I don't want to eat," the boy said.

He stood before his father, very angry, and then suddenly turned and ran. He ran all the way to town and walked along every street looking for his bike. After an hour he walked home, ate his supper, and went to bed.

He was now eleven years old.

One evening in August he was playing handball with Nick Roma against the wall of the Telephone Building. Nick made a man-killer, a truck turned into the alley, bumped the ball, and carried it down the alley. The boy went after the ball. It had fallen down a small flight of stairs into a narrow passageway where there were garbage cans and boxes full of ashes. He looked for the ball. In a corner he saw a bicycle frame, with the paint scratched off. He turned the frame upside down and read the number. It had been hammered, but he could still read the 13 and the R.

He stood in the dark passageway, holding the old frame. His friend Nick Roma came up and said, "Where's the ball?"

"It's lost," the boy said. "I found my bike. They took everything off of it."

"Is the frame all right?" Nick said.

"It's all right," the boy said, "but what good is a frame without the other stuff?"

"It's worth *something*," Nick said.

"I'd like to get the guy who stole it," the boy said.

Paul Armer came walking down the alley and saw the two boys with the bicycle frame.

He examined the frame with them.

"What do you want for it, Ike?" he said.

"I don't know," the boy said.

He was angry and broken-hearted.

"It was my bike," he said to Paul. "Then they stole it. We were playing handball, I went to get the ball and I found the frame. They took everything off of it and threw it in here."

"Where did the ball go?" Nick said.

"To hell with the ball," Ike said.

"I'll give you a dollar for it," Paul Armer said.

"All right," the boy said.

A week later when he saw the bike again, painted and with new parts, he became angry again and said to himself, "If I ever get the guy who stole it!"

THE THIRD DAY
AFTER CHRISTMAS

DONALD EFAW, who was six years old plus three months, was standing on the corner of 3rd Avenue and 37th Street where his angry father Harry had asked him an hour ago to wait a minute while he stepped into the store for some stuff for Alice who was sick in bed, coughing and crying. Alice was three and she had kept everybody awake all night. Donald's angry father Harry hadn't liked the noise at all and he'd blamed it on Mama. Mama's name was Mabelle. "Mabelle Louisa Atkins Fernandez before I married Harry Efaw," the boy had once heard his mother say to a man who had come to fix the broken window in the kitchen. "My husband is part-Indian on his mother's side, and I'm part-Indian on my father's. Fernandez sounds more Spanish or Mexican than Indian, but my father was part-Indian just the same. We never lived among them, though, the way some part-Indians do. We always lived in cities."

The boy wore overalls and an old checkered coat his father had outgrown that might have been an overcoat for him if it hadn't been so ill-fitting. The sleeves had been cut to fit the boy, but that was all. The pockets were out of reach, so the boy rubbed his hands to keep them warm. It was eleven o'clock in the morning now.

Donald's father had gone into the place, and pretty soon he would come out and they'd walk home and Mama would give Alice some of the stuff—milk and medicine—and she'd stop crying and coughing and Mama and Papa would stop fighting.

The place was Haggerty's. It had an entrance on the corner and another on the side street. Harry Efaw had used the 37th Street exit five minutes after he had gone in. He hadn't *forgotten* the boy in the street, he had just wanted to get away from him for awhile, and from the rest of them, too. He had had one little shot of rye that had cost too much and that was all. It had cost a quarter and that was too much for one little shot of rye. He had gulped the drink down and hurried out of the place and walked away, planning to come back after a few minutes to pick the boy up and then buy the food and medicine and go back home to see if something could be done about the little girl's sickness, but somehow or other he had gone right on walking.

At last Donald stepped into the place and saw that it was not like any other store he had ever seen. The man in the white coat looked at him and said, "You can't come in here. Go on home."

"Where's my father?"

"Is this boy's father in the house?" the man called out, and everybody in the place, seven men, turned and looked at Donald. They looked only a moment and then went back to their drinking and talking.

"Your father's not here," the man said, "whoever he is."

"Harry," Donald said. "Harry Efaw."

"I don't know anybody named Harry Efaw. Now, go on home."

"He told me to wait outside a minute."

"Yes, I know. Well, a lot of fellows come in here for a drink and then go. I guess that's what he did. If he told you to wait outside, you'd better do it. You can't stay in here."

"It's cold outside."

"I know it's cold outside," the bartender said. "But you can't stay in here. Wait outside like your father told you to, or go home."

"I don't know how," the boy said.

"Do you know the address?"

The boy obviously didn't know the meaning of the question, so the bartender tried to put it another way.

"Do you know the number of the house and the name of the street?"

"No. We walked. We came for medicine for Alice."

"Yes, I know," the bartender said patiently. "And I know it's cold outside, too, but you'd better get out of here just the same. I can't have small boys coming into this place."

A sickly man of sixty or so who was more than half-drunk and half-dead got up from his table and went to the bartender.

"I'll be glad to get the boy home if he can show me the way."

"Sit down," the bartender said. "The boy doesn't know the way."

"Maybe he does," the man said. "I've had children of my own and the street's no place for a small boy. I'll be glad to get him home to his mother."

"I know," the bartender said. "But just go sit down."

"I'll take you home, sonny," the old man said.

"Sit down," the bartender almost shouted, and the old man turned in astonishment.

"What do you take me for, anyway?" he said softly. "The boy's scared and cold and needs his mother."

"Will you please sit down?" the bartender said. "I know all about the boy. And you're not the man to get him home to his mother, either."

"*Somebody's* got to get him home to his mother," the old man said softly, and then belched. He was in the kind of worn and lumpy clothing the bartender knew had been given to him by a charitable institution. He probably had another thirty or forty cents to spend for beer, money he'd gotten by begging, most likely.

"It's the third day after Christmas," the old man went on. "It's not so long after Christmas any of us has got a right to forget trying to help a small boy home."

"Ah, what's the matter?" another drinker asked from his chair.

"Nothing's the matter," the bartender said. "This boy's father asked him to wait for him outside, that's all." The bartender turned to Donald Efaw. "If you don't know how to get home, just wait outside like your father told you to, and pretty soon he'll be back and he'll take you home. Now, go on and get out of here."

The boy left the place and began standing where he had already stood more than an hour. The old man began to follow the boy. The bartender swung himself over the bar, caught the old man by the shoulders at the swinging doors, twisted him around and walked him back to his chair.

"Now sit down," he said softly. "It's not your place to worry about the boy. Keep your worry for yourself. I'll see that nothing happens to him."

"What do you take me for, anyway?" the old man said again.

At the swinging doors for a look up and down the street the bartender, a short, heavy Irishman in his early fifties, turned and said, "Have you had a look at yourself in a mirror lately? You wouldn't get to the next corner holding the hand of a small boy."

"Why not?" the old man demanded.

"Because you don't look like any small boy's father or grandfather or friend or anything else."

"I've had children of my own," the old man said feebly.

"I know," the bartender said. "But just sit still. Some people are allowed to be kind to children and some aren't, that's all."

He took a bottle of beer to the old man's table and set it down by the old man's empty glass.

"Here's a bottle on me," he said. "I'm allowed to be kind to old men like yourself once in awhile, and you're allowed to be kind to bartenders like me once in awhile, but you're not allowed to be kind to a small boy whose father is some place in the neighborhood, most likely. Just sit still and drink your beer."

"I don't want your dirty beer," the old man said. "You can't hold *me* prisoner in your dirty saloon."

"Just sit still until the boy's father comes and takes him home, and then you can get out of here as fast as you like."

"I want to get out of here *now*," the old man said. "I don't have to take insults from anybody in this whole world. If I told you a few things about who I am I guess you wouldn't talk to me the way you've been talking."

"All right," the bartender said. He wanted to keep things from getting out of hand, he didn't want a fuss, and he felt he might be able to humor the old man out of his wish to be helpful to the boy. "Tell me a few things about who you are and maybe I won't talk to you the way I've been talking."

"I'll say you won't," the old man said.

The bartender was glad to notice that the old man was pouring beer into his glass. He watched the old man drink the top third of the glass, and then the old man said, "My name is Algayler, that's what it is."

He drank some more of his beer and the bartender waited for him to go on. He was standing at the end of the bar now, so he could keep his eye on the boy in the street. The boy was rubbing his hands together, but it was all right. He was a boy who had been toughened by hard times of all kinds, and this waiting in the street for his father wasn't going to be too much for him.

"Algayler," the old man said again, and he went on softly. The bartender couldn't hear what he was saying now, but that didn't matter because he knew the old man would be all right from now on. He was back in himself altogether again where he belonged.

A woman who had been coming to the saloon every day now around noon for a week or so came in with a fox-terrier on a leash and said,

"There's a small boy standing out front in the cold. Now, whose boy is he?"

The woman clamped her false teeth together as she looked over the drinkers, and her dog danced around her feet getting used to the warmth of the place.

"He's all right," the bartender said. "His father's gone on an errand. He'll be back in a minute."

"Well, he'd *better* be back in a minute," the woman said. "If there's one thing I can't stand it's a father who leaves a boy standing in the street."

"Algayler," the old man turned and said in a very loud voice.

"What did you say to me, you drunken old bum?" the woman said. Her dog moved toward the old man, tightening the leash, and barked several times.

"It's all right," the bartender said politely. "He only said his name."

"Well, it's a good thing he didn't say something else," the woman said, clamping down on her false teeth again.

The dog calmed down a little, too, but still had to dance about because of the warmth. He was wearing the coat she always strapped on him in the cold weather, but it never did his feet any good, and it was his feet that felt the cold the most.

The bartender poured beer into a glass for the woman and she began to drink, standing at the bar. Finally, she got up on a stool to take things easy, and the dog stopped dancing to look around the place.

The bartender took Algayler another bottle of free beer and without a word, or even a glance, they were agreed that they could get along on this basis.

A man of thirty-five or so whose face and neatly trimmed moustache seemed faintly familiar came in from the 37th Street entrance and asked for a shot of bourbon, and after the drink had been poured, the bartender said very quietly so that no one else would hear him, "That wouldn't be your son standing outside, would it?"

The man had lifted the small glass to his lips, looking at it, but now, having heard the question, he looked away from the glass to the bartender, then swallowed the drink quickly, and without a word moved to the front window to have a look at the boy. At last he turned to the bartender and shook his head. He wanted another and had it, and then went out and walked past the boy, hardly noticing him.

After finishing the second free bottle of beer Algayler began to doze in his chair, and the woman with the fox-terrier began to tell the bartender something about her dog.

"I've had Tippy all his life," she said, "and we've been together the whole time. Every minute of it."

A fellow under thirty in pretty good clothes came in at a quarter after twelve and asked for Johnny Walker Black Label over ice with a water chaser, but quickly settled for Red Label, and after finishing the drink said, "Where's the television?"

"We don't have any."

"No television?" the man said cheerfully. "What kind of a bar is this, anyway? I didn't know there was a bar in New York that didn't have a television. What do people look at in here, anyway?"

"All we've got is the phonograph."

"Well, O.K., then," the man said. "If that's all you've got, that's all you've got. What would you like to hear?"

"Suit yourself."

The man studied the titles of the various records that were in the machine and then said, "How about Benny Goodman doing *Jingle Bells?*"

"Suit yourself," the bartender said.

"O.K.," the man said, putting a nickel into the slot. "*Jingle Bells* it is."

The machine began to work as the man sat at the bar again and the bartender fixed him another Red Label over ice. The music began and after listening a moment the man said, "That ain't *Jingle Bells,* that's something else."

"You pressed the wrong number."

"Well," the man said pleasantly, "no matter. No matter at all. That ain't a bad number, either."

The boy came in again but the machine was making too much noise for the bartender to be able to tell him to get out without shouting at him, so he went to the boy and led him out to his place in the street.

"Where's my father?" Donald Efaw said.

"He'll be back in a minute. You just stay out here."

This went on until half past two when snow began to fall. The bartender chose an appropriate moment to go out and bring the boy in. He began to make trips to the kitchen fetching the boy things to eat. The boy sat on a box, behind the bar, out of sight, and ate off the top of another box.

After eating, the boy began to fall asleep, so the bartender fixed him a place to stretch out on on some empty beer cases, using his overcoat for a mattress and three old aprons out of the laundry bag and his street coat for covering. He and the boy hadn't said a word since he had brought the boy in, and now, stretched out, on the verge of falling asleep, the boy almost smiled and wept at the same time.

The morning drinkers were gone now, including Algayler and the woman with the false teeth and the fox-terrier, and the trade changed once again while the boy slept.

It was a quarter to five when the boy sat up. He remembered the bartender after a moment, but again they didn't speak. He sat up, as if he were in his bed at home, and then, after dreaming with his eyes open for ten minutes, stepped down.

It was dark outside now and it was snowing the way it does in a storm. The boy watched the snow a moment and then turned and looked up at the bartender.

"Did my father come back?" he said.

"Not yet," the bartender said.

He knelt down to talk to the boy.

"I'll be through work in a few minutes, and if you can show me your house when you see it, I'll try to get you home."

"Didn't my father come back?"

"No, he didn't. Maybe he forgot where he left you."

"He left me right here," the boy said, as if that were something impossible to forget. "Right out front."

"I know."

The night bartender came out of the kitchen in his white coat and noticed the boy.

"Who's that, John? One of your kids?"

"Yeah," the bartender said because he didn't want to try to tell the other bartender what had happened.

"Where'd he get that coat?"

The boy winced and looked at the floor.

"It's one of *my* old coats," the bartender said. "He's got his own of course, but this is the coat he *likes* to wear."

The boy looked up at the bartender suddenly, amazed.

"Yeah, that's the way it is with kids, John," the night bartender said. "Always wanting to be like the old man."

"That's right," the other said.

He took off his white coat and got into his street coat and overcoat, and took the boy by the hand.

"Good night," he said, and the night bartender answered him and watched him step out into the street with the boy.

They walked together in silence three blocks and then stepped into a drug store and sat at the counter.

"Chocolate or vanilla?"

"I don't know."

"One chocolate, one vanilla ice cream soda," the bartender said to the soda jerk, and when the drinks were set down on the counter the bartender went to work on the vanilla. The boy did all right on the other, and then they stepped out into the snow again.

"Now, try to remember which way you live. Can you do that?"

"I don't *know* which way."

The bartender stood in the snow, trying to think what to do, but the going was tough, and he got nowhere.

"Well," he said at last, "do you think you could spend the night at my house with my kids? I've got two boys and a little girl. We'll make a place for you to sleep, and tomorrow your father will come and get you."

"Will he?"

"Sure he will."

They walked along in the silent snow and then the bartender heard the boy begin to cry softly. He didn't try to comfort the boy because he knew there was no comforting him. The boy didn't let himself go, though, he just cried softly, and moved along with his friend. He had heard about strangers and he had heard about enemies and he had come to believe that they were the same thing, but here was somebody he had never seen before who was neither a stranger nor an enemy. All the same it was awful lonesome without his angry father.

They began to go up some steps that were covered with snow and the boy's friend said, "This is where we live. We'll have some hot food and then you can go to bed until tomorrow when your father will come and get you."

"When will he come?" the boy said.

"In the morning," his friend said.

When they stepped into the light of the house the bartender saw that the boy was finished crying, perhaps for the rest of his life.

SEVENTY THOUSAND
ASSYRIANS

I HADN'T had a haircut in forty days and forty nights, and I was beginning to look like several violinists out of work. You know the look: genius gone to pot, and ready to join the Communist Party. We barbarians from Asia Minor are hairy people: when we need a haircut, we *need* a haircut. It was so bad, I had outgrown my only hat. (I am writing a serious story, perhaps one of the most serious I shall ever write. That is why I am being flippant. Readers of Sherwood Anderson will begin to understand what I am saying after a while; they will know that my laughter is rather sad.) I was a young man in need of a haircut, so I went down to Third Street (San Francisco), to the Barber College, for a fifteen-cent haircut.

Third Street, below Howard, is a district; think of the Bowery in New York, Main Street in Los Angeles: think of old men and boys, out of work, hanging around, smoking Bull Durham, talking about the government, waiting for something to turn up, simply waiting. It was a Monday morning in August and a lot of the tramps had come to the shop to brighten up a bit. The Japanese boy who was working over the free chair had a waiting list of eleven; all the other chairs were occupied. I sat down and began to wait. Outside, as Hemingway (*The Sun Also Rises, A Farewell to Arms, Death in the Afternoon, Winner Take Nothing*) would say, haircuts were four bits. I had twenty cents and a half pack of Bull Durham. I rolled a cigarette, handed the pack to one of my contemporaries who looked in need of nicotine and inhaled the dry smoke, thinking of America, what was going on politically, economically, spiritually. My contemporary was a boy of sixteen. He looked Iowa; splendid potentially, a solid American, but down, greatly down in the mouth. Little sleep, no change of clothes for several days, a little fear, etc. I wanted very much to know his name. A writer is always wanting to get the reality of faces and figures. Iowa said, 'I just got in from Salinas. No work in the lettuce fields. Going north now, to Portland; try to ship out.' I wanted to tell him how it was with me: rejected story from *Scribner's*, rejected essay from *The Yale Review*, no money for decent cigarettes, worn shoes, old shirts, but I was afraid to make something of my own troubles. A writer's troubles are always boring, a bit unreal. People are apt to feel, *Well, who asked you to write in the first place?* A man must pretend not to be a writer. I said, 'Good luck, north.' Iowa shook his head. 'I know better. Give it a try, anyway. Nothing to lose.' Fine boy, hope he isn't dead, hope he hasn't frozen, mighty cold these days (December, 1933), hope he hasn't gone down; he deserved to live. Iowa, I hope you got work in Portland; I hope you are earning money; I hope you have rented a clean room with a warm bed in it; I hope you are sleeping nights, eating regularly, walking along like a human being, being happy. Iowa, my good wishes are with you. I have said a number of prayers for you. (All the same, I think he is dead by this time. It was in him the day I saw him, the low malicious face of the beast, and at the same time all the theatres in America were showing, over and over again, an animated film-cartoon in which there was a song called 'Who's Afraid of the Big Bad Wolf?', and that's what it amounts to: people with money laughing at the death that is crawling slyly into boys like young Iowa, pretending that it isn't there, laughing in warm theatres. I have prayed for Iowa, and I consider myself a coward. By this time he must be dead, and I am sitting in a small room, talking about him, only talking.)

I began to watch the Japanese boy who was learning to become a barber. He was shaving an old tramp who had a horrible face, one of those faces that emerge from years and years of evasive living, years of being unsettled, of not belonging anywhere, of owning nothing, and the Japanese boy was holding his nose back (his own nose), so that he would not smell the old tramp. A trivial point in a story, a bit of data with no place in a work of art, nevertheless, I put it down. A young writer is always afraid some significant fact may escape him. He is always wanting to put in everything he sees. I wanted to know the name of the Japanese boy. I am profoundly interested in names. I have found that those that are unknown are the most genuine. Take a big name like Andrew Mellon. I was watching the Japanese boy very closely. I wanted to understand from the way he was keeping his sense of smell away from the mouth and nostrils of the old man what he was thinking, how he was feeling. Years ago, when I was seventeen, I pruned vines in my uncle's vineyard, north of Sanger, in the San Joaquin Valley, and there were several Japanese working with me, Yoshio Enomoto, Hideo Suzuki, Katsumi Sujimoto, and one or two others. These Japanese taught me a few simple phrases, *hello, how are you, fine day, isn't it, good-bye,* and so on. I said in Japanese to the barber student, "How are you?" He said in Japanese, "Very well, thank you." Then, in impeccable English, "Do you speak Japanese? Have you lived in Japan?" I said, "Unfortunately, no. I am able to speak only one or two words. I used to work with Yoshio Enomoto, Hideo Suzuki, Katsumi Sujimoto; do you know them?" He went on with his work, thinking of the names. He seemed to be whispering, "Enomoto, Suzuki, Sujimoto." He said, "Suzuki. Small man?" I said, "Yes." He said, "I know him. He lives in San Jose now. He is married now."

I want you to know that I am deeply interested in what people remember. A young writer goes out to places and talks to people. He tries to find out what they remember. I am not using great material for a short story. Nothing is going to happen in this work. I am not fabricating a fancy plot. I am not creating memorable characters. I am not using a slick style of writing. I am not building up a fine atmosphere. I have no desire to sell this story or any story to *The Saturday Evening Post* or to *Cosmopolitan* or to *Harper's*. I am not trying to compete with the great writers of short stories, men like Sinclair Lewis and Joseph Hergesheimer and Zane Grey, men who really know how to write how to make up stories that will sell. Rich men, men who understand all the rules about plot and character and style and atmosphere and all that stuff. I have no desire for fame. I am not out to win the Pulitzer Prize or the Nobel Prize or any other prize. I am out here in the far West, in San Francisco, in a small room on Carl Street, writing a letter to common people, telling them in simple language things they already know. I am merely making a record, so if I wander around a little, it is because I am in no hurry and because I do not know the rules. If I have any desire at all, it is to show the brotherhood of man. This is a big statement and it sounds a little precious. Generally a man is ashamed to make such a statement. He is afraid sophisticated people will laugh at him. But I don't mind. I'm asking sophisticated people to laugh. That is what sophistication is for. I do not believe in races. I do not believe in governments. I see life as one life at one time, so many millions simultaneously all over the earth. Babies who have not yet been

taught to speak any language are the only race of the earth, the race
of man: all the rest is pretence, what we call civilization, hatred, fear,
desire for strength. . . . But a baby is a baby. And the way they
cry, there you have the brotherhood of man, babies crying. We grow
up and we learn the words of a language and we see the universe
through the language we know, we do not see it through all languages
or through no language at all, through silence, for example, and we
isolate ourselves in the language we know. Over here we isolate ourselves in English, or American as Mencken calls it. All the eternal
things, in our words. If I want to do anything, I want to speak a
more universal language. The heart of man, the unwritten part of
man, that which is eternal and common to all races.

Now I am beginning to feel guilty and incompetent. I have used
all this language and I am beginning to feel that I have said nothing.
This is what drives a young writer out of his head, this feeling that
nothing is being said. Any ordinary journalist would have been able
to put the whole business into a three-word caption. Man is man,
he would have said. Something clever, with any number of implications. But I want to use language that will create a single implication. I want the meaning to be precise, and perhaps that is why
the language is so imprecise. I am walking around my subject, the
impression I want to make, and I am trying to see it from all angles,
so that I will have a whole picture, a picture of wholeness. It is the
heart of man that I am trying to imply in this work.

Let me try again: I hadn't had a haircut in a long time and I was
beginning to look seedy, so I went down to the Barber College on
Third Street, and I sat in a chair. I said, "Leave it full in the back.
I have a narrow head and if you do not leave it full in the back,
I will go out of this place looking like a horse. Take as much as you
like off the top. No lotion, no water, comb it dry." Reading makes
a full man, writing a precise one, as you see. This is what happened.
It doesn't make much of a story, and the reason is that I have left
out the barber, the young man who gave me the haircut.

He was tall, he had a dark serious face, thick lips, on the verge
of smiling but melancholy, thick lashes, sad eyes, a large nose. I saw
his name on the card that was pasted on the mirror, Theodore Badal.
A good name, genuine, a good young man, genuine. Theodore Badal
began to work on my head. A good barber never speaks until he has
been spoken to, no matter how full his heart may be.

"That name," I said, "Badal. Are you an Armenian?" I am an

Armenian. I have mentioned this before. People look at me and begin to wonder, so I come right out and tell them, "I am an Armenian," I say. Or they read something I have written and begin to wonder, so I let them know. "I am an Armenian," I say. It is a meaningless remark, but they expect me to say it, so I do. I have no idea what it is like to be an Armenian or what it is like to be an Englishman or a Japanese or anything else. I have a faint idea what it is like to be alive. This is the only thing that interests me greatly. This and tennis. I hope some day to write a great philosophical work on tennis, something of the order of *Death in the Afternoon*, but I am aware that I am not yet ready to undertake such a work. I feel that the cultivation of tennis on a large scale among the peoples of the earth will do much to annihilate racial differences, prejudices, hatred, etc. Just as soon as I have perfected my drive and my lob, I hope to begin my outline of this great work. (It may seem to some sophisticated people that I am trying to make fun of Hemingway. I am not. *Death in the Afternoon* is a pretty sound piece of prose. I could never object to it as prose. I cannot even object to it as philosophy. I think it is finer philosophy than that of Will Durant and Walter Pitkin. Even when Hemingway is a fool, he is at least an accurate fool. He tells you what actually takes place and he doesn't allow the speed of an occurrence to make his exposition of it hasty. This is a lot. It is some sort of advancement for literature. To relate leisurely the nature and meaning of that which is very brief in duration.)

"Are you an Armenian?" I asked.

We are a small people and whenever one of us meets another, it is an event. We are always looking around for someone to talk to in our language. Our most ambitious political party estimates that there are nearly two million of us living on the earth, but most of us don't think so. Most of us sit down and take a pencil and a piece of paper and we take one section of the world at a time and imagine how many Armenians at the most are likely to be living in that section and we put the highest number on the paper, and then we go on to another section, India, Russia, Soviet Armenia, Egypt, Italy, Germany, France, America, South America, Australia, and so on, and after we add up our most hopeful figures the total comes to something a little less than a million. Then we start to think how big our families are, how high our birthrate and how low our deathrate (except in times of war when massacres increase the deathrate), and we begin to imagine how rapidly we will increase if we are left alone a quarter of a century, and we feel pretty happy. We always leave out earthquakes, wars, massacres, famines, etc., and it is a mistake. I remember the Near East Relief drives in my home town. My uncle used to be our orator and he used to make a whole auditorium full of Armenians weep. He was an attorney and he was a great orator. Well, at first the trouble was war. Our people were being destroyed by the enemy. Those who hadn't been killed were homeless and they were starving, *our own flesh and blood*, my uncle said, and we all wept. And we gathered money and sent it to our people in the old country. Then after the war, when I was a bigger boy, we had another Near East Relief drive and my uncle stood on the stage of the Civic Auditorium of my home town and he said, "Thank God this time it is not the enemy, but an earthquake. God has made us suffer. We have worshipped Him through trial and tribulation, through suffering and disease and torture and horror and (my uncle began to weep, began to sob) through the madness of despair, and now He has done this thing, and still we praise Him, still we worship Him. We do not understand the ways of God.' And after the drive I went to my uncle and I said, "Did you mean what you said about God?" And he said, "That was oratory. We've got to raise money. What God? It is nonsense." "And when you cried?" I asked, and my uncle said, "That was real. I could not help it. I had to cry. Why, for God's sake, why must we go through all this God damn hell? What have we done to deserve all this torture? Man won't let us alone. God won't let us alone. Have we done something? Aren't we supposed to be pious people? What is our sin? I am disgusted with God. I am sick of man. The only reason I am willing to get up and talk is that I don't dare keep my mouth shut. I can't bear the thought of more of our people dying. Jesus Christ, have we done something?"

I asked Theodore Badal if he was an Armenian.

He said, "I am an Assyrian."

Well, it was something. They, the Assyrians, came from our part of the world, they had noses like our noses, eyes like our eyes, hearts like our hearts. They had a different language. When they spoke we couldn't understand them, but they were a lot like us. It wasn't quite as pleasing as it would have been if Badal had been an Armenian, but it was something.

"I am an Armenian," I said, "I used to know some Assyrian boys in

my home town, Joseph Sargis, Nito Elia, Tony Saleh. Do you know
any of them?"

"Joseph Sargis, I know him," said Badal. "The others I do not
know. We lived in New York until five years ago, then we came
out west to Turlock. Then we moved up to San Francisco."

"Nito Elia," I said, "is a Captain in the Salvation Army." (I don't
want anyone to imagine that I am making anything up, or that I
am trying to be funny.) "Tony Saleh," I said, "was killed eight years
ago. He was riding a horse and he was thrown and the horse began
to run. Tony couldn't get himself free, he was caught by a leg, and
the horse ran around and around for a half-hour and then stopped,
and when they went up to Tony he was dead. He was fourteen at
the time. I used to go to school with him. Tony was a very clever
boy, very good at arithmetic."

We began to talk about the Assyrian language and the Armenian
language, about the old world, conditions over there, and so on. I
was getting a fifteen-cent haircut and I was doing my best to learn
something at the same time, to acquire some new truth, some new
appreciation of the wonder of life, the dignity of man. (Man has
great dignity, do not imagine that he has not.)

Badal said, "I cannot read Assyrian. I was born in the old country,
but I want to get over it."

He sounded tired, not physically but spiritually.

"Why?" I said. "Why do you want to get over it?"

"Well," he laughed, "simply because everything is washed up
over there." I am repeating his words precisely, putting in nothing
of my own. "We were a great people once," he went on. "But that
was yesterday, the day before yesterday. Now we are a topic in ancient
history. We had a great civilization. They're still admiring it. Now I
am in America learning to cut hair. We're washed up as a race, we're
through, it's all over, why should I learn to read the language? We
have no writers, we have no news—well, there is a little news: once
in a while the English encourage the Arabs to massacre us, that is all.
It's an old story, we know all about it. The news comes over to us
through the Associated Press, anyway."

These remarks were painful to me, an Armenian. I had always
felt badly about my own people being destroyed. I had never heard
an Assyrian speaking in English about such things. I felt great love
for this young fellow. Don't get me wrong. There is a tendency these
days to think in terms of pansies whenever a man says that he has

affection for man. I think now that I have affection for all people, even for the enemies of Armenia, whom I have so tactfully not named. Everyone knows who they are. I have nothing against any of them because I think of them as one man living one life at a time, and I know, I am positive, that one man at a time is incapable of the monstrosities performed by mobs. My objection is to mobs only.

"Well," I said, "it is much the same with us. We, too, are old. We still have our church. We still have a few writers, Aharonian, Isahakian, a few others, but it is much the same."

"Yes," said the barber, "I know. We went in for the wrong things. We went in for the simple things, peace and quiet and families. We didn't go in for machinery and conquest and militarism. We didn't go in for diplomacy and deceit and the invention of machine-guns and poison gases. Well, there is no use being disappointed. We had our day, I suppose."

"We are hopeful," I said. "There is no Armenian living who does not still dream of an independent Armenia."

"Dream?" said Badal. "Well, that is something. Assyrians cannot even dream any more. Why, do you know how many of us are left on earth?"

"Two or three million," I suggested.

"Seventy thousand," said Badal. "That is all. Seventy thousand Assyrians in the world, and the Arabs are still killing us. They killed seventy of us in a little uprising last month. There was a small paragraph in the paper. Seventy more of us destroyed. We'll be wiped out before long. My brother is married to an American girl and he has a son. There is no more hope. We are trying to forget Assyria. My father still reads a paper that comes from New York, but he is an old man. He will be dead soon."

Then his voice changed, he ceased speaking as an Assyrian and began to speak as a barber: "Have I taken enough off the top?" he asked.

The rest of the story is pointless. I said *so long* to the young Assyrian and left the shop. I walked across town, four miles, to my room on Carl Street. I thought about the whole business: Assyria and this Assyrian, Theodore Badal, learning to be a barber, the sadness of his voice, the hopelessness of his attitude. This was months ago, in August, but ever since I have been thinking about Assyria, and I have been wanting to say something about Theodore Badal, a son of an ancient race, himself youthful and alert, yet hopeless. Seventy thousand Assyrians, a mere seventy thousand of that great people, and all the others quiet in death and all the greatness crumbled and ignored, and a young man in America learning to be a barber, and a young man lamenting bitterly the course of history.

Why don't I make up plots and write beautiful love stories that can be made into motion pictures? Why don't I let these unimportant and boring matters go hang? Why don't I try to please the American reading public?

Well, I am an Armenian. Michael Arlen is an Armenian, too. He is pleasing the public. I have great admiration for him, and I think he has perfected a very fine style of writing and all that, but I don't want to write about the people he likes to write about. Those people were dead to begin with. You take Iowa and the Japanese boy and Theodore Badal, the Assyrian; well, they may go down physically, like Iowa, to death, or spiritually, like Badal, to death, but they are of the stuff that is eternal in man and it is this stuff that interests me. You don't find them in bright places, making witty remarks about sex and trivial remarks about art. You find them where I found them, And they will be there forever, the race of man, the part of man, of Assyria as much as of England, that cannot be destroyed, the part that earthquake and war and famine and madness and everything else cannot destroy.

This work is in tribute to Iowa, to Japan, to Assyria, to Armenia, to the race of man everywhere, to the dignity of that race, the brotherhood of things alive. I am not expecting Paramount Pictures to film this work. I am thinking of seventy thousand Assyrians, one at a time, alive, a great race. I am thinking of Theodore Badal, himself seventy thousand Assyrians and seventy million Assyrians, himself Assyria, and man, standing in a barber's shop, in San Francisco, in 1933, and being, still, himself, the whole race.

THE INSURANCE SALESMAN,
THE PEASANT,
THE RUG MERCHANT,
AND THE POTTED PLANT

ARSHAG GOROBAKIAN was a small man who earned his living as a salesman for the New York Life Insurance Company. He worked exclusively among his own people, the Armenians. In twenty years, he often told a new client, I have sold three hundred policies, and so far two hundred of my clients have died. He did not utter this remark with sorrow and it was not intended to be a commentary on the sadness of life. On the contrary, Gorobakian's smile indicated that what he meant by two hundred of them dying was simply that these were men who had cheated death of its awful victory, and at the same time made a monkey out of the New York Life Insurance Company. All shrewd men, he often told a new client. Men like yourself, in all things practical and brilliant. They said to themselves, Yes, we shall die, there is no way out of that, let us face the facts.

Here the insurance salesman would bring the printed charts and statistics out of his inside coat pocket and say, Here are the facts. You are forty-seven years of age, and by the grace of God in good health. According to the facts you will be dead in five years.

He would smile gently, sharing with the new client the thrill of dying in five years and earning thereby an enormous sum of money. In five years, he would say, you will have paid my company three hundred and eighty-seven dollars, and on dying you will have earned twenty thousand dollars, or a net profit of nineteen thousand six hundred and thirteen dollars.

That, he would say, is a fair profit on any investment.

Once, however, he talked to a peasant in Kingsburg who didn't believe he would be dead in five years.

Come back in seventeen or eighteen years, the peasant said.

But you are sixty-seven years old now, the insurance salesman said.

I know, the peasant said. But I shall not be swindled in an affair like this. I shall be alive twenty years from now. I have planted three hundred new olive trees and I know I shall not be dead until they are full grown. Not to mention the mulberry trees, and the pomegranate trees, and the walnut and almond trees.

No, the peasant said, the time is not ripe for a bargain of this sort. I know I shall be alive twenty years from now. I can feel it in my bones. Shall I say something?

Yes, the insurance salesman said.

I shall live *thirty* years longer, not twenty. You will admit I should be cheated in a deal of this sort.

The insurance salesman was small, courteous, quiet-spoken, and never aggressive.

I can see, he said, that you are a man of giant strength——

Giant strength? the peasant roared. Shall I say something?

The insurance salesman nodded.

What you say is the truth, he said. I am a man of giant strength. What death? Why should I die? For what reason, countryman? I am in no hurry. Money? Yes. It is good. But I am not going to die.

The insurance salesman smoked his cigar calmly, although inwardly he was in a state of great agitation, like a routed cavalry officer trying desperately to round up his men and organize another offensive.

Death to you? he said to the peasant. God forbid. In all my life I have never wished another man's death. Life is what we enjoy. The taste of the watermelon in the summer is the thing we cherish.

May I say something? the peasant interrupted.

Again the insurance salesman nodded.

What you say is true, he said. The thing we cherish is the taste of the watermelon in the summertime. And bread and cheese and grapes in the cool of evening, under the trees. Please go on.

I do not wish any man's departure from this warm scene of life, the insurance salesman said. We must face the facts, however.

He shook the documents in his hand.

Our world is a crazy world, he said. You are a strong man. You enjoy the taste of the watermelon. You are walking in the city. An automobile strikes you and where are you? You are dead.

The peasant frowned.

Ah, yes, he said. The automobile.

In the event that you are killed accidentally, which God forbid, the insurance salesman said, you will be rewarded doubly.

The confounded automobiles, the peasant said. I shall be very careful in the streets.

We are all careful, the insurance salesman said, but what good does it do us? More people are killed in every year in automobile accidents than in one year of a great war.

May I say something? the peasant said.

Say it, the insurance salesman said.

I have half a mind to be protected, the peasant said. I have half a mind to take out an insurance policy.

That is a wise plan, the insurance salesman said.

The peasant purchased a policy and began making payments. Two years later he called the insurance salesman to his house and reprimanded him severely, although politely. He complained that although he had spent several hundred dollars, he had not so much as come anywhere near being killed, which he considered very odd.

I do not want the policy any longer, he said.

The insurance salesman told the ironic story of another man who gave up his policy after two years, and three weeks later was gored to death by an angry bull. But the peasant was not impressed with the story.

May I say something? he said. There is no bull in the world strong enough to gore me. I would break his neck. No thank you, I do not want to be insured. I have made up my mind not to die, even for a profit. I have had a hundred chances of walking in front of an automobile, but always I have stepped back cautiously and allowed it to go by.

That was fourteen years ago, and the peasant, a man named Hakimian, is still alive.

The insurance salesman, however, preferred people more enlightened than peasants. He himself was a graduate of college. His preference was for men with whom he could talk for hours about other things, and then little by little move in with the insurance speech. He would often drive two hundred miles to San Francisco to talk with a dentist who had graduated from college.

Once he decided to drive his Buick across the country to Boston. It was a journey of ten days. Along the way there would be much to see, and in Boston he would visit his sister and her husband and their eleven children. He drove to Boston, visited his sister and her family, and met a rug merchant who was a college graduate. Three times in ten days he called at this man's home and carried on pleasant conversations. The man's name was Haroutunian and he was extremely fond of conversation. The insurance salesman found him brilliant on all subjects. But when the subject of life insurance was introduced he discovered that his friend was, bluntly, in no mood for it. At least, not for the present.

The time came for the insurance salesman to return to California. Before departing he was paid a visit by the rug merchant, Haroutunian, who was carrying a small potted plant.

My friend, the rug merchant said, I have a brother in Bakersfield which is near where you live. I have not seen him in twenty years. Will you do me a favor?

Of course, the insurance salesman said.

Carry this plant to my brother with my greetings, the rug merchant said.

Gladly, the insurance salesman said, what plant is this?

I do not know, the rug merchant said, but the leaf has a wonderful odour. Smell it.

The insurance salesman smelled the plant and was disappointed in the smell of the leaf.

It is truly a heavenly smell, he said.

The rug merchant gave the insurance salesman the name and address of his brother, and then said:

One more thing. The agricultural department in each state demands that a plant being transported be examined for plant insects. There are none on this plant, but the law is the law. You will have to stop a minute at the agricultural department of each state. A formality.

Oh, the insurance salesman said.

His word had been given, however, so he put the plant into his car and made his departure from Boston.

He was a very law-abiding man and the plant caused him quite a little trouble. Very often even after he had found the agricultural department of each state, the inspector was out of town and wouldn't be back for several days.

The result of the whole thing was that the insurance salesman got home in twenty-one days instead of ten. He drove a hundred miles to Bakersfield and found the rug merchant's brother.

The plant was safe and was now growing small red blossoms that gave off an odour which to the insurance salesman was extremely unpleasant.

Three thousand six hundred and seventy-eight miles I have carried this wonderful plant, the insurance salesman said, from the home of your brother in Boston to your home in Bakersfield. Your brother sends greetings.

The rug merchant's brother liked the plant even less than the insurance salesman did.

I do not want the plant, he said.

The insurance salesman was a man who was hardly ever amazed by anything. He accepted the brother's indifference and took the plant home with him.

He planted it in the finest soil in his back-yard, bought fertilizer for it, watered it, and took very good care of it.

It is not the plant, he told a neighbour. It nauseates me. But some day I shall perhaps be going back to Boston to visit my sister and when I see the rug merchant again I know he shall ask about the plant and I shall be pleased to tell him that it is flourishing. I feel that I have as good a chance as any man to sell him an insurance policy some day.

THE BEGGARS

I WAS a traveler once and I went to Europe.

I went right out and saw the world. Everywhere I went I saw the same thing. The world and beggars. I saw every variety of beggar there is. I saw rich beggars and poor beggars, proud beggars and humble beggars, fat beggars and thin beggars, healthy beggars and sick beggars, whole beggars and crippled beggars, wise beggars and stupid beggars.

I saw amateur beggars and professional beggars. A professional beggar is a beggar who begs for a living. He begs for money with which to buy bread.

Every man alive in the world is a beggar of one sort or another, every last one of them, great and small. The priest begs God for grace, and the king begs something for something. Sometimes he begs the people for loyalty, sometimes he begs God to forgive him. No man in the world can have endured ten years without having begged God to forgive him.

I saw gay beggars and sad beggars.

One of the gayest little beggars I ever saw was a Russian boy of nine or ten who met the trains at the station of a little village south of Kiev on the way to Kharkov. He met the train on which I was a passenger very early one morning and inasmuch as everybody aboard the train seemed asleep, he sang in a very loud voice and wakened a number of the passengers, including me. He sang like a gay cock in the morning. He sang like an angel. He was in rags and had no shoes, but his face was the shining face of an angel, and his voice was the voice of one. It was the loudest, purest, simplest, strongest, gayest, most fearless voice I have ever heard, and the song he sang was. I did not understand the words of the song but I understood the music. I guess the words came to just about the same thing: gayety, joy, pride, delight, simplicity, poise, strength, fearlessness. A beggar boy, doubtless an orphan, a *bezhprizoni*, homeless, without father or mother, uncle or aunt, brother or sister or cousin

or friend. Friend? He had as many friends as there were people in
the world, good and evil.

I was sleeping on the wooden bench, in the third class section
of the train, and early in the morning his voice wakened me and I
got up, delighted with the world and the Soviet Socialist Union of
Republics, or whatever it's called.

The black Caucasian peasant who slept on the opposite bench
wakened too. He lighted a Russian cigarette, inhaled, yawned, and
began to smile. He pointed, as if toward the voice, and said something in Russian.

The song this little Russian sang is impossible to describe, and
impossible to forget: it began strong, almost violently, at the top
of his voice; nevertheless, like the crow of a cock, which becomes
at the end almost impossibly strong with morning delight, every
now and then it reached a newer, an almost unbelievable, and greater,
strength and gayety and joyousness.

I got up and stretched my muscles and lighted a Russian cigarette.
Then I hurried to the first window and lifted it and looked down
on the singer, who was looking up at the train, singing, laughing,
lifting himself upward exactly as the cock does. And until I arrived
not a soul had come to the windows to see and hear him. He had
been singing to the train.

There was sadness in the song but it was the kind of sadness
which has not forgotten gayety. The boy was tough, lithe, hard,
supple, blond, and brown with exposure to sun and wind and the
world. He sang the song through once and then stood smiling at me
and I began to hurry through my pockets for Russian money. The
black Caucasian peasant came to another window and lifted it and
looked out and said a few words to the boy. I don't know what it was,
but it was a question. He perhaps asked the boy what his name
was. The boy answered the peasant in a few words, and then I
showed the coins and when I dropped them he caught them neatly
and thanked me in Russian and began to sing the same song all
over again which was exactly what I had wanted him to do.

He wakened quite a few people before the train began to move
away. Everybody was delighted with him. It is impossible to forget
that kind of singing, and I daresay it is impossible to hear that kind
of singing twice in a lifetime. That kind of singing comes out of the
whole heart of a race, the whole strength and suffering of an age.
I could go back to Russia a hundred times in the next fifty years

and I doubt very much if I should ever again hear that kind of singing.

This was one of the things that pleased me very much about Russia.

I went to Edinburgh in Scotland and found a fairly good hotel on the slope of a hill, on a very old and narrow street, and my room had a view of the street. Edinburgh is a gray sombre city. There are beggars in Edinburgh too.

A group of three of them came around the curve of this street and stopped in front of my hotel and began to perform. These beggars were three young men. One beat a big drum, another played a banjo, and the third, who was the greatest artist of all, the greatest beggar of all, sang through a megaphone and then tap-danced. Right in the street. Right in the world. Right on the stage of the world-theatre. That kind of music is magnificent in the world. I don't know how it would be in a theatre, but I doubt very much if it would be half as magnificent. That kind of music needs the world for a stage. These are the things which delight the traveler. These are the human things. I didn't visit any of the places travelers visit. I wanted to know about people living in the world. These voices of the beggars are things I remember with gladness. And this team of beggars was a great team. The drummer, the banjo-player, and the singer and dancer. In that gray sombre city, Edinburgh, in that profound and noble city, these three beggars smashed the quiet of centuries with deep, melancholy, Scotch anger. They didn't play and sing Scotch music. There was no bag-pipe. These young men were in ordinary every-day clothes, except the singer and dancer. The singer and dancer wore a cutaway coat and a derby.

He sang only the chorus of a song. The music would go along, reach the chorus, he would put the megaphone to his lips and sing; and after he had sung the chorus, he would dance the chorus. He danced like a man who was very angry, not waiting for his feet to fall after he had lifted them, but putting them down with great speed, great energy, great anger, and he didn't dance in one place, he went down the slope of the street, then turned around and danced up the slope, and it was great stuff. He sang something I tried very hard to remember, but all that I remembered was this: *Ha ya hika, waka ho,* and much more in this same kind of language.

The police drove away the three beggars and I got my hat and coat and ran downstairs and followed them. I gave the singer a half crown piece and talked to him. Did the police always go after them? Yes; only sometimes the police put them in jail. It all depended on the location. Couldn't get too close to business streets. Everywhere else the police only kept making them move on. The team went five blocks away and then stopped and again began to perform. They had only one song, this *Ya ya hika, waka ho*. I thought it must be some song these boys had made up, so I asked the singer and dancer. No, it was an American song. He named the song. Then when he sang the song again I listened very carefully, but it wasn't the American song; not any more. I knew the American song: it didn't go that way. It didn't have one-tenth of the anger in it that this song had.

In London I got a third-floor room in a traveler's hotel, and the room overlooked the street. There were a number of kinds of beggars who passed along this street. Organ-grinders mostly, but flower-sellers too. There was a big cockney lady of fifty or so who had a bunch of roses, and she passed along this street very slowly and called to the people in the hotels. The way she did it broke my heart. All she did was say, *Buy a pretty rose, a lovely garden rose,* and so on over and over again, but her voice, that is the unforgettable thing.

It was the saddest and loveliest and most tragic voice I had ever heard, and her language was cockney. She uttered her words half in speech and half in song. It was very touching, very sorrowing, very beautiful, and a thing to remember.

There were all kinds of beggars in the world when I left home and went traveling. Most of them irritated me very much, especially the rich ones, the fat ones, the whole ones, the pompous ones, but the real beggars, the noble beggars, the gay beggars, the angry beggars, either saddened or delighted me.

Their voices I shall never forget.

THE FILIPINO
AND THE DRUNKARD

THIS loud-mouthed guy in the brown camel-hair coat was not really mean, he was drunk. He took a sudden dislike to the small well-dressed Filipino and began to order him around the waiting room, telling him to get back, not to crowd up among the white people. They were waiting to get on the boat and cross the bay to Oakland. If he hadn't been drunk no one would have bothered to notice him at all, but as it was, he was making a commotion in the waiting room, and while everyone seemed to be in sympathy with the Filipino, no one seemed to want to bother about coming to the boy's rescue, and the poor Filipino was becoming very frightened.

He stood among the people, and this drunkard kept pushing up against him and saying, I told you to get back. Now get back. Go away back. I fought twenty-four months in France. I'm a real American. I don't want you standing up here among white people.

The boy kept squeezing nimbly and politely out of the drunkard's way, hurrying through the crowd, not saying anything and trying his best to be as decent as possible. He kept dodging in and out, with the drunkard stumbling after him, and as time went on the drunkard's dislike grew and he began to swear at the boy. He kept saying, You fellows are the best-dressed men in San Francisco, and you make your money washing dishes. You've got no right to wear such fine clothes.

He swore a lot, and it got so bad that a lot of ladies had to imagine they were deaf and weren't hearing any of the things he was saying.

When the big door opened, the young Filipino moved swiftly among the people, fleeing from the drunkard, reaching the boat before anyone else. He ran to a corner, sat down for a moment, then got up and began looking for a more hidden place. At the other end of the boat was the drunkard. He could hear the man swearing. He looked about for a place to hide, and rushed into the lavatory. He went into one of the open compartments and bolted the door.

The drunkard entered the lavatory and began asking others in the room if they had seen the boy. He was a real American, he said. He had been wounded twice in the War.

In the lavatory he swore more freely, using words he could never use where women were present. He began to stoop and look beyond the shut doors of the various compartments. I beg your pardon, he said to those he was not seeking, and when he came to the compartment where the boy was standing, he began swearing and demanding that the boy come out.

You can't get away from me, he said. You got no right to use a place white men use. Come out or I'll break the door.

Go away, the boy said.

The drunkard began to pound on the door.

You got to come out sometime, he said. I'll wait here till you do.

Go away, said the boy. I've done nothing to you.

He wondered why none of the men in the lavatory had the decency to calm the drunkard and take him away, and then he realized there were no other men in the lavatory.

Go away, he said.

The drunkard answered with curses, pounding the door.

Behind the door, the boy's bitterness grew to rage. He began to tremble, not fearing the man but fearing the rage growing in himself. He brought the knife from his pocket and drew open the sharp blade, holding the knife in his fist so tightly that the nails of his fingers cut into the flesh of his palm.

Go away, he said. I have a knife. I do not want any trouble.

The drunkard said he was an American. Twenty-four months in France. Wounded twice. Once in the leg, and once in the thigh. He would not go away. He was afraid of no dirty little yellow-belly Filipino with a knife. Let the Filipino come out, he was an American.

I will kill you, said the boy. I do not want to kill any man. You are drunk. Go away.

Please do not make any trouble, he said earnestly.

He could hear the motor of the boat pounding. It was like his rage pounding. It was a feeling of having been humiliated, chased about and made to hide, and now it was a wish to be free, even if he had to kill. He threw the door open and tried to rush beyond the man, the knife tight in his fist, but the drunkard caught him by the sleeve and drew him back. The sleeve of the boy's coat ripped, and the boy turned and thrust the knife into the side of the drunkard, feeling it scrape against rib-bone. The drunkard shouted and screamed at once, then caught the boy at the throat, and the boy began to thrust the knife into the side of the man many times, as a boxer jabs in the clinches.

When the drunkard could no longer hold him and had fallen to the floor, the boy rushed from the room, the knife still in his hand, blood dripping from the blade, his hat gone, his hair mussed, and the sleeve of his coat badly torn.

Everyone knew what he had done, yet no one moved.

The boy ran to the front of the boat, seeking some place to go, then ran back to a corner, no one daring to speak to him, and everyone aware of his crime.

There was no place to go, and before the officers of the boat arrived he stopped suddenly and began to shout at the people.

I did not want to hurt him, he said. Why didn't you stop him? Is it right to chase a man like a rat? You knew he was drunk. I did not want to hurt him, but he would not let me go. He tore my coat and tried to choke me. I told him I would kill him if he would not go away. It is not my fault. I must go to Oakland to see my brother. He is sick. Do you think I am looking for trouble when my brother is sick? Why didn't you stop him?

THE WORLD'S CHAMPION
ELEVATOR OPERATOR

LORD GOD, how he could meet the floor, open the door, let out the passenger, close the door, and go right on up to the top floor, every little detail perfectly timed, executed, and rounded out with small, humble indications of kindness, humility, generosity, and natural goodness, a certain way of letting the hand fall after the door had been swung inward, another way of bowing the head, partly in recognition of the importance of the passenger, a dentist or a lawyer, Doc Morrow or Will Colinet, and partly in recognition of the beauty of the performance, the skill, the accuracy, the grace and ease.

The awful syncopation.

Everybody marveled at the way he handled the elevator. Almost every man of any importance in town had stepped into his car at one time or another and noticed the magnificent way he met the floor, easing up to it gently, stopping gently, the car swaying up and down gently, especially in the summer when it was very hot and quiet and a man could dream clearly. Big men like Judge Cleary had openly admired his talent.

Elmer, Judge Cleary told him one day, I wouldn't be at all surprised if you're the best elevator operator in town.

Elmer never bothered to notice how nicely he was doing his work, he just did it and let it go at that. He didn't think about it one way or another, just dreamed along all day and then went home. But when Judge Cleary said what he said Elmer got to thinking.

Lord God, he thought, I guess I didn't graduate from high school for nothing.

He hadn't done all them hard lessons and got good grades in everything for nothing. Maybe he didn't know it, but maybe he was something new in the way of an elevator operator. He got the same pay as Alvin Hill, who was over fifty and always tired and sullen, but he figured he was a better elevator operator than old Hill at a ratio of at least two to one. And all he got was fifteen dollars a week. Well, that was all right. Rent, food, clothing, Sunday paper, radio, and all bills paid, except in case of illness like when Mary went to the hospital and died, sixteen months old, his only child. And the funeral, Lord God, all the rest of it. He was still paying fifty cents a week for the ground in the cemetery. At the rate he was going he guessed he'd be paying for that ground till he died and that wouldn't be for at least fifty years. He was twenty-nine, and his father died at the age of eighty-seven, his grandfather at the age of ninety-two, and his grandmothers long past a hundred.

Nobody ever could figure out how his old Pa kept right on being good that way. They never could understand all them kids in the house in Billings with his old Pa hardly able to walk straight on account of drink and fast living. Relatives with money and lots of advice used to drive up to that old house every five or six years and count the kids.

These kids all your kids, Tom? they'd say, Or what?

My kids? his old Pa would say to them. Go away with your big cars and sarcastic talk. Eleven boys and six girls is no family.

And sure enough there was another girl two years after he died. Elmer himself remembered his oldest brother as a man of forty with five kids of his own who wouldn't move away from the house in Billings because he was afraid. Pa and Ma both tried to kick him out, but Sam wouldn't go. Cried like a baby. And his own kids laughed at him.

That was before the war though.

When Sam went to France to be a soldier they didn't think it was so funny. And when he came back six months later with a scratch on his forehead, they were terrified. Sam was fighting the Germans late one night and was running in what seemed to be the direction of the enemy. He bumped his head on the floor, got up and swung at the bartender who turned around and hit him over the head with his crutch, and Sam was declared wounded. Somehow or other they gave him some kind of a test in the hospital and sent him home. He didn't know who the enemy was, what country he was in, or the name of the President of the United States. George Washington, he said. The kids were broken-hearted when they saw the big scratch on his forehead.

So when Judge Cleary said what he said, Elmer got to thinking about his ancestors and relatives and how they were all remarkable people, how it was in the blood, just natural for them to be different, and he figured he'd challenge every elevator operator in town to a contest. Fifty cents entrance fee and the winner to get all the money, ten percent for charity. Old Alvin Hill, of course, didn't like the idea from the start and wanted to know why in hell he should throw away his good money.

Well, Elmer said, if you're satisfied to be challenged and not accept the challenge, why that's your affair.

They talked while they operated, shouting to one another, but only when there were no passengers going up or down. That was often, especially in the summer, but the elevators had to keep their schedules. Passengers or no passengers, they went up and down, six floors up and six down.

Who in hell ever heard of an elevator driving contest? old Hill said. I guess you've plumb gone out of your head. What do you think you are? An aviator or something?

Well, said Elmer, while the elevators were about to pass at the third floor, I'm a damn sight better elevator operator than you'll ever be, or any of your kids either.

Either, Elmer said again.

It was September and mighty hot. Everybody in town was sleeping, either stretched out, or in a chair at a desk. They hadn't had more than a passenger each for over an hour. Elmer had taken up an old lady he had never before seen and directed her to Will Colinet's law office and she hadn't come out yet, so he figured both of them were sleeping the afternoon away. And old Hill had taken up a small Armenian with a toothache to Doc Morrow's painless extraction emporium, a room no bigger than a closet, full of junk run by electricity and capable of hurting a man to death.

The two cars passed, one going down, the other up. The doors opened, one on the ground floor, the other on the top floor. There was no passenger for either, and no ring, so all they had to do was get each car in motion again, one coming down to find out if anybody was awake in town, the other going up, just for fun, most likely.

Old Alvin Hill didn't like Elmer's attitude. It was mighty hot too. He never felt so shamefully young in all his life and all he kept dreaming about was the fine fat legs of Will Colinet's private secretary. He just wished he could get her somewhere private with lots of elbow-room all around. Well, that was crazy and it made him feel pretty sore at Elmer for nagging at him.

You keep my God damn kids out of this, he said, or I'll stop my car and bust you in the mouth.

Elmer hated to have a man who hadn't graduated from high school talk to him in that tone of voice so he said, You crack me in the mouth, and I'll bust your head open at the left ear.

They both felt more alive than at any other time of the year, and all old Alvin wanted was Will Colinet's private secretary in the country, and all Elmer wanted was the world's championship title as best all-around elevator operator.

Old Alvin stopped his car on the second floor and Elmer stopped his on the third. Old Alvin challenged Elmer to come down a floor and meet him. He took a couple of swipes at the imaginary and pathetic figure of Elmer, dreaming mostly of the legs of Will Colinet's secretary and feeling young enough to get sent up to San Quentin for some crazy act of love and passion. Elmer, on the other hand, wanted to know why he, who had graduated from high school, should go down a floor to met old Alvin. He asked very politely why old Alvin shouldn't come up to the third floor and get his head busted open at the left ear.

Head busted open? said old Alvin. You and who else?

Just me, said Elmer, and you know it.

That's what you think, said old Alvin. Come on down and see what happens.

Elmer remembered all the agony he went through getting good grades at high school, all the painful copying and writing answers on his cuff and little pieces of paper, and it burned him up to think an ignorant man like old Alvin was telling him to go down a floor and get himself slaughtered, so he ran down the stairs, instead of going down in his car, and old Alvin was there, all primed to lay him out cold. Elmer took a wild swipe at old Alvin and hit the wall with his fist, and old Alvin kicked at Elmer and lost his shoe.

Then the bell rang and old Alvin started for his car because he believed it was his duty to answer that bell, no matter what happened, but Elmer stood in front of the door and put out his fists like John L. Sullivan or somebody twice as good, and old Alvin said, We'll get fired. God damn it, get out of the way, or we'll both get fired.

Old Alvin felt terrible about wanting Will Colinet's secretary because everything seemed mighty dangerous and if that was John Fowler ringing the bell, they sure as hell *would get* fired because John

Fowler owned the building, fired and hired, and hated anybody who didn't do his work well.

Elmer was feeling too good to let old Alvin get into his car because he knew old Alvin was scared to death and this made Elmer feel better than when he won seven dollars on a Chinese lottery ticket, and he never stopped to think about what would happen in case he really did get fired for not letting old Alvin get in his car and answer the ring.

He just asked old Alvin to walk into suicide if he felt like it, and old Alvin began to beg him to get out of the way. The bell rang a dozen times while Elmer kept his fists stuck out in front of him like the world's champion of everything.

He felt even better than the time he ate two whole watermelons one Sunday afternoon while his wife was in the hospital having the baby that died.

Then old Alvin made for the stairs, figuring he'd go up to the third floor and answer the ring in Elmer's car, but Elmer caught him by the right leg and old Alvin fell backwards on Elmer, and Elmer got knocked unconscious on account of his head bumping old Alvin's head, and old Alvin got knocked unconscious too. Then, just for spite, everybody in the building wanted to get out, and everybody out of the building wanted to get in, and the bells were ringing like merry Christmas. Elmer and old Alvin were dead to the world and smiling.

John Fowler himself threw the bucket of water on Elmer and old Alvin that brought them around, and he himself asked what the crazy idea was. Well, Elmer wanted to mention his high school education, but couldn't, and old Alvin knew he couldn't give out any information about his affair with Will Colinet's secretary, so neither one of them said anything.

Finally Elmer said, Mr. Fowler, you know I graduated from high school.

What about it? Mr. Fowler said. I didn't.

Elmer felt ten times as bad now as he had felt good when he was holding off old Alvin by sticking his fists out in front of him, and he couldn't figure out anything more to say.

I thought it would be a good idea to have an elevator operator's contest, Pete said.

What the hell for? Mr. Fowler said.

Because I figure I'm the best elevator operator in town, Elmer said, only he felt lousier than ever because most of the time he was not like that, he was polite and humble and never talked out of turn like that.

You're the best elevator operator in town? Mr. Fowler said. You're out of your head. You're the worst in town, the worst anywhere. What in hell do you mean by fighting old Alvin?

Elmer felt like doing one of two things, crying, or busting Mr. Fowler's head open at the left ear. So he started to cry. He could tell now how bad it was, all around, and he didn't want to go home and tell Annie he had lost his job because she would just naturally kill him or raise enough female hell to make him commit suicide.

Mr. Fowler looked disgusted and had to light a cigar. Old Alvin just sat in the office and dreamed, and by God, even with the big bump on his head, all he could dream about was the fat legs of Will Colinet's secretary.

That's all.

So the old man, Mr. Fowler, said he would give each of them another chance, and the next day they went to work again. Things looked terrible for three months; Elmer just couldn't get into the swing of things again. The cold days of winter came, and it was terrible. He had to ask passengers all day to step up or step down and not more than a dozen times a day did he ever meet the floor perfectly, and even when he did, the car didn't ease up to the floor gently and sway gently the way it used to when he felt good and knew his high school education hadn't been in vain. On top of this he wasn't swinging the door inward the clean and easy way he used to, and when somebody made some remark to him about the weather he hadn't any sort of answer at all. Not more than half a year ago he would have come right back at them with every kind of lively and pleasant remark imaginable.

Besides, Annie was pregnant. Everything was haywire. He was still paying fifty cents a week for the ground in the cemetery, and there never was a dime left over, and his high school education looked like the worst waste of time of anything in his life, worse than the time he went all the way to San Francisco, over two hundred miles, and tried a whole month to live in the big city and nearly died of pneumonia and dreams of small towns.

He just took the elevator up to the sixth floor and down to the street floor and up and down, and didn't think any more about the championship, and felt terrible all the time, and didn't answer the people who mentioned the weather.

Then all of a sudden while he was coming down from the fifth floor with a woman in the car who had perfume on her he realized it was June and summer was coming, and he felt pretty good. God, how he eased the car down to the ground floor, and how it swayed when it got there, just like last year, and how nice the lady smelled. By God, there was nothing in the world to stop him from using his high school education. About the middle of August he was right back there in his old stride, meeting the floor perfectly, swinging the door inward perfectly, letting his hand fall the right way, bowing his head, coming right back at them with all kinds of cheerful remarks about the weather and everything else, the car swaying gently, the town nice and small, the climate hot, and himself damn near the world's champion of everything.

FINLANDIA

I WAS walking down Annankatu Street in Helsingfors when I saw two horns, a cello, a violin, and a picture of Beethoven in a store window, and remembered music. You go out into the world and all you see is telegraph poles and city streets, and all you hear is the train moving and automobile horns. You see multitudes of people trying to do all sorts of things, and in restaurants and in the streets you hear them talking anxiously. You forget music, and then all of a sudden you remember music.

Jesus Christ, you say. There is nothing else. After the train stops and you get off, or the ship docks and you walk down the gangplank, or the airplane comes down to the earth and lets you put your feet where they belong, there is nothing. You have arrived and you are nowhere. The name of the city is on the map. It is in big letters on the railway station. And the name of the country is on the new coins which buy bread, but you are nowhere and the more places you reach the more you understand that there is no geographical destination for man.

To hell with this, you say. London, and nothing. Paris, and nowhere. Vienna, and nothing. Moscow. The same. Dialectical materialism. Class consciousness. Revolution. Comrades. Baloney.

Nothing. Nowhere.

There is no place to go in that direction. And it breaks your heart. Jesus, you say. This is the world. These are the places of the world. What's the matter? Everything is haywire. And in the streets of every new city you feel again the world's dumb agony.

In Helsingfors it is not so bad, although there is private ownership of property in Finland. People own small objects. In the market those who own fish, sell fish, those who own tomatoes, sell tomatoes. Maybe it is Capitalism, but even so you can't find anything wrong with the people.

When I saw the cornet and the trombone and the cello and the violin and the picture of Beethoven, I felt very mournful. The shape

of the cornet is no small triumph, and even a tin violin is a poem of
an idea.

I went into the store and asked the girl in English if I could listen
to some phonograph records of Finnish music. The girls of Finland
are quiet, healthy, beautiful. Their mothers and fathers are Lutherans
and believe in God. The girls look as if they also believe, but even if
they don't, they probably go to church every Sunday and sing, and it
amounts to the same thing. They aren't fanatics, but they probably
go to church because it is all right. It is rather nice. Everybody is
there, and the old Sunday mood of the world quiets the harsh noises
and irritations of week days, and by the time the sermon is over everybody feels less important than on week days and there are no hard
feelings. You own the bank. Good. Keep it. I have a bicycle. You are
the mayor. Good. I am a clerk in an office. No hard feelings, and the
Sunday sun is bright.

In Russia, though, there is no such thing as Sunday. The girls of
Russia burst into false laughter every time a movie puts over a little
anti-religious propaganda because they know it is not true, there were
never any saints, religion is the opium of the people, Karl Marx is the
closest thing to a saint the world has ever known, Trotzky is a rat,
Lenin was almost the second coming of Jesus, and Comrade Stalin
is something amazing. As a result the girls of Russia don't look very
good. They are so wise it has spoiled their complexions. All the same,
Russia is at least a thousand years ahead of Finland. Look at the
things they are doing. Building cities. Creating a classless society. Calling everybody Comrade. Years and years ahead. The girls look pretty
bad, though.

The girl in the music store in Helsingfors was very old-fashioned.
She was polite. She didn't know anything about creating a classless
society, so she had time enough to do one small thing at a time, instead of doing nothing at all, and that loudly, the way it is in Russia.
Not all the time of course. There are some girls in Russia who are almost like the girls of Finland, but these are the ones who are not
militant. It's Dictatorship of the Proletariat, so it's Dictatorship of
the Proletariat, and they go on living their private lives. These kind
will never be leaders. They will never elevate the lives of the peasants.
They are very unimportant. But most of the girls in Russia a traveler
meets smell dialectical. It's something like the smell of a weed you
know is poison.

Jean Sibelius, I said to the girl in the music store. *Finlandia.*

Two months ago Helsingfors was very far from where I was. I was
in a room in the Great Northern Hotel in Manhattan, 517, with
bath. Helsingfors? Where's that, anyway? Now I am in Helsingfors,
and the only thing I know about the location of Manhattan is that
you get into a boat and after six days, if the boat is fast, you see the
skyline of Manhattan, and there you are. It is the same with Helsingfors or anywhere else. You are so many feet and so many inches off
the cement pavement. The sky is over you. The sun comes up in the
morning. In Manhattan, of course, it gets darker in the summer than
it does in Helsingfors in the summer. It never gets very dark in the
summer in Helsingfors. At midnight it is still pretty light, and a couple
of hours later the sun comes up again.

And it is fine. It is tremendous. It is the crazy world. The urban
corners of what is affectionately known as civilization. A cornet, a
trombone, a cello, and a violin in a store window. And of course music
is the most effective opium of the people there is, unless it is composed by a dialectical materialist. Then nobody knows what it is. But
if it is good, then the boy who did the job is fooling somebody,
maybe Marx.

All I wanted was music. No dialectics. Just the simple old-fashioned
fury of one man alone, fighting it out alone, wrestling with God, or
with the whole confounded universe, throwing himself into silence
and time, and after sweating away seven pounds of substance, coming out of the small room with something detached, of itself, alive,
timeless, crazy, magnificent, delirious, blasphemous, pious, furious,
kindly, not the man, not all men, but a thing by itself, incredibly
complete, an incision of silence and emptiness, and then sound and
the shapes of things without substance. Music. A symphony.

Finlandia, I said. The word was strong and good, and I was there.
I am in Finland, I thought. This store is on Annankatu Street in Helsingfors. Jean Sibelius lives in Finland. It was here that he composed
Finlandia, and in American five years ago I heard *Finlandia*, and I
have been hearing it ever since, and the ear of man will never cease
hearing it.

It is no small thing to hear *Finlandia* in Helsingfors.

The girl was very pious, changing the needle, letting it touch the
record, winding the phonograph. She went away six paces and stood
humbly listening. After the silence the music began to leap out into
the world again. Finland.

O Jesus Christ, there is no geographic destination for man. And the music charged into the chaos of the world, smashing hell out of error, ignoring waste, and creating a classless society. Last year in England the king listened and knew the truth, and tomorrow in Nebraska a child will listen and know the truth, and it will be the same with kings and children a hundred years from now, or a thousand.

I smoked four cigarettes, and then this great work of Jean Sibelius ended. The silence that had existed before the music began came into existence again, and now it was no longer *Finlandia* but Finland, Helsingfors. The girl could not speak English, but she also could not say anything in Finnish. She smiled, almost weeping. Then she hurried away and returned with an album containing the records of a whole symphony by Sibelius.

No, I said. It was very kind of you to let me hear *Finlandia* in Helsingfors. I cannot buy. I am only here on my way back to America. I am sailing tomorrow for Stockholm.

I brought some marks from my pocket and asked if I could pay for hearing *Finlandia*.

This, the appearance of money, spoiled everything. Now the girl not only did not understand what I was saying, she did not understand the *meaning* of what I was saying. She could not understand how I felt. With the music she knew and she didn't need to understand the words.

She wanted to give me something for the money.

No, I said. This money is for hearing *Finlandia*.

This was too much. She went away and returned with a girl who spoke English.

I explained everything, and the girl who knew English interpreted to the girl who did not, and we all laughed.

No no, said the girl who spoke English. Would you like to hear some more of Sibelius?

No, I said. I want to remember *Finlandia* in Helsingfors. Do you know Jean Sibelius?

Yes, of course, said the girl.

The other girl stood by watching our faces.

What sort of a man is he? I said.

Big, said the girl. He is very big. He comes to this store very often.

He lives in Helsingfors?

Yes.

Look, I said. I am in Helsingfors today and I may never be here again. Tomorrow I am going to Stockholm. I am an American, and I am supposed to be a writer. Do you think Jean Sibelius would see me?

But wait a minute. Let me explain.

The first time I heard *Finlandia*, five years ago in American, I got up from the chair, pushed over the table, knocked some plaster out of the wall, and said, Jesus Christ, who is this man? Now, it was almost the same. It is not every day that I am in Helsingfors, and it is not every century that Jean Sibelius is in Helsingfors the same day.

Yes, said the girl. Wait a moment, please. I will get the number.

And she went upstairs. She returned running.

Jean Sibelius is in Jarvenpaa, she said.

How far is that from Helsingfors? I said.

One hour, said the girl.

I wrote the name of the place on an envelope and hurried away. The two Finnish girls walked all the way to the door with me. They were almost as excited as I was. From America, and he has heard *Finlandia*. Music is international. (And it is. Even the word music is. If you say bread in English, many people will not know what you mean, but if you say music, they will know.)

I thought I would send a telegram. I tried to write one but it sounded lousy. It doesn't mean a thing in a telegram.

I asked the hotel clerk if I could reach Jean Sibelius by telephone. I felt like a fool. Such a thing is ridiculous.

Of course, he said.

And before I knew it I was talking to him over the telephone.

I am from America, I said. Everybody in America likes your music.

I am at this place in the country, he said in English. Come at seven.

It was half past four, and it took an hour to get to Jarvenpaa, so that left me about an hour in which to try to figure out what the hell was going on. Who am I to see Jean Sibelius? What can I say to the man who composed *Finlandia*, and what will he have to say to me? He is seventy years old and I am twenty-seven. I was born in America. I am a punk writer, and he is a great composer, Jesus Christ.

But that's music for you. I didn't know what I was doing.

It is *Finlandia*. And it was Finland. The girls were beautiful and very quiet and very polite. It is a writer's job to try to find out how these things happen: that music, and the clean innocent faces of the girls of Finland.

I went up to my room at the Torni Hotel and tried to think of some questions to ask Jean Sibelius, but nothing is more disgusting than a question, and the ones I wrote were the worst questions anybody ever thought of asking anybody else. They were long involved questions, asking if perhaps it is true that all art forms are inherent in nature and all the artist can do is reveal these forms, and what effect does the world of man, the world of cities, trains, ships, skyscrapers, factories, machines, noises, have on a composer, and if music should have a function, and what is the quality which most nearly makes a competent composer a great composer, his spiritual heritage, his race, the experiences and remembrances of his race, his own personal experiences, or simply much energy, some anger, and the will or impulse to declare his mortality at a certain time and thus to be immortal?

Jesus Christ.

And God forgive me I actually asked the questions.

It was an old Buick going like a bat out of hell through the clean landscape of Finland, and along the roads were boys on bicycles, girls walking, and farmers going home on carts. Clear air. Fresh green growing things. Clean sky. Cool clean lakes. Cool trees. Grass. The place of *Finlandia*.

It is not easy to explain. It is not only these things, but something more. Maybe it is because there is hardly any night at all during the summer. Maybe it is because they are Lutherans, and have a church, and believe. Maybe it is because Finland is north. Cool. Quiet. Blond. Blue eyes. I don't know what the hell it is.

It was a country house in this landscape. The cab-driver stopped the car in the country and asked three young girls where was the road to the house of Jean Sibelius. The girls told him he had traveled too far. It was about a quarter of a kilometre back. In Finland everybody knows about Jean Sibelius and many people in and around Helsingfors have spoken with him.

Don't get this wrong. I mean something. Don't get the idea I mean it is remarkable that many people have spoken with Jean Sibelius or that it is splendid of him to know so many people. I mean it is all the same. These are the people of Finland. Jean Sibelius is the big man who makes music, and the others are the others, and it is the same. They are all alive in Finland.

I went into the house all mixed up. The maid was waiting for me and welcomed me in Finnish. He was seated, talking to a young man, an American-Finn from California, and he got up, and then it was the thing I was after, *Finlandia,* Jean Sibelius, seventy years old, and timeless, and a child, the smile, the fury of politeness, *yes yes yes,* the strong hand, the introduction to his friend, the strong gesture, the energy, sit down, and Jesus Christ, what about those crazy questions? I couldn't talk, I had to say my piece and scram and I wanted to do so, so I began to explain about the questions, stumbling, a very big man, and I don't mean bulk alone, and I was from America, eleven hours in Helsingfors.

He answered the God damn questions, and it was great. Yes, yes, silence. Silence is everything. (He jumped up, his big hands trembling and got a can of cigars. Cigar? And then he shouted for whiskey, and in a moment the maid came into the room with whiskey.) Music is like life. It begins and ends in silence. He made a wild gesture, every nerve of his body alive. Drink whiskey, he said. I didn't know what to do. I poured a drink for his young friend, and another for myself, and we drank.

The world of cities, I said. Trains, ships, skyscrapers, subways, airplanes, factories, machines, noises, what effect?

I felt like a fool.

He was furious and began to speak in his native tongue.

He cannot answer, said the young man. Music speaks for him. It is all in the music.

I am sorry about these questions, I said. I'll leave out some of them.

He spoke in Finnish, and the young man interpreted: Beauty and truth, but he does not like the words. Not the words. It is something different in music. Everybody says beauty and truth. He is no prophet. Only a composer.

And the angry-kindly smile in the ferociously stark face.

Drink whiskey, he said in English.

I went on to the one about what is it that makes the man great. No, he said in English. You cannot talk about such a thing.

It was swell. It was the real thing. It was too silly to talk. He was too wise to fool with words. He put it down in music. I felt swell because he was so young, so much a boy, so excited, nervous, energetic, impatient, so amazingly innocent, and on the way back to Helsingfors I began to see in the landscape of Finland the clean clear music of *Finlandia.*

HELSINGFORS, FINLAND. *July,* 1935.

A COLD DAY

Dᴇᴀʀ ᴍ—,

I want you to know that it is very cold in San Francisco today, and that I am freezing. It is so cold in my room that every time I start to write a short story the cold stops me and I have to get up and do bending exercises. It means, I think, that something's got to be done about keeping short story writers warm. Sometimes when it is very cold I am able to do very good writing, but at other times I am not. It is the same when the weather is excessively pleasant. I very much dislike letting a day go by without writing a short story and that is why I am writing this letter: to let you know that I am very angry about the weather. Do not think that I am sitting in a nice warm room in sunny California, as they call it, and making up all this stuff about the cold. I am sitting in a very cold room and there is no sun anywhere, and the only thing I can talk about is the cold because it is the only thing going on today. I am freezing and my teeth are chattering. I would like to know what the Democratic party ever did for freezing short story writers. Everybody else gets heat. We've got to depend on the sun and in the winter the sun is undependable. That's the fix I am in: wanting to write and not being able to, because of the cold.

One winter day last year the sun came out and its light came into my room and fell across my table, warming my table and my room and warming me. So I did some brisk bending exercises and then sat down and began to write a short story. But it was a winter day and before I had written the first paragraph of the story the sun had fallen back behind clouds and there I was in my room, sitting in the cold, writing a story. It was such a good story that even though I knew it would never be printed I had to go on writing it, and as a result I was frozen stiff by the time I finished writing it. My face was blue and I could barely move my limbs, they were so cold and stiff. And my room was full of the smoke of a package of Chesterfield cigarettes, but even the smoke was frozen. There were clouds of it in my room, but my room was very cold just the same. Once, while I was writing, I thought of getting a tub and making a fire in it. What I intended to do was to burn a half dozen of my books and keep warm, so that I could write my story. I found an old tub and I brought it to my room, but when I looked around for books to burn and I couldn't find any. All of my books are old and cheap. I have about five hundred of them and I paid a nickel each for most of them, but when I looked around for titles to burn, I couldn't find any. There was a large heavy book in German on anatomy that would have made a swell fire, but when I opened it and read a line of that beautiful language, *sie bestehen aus zwei. Hüftgelenkbeugemuskeln des Oberschenkels, von denen der eine breitere,* and so on, I couldn't do it. It was asking too much. I couldn't understand the language, I couldn't understand a word in the whole book, but it was somehow too eloquent to use for a fire. The book had cost me five cents two or three years ago, and it weighed about six pounds, so you see that even as fire wood it had been a bargain and I should have been able to tear out its pages and make a fire.

But I couldn't do it. There were over a thousand pages in the book and I planned to burn one page at a time and see the fire of each page, but when I thought of all that print being effaced by fire and all that accurate language being removed from my library, I couldn't do it, and I still have the book. When I get tired of reading great writers, I go to this book and read language that I cannot understand, *während der Kindheit ist sie von birnförmiger Gestalt und liegt vorzugsweise in der Bauchhöhle.* It is simply blasphemous to think of burning a thousand pages of such language. And of course I haven't so much as mentioned the marvelous illustrations.

Then I began to look around for cheap fiction.

And you know the world is chock full of such stuff. Nine books out of ten are cheap worthless fiction, inorganic stuff. I thought, well, there are at least a half dozen of those books in my library and I can burn them and be warm and write my story. So I picked out six books and together they weighed about as much as the German anatomy book. The first was *Tom Brown At Oxford: A Sequel to School Days At Rugby,* Two Volumes in One. The first book had 378 pages, and the second 430, and all these pages would have made a small fire that would have lasted a pretty long time, but I had never read the book and it seemed to me that I had no right to burn a book I hadn't even read. It looked as if it ought to be a book of cheap prose, one worthy of being burned, but I couldn't do it. I read, *The belfry-tower rocked and reeled, as that peal rang out, now merry, now scornful, now plaintive, from those narrow belfry windows, into the bosom of the soft southwest wind, which was playing round the old gray tower of Englebourn church.* Now that isn't exactly tremendous prose, but it isn't such very bad prose either. So I put the book back on the shelf.

The next book was *Inez: A Tale of the Alamo,* and it was dedicated to The Texan Patriots. It was by the author of another book called *Beulah,* and yet another called *St. Elmo.* The only thing I knew about this writer or her books was that one day a girl at school had been severely reprimanded for bringing to class a book called *St. Elmo.* It was said to be the sort of book that would corrupt the morals of a young girl. Well, I opened the book and read, *I am dying; and, feeling as I do, that few hours are allotted me, I shall not hesitate to speak freely and candidly. Some might think me deviating from the delicacy of my sex; but, under the circumstances, I feel that I am not. I have loved you long, and to know that my love is returned, is a source of deep and unutterable joy to me.* And so on.

This was such bad writing that it was good, and I decided to read the whole book at my first opportunity. There is much for a young writer to learn from our poorest writers. It is very destructive to burn bad books, almost more destructive than to burn good ones.

The next book was *Ten Nights In A Bar Room, and What I Saw There* by T. S. Arthur. Well, even this book was too good to burn. The other three books were by Hall Caine, Brander Matthews, and Upton Sinclair. I had read only Mr. Sinclair's book, and while I didn't like it a lot as a piece of writing, I couldn't burn it because the print was so fine and the binding so good. Typographically it was one of my best books.

Anyway, I didn't burn a single page of a single book, and I went on freezing and writing. Every now and then I burned a match just to remind myself what a flame looked like, just to keep in touch with the idea of heat and warmth. It would be when I wanted to light another cigarette and instead of blowing out the flame I would let it burn all the way down to my fingers.

It is simply this, that if you have any respect for the mere idea of books, what they stand for in life, if you believe in paper and print, you cannot burn any page of any book. Even if you are freezing. Even if you are trying to do a bit of writing yourself. You can't do it. It is asking too much.

Today it is as cold in my room as the day I wanted to make a fire of books. I am sitting in the cold, smoking cigarettes, and trying to get this coldness onto paper so that when it becomes warm again in San Francisco I won't forget how it was on the cold days.

I have a small phonograph in my room and I play it when I want to exercise in order to keep warm. Well, when it gets to be very cold in my room this phonograph won't work. Something goes wrong inside, the grease freezes and the wheels won't turn, and I can't have music while I am bending and swinging my arms. I've got to do it without music. It is much more pleasant to exercise with jazz, but when it is very cold the phonograph won't work and I am in a hell of a fix. I have been in here since eight o'clock this morning and it is now a quarter to five, and I am in a hell of a mess. I hate to let a day go by without doing something about it, without saying something, and all day I have been in here with my books that I never read, trying to get started and I haven't gotten anywhere. Most of the time I have been walking up and down the room (two steps in any direction brings you to a wall) and bending and kicking and swinging my arms. That's practically all I have been doing. I tried the phonograph a half dozen times to see if the temperature hadn't gone up a little, but it hadn't, and the phonograph wouldn't play music.

I thought I ought to tell you about this. It's nothing important. It's sort of silly, making so much of a little cold weather, but at the same time the cold is a fact today and it is the big thing right now and I am speaking of it. The thing that amazes and pleases me is that my typewriter hasn't once clogged today. Around Christmas when we had a very cold spell out here it was always clogging, and the more I oiled it the more it clogged. I couldn't do a thing with it. The reason was that I had been using the wrong kind of oil. But all this time that I have been writing about the cold my typewriter has been doing its work excellently, and this amazes and pleases me. To think that in spite of the cold this machine can go right on making the language I use is very fine. It encourages me to stick with it, whatever happens. If the machine will work, I tell myself, then you've got to work with it. That's what it amounts to. If you can't write a decent short story because of the cold, write something else. Write anything. Write a long letter to somebody. Tell them how cold you are. By the time the letter is received the sun will be out

again and you will be warm again, but the letter will be there men-
tioning the cold. If it is so cold that you can't make up a little ordinary
Tuesday prose, why, what the hell, say anything that comes along,
just so it's the truth. Talk about your toes freezing, about the time you
actually wanted to burn books to keep warm but couldn't do it, about
the phonograph. Speak of the little unimportant things on a cold
day, when your mind is numb and your feet and hands frozen. Mention the things you wanted to write but couldn't. This is what I have
been telling myself.

After coffee this morning, I came here to write an important story.
I was warm with the coffee and I didn't realize how really cold it
was. I brought out paper and started to line up what I was going
to say in this important story that will never be written because once
I lose a thing I lose it forever, this story that is forever lost because
of the cold that got into me and silenced me and made me jump up
from my chair and do bending exercises. Well, I can tell you about
it. I can give you an idea what it was to have been like. I remember
that much about it, but I didn't write it and it is lost. It will give
you something of an idea as to how I write.

I will tell you the things I was telling myself this morning while I
was getting this story lined up in my mind:

Think of America, I told myself this morning. The whole thing.
The cities, all the houses, all the people, the coming and going, the
coming of children, the going of them, the coming and going of men
and death, and life, the movement, the talk, the sound of machinery,
the oratory, think of the pain in America and the fear and the deep
inward longing of all things alive in America. Remember the great
machines, wheels turning, smoke and fire, the mines and the men
working them, the noise, the confusion. Remember the newspapers
and the moving picture theatres and everything that is a part of this
life. Let this be your purpose: to suggest this great country.

Then turn to the specific. Go out to some single person and dwell
with him, within him, lovingly, seeking to understand the miracle
of his being, and utter the truth of his existence and reveal the
splendor of the mere fact of his being alive, and say it in great prose,
simply, show that he is of the time, of the machines and the fire and
smoke, the newspapers and the noise. Go with him to his secret and
speak of it gently, showing that it is the secret of man. Do not deceive. Do not make up lies for the sake of pleasing anyone. No one
need be killed in your story. Simply relate what is the great event of

all history, of all time, the humble, artless truth of mere being. There is no greater theme: no one need be violent to help you with your art. There *is* violence. Mention it of course when it is time to mention it. Mention the war. Mention all ugliness, all waste. Do even this lovingly. But emphasize the glorious truth of mere being. It is the major theme. You do not have to create a triumphant climax. The man you write of need not perform some heroic or monstrous deed in order to make your prose great. Let him do what he has always done, day in and day out, continuing to live. Let him walk and talk and think and sleep and dream and awaken and walk again and talk again and move and be alive. It is enough. There is nothing else to write about. You have never seen a story in life. The events of life have never fallen into the form of the short story or the form of the poem, or into any other form. Your own consciousness is the only form you need. Your own awareness is the only action you need. Speak of this man, recognize his existence. Speak of man.

Well, this is a poor idea of what the story was to have been like. I was warm with coffee when I was telling myself what and how to write, but now I am freezing, and this is the closest I can come to what I had in mind. It was to have been something fine, but now all that I have is this vague remembrance of the story. The least I can do is put into words this remembrance. Tomorrow I will write another story, a different story. I will look at the picture from a different viewpoint. I don't know for sure, but I may feel cocky and I may mock this country and the life that is lived here. It is possible. I can do it. I have done it before, and sometimes when I get mad about political parties and political graft I sit down and mock this great country of ours. I get mean and I make man out to be a rotten, worthless, unclean thing. It isn't man, but I make out as if it is. It's something else, something less tangible, but for mockery it is more convenient to make out that it is man. It's my business to get at the truth, but when you start to mock, you say to hell with the truth. Nobody's telling the truth, why should I? Everybody's telling nice lies, writing nice stories and novels, why should I worry about the truth. There is no truth. Only grammar, punctuation, and all that rot. But I know better. I can get mad at things and start to mock, but I know better. At its best, the whole business is pretty sad, pretty pathetic.

All day I have been in this room freezing, wanting to say something solid and clean about all of us who are alive. But it was so cold I couldn't do it. All I could do was swing my arms and smoke cigarettes and feel rotten.

Early this morning when I was warm with coffee I had this great story in my mind, ready to get into print, but it got away from me.

The most I can say now is that it is very cold in San Francisco to-day, and I am freezing.

THE HUMAN COMEDY

CHAPTER 1 *Ulysses*

The little boy named Ulysses Macauley one day stood over the new gopher hole in the backyard of his house on Santa Clara Avenue in Ithaca, California. The gopher of this hole pushed up fresh moist dirt and peeked out at the boy, who was certainly a stranger but perhaps not an enemy. Before this miracle had been fully enjoyed by the boy, one of the birds of Ithaca flew into the old walnut tree in the backyard and after settling itself on a branch broke into rapture, moving the boy's fascination from the earth to the tree. Next, best of all, a freight train puffed and roared far away. The boy listened, and felt the earth beneath him tremble with the moving of the train. Then he broke into running, moving (it seemed to him) swifter than any life in the world.

When he reached the crossing he was just in time to see the passing of the whole train, from locomotive to caboose. He waved to the engineer, but the engineer did not wave back to him. He waved to five others who were with the train, but not one of them waved back. They might have done so, but they didn't. At last a Negro appeared leaning over the side of a gondola. Above the clatter of the train, Ulysses heard the man singing:

> "Weep no more, my lady. O weep no more today
> We will sing one song for the old Kentucky home
> For the old Kentucky home far away"

Ulysses waved to the Negro too, and then a wondrous and unexpected thing happened. *This* man, black and different from all the others, waved back to Ulysses, shouting: "Going home, boy—going back where I belong!"

The small boy and the Negro waved to one another until the train was almost out of sight.

Then Ulysses looked around. There it was, all around him, funny and lonely—the world of his life. The strange, weed-infested, junky, wonderful, senseless yet beautiful world. Walking down the track came an old man with a rolled bundle on his back. Ulysses waved to this man too, but the man was too old and too tired to be pleased with a small boy's friendliness. The old man glanced at Ulysses as if both he and the boy were already dead.

The little boy turned slowly and started for home. As he moved, he still listened to the passing of the train, the singing of the Negro, and the joyous words: "Going home, boy—going back where I belong!" He stopped to think of all this, loitering beside a china-ball tree and kicking at the yellow, smelly, fallen fruit of it. After a moment he smiled the smile of the Macauley people—the gentle, wise, secret smile which said *Yes* to all things.

When he turned the corner and saw the Macauley house, Ulysses began to skip, kicking up a heel. He tripped and fell because of this merriment, but got to his feet and went on.

His mother was in the yard, throwing feed to the chickens. She watched the boy trip and fall and get up and skip again. He came quickly and quietly and stood beside her, then went to the hen nest to look for eggs. He found one. He looked at it a moment, picked it up, brought it to his mother and very carefully handed it to her, by which he meant what no man can guess and no child can remember to tell.

CHAPTER 2 *Homer*

His brother Homer sat on the seat of a secondhand bicycle which struggled bravely with the dirt of a country road. Homer Macauley wore a telegraph messenger's coat which was far too big and a cap which was not quite big enough. The sun was going down in a somnolence of evening peace deeply cherished by the people of Ithaca. All about the messenger orchards and vineyards rested in the old, old earth of California. Even though he was moving along swiftly, Homer was not missing any of the charm of the region. Look at that! he kept saying to himself of earth and tree, sun and grass and cloud. Look at that, will you? He began to make decorations with the

movements of his bike and, to accompany these ornaments of movement, he burst out with a shouting of music—simple, lyrical and
ridiculous. The theme of this opera was taken over in his mind by the
strings of an orchestra, then supplemented by the harp of his mother
and the piano of his sister Bess. And finally, to bring the whole family together, an accordion came into the group, saying the music with
a smiling and somber sweetness, as Homer remembered his brother
Marcus.

Homer's music fled before the hurrying clatter of three incredible
objects moving across the sky. The messenger looked up at these
objects, and promptly rode into a small dry ditch. Airplanes, Homer
said to himself. A farmer's dog came swiftly and with great importance, barking like a man with a message. Homer ignored the message,
turning only once to spoof the animal by saying "Arp, Arp!" He
seated himself on the bicycle again and rode on.

When he reached the beginning of the residential district of the
city, he passed a sign without reading it:

ITHACA, CALIFORNIA

EAST, WEST—HOME IS BEST

WELCOME, STRANGER

He stopped at the next corner to behold a long line of Army trucks
full of soldiers roll by. He saluted the men, just as his brother
Ulysses had waved to the engineer and the hoboes. A great many
soldiers returned the messenger's salute. Why not? What did they
know about anything?

CHAPTER 3   *You Go Your Way, I'll Go Mine*

The messenger got off his bicycle in front of the house of Mrs. Rosa
Sandoval. He went to the door and knocked gently. He knew almost
immediately that someone was inside the house. He could not hear
anything, but he was sure the knock was bringing someone to the door
and he was most eager to see who this person would be—this woman
named Rosa Sandoval who was now to hear of murder in the world
and to feel it in herself. The door was not a long time opening, but

there was no hurry in the way it moved on its hinges. The movement of the door was as if, whoever she was, she had nothing in the
world to fear. Then the door was open, and there she was.

To Homer the Mexican woman was beautiful. He could see that
she had been patient all her life, so that now, after years of it, her
lips were set in a gentle and saintly smile. But like all people who
never receive telegrams the appearance of a messenger at the front
door is full of terrible implications. Homer knew that Mrs. Rosa
Sandoval was shocked to see him. Her first word was the first word
of all surprise. She said "Oh," as if instead of a messenger she had
thought of opening the door to someone she had known a long time
and would be pleased to sit down with. Before she spoke again she
studied Homer's eyes and Homer knew that she knew the message
was not a welcome one.

"You have a telegram?" she said.

It wasn't Homer's fault. His work was to deliver telegrams. Even
so, it seemed to him that he was part of the whole mistake. He felt
awkward and almost as if he *alone* were responsible for what had
happened. At the same time he wanted to come right out and say,
"I'm only a messenger, Mrs. Sandoval. I'm very sorry I must bring
you a telegram like this, but it is only because it is my work to do so."

"Who is it for?" the Mexican woman said.

"Mrs. Rosa Sandoval, 1129 G Street," Homer said. He extended
the telegram to the Mexican woman, but she would not touch it.

"Are you Mrs. Sandoval?" Homer said.

"Please," the woman said. "Please come in. I cannot read English.
I am Mexican. I read only *La Prensa* which comes from Mexico
City." She paused a moment and looked at the boy standing awk-
wardly as near the door as he could be and still be inside the house.

"Please," she said, "what does the telegram say?"

"Mrs. Sandoval," the messenger said, "the telegram says—"

But now the woman interrupted him. "But you must *open* the
telegram and *read* it to me," she said. "You have not opened it."

"Yes, ma'am," Homer said as if he were speaking to a school
teacher who had just corrected him.

He opened the telegram with nervous fingers. The Mexican woman
stooped to pick up the torn envelope, and tried to smooth it out. As
she did so she said, "Who sent the telegram—my son Juan
Domingo?"

"No, ma'am," Homer said. "The telegram is from the War Department."

"War Department?" the Mexican woman said.

"Mrs. Sandoval," Homer said swiftly, "your son is dead. Maybe it's a mistake. Everybody makes a mistake, Mrs. Sandoval. Maybe it wasn't your son. Maybe it was somebody else. The telegram *says* it was Juan Domingo. But maybe the telegram is wrong."

The Mexican woman pretended not to hear.

"Oh, do not be afraid," she said. "Come inside. Come inside. I will bring you candy." She took the boy's arm and brought him to the table at the center of the room and there she made him sit.

"All boys like candy," she said. "I will bring you candy." She went into another room and soon returned with an old chocolate candy box. She opened the box at the table and in it Homer saw a strange kind of candy.

"Here," she said. "Eat this candy. All boys like candy."

Homer took a piece of the candy from the box, put it into his mouth, and tried to chew.

"You would not bring me a bad telegram," she said. "You are a good boy—like my little Juanito when he was a little boy. Eat another piece." And she made the messenger take another piece of the candy.

Homer sat chewing the dry candy while the Mexican woman talked. "It is our own candy," she said, "from cactus. I make it for my Juanito when he come home, but *you* eat it. You are my boy too."

Now suddenly she began to sob, holding herself in as if weeping were a disgrace. Homer wanted to get up and run but he knew he would stay. He even thought he might stay the rest of his life. He just didn't know what else to do to try to make the woman less unhappy, and if she had *asked* him to take the place of her son, he would not have been able to refuse, because he would not have known how. He got to his feet as if by standing he meant to begin correcting what could not be corrected and then he knew the foolishness of this intention and became more awkward than ever. In his heart he was saying over and over again, "What can I do? What the hell can *I* do? I'm only the messenger."

The woman suddenly took him in her arms, saying, "My little boy, my little boy!"

He didn't know why, because he only felt wounded by the whole thing, but for some reason he was sickened through all his blood and thought he would need to vomit. He didn't *dislike* the woman or anybody else, but what was happening to her seemed so wrong and so full of ugliness that he was sick and didn't know if he ever wanted to go on living again.

"Come now," the woman said. "Sit down here." She forced him into another chair and stood over him. "Let me look at you," she said. She looked at him strangely and, sick everywhere within himself, the messenger could not move. He felt neither love nor hate but something very close to disgust, but at the same time he felt great compassion, not for the poor woman alone, but for all things and the ridiculous way of their enduring and dying. He saw her back in time, a beautiful young woman sitting beside the crib of her infant son. He saw her looking down at this amazing human thing, speechless and helpless and full of the world to come. He saw her rocking the crib and he heard her singing to the child. Now look at her, he said to himself.

He was on his bicycle suddenly, riding swiftly down the dark street, tears coming out of his eyes and his mouth whispering young and crazy curses. When he got back to the telegraph office the tears had stopped, but everything else had started and he knew there would be no stopping them. "Otherwise I'm just as good as dead myself," he said, as if someone were listening whose hearing was not perfect.

CHAPTER 4   *A Speech on the Human Nose*

Miss Hicks waited for Helen to take her seat and then looked over the faces of her pupils. "Now," she said, "what have we learned?"

"That people all over the world have noses," Homer said.

Miss Hicks was not upset by this reply and took it for what it was worth. "What else?" she said.

"That noses," Homer said, "are not only for blowing or to have colds in but also to keep the record of ancient history straight."

Miss Hicks turned away from Homer and said, "Someone else, please. Homer seems to have been carried away by the noses."

"Well, it's in the book, isn't it?" Homer said. "What do *they* mention it for? It must be important."

"Perhaps," Miss Hicks said, "you would like to make an extemporaneous speech on the nose, Mr. Macauley."

"Well," Homer said, "maybe not exactly a speech—but ancient history tells us one thing." Slowly now, and with a kind of unnecessary emphasis, he continued, "People have always had noses. To prove it all you have to do is look around at everybody in this classroom." He looked around at everybody. "Noses," he said, "all over the place." He stopped a moment to decide what else would be possible to say on this theme. "The nose," he decided to say, "is perhaps the most ridiculous part of the human face. It has always been a source of embarrassment to the human race, and the Hittites probably beat up on everybody because their noses were so big and crooked. It doesn't matter who invented the sundial because sooner or later somebody invents a watch. The important thing is, Who's got the noses?"

Joe the comedian, listened with profound interest and admiration, if not envy. Homer continued.

"Some people," he said, "talk through their noses. A great many people snore through their noses, and a handful of people whistle or sing through them. Some people are led around by their noses, others use the nose for prying and poking into miscellaneous places. Noses have been bitten by mad dogs and movie actors in passionate love stories. Doors have been slammed on them and they have been caught in egg-beaters and automatic record changers. The nose is stationary, like a tree, but being on a movable object—the head—it suffers great punishment by being taken to places where it is only in the way. The purpose of the nose is to smell what's in the air, but some people sniff with the nose at other people's ideas, manners, or appearances." He turned and looked at Hubert Ackley III and then at Helen Eliot, whose nose, instead of moving upward, for some reason went slightly downward. "These people," he said, "generally hold their noses toward heaven, as if that were the way to get in. Most animals have nostrils but few have noses, as we understand noses, yet the sense of smell in animals is more highly developed than in man—who has a nose, and no fooling." Homer Macauley took a deep breath and decided to conclude his speech. "The most important thing about the nose," he said, "is that it makes trouble, causes wars, breaks up old friendships, and wrecks many happy homes. *Now* can I go to the track meet, Miss Hicks?"

The ancient-history teacher, although pleased with this imaginative discourse on a trivial theme, would not allow its success to interfere with the need for her to maintain order in her classroom. "You will stay in after school, Mr. Macauley," she said, "and *you*, Mr. Ackley. Now that we have disposed of the matter of noses, someone else please comment on what we have read."

There were no comments.

"Come, come now," Miss Hicks said. "Somebody else comment— *anybody*."

Joe the comedian answered the call. "Noses are red," he said, "violets are blue. This class is dead. And in all probability so are you."

"Anyone else?" Miss Hicks said.

"Big noses are generally on navigators and explorers," a girl said.

"All two-headed boys have two noses," Joe said.

"The nose is never on the back of the head," one of Joe's admirers said.

"Somebody else," Miss Hicks said. She turned to a boy and said his name. "Henry?"

"I don't know anything about noses," Henry said.

Joe turned to Henry. "All right," he said, "who is Moses?"

"Moses was in the Bible," Henry said.

"Did he have a nose?" Joe said.

"Sure he had a nose," Henry said.

"All right, then," Joe said. "Why don't you say, 'Moses had a nose as big as most noses'? This is an ancient history class. Why don't you try to learn something once in a while? Moses—noses—ancient— history. Catch on?"

Henry tried to catch on. "Moses noses," he said. "No, wait a minute. Moses's nose was a big nose."

"Ah," Joe said. "You'll never learn anything. You'll die in the poorhouse. Moses had a nose as big as most noses! Henry, you've got to get that straight. Now think about it."

"All right, now," Miss Hicks said, "anybody else?"

"The hand is faster than the eye," Joe said, "but only the nose runs."

"Miss Hicks," Homer said, "you've got to let me run the two-twenty low hurdles."

"I'm not interested in *any* kind of hurdles," Miss Hicks said. "Now, anyone else?"

"Well," Homer said, "I brought this class to life for you, didn't I? I've got them all talking about noses, haven't I?"

"That's beside the point," the ancient-history teacher said. "Somebody else now?"

But it was too late. The class bell rang. Everyone got up to leave for the track meet except Homer Macauley and Hubert Ackley III.

CHAPTER 5   *The Apricot Tree*

Ulysses Macauley was up very early, skipping through the morning's first sunlight toward the yard of a man who owned a cow. When he reached the yard, Ulysses saw the cow. The small boy stood and watched the cow a long time. At last the man who owned the cow came out of the small house. He was carrying a bucket and a stool. The man went straight to the cow and began to milk. Ulysses moved in closer until finally he was directly behind the man. Still, he couldn't see enough, so he knelt down, almost under the cow. The man saw the boy but did not say anything. He went right on milking. The cow, however, turned and looked at Ulysses. Ulysses looked back at the cow. It seemed that the cow did not like to have the boy so close. Ulysses got out from under the cow, walked away, and watched from near by. The cow, in turn, watched Ulysses, so that the small boy believed they were friends.

On his way home, Ulysses stopped to watch a man who was building a barn. The man was high-strung, nervous, impatient, and should never have undertaken the work. He labored furiously, making all kinds of mistakes, while Ulysses watched and did not understand.

Ulysses got back to Santa Clara Avenue just in time to see Mr. Arena go off to work on his bicycle. Mary Arena waved to him from the porch and then went back into the house.

It was Saturday morning in Ithaca, the school boys' happiest day. Out of a house not far away came a boy of eight or nine. Ulysses waved to him and the boy waved back. This boy was Lionel Cabot, the neighborhood half-wit, but all the same a great human being, faithful, generous and sweet-tempered. After a moment Lionel looked over at Ulysses again, and, for want of something better to do, waved again. Ulysses waved back. This continued at frequent intervals until August Gottlieb came out of his house next door to Ara's Market.

Auggie had been the leader of the neighborhood boys since Homer

Macauley had retired from that position at the age of twelve. The new leader looked around for his followers. He rejected Lionel as too dumb and Ulysses as too little, but waved a greeting to each of them nevertheless. He then went out to the middle of the street and whistled, newsboy style. It was a loud whistle, very authoritative, very commanding, and absolutely final. Auggie waited with the confidence of a man who knows what he is doing and what results he is going to get. Immediately windows were opened and replies were whistled. Soon a number of boys came running to the corner. In less than three minutes the gang was together—Auggie Gottlieb, the leader, Nickie Paloota, Alf Rife, and Shag Manoogian.

"Where are we going, Auggie?" Nickie said.

"To see if Henderson's apricots are ripe," Auggie said.

"Can I come, Auggie?" Lionel said.

"O.K., Lionel," Auggie said. "If they're ripe, will you steal some?"

"It's a sin to steal," Lionel said.

"Not apricots," Auggie said, making an important distinction. "Ulysses," he said, "you go home. This is not for little boys. It's dangerous."

Ulysses moved away three steps, stopped and watched. He wasn't hurt or offended by Auggie's orders. He understood the code. He was just not old enough yet, that's all. But while he respected the law, he couldn't resist wanting to be in the gang anyhow.

The boys started off for Henderson's. Instead of going by way of streets and sidewalks, they took alleys, crossed empty lots, and climbed over fences. They wanted to get there the hard way, the adventurous way. Not far behind, at a safe distance, Ulysses followed.

"Ripe apricots are just about the best-tasting fruit in the world," Auggie said to the members of his gang.

"Do apricots get ripe in March?" Nickie Paloota said.

"It's almost April," Auggie said. "*Early* apricots get ripe in no time if the sun shines a lot."

"It's been raining lately, though," Alf Rife said.

"Where do you think apricots get their juice from?" Auggie said. "From water—from rain. Rain is just as important as sunshine to apricots."

"Sunshine in the daytime, rain at night," Shag Manoogian said. "Warm them up, give them water. I'll bet there's a lot of ripe apricots on the tree."

"Boy, I hope so," Alf Rife said.

"It's too early for apricots," Nickie Paloota said. "They weren't ripe last year until June."

"That was last year," Auggie said. "This is this year."

From a distance of about one hundred yards the boys stopped to admire the famous apricot tree—all green and pretty, very old and very big. It stood in the corner of Henderson's backyard. For ten years the boys of the neighborhood had raided old man Henderson's apricot tree. In the broken-down house every spring Mr. Henderson had watched their coming with fascination and delight—always satisfying the boys by appearing at the last minute and scaring them away. Now in the house at a curtained window Mr. Henderson looked up from his book.

"Well, look at that!" he said to himself. "Coming to steal apricots in March, in the dead of Winter. Look at them!" He peeked out at the boys again, whispering as if he were one of them. "Coming to get apricots off old man Henderson's tree," he said. "Here they come. Slowly, now. Ha-ha," he laughed, "look at them! And look at that little one! Surely not more than four years old. He's a new one. Come on, come on! Come to the wonderful old tree. If I could ripen the apricots for you to steal, I'd do it—"

Mr. Henderson watched the boys as Auggie instructed, directed and led the attack. The boys surrounded the tree cautiously, fearfully, and with a mingling in their hearts of hope and fear. Even if the apricots were green, they were on Henderson's tree and belonged to him, and therefore their coming for the apricots was the same as if the apricots were ripe—therefore they *hoped* the apricots *were* ripe. But they were afraid, too. They were afraid of Henderson, they were afraid of sin, of capture and guilt, and they were afraid they were a little too early. They were afraid the apricots weren't ripe yet.

"Maybe he ain't home, Auggie," Nickie Paloota whispered as the boys almost reached the tree.

"He's home," Auggie said. "He's *always* home. He's hiding, that's all. It's a trap. He wants to catch us. Careful, everybody. There's no telling where he'll be. Ulysses, you go home."

Obediently Ulysses retreated three steps and stopped to watch the magnificent duel with the magnificent tree.

"Are they ripe, Auggie?" Shag said. "Do you see any color?"

"Only green," Auggie said. "That's leaves. The apricots are underneath. Easy now, everybody. Where's Lionel?"

"Here I am," Lionel whispered. He was terribly afraid.

"Well," Auggie said, "be on your toes. If you see old man Henderson, run!"

"Where is he?" Lionel said as if Henderson might be invisible or no bigger than a rabbit, something likely to jump up suddenly out of the grass.

"What do you mean where is he?" Auggie said. "He's in the house, I guess. But you can never tell about Henderson. He might be hiding outside some place, waiting to take us by surprise."

"Are *you* going to climb the tree, Auggie?" Alf Rife said.

"Who else?" Auggie said. "Sure I'm going to climb the tree, but let's see if the apricots are ripe first."

"Ripe or green," Shag Manoogian said, "we want to steal at least *some* of them, Auggie."

"Don't worry," Auggie said. "We will. If they're ripe, we'll steal a *lot* of them."

"What are you going to say at Sunday School tomorrow, Auggie?" Lionel said.

"Stealing apricots isn't stealing, like stealing in the Bible, Lionel," Auggie said. "This is different."

"Then what are you scared of?" Lionel said.

"Who's scared?" Auggie said. "We've just got to be careful, that's all. What's the use getting caught if you can get away?"

"I don't see any ripe apricots," Lionel said.

"You see a tree, don't you?" Auggie said.

"I see a tree, all right," Lionel said. "That's *all*, though—just a big tree—all green. It sure is pretty, too, Auggie."

Now the gang was almost under the tree. Ulysses followed not far behind. He was absolutely unafraid. He didn't understand at all, but he was sure this was very important stuff—something about trees, something about apricots. The boys studied the branches of the old apricot tree, green with fine young leaf. The apricots were all very small, very green, and obviously very hard.

"Not ripe yet," Alf Rife said.

"Yeah," Auggie admitted. "I guess they need a couple days more. Maybe next Saturday."

"Next Saturday—*sure*," Shag said.

"There's a *lot* of them, though," Auggie said.

"We can't go back empty-handed, Auggie," Shag said. "We've got to get at least *one* of them—green or ripe—*one* of them anyway."

"O.K.," Auggie said. "I'll get it. Now the rest of you be ready to run." Auggie dashed to the tree, swung up into it on one of its lower branches while the gang and Mr. Henderson and Ulysses watched with fascination, amazement, and admiration. Then Mr. Henderson stepped out of the house onto the back-porch steps. All the boys went off like a school of startled minnows.

"Auggie!" Shag Manoogian shouted. "*Henderson!*"

Like a frightened orang-outang in the jungle, Auggie bounced around in the tree, hung from a branch, and then dropped to the ground. He was running almost before his feet touched the ground, but he noticed Ulysses and stopped suddenly, shouting at the boy, "Ulysses! Run—*run!*"

Ulysses, however, didn't budge. He couldn't figure it out. Auggie rushed back to the small boy, lifted him off his feet, and ran with him while Henderson watched. When all the boys had disappeared and everything was quiet again, the old man smiled and looked up into the tree. Then he turned around and went back into the house.

CHAPTER 6 *At the Public Library*

The good friends, Lionel and Ulysses, walked toward the public library. A block before them a funeral procession emerged from the First Ithaca Presbyterian Church. Pallbearers carried a plain casket to an old Packard hearse. Following the casket the two boys saw a handful of mourners.

"Come on, Ulysses," Lionel said, "it's a funeral! Somebody's dead." They ran, Lionel holding Ulysses by the hand, and very soon they were at the center of everything.

"That's the casket," Lionel whispered. "Somebody's dead in there. I wish I knew who it is. See the flowers. They give them flowers when they die. See them crying. Those are the people who knew him."

Lionel turned to a man who wasn't very busy crying. The man had just blown his nose and touched his handkerchief to the corners of his eyes.

"Who's dead?" Lionel asked the man.

"It's poor little Johnny Merryweather, the hunchback," the man said.

Lionel turned to Ulysses. "It's poor little Johnny Merryweather, the hunchback," Lionel said.

"Seventy years old," the man said.

"Seventy years old," Lionel said to Ulysses.

"Sold popcorn on the corner of Mariposa and Broadway for thirty years," the man said.

"Sold popcorn on the corner of—" Lionel stopped suddenly and looked at the man. He almost shouted. "You mean the popcorn man?" Lionel said.

"Yes," the man said, "Johnny Merryweather—gone to his rest."

"I knew *him!*" Lionel shouted. "I bought popcorn off of him many times! Did *he* die?"

"Yes," the man said, "he died peacefully. Died in his sleep. Gone to his Maker."

"I knew Johnny Merryweather!" Lionel said, almost crying. "I didn't know his name was Johnny Merryweather, but I knew him."

Lionel turned to Ulysses and put his arm around his friend. "It's Johnny," he almost wept. "Johnny Merryweather, gone to his Maker. One of my best friends, gone to his rest."

The hearse drove away and very soon there was no one in front of the church except Lionel and Ulysses. Somehow it seemed wrong for Lionel to leave the place where he learned that the man who had died, the man in the casket, was a man he knew, even though he had never known that the man's name was Johnny Merryweather. At last, however, he decided that he couldn't stand in front of the church forever, even if he had bought popcorn off of Johnny Merryweather many times—so, thinking of the popcorn, almost tasting it again, he went on down the street with his friend Ulysses, still headed for the public library.

When the two boys entered this humble but impressive building, they entered an area of profound and almost frightening silence. It seemed as if even the walls had become speechless, and the floor and the tables, as if silence had engulfed everything in the building. There were old men reading newspapers. There were town philosophers. There were high school boys and girls doing research, but everyone was hushed, because they were seeking wisdom. They were near books. They were trying to find out. Lionel not only whispered, he moved on tiptoe. Lionel whispered because he was under the impression that it was out of respect for books, not consideration for readers. Ulysses followed him, also on tiptoe, and they explored the library, each finding many treasures, Lionel—books, and Ulysses—people. Lionel didn't read books and he hadn't come to the public library to get any for himself. He just liked to *see* them—the thousands of them. He pointed out a whole row of shelved books to his friend and then he whispered, "All of these—and these. And these. Here's a red one. All these. There's a green one. All these."

Finally Mrs. Gallagher, the old librarian, noticed the two boys and went over to them. *She* didn't whisper, however. She spoke right out, as if she were not in the public library at all. This shocked Lionel and made a few people look up from the pages of their books.

"What are you looking for, boy?" Mrs. Gallagher said to Lionel.

"Books," Lionel whispered softly.

"What books are you looking for?" the librarian said.

"All of them," Lionel said.

"All of them?" the librarian said. "What do you mean? You can't borrow more than four books on one card."

"I don't want to borrow *any* of them," Lionel said.

"Well, what in the world *do* you want with them?" the librarian said.

"I just want to look at them," Lionel said.

"Look at them?" the librarian said. "That is not what the public library is for. You can look *into* them, you can look *at* the pictures in them, but what in the world do you want to look at the outsides of them for?"

"I like to," Lionel whispered. "Can't I?"

"Well," the librarian said, "there's no law against it." She looked at Ulysses. "And who's this?" she said.

"This here's Ulysses," Lionel said. "He can't read."

"Can you?" the librarian said to Lionel.

"No," Lionel said, "but he can't either. That's why we're friends. He's the only other man I know who can't read."

The old librarian looked at the two friends a moment and in her mind said something which very nearly approached a kind of delicious cursing. This was something brand new in all the years of her experience at the public library. "Well," she said at last, "perhaps it's just as well that you *can't* read. *I* can read. I have been reading books for the past sixty years, and I can't see as how it's made any great difference. Run along now and look at the books as you please."

"Yes, ma'am," Lionel said.

The two friends moved off into still greater realms of mystery and adventure. Lionel pointed out more books to Ulysses. "These," he said. "And those over there. And these. All books, Ulysses." He stopped a moment to think. "I wonder what they say in all these books." He pointed out a whole vast area of them, five shelves full of them. "All these," he said—"I wonder what they say." Finally he discovered a book that looked very pretty from the outside. Its cover was green, like fresh grass. "And this one," he said, "this one is pretty, Ulysses."

A little frightened at what he was doing, Lionel lifted the book out of the shelf, held it in his hands a moment and then opened it. "There, Ulysses!" he said. "A book! There it is! See? They're saying something in here." Now he pointed to something in the print of the book. "There's an 'A,'" he said. "That's an 'A' right there. There's another letter of some sort. I don't know what that one is. Every letter's different, Ulysses, and every word's different." He sighed and looked around at all the books. "I don't think I'll ever learn to read," he said, "but I sure would like to know what they're saying in there. Now here's a picture," he said. "Here's a picture of a girl. See her? Pretty, isn't she?" He turned many pages of the book and said, "See it? More letters and words, straight through to the end of the book. This is the pubalic liberry, Ulysses," he said. "Books all over the place." He looked at the print of the book with a kind of reverence, whispering to himself as if he were trying to read. Then he shook his head. "You can't know what a book says, Ulysses, unless you can read, and I can't read," he said.

He closed the book slowly, put it back in its place, and together the two friends tiptoed out of the library. Outside, Ulysses kicked up his heel because he felt good, and because it seemed he had learned something new.

CHAPTER 7   *Mr. Mechano*

After their adventure in the public library, Lionel and Ulysses continued to explore Ithaca. At sundown they found themselves standing at the very front of a small crowd of idlers and passers-by, watching a man in the window of a third-rate drug store. The man moved like a piece of machinery, although he *was* a human being. He looked, however, as if he had been made of wax instead of flesh. He seemed inhuman and in fact he looked like nothing so much as an upright, unburied corpse still capable of moving. The man was the most incredible thing Ulysses had seen in all of his four years of life in the world. No light came out of the man's eyes. His lips were set as if they would never part.

The man was engaged in advertising *Dr. Bradford's Tonic.* He worked between two easels. On one easel was a sign on which this message had been printed: "Mr. Mechano—The Machine Man— Half Machine, Half Human. More Dead Than Alive. $50 if you can make him smile. $500 if you can make him laugh." On the other easel Mr. Mechano placed pasteboard cards which he took in an extremely mechanical fashion from the small table in front of the easel. On these cards were printed various messages urging people to buy the patent medicine which Dr. Bradford had invented and thereby to become more alive. After each new card had been placed on the easel Mr. Mechano pointed at each word of the message on the card with a pointer. When all ten of the cards had been placed on the easel, Mr. Mechano removed them all and put them back on the table and began the procedure all over again.

"It's a man, Ulysses," Lionel said to his friend. "I can see him. It's not a machine, Ulysses. It's a man! See his eyes? He's alive. See him?"

The card Mr. Mechano had just placed on the easel read: "Don't drag yourself around half dead. Enjoy life. Take Dr. Bradford's Tonic and feel like a new man."

"There's another card," Lionel said. "It says something on that card." Suddenly he was weary and eager to get home. "Come on, Ulysses," he said, "let's go. We've seen him go through all the cards three times. Let's go home. It's almost night now." He took his friend by the hand, but Ulysses drew his hand away.

"Come on, Ulysses!" Lionel said. "I've got to go home now. I'm hungry." But Ulysses did not want to go. It seemed that he did not even *hear* Lionel's words.

"I'm going, Ulysses," Lionel challenged. He waited for Ulysses to turn and go with him, but the boy did not budge. A little hurt and amazed by this betrayal of friendship, Lionel began to walk home, turning every three or four steps to see if his friend was not going to join him after all. But no, Ulysses wanted to stay and watch Mr. Mechano. Lionel felt deeply wounded as he continued his journey home. "I thought he was my best friend in the whole world," he said.

Ulysses stood among the handful of people watching Mr. Mechano until at last only he and an old man were left. Mr. Mechano went right on picking up the cards and putting them on the easel. He went right on pointing to each word on each card. Soon the old man went away too, and then only Ulysses stood on the sidewalk looking up at the strange human being in the window of the drug store. It was growing dark now. When the street lights came on, Ulysses came out of the trance of fascination into which the vision of Mr. Mechano had placed him. It was almost as if he had become hypnotized by the sight of the man. Now, out of the trance, he looked around. Day had ended and everybody had gone— The only thing left anywhere was something for which he had no word—Death.

The small boy looked back suddenly at the mechanical man. It seemed then that the man was looking at *him*. There was swift and fierce terror in the boy. Suddenly he was running away. The few people he saw in the streets now seemed full of death, too, like Mr. Mechano. They seemed suddenly ugly, not beautiful, as they had always seemed before. Ulysses ran until he was almost exhausted. He stopped, breathing hard and almost crying. He looked around, feeling a deep silent steady horror in all things—the horror of Mr. Mechano—Death! He had never before known fear of *any* kind, let alone fear such as this, and it was the most difficult thing in the world for him to know what to do. His poise was all gone—scattered by the fear of the horror catching up with *him*, and he began to run again. This time as he ran he said to himself, almost crying, "Papa, Mama, Marcus, Bess, Homer! Papa, Mama, Marcus, Bess, Homer!"

The world was surely wonderful and it was surely full of good things to be seen again and again, but now the world was a thing to escape, only he could think of no direction to take. He wanted swiftly to reach somebody of his family.. He stood panic-stricken, and then began moving a few steps in one direction and then a few in another, feeling all around him a presence of incredible disaster, a disaster he could escape only by reaching his father, his mother, one of his brothers, or his sister. And then, instead of reaching one of these, he saw far down the street the leader of the neighborhood gang, August Gottlieb. The newsboy was standing on a deserted street corner, calling out the headline as if the area around him were full of people who must be told what had happened that day in the world. Hollering headlines had always seemed slightly ridiculous to August Gottlieb because, for one thing, the headlines were always about murder of one sort or another and, for another, because it seemed somehow a thing of bad taste to go about among people in the streets of Ithaca lifting his voice. Consequently, the newsboy felt pleased when at last he discovered that the streets were deserted. Without even knowing that he was doing such a thing, whenever the streets had become empty of the people of Ithaca, August Gottlieb, as if grateful for his almost solitary inhabitance of the city, lifted his voice more powerfully than ever, calling out the day's miserable news. What could a man do about the news—sell a paper, and make a few pennies? Is that what he could do about it? Wasn't it foolish for him to cry out the daily message of mistake as if it were glad tidings? Wasn't it shameful for the people to be so steadily unimpressed with the nature of every day's news? Sometimes even in his sleep the newsboy dreamed of calling out the headlines of the world's news, but there, in that inner area of experience, he felt mockery and contempt for the nature of the news, and when he shouted, it was always from a great height, and beneath him always were multitudes engaged in activities of error and crime. But the minute they heard his roaring voice, they stopped in their tracks to look up at him, and then he always shouted, "Now go back, go back where you belong! Stop your murder! Plant trees instead!" He had always loved the idea of planting a tree.

When Ulysses saw August Gottlieb on the street corner, much of the terror in his heart passed away and he began to feel that it would not be years and years before he might again find goodness and love in the world. The little boy wanted to shout out to August Gottlieb, but he couldn't make a sound. Instead, he ran with all his might to the newsboy and flung himself upon him in an embrace so forceful that it almost knocked Auggie down.

"Ulysses!" the newsboy said. "What's the matter? What are you crying about?"

Ulysses looked up into the eyes of the newsboy, but still he could not speak.

"You're scared, Ulysses," Auggie said. "Well, don't be scared—there's nothing to be scared of. Now don't cry, Ulysses. You don't have to be scared." But still the boy could not stop sobbing. "Now don't cry any more," Auggie said, and waited for Ulysses to stop. Ulysses tried very hard not to cry and soon the sobs came at infrequent intervals, each sob like a hiccup. Then Auggie said, "Come on, Ulysses, we'll go to Homer."

At the sound of that name, the name of his brother, Ulysses smiled, and then hiccuped another sob. "Homer?" he said.

"Sure," Auggie said. "Your brother. Come on."

It was almost too wonderful for the little boy to believe. "Going to see Homer?" he said.

"Sure," Auggie said. "The telegraph office is just around the corner."

August Gottlieb and Ulysses Macauley walked around the corner to the telegraph office. They found Homer seated at the delivery desk. When Ulysses saw his brother, a wonderful thing happened to his face. All the terror left his eyes, because now he was home.

When Homer saw his brother, he got up and went to the boy and lifted him in his arms. He turned to Auggie. "What's the matter?" he said. "What's Ulysses doing in town at this hour?"

"He got lost, I guess," Auggie said. "He was crying."

"Crying?" Homer said, and then hugged his brother, just as Ulysses hiccuped another sob. "All right, Ulysses," he said. "Don't cry any more. I'll take you home on my bike. Now, don't cry."

CHAPTER 8 *A Letter from Marcus to His Brother Homer*

This Saturday was one of the longest and most eventful days of Homer Macauley's life. Little things began to take on fresh importance and to mean something which he could understand. The sleep of last night, troubled and full of grief, was now forever a part of his wakefulness. He had tried with all his might to keep the messenger of Death from reaching Ithaca and its people. He had dreamed that, but now it was no longer a dream.

The letter from his brother Marcus was with him, unopened, waiting to be read.

He came into the telegraph office, limping, tired and eager to rest. He looked at the call sheet and there were no calls to take. He looked on the incoming telegram hook and there were no telegrams to deliver. His work was done. All was clear. He went to the old telegraph operator and said, "Mr. Grogan, would you like to chip in with me tonight for two day-old pies—apple and cocoanut cream?"

The old telegraph operator was by this time more than half drunk. "I'll chip in, boy," he said, "but I'll not have any of the pies—thanks just the same."

"If *you* don't want any of the pies, Mr. Grogan," Homer said, "I don't want any either. I thought *you* might be hungry. I'm not hungry at all. I haven't had a chance to take it easy all day until now. But I'm not hungry. It seems funny. You'd think a fellow would get hungry working all day and all night, but he doesn't. I had a bowl of chili at six tonight and that's all."

"How's your leg?" Grogan said.

"O.K.," Homer said. "I've forgotten all about it. I get around all right." He looked curiously at the old telegraph operator and then said very softly, "Are you drunk, Mr. Grogan?" He spoke earnestly and the old man was not offended or hurt.

"Yes, I am, boy," Mr. Grogan said. He went to his chair and sat down. After a moment he looked over at the boy across the table from him, not sitting but standing there. "I feel a lot better when I'm drunk," the old telegraph operator said. Then he brought the bottle out and took a good long drink. "I'm not going to tell you never to take a drink," he said. "I'm not going to say, as so many old fools do—*Learn a lesson from me. Look what drink did to me*—that would be a lot of nonsense. You're getting around now, seeing a lot of things—a lot of things you never saw before. Well, let me tell you something. Anything that concerns people—be very careful about it. If you see something you're sure is wrong, don't be sure. If it's people, be very careful. Now, you'll forgive me, but I must tell you, because you're a man I respect, so I don't mind trying to tell you that it's not right, it's foolish, to criticize the way any people happen to be. I haven't the slightest idea who you are—where you're from—how you came about—what made you the way you are—but I feel pleased about these things and I'm grateful. As a man gets closer to the end of his time he feels more and more grateful for the good people who're going to go on when he's gone. I might not be telling you this if I weren't drunk, so that alone is a good example of why it's wrong to have ideas about people who do things that everyone likes to feel aren't right. It's very important for me to tell you these things and for you to know them. Therefore, it is a good thing that I *am* drunk and that I am telling you. Can you understand what I'm saying?"

"I'm not sure, Mr. Grogan," Homer said.

"I'm telling you," the old telegraph operator said, "something that may embarrass you. And I could not tell you unless I were drunk. I'm telling you this—be grateful for yourself. Yes, for *yourself.* Be thankful. Understand that what a man is is something he *can* be grateful for, and *ought* to be grateful for, because if he is good, his goodness is not his alone, it's mine too, and the other fellow's. It's his only to protect and to spread around for me and for everybody else in the world. What you have is good, so be thankful for it. It will be welcomed by everyone you meet at one time or another. They will know you the minute they see you."

Now for some reason Homer remembered the girl at Bethel Rooms and the way she spoke to him, and as he remembered the old telegraph operator went on.

"They will know that you will not betray them or hurt them. They will know that you will not despise them after the whole world has despised them. They will know that you will see in them what the world has failed to see. You must know about that. You must not be embarrassed by it. You are a great man, fourteen years old. Who has made you great, nobody knows, but as it is true, know that it is true, be humble before it, and protect it. Do you understand?"

The messenger was extremely embarrassed, and it was very difficult for him to say, "I guess so, Mr. Grogan."

The old telegraph operator went on: "Then, I thank you. I have watched you, sober and drunk, since you came to work here, and, sober *or* drunk, I have recognized you. I have worked in cities in every part of the world. In my youth I wanted to reach many cities, and I reached them. All my life I have watched for you everywhere I have gone, and I have found you in many places—many out-of-the-way places—in many unknown people. I have found *something* of you in every man I have ever met, but most often it has not been enough. Now, in Ithaca, on my way home, I have found you again, better than ever, greater than ever. So, if you understand, I thank you. What is that you're holding—a letter? I have finished. Go ahead. Read your letter, boy."

"It's a letter from my brother Marcus," Homer said. "I haven't had a chance to open it yet."

"Then open it," the old telegraph operator said. "Read the letter from your brother. Read it aloud."

"Would you like to hear it, Mr. Grogan?" Homer said.

"Yes, if I may, I would like very much to hear it," the old telegraph operator said, and then took another drink.

Homer Macauley tore open the envelope of the letter from his brother Marcus, brought out the letter, unfolded it, and began to read, speaking very slowly.

"Dear Homer:" he read. "First of all, everything of mine at home is yours—to give to Ulysses when you no longer want them: my books, my phonograph, my records, my clothes when you're ready to fit into them, my bicycle, my microscope, my fishing tackle, my collection of rocks from Piedra, and all the other things of mine at home. They're yours rather than Bess's as you are now the man of the Macauley family of Ithaca. The money I made last year at the packing house I have given to Ma of course, to help out. It is not nearly enough, though, and soon Ma and Bess will be thinking of going to work. I cannot ask you not to allow them to go to work, but I am hoping that you yourself will not allow them to do so. I believe that you will not, as I know I would not. Ma would want to go to work, of course, and so would Bess. But that is all the more reason for you not to let them. I don't know how you are going to be able to keep our famliy together and go to high school at the same time, but I believe you will find a way. My Army pay goes to Ma, except for a few dollars that I must have, but this money is not enough. It is not easy for me to hope for so much from you, when I myself did not begin to work until I was nineteen, but somehow I believe that you will be able to do what I could not do.

"I miss you of course and I think of you all the time. I am happy, and even though I have never believed in wars—and know them to be foolish, even when they are necessary—I am proud that I am serving my country—which to me is Ithaca, our home, and all of the Macauleys. I do not recognize any enemy which is human, for no human being can be my enemy. Whoever he is, whatever color he is, however mistaken he may be in what he believes, he is my friend, not my enemy, for he is no different from myself. My quarrel is not with *him*, but with that in him which I seek to destroy in myself first.

"I do not feel like a hero. I have no talent for such feelings. I hate no one. I do not feel patriotic either, for I have always loved my country, its people, its towns, my home, and my family. I would rather I were not in the Army. I would rather there were no War, but as I *am* in the Army and as there *is* a War, I have long since made up my mind to be the best soldier it is possible for me to be. I have no idea what is ahead, but whatever it is I am humbly ready for it. I am terribly afraid—I must tell *you* this—but I know that when the time comes I shall do what is expected of me, and maybe even more than what is expected of me, but I want you to know I shall be obeying no command other than the command of my own heart. With me will be boys from all over America, from thousands of towns like Ithaca. I may be killed in this War. I must come right out and tell you this. I don't like the idea at all. More than anything else in the world I want to come back to Ithaca, and spend many long years with you and with my mother and sister and brother. I want to come back for Mary and a home and a family of my own. It is very likely that we shall be leaving soon—for action. Nobody knows where the action will be, but it is understood that we shall soon be leaving. Therefore, this may be my last letter to you for some time. I hope it is not the last of all. If it is, hold us together. Do not believe I am gone. Do not let the others believe it. My friend here is an orphan—a foundling— it is very strange that of all the boys here *he* should become my friend. His name is Tobey George. I have told him about Ithaca and our family. Some day I shall bring him to Ithaca with me. When you read this letter, do not be unhappy. I am glad that I am the Macauley who is in the War, for it would be a pity and a mistake if it were you.

"I can write to you what I could never say in words. You are the best of the Macauleys. You must go on being the best. Nothing must ever stop you. You are fourteen years old, but you must live to be twenty and then thirty and forty and fifty and sixty. You must live, in the years of your life, forever. I believe you will. I shall always be watching you. You are what we are fighting the War for. Yes, *you*— my brother. How could I ever tell you such things if we were together? You would jump on me and wrestle with me and call me a fool, but even so everything I have said is true. Now I will write your name here, to remind you: Homer Macauley. That's who you are. I miss you very much. I can't wait until I see you again. When that happens, when we meet again, I will let you wrestle me and put me down on my back in the parlor in front of Ma and Bess and Ulysses and maybe Mary even—I'll let you do that because I wil be so glad to see you again. God bless you. So long. Your brother, Marcus."

While he was reading the letter the messenger sat down. He read very slowly, gulping many times, and becoming sick many times as he had been sick first in the house of the Mexican mother and then the night that he had cried while riding his bicycle around Ithaca after work. Now he got up. His hands were trembling. He bit the corner of his lip and looked over at the old telegraph operator, who was as deeply moved by the letter as the messenger himself. He spoke very softly. "If my brother is killed in this stupid War," he said, "I shall spit at the world. I shall hate it forever. I won't be good. I shall be the worst of them all, the worst that ever lived."

He stopped suddenly and tears came to his eyes. He hurried to the locker behind the repeater rack, took off his uniform and got into his regular clothes. He was running out of the office almost before his clothes had been properly arranged.

The old telegraph operator sat a long time. It was very quiet when he shook himself at last, finished the rest of the bottle, got up and looked around the office.

CHAPTER 9 *The End and the Beginning*

The limping soldier who got off the train which brought Danny Booth and Henry Rife home to Ithaca, began to walk around the town. He walked slowly, looking at everything, and talking to himself.

"This is Ithaca!" he said. "There's the depot—the Santa Fé—and there's the Ithaca sky over it. There's the Kinema Theatre, with the wonderful people of Ithaca standing in line. This is the Public Library. There's the Presbyterian Church. There's Ithaca High School, and this is the athletic field. There's Santa Clara Avenue and Ara's Market, and there's the house! There it is. There's my home!"

The soldier stood staring at the house a long time. "Ma and Bess," he said, "Homer and Ulysses. Mary next door, and her father, Mr. Arena." No thought said what was now said, only blood. "Ithaca, oh, Ithaca!" The soldier moved on. "There's the courthouse park," he said. "Here's the city jail with the prisoners at the windows. And there are a couple of Ithaca men pitching a game of horseshoes." The soldier walked slowly toward the two men and leaned against the wire fence.

Homer Macauley and Thomas Spangler pitched horseshoes in silence, not even counting points. It was too dark now for the game, but they went on pitching. Homer started when he noticed the soldier leaning against the fence. For some reason it seemed to him that he knew this soldier. He moved toward the young man, looking into his face.

"Excuse me for staring," he said. "I thought I knew you."

"That's all right," the soldier said.

"Would you care to *pitch* a game?" Homer said. "You can take my place. It's a little dark, of course."

"No, thanks," the soldier said, "you go ahead. I'll just watch."

"I don't think I've ever seen you before," Homer said. "Is Ithaca your home?"

"Yes, it is," the soldier said. "I've come back—to stay."

"You mean," Homer said, "you don't have to go back to the War?"

"No," the soldier said, "they've sent me home—for good. I got off the train a couple of hours ago. I've been walking around the town, looking at everything again."

"Well, why don't you go home?" Homer said. "Don't you want your family to know you're here?"

"I'll go home," the soldier said. "Of course I want my family to know I'm here. I'll go home little by little. I want to see as much as I can, first. I can't see enough of it. I can't believe I'm here. I'll walk around some more and then I'll go home."

The soldier went off slowly, limping. Homer Macauley stared after him, wondering.

"I don't know," he said to Spangler, "I seem to think I know that fellow. I don't feel like pitching any more, Mr. Spangler," he said. And then after a moment he said, "What shall I do? What am I going to tell them? They're waiting for me at home now. I know they are. I told them I'd be home for supper. How am I going to go into the house and look at them? They'll know everything the minute they see me. I don't *want* to tell them, but I know they'll know."

Spangler put his arm around Homer. "Wait," he said. "Don't go home just yet. Sit down here. Wait awhile. It takes a little time."

They sat quietly on a park bench, not talking. After a while Homer said, "What am I waiting for?"

"Well," Spangler said, "you're waiting for the part of *him* that died to die in you, too—the part that's only flesh—the part that comes and goes. That dying is hurting you now, but wait awhile. When the pain becomes death and leaves you, the rest will be lighter and better than ever. It takes a little time, and as long as you live it will take a little time, again and again, but each time it goes it will leave you closer than ever to the best that is in all men. Be patient with it, you will go home at last with no death in you. Give it time to go. I'll sit with you here until it's gone."

"Yes, sir," Homer said. The manager of the telegraph office and the messenger sat in the courthouse park of Ithaca, waiting.

Now the strings of the harp in the Macauley house soothed the pain out of all things. The face of the one who plucked the strings of the harp was a face radiant and strong and full of love. The girl who played the piano was one whose heart was earnest and innocent, and the girl who sang was one whose spirit was gentle and sweet. The small boy listening listened with the ears of all the living and watched with eyes full of faith in all things. The young man sitting on the steps of the front porch, the soldier, the boy who had come home to a town he had never before seen, to a house he had never before entered, to a family he had never known—was everybody. And he *was* home. Ithaca *was* the place of his birth. The house *was* the house he grew up in. The family inside the house *was* his family.

Suddenly Ulysses Macauley was standing at the open front door, pointing. His sister Bess went over to see what it was. She turned to her mother. "Ma," she said, "somebody's sitting on our front-porch steps."

"Well," Mrs. Macauley said, "go on out to him, Bess, and ask him in—whoever he is. You needn't be afraid."

Bess Macauley went out onto the porch. "Won't you come in?" she said to the soldier. "My mother would like you to come in."

The soldier turned slowly and looked up at the girl. He spoke very quietly. "Bess," he said. "Sit down beside me! Sit down beside me until I am quiet inside and able to stand again. My legs are trembling, and if I try to stand you, I'll fall. Sit beside me, Bess."

The girl sat down on the steps beside the young man. "How do you know my name?" she said softly. "Who are you?"

"I don't know who I am," the soldier said, "but I know who *you* are, and who your mother is, and who your brothers are. Sit close to me, Bess—until I quiet down."

"Do you know my brother Marcus?" Bess said.

"Yes," the soldier said. "Your brother gave me my life—a place of birth—a family. Yes, I know him—he is *my* brother, too."

"Where is Marcus?" Bess said. "Why hasn't he come home with you?"

"Bess," the soldier said. He handed the girl a ring Marcus Macauley had given him. "Your brother Marcus sent you this."

Bess Macauley did not speak for some time and then she said, "Is Marcus dead?" Her voice was hushed, not excited.

"No," the soldier said. "Bess, believe me." He kissed the girl on the mouth. "He is not dead."

Homer Macauley came walking down the street. His sister Bess ran out to him. "Homer!" she said. "He's come from Marcus. They were friends. He's sitting on our steps." She turned and ran into the house.

Homer Macauley stood looking at Tobey George. "Tobey?" he said. "I thought I knew you when we talked in the park." He waited a moment and then said. "The telegram came this afternoon. I have it in my pocket. What are we going to do?"

"Tear it up, Homer," the soldier said. "Throw it away. It's not true, tear it up."

Homer brought the telegram out of his pocket and swiftly tore it up. He put the small pieces back into his pocket—to keep, forever.

"Please help me up," the soldier said. "We'll go into the house together." Homer Macauley leaned down to Tobey George, the orphan who had come home at last, and the soldier took the messenger by the shoulders and slowly got to his feet.

Now Homer lifted his voice. There was no sadness in his words or in his way of saying them. "Ma!" he said. "Bess! Mary! play some music. The soldier's come home! Welcome him!"

The music began.

"Let me stand here a moment and listen," the soldier said.

Homer Macauley and Tobey George listened to the music, each of them smiling, the soldier with a tender painfulness and the messenger with a kind of happiness he could not yet understand.

Mary Arena began to sing now, and then Ulysses Macauley came out of the house and took the hand of the soldier. When the song ended, Mrs. Macauley and Bess and Mary came to the open door. The mother, standing, looking at her two remaining sons, one on each side of the stranger, the soldier who had known her son who was now dead, smiled and understood. She smiled at the *soldier*. Her smile was for him who was now himself her son. She smiled as if he were Marcus himself and the soldier and his two brothers moved toward the door, toward the warmth and light of home.

THE SLAUGHTER
OF THE INNOCENTS

ACT ONE

SCENE 1

The place is Crookshank's Food and Drink, adjoining a parking lot.
ARCHIE CROOKSHANK *himself, a man of sixty or so who came over from*
London twenty years ago, is studying some papers, as HE *straightens a*
chair at a table. A young WOMAN *comes in.*

ARCHIE: What is it now? What do you want in here?

GIRL: What do I want, Archie? That's a nice question to ask a customer. I want a drink, that's what I want.

ARCHIE: You do, do you? Well, read the sign. (HE *points*)

GIRL: (*Reading*) Court of Justice. What's that mean?

ARCHIE: What's it mean? It means you can't have a drink, that's what
it means. Not in here, at any rate.

GIRL: Oh, don't be silly, Archie. Get behind the bar now, and pour
me a shot of whiskey like you've done almost a whole year now.

ARCHIE: I'll get behind the bar, I will. I'll ask you to get out of here,
that's what I'll do.

GIRL: (*Astonished*) Well, if you've fallen to common rudeness, if
you've turned out like everybody else in the world and made
yourself and your place that I've taken all along, one for a friend
and the other for a friend's place, the same as others and their
places, then I *will* go, Archie, and say to myself, Well, there's
another of them turned out like all the others.

ARCHIE: Will you stop your jabbering, please? Now, isn't the sign over
the door outside, too? Then why do you come in here? The place
is a Court of Justice now.

168

GIRL: I saw the sign. I thought somebody had put it up to make you mad or give you a laugh. It's not a very large sign and your own sign's still there, too, and much larger, Crookshank's Food and Drink.

ARCHIE: All the same, the place is a Court of Justice.

GIRL: Since when?

ARCHIE: Since three o'clock this morning when they got me up out of bed, right upstairs there, and told me so. They gave me these printed instructions, they gave me spoken instructions, they gave me *hinted* instructions, and they gave me every other kind, too.

GIRL: Who was it did it, Archie?

ARCHIE: Who was it did it? (*Points at sign.*) Step over there and read for yourself who was it did it. They'll be here in a minute. I've set the clock, just as I was instructed to do. Court opens at ten. It's a quarter to now, so you'd better get out.

GIRL: Let me stay, Archie. Let me watch. I've never seen them do. I hear the lawyers aren't lawyers, the judges aren't judges, and nobody knows anything about anything, but they all go to work just the same, as if they *did* know. God help anybody who's unlucky enough to fall into their hands.

ARCHIE: *You'll* be the unlucky one when you fall into their hands.

GIRL: Why would I fall into their hands? I'm no enemy of the Republic.

ARCHIE: Is that so? Well, just run down the list of people they call enemies. Here. Run down for yourself. (HE *shows her the list, running his finger down the page, stopping suddenly*) Read *that* for yourself.

GIRL: I don't like the language they use. I think they might have chosen a more courteous way of putting it. They can't prove a thing, anyway. Let me stay and watch.

ARCHIE: This is no sideshow, girl.

GIRL: We've been friends for so long, Archie. If I can't have a drink, at least let me stay and watch. I swear to God I *am* lonely. I've nowhere else to go and I *had* counted on coming here for a rest.

ARCHIE: The place isn't the same any more. Now, get out before you fall into their hands.

GIRL: You *do* have love in your heart, Archie. If it weren't that you were thinking of me, I know you'd let me stay, and I appreciate it. I appreciate it very much.

ARCHIE: If you appreciate it, get going, will you?

GIRL: Yes, Archie. (SHE *turns to go*) Well, goodbye. I'm going to miss the place, Archie.

ARCHIE: Miss the place? What for? (HE *fumbles through the papers*) It's just for today. I don't remember reading anything that said it was for more than one day.

GIRL: Did you read anything that said it was for today *only?*

ARCHIE: No.

GIRL: Then it's for as long as they like. Maybe for ever.

ARCHIE: No, they can't do that. I've got customers. I've built up a nice little business. Of course it's just for today.

GIRL: I *hope* so, Archie.

ARCHIE: Go on, now. Go on. Don't try to upset me the first thing in the morning.

GIRL: *Me*, Archie? Try to upset you? How can you say such a thing? There's no use trying to hide from the truth, though. *You've* fallen into their hands.

ACRHIE: The hell I have.

GIRL: Then why have they come here instead of some place that would be more suitable for a Court of Justice?

ARCHIE: The parking lot next door, that's why. They said so themselves. The high brick walls of the warehouse surrounding the parking lot, that's why they've come here.

GIRL: What's the parking lot and the high brick wall got to do with anything?

ARCHIE: Well, they were out there with red flares this morning, talking about it. The Judge is going to stand back there where I stand. The lawyers are going to sit at these eating tables, and walk back and forth in front of the bar. The prisoners are going to stand over there, one at a time.

GIRL: What about the parking lot next door?

ARCHIE: I don't know. I guess that's where they'll keep the prisoners. Whatever it's for, you'd better get out.

GIRL: I'm scared, Archie. There's so many people killing themselves these days. Shooting themselves, or swallowing pills, or jumping out of buildings, or driving their cars into other cars or over cliffs, and so many killing their kids, too, and their husbands and wives and mothers and fathers. Every time you look at a paper you read about half a dozen more of them, people you don't know, but you know they're wives and mothers or husbands and fathers. I'm scared of it, Archie.

ARCHIE: All right now, take it easy.

GIRL: I get awful lonesome in the streets, Archie. I keep looking for a place to rest, and this is the only place I've ever found. My room isn't like this place, it's like the places *they* must be in when they kill themselves because the minute I'm alone in my room I swear to God, Archie, I keep thinking I've got to do it, too. I've *got to*, there's nothing else to do, nothing else to do any more, it's too late now, it's no use now. And then I remember this place and I say to myself, Archie's'll be open in five or six hours. Try it once more. You never know. Tomorrow may be the good day. Something may turn up tomorrow. Somebody may turn up. I don't like what's happening, Archie. The minute I stepped in here this morning you hollered at me. You never did that before.

ARCHIE: They never made a Court of Justice out of my place before, either. You better go.

GIRL: I'm scared, Archie. Don't you understand? I'm afraid if I go I'll go forever. And I don't want to. I really don't want to. There's other places nicer than this if it comes to furniture. There's churches to go to, but they're not for me. There's the places where people are busy selling or buying, but they're not for me, either. There's the cheerful parks with the cheerful flowers and birds—I guess they're cheerful—but they're not for me. There's the libraries to sit in and read, but nothing I ever found to read was for me. This is the only place I ever found that *was* for me. For me, *too*, Archie. It wasn't home, but it was something like it. I could come in here and rest anyway. I could pretend here, Archie. The whiskey could help me believe I still had something to wait for, something *worth* waiting for. I've had whiskey in a lot of other places but it didn't mean anything like what it means to me here. (*Desperately*) Archie!

ARCHIE: Ah, what's the matter with you?

GIRL: Something's happening to all of us. Something terrible's happening to all of us and I'm scared to death of it. I wish to God I wasn't so weak, so I could work as a waitress or something, but I'm weak, Archie. I get tired. My back hurts, my legs hurt, my arms hurt, my head aches. In a half hour I'm ready to faint. I don't know why. I'm just weak, I guess. Weak and scared. I don't want to go. I'm afraid to go, Archie.

ARCHIE: There's nothing to be afraid of. They'll only be here today, and then tomorrow you can come back and everything'll be all right again.

GIRL: They'll stay, Archie. Once they're here, they'll stay. If they're down to saloons now—if they've used up all the schools and churches and museums for Courts of Justice and they're down to saloons, they'll stay, Archie.

ARCHIE: Better not let anybody hear you talk that way.

GIRL: I know, Archie. I know what to say when I'm talking to anybody but you, anybody else in the whole world, but now I'm talking to *you*, and I say they'll stay.

ARCHIE: For God's sake, girl, there's somebody at the door. Now, hurry—get out.

GIRL: Goodbye, Archie. Good luck.

(TWO GUARDS *carrying rifles with bayonets attached to them come in, followed by a very tall and thin* MAN *of sixty or so who wears the same uniform as the guards, but with many decorations.* HE *notices the girl.*)

GOVERNMENT MAN: Your daughter, I presume, Mr. Crookshank. Well, there's work for *her* to do, too.

ARCHIE: Just a minute, General.

GOVERNMENT MAN: If you please, Mr. Crookshank, I will need the services of your daughter. Your name, Miss?

GIRL: Rose.

GOVERNMENT MAN: Rose Crookshank. Your work, your trade, or your profession?

ROSE: I—I help my father.

GOVERNMENT MAN: Very good. Now, Miss Crookshank, you will stand there please and serve as witness on behalf of the people. We have dispensed with the time-wasting jury system, but whenever possible or convenient we install a witness on behalf of the people. Raise your right arm please. (SHE *does so.*) Say the following words. I, Rose Crookshank, swear that I have lived faithfully not for myself but for *all* of the people.

ROSE: (*mumbling swiftly*) I, Rose Crookshank, swear that I have lived faithfully not for myself but for all of the people.

GOVERNMENT MAN: Very good. (*To* ARCHIE) I see all is in order, Mr. Crookshank.

ARCHIE: I was wondering—

GOVERNMENT MAN: Yes?

ARCHIE: Well, I was wondering how long I might have the honor—

GOVERNMENT MAN: How long? Why, until justice had been done, of course.

ARCHIE: (*dazed*) Yes, sir.

GOVERNMENT MAN: Guards, you may bring in the court now, including the first Accused. (*The* GUARDS *go out. The* GOVERNMENT MAN *goes to the bar. The* OTHERS *come in, including a* YOUNG MAN *who is the Accused.*) (*To the young man*) You will stand here.

ACCUSED: Yes, sir. (HE *goes behind the bar.*)

GOVERNMENT MAN: The procedure will be the usual one. The Accused are outside waiting, are they not?

ACCUSED: Yes, sir.

GOVERNMENT MAN: (*to one man*) That is the desk for the Attorney for the People. (*To another*) That is the desk for the Attorney for the Accused. (THEY *go to their desks.*) That is the desk for the Bailiff. The People's Attorney will inform the Court what the nature of the crime is. The Attorney for the Accused will answer on behalf of the Accused. The Bailiff will await the Court's decision, stamp the Accused's papers, and the Accused will be removed through that door to the parking lot. The troops are there, are they not?

BAILIFF: Yes, sir.

GOVERNMENT MAN: They will do their work immediately in each case. Now, the Accused will stand there.

(HE *has said this to a man who apparently has seemed to him to be the one who looks the most guilty of something or other.*)

JUDGE: (*pointing to the man behind the bar*) He is the Accused, sir.

GOVERNMENT MAN: Who are *you?*

JUDGE: I am the Judge, sir.

GOVERNMENT MAN: Very well. (*To the* ACCUSED) Please stand there. (*To the* JUDGE) Please stand behind the bar. (*To everybody*) Mr. Crookshank and his daughter Rose will remain in Court, the father to serve the Court, the daughter to witness on behalf of the people. I think that is all. (*To* JUDGE) Begin, then.

JUDGE: First Accused, please.

PEOPLE'S ATTORNEY: (*lifting several sheets of paper from a stack of papers*) *Edward Ellington. Is that your name?*

ACCUSED: Yes, sir.

PEOPLE'S ATTORNEY: The Accused is twenty-seven years of age. Unmarried. No children. Attempted to assassinate a Clerk in the Office of Employment. (HE *stops abruptly.*)

JUDGE: Go on, please.

PEOPLE'S ATTORNEY: That is all, sir.

JUDGE: What weapon or weapons?

PEOPLE'S ATTORNEY: There is no mention of a weapon.

JUDGE: Attorney for the Accused.

ACCUSED'S ATTORNEY: Yes, sir.

JUDGE: Proceed, please.

ACCUSED'S ATTORNEY: Inform the Court in your own words what happened.

ACCUSED: Well, I'd go out and get a job and somebody from the Office of Employment would come and get me fired. They said I had to get a job through the Office of Employment. I went there every morning at seven and stayed until seven at night for three months but the clerk never gave me a job. One day I asked him when I'd get a job. He said never, as far as he was concerned. I said why. He said I had already taken three illegal jobs and his orders were to give jobs to those who had not taken illegal jobs. I asked him how I was going to live. You don't have to live, he said. This made me mad because I was trying my best to abide by the rules, so I said, Neither do you. I took him by the shoulders and dragged him across the counter.

JUDGE: Go on.

ACCUSED: He screamed and kicked. We stumbled and fell. The Guards came. One of them hit him on top of the head with a stick. They picked him up and went off with him. I went to my room. I had what was left of a loaf of bread for supper, then went to sleep. In the middle of the night—last night—some Guards came and took me away.

JUDGE: People's Attorney, are you satisfied the Accused is guilty?

PEOPLE'S ATTORNEY: I am.

JUDGE: Attorney for the Accused, are you?

ATTORNEY FOR ACCUSED: The Accused, may it please the Court, did not strike the Clerk of the Office of Employment.

PEOPLE'S ATTORNEY: He himself has confessed that he grabbed the Clerk by the shoulders. Isn't that so?

ATTORNEY FOR ACCUSED: He was angry. I question if he actually meant to assassinate the Clerk.

JUDGE: Attorney for the Accused, you will please leave the passing of judgment to the Court.

ATTORNEY FOR ACCUSED: Yes, sir.

JUDGE: (*to the Accused*) Is there anything you wish to say?

ACCUSED: I only wanted to do the right thing. I only wanted to abide by the rules. I only wanted to get a legal job, so I wouldn't lose it, because I want to get married and have a family.

JUDGE: Anything else?

ACCUSED: I've never looked for trouble.

JUDGE: He said to you, You don't have to live, and you said to him, Neither do you. And then you attacked him. (*Pause*) Answer the Court, please. And then you attacked him. Is that right?

ACCUSED: I dragged him across the counter.

JUDGE: Guilty. (*Slight pause*) Guards.

GOVERNMENT MAN: One moment. All Accused are permitted to make a last request. (*To the* ACCUSED) The usual is a cigarette. Here, because of the setting, a drink is permissible. Inform the Court of your last request.

ACCUSED: I'd like a good meal.

GOVERNMENT MAN: That would take too long. A drink or a cigarette?

ACCUSED: Well, I'd like a drink first and a cigarette afterwards, then.

GOVERNMENT MAN: I think that is permissible. Mr. Crookshank will manage these matters.

ARCHIE: (*goes to end of bar*) What'll you have, son?

ACCUSED: Brandy.

GOVERNMENT MAN: You will keep an account of the drinks, Mr. Crookshank, on Form 333, for remuneration by the Government.

ARCHIE: (*Pours drink, hands it to* ACCUSED, *who gulps it down*) Another?

GOVERNMENT MAN: The Government will pay for only one drink per Accused, Mr. Crookshank. You yourself, however, may offer a second at your own expense if you like.

ARCHIE: (*Pours another, hands it to the* ACCUSED, *who gulps it down again*) What kind of cigarettes do you smoke?

ACCUSED: Any kind just now, Mr. Crookshank. Thanks. (HE *takes a cigarette from Archie's pack.* ARCHIE *lights it.*)

GOVERNMENT MAN: Very good. Proceed, Guards. (*The Guards go off with the* ACCUSED.) The Court will occupy itself with routine work until each Accused is *corrected*. At that time another Accused will be brought in for judgment. Is that understood?

EVERYBODY: Yes, sir.

POWERFUL VOICE: Guards of the Republic, for the people!

CHORUS OF VOICES: For the people!

(*A volley of shots is heard.*)

GOVERNMENT MAN: Proceed, then.

JUDGE: The next Accused, please.

(*The* GUARDS *bring in a very old man.*)

GOVERNMENT MAN: Very good. You will recess from one to one-thirty.
    Mr. Crookshank will attend to food for all, for which he will be
    remunerated by the Government. Court adjourns at five. You will
    move a great deal swifter once you have gotten organized. You
    will *have* to. This is a state of emergency. In and out, in and out.
    Proceed, then.

ARCHIE: Excuse me, sir, I would like permission to run my establish-
    ment when court adjourns.

GOVERNMENT MAN: Food and drink, is that it?

ARCHIE: Yes, sir.

GOVERNMENT MAN: Lodging?

ARCHIE: No, sir.

GOVERNMENT MAN: Just yourself and your daughter, then, living up-
    stairs?

ARCHIE: (*slowly*) Yes, sir.

GOVERNMENT MAN: Court opens at ten, closes at five. From five to
    one—that's one in the morning—a period of eight hours out of
    every twenty-four—the place may resume normal business. But
    you will see to it, Mr. Crookshank, that everything is in order for
    swift action by ten each morning.

ARCHIE: Yes, sir.

GOVERNMENT MAN: Proceed, then.

ACCUSED OLD MAN: What about me? What are you going to do with
    me? What did I do? I'm seventy-two years old. What did I do
    wrong?

SCENE 2

It is two minutes to five. The JUDGE, the ATTORNEYS, the BAILIFF
with the rubber stamp, and the Court GUARDS *are in their places.*

VOICE: Guards of the Republic, for the people!

CHORUS OF VOICES: For the people!

(A *volley of shots is heard.*)

JUDGE: The next Accused, please.

ARCHIE: You haven't got time for another one. It's two minutes to five.

JUDGE: Guards, the next Accused, please! (*The* GUARDS *go out quickly.*) A great deal can be done in two minutes, Mr. Crookshank, as you will see. The value of two minutes to the Government is— (*The* GUARDS *come in with an angry* YOUNG MAN *who glares with contempt at the Judge, the Lawyers, the Bailiff and everybody else.*) Let's make it snappy, please.

PEOPLE'S ATTORNEY: Joseph Moore. Thirty-one years of age. Long history of social irresponsibility. Unmarried. No children. Attempted to commit suicide.

JUDGE: Faster, please. Suicide by what mean?

PEOPLE'S ATTORNEY: Excessive drinking.

JUDGE: Attorney for the Accused.

ATTORNEY FOR ACCUSED: It is not scientifically established how much drinking constitutes—

JUDGE: Make it routine, please.

ATTORNEY FOR ACCUSED: I am satisfied simply from looking at the accused that he—

JUDGE: Guilty. (*To the Accused*) Is there anything you wish to say?

ACCUSED: Yes. (*Slight pause.*)

JUDGE: Then say it. What are you waiting for?

ACCUSED: Happy birthday.

JUDGE: Happy birthday? We haven't time for riddles. The government generously allots you a moment in which to speak, but not in riddles. Say what you wish to say.

ACCUSED: Happy birthday.

JUDGE: You may have a drink and a cigarette.

ACCUSED: Happy birthday.

JUDGE: Proceed, Guards. (*The* GUARDS *hurry off with the* MAN, *who stops at the door, turns, and says: Anybody—anybody at all— don't forget—please.*) Hurry, Guards! (*The* GUARDS *move* HIM *out.*)

VOICE: Guards of the Republic, for the people!

ACCUSED'S VOICE: Happy birthday!

CHORUS OF VOICES: For the people!

(*A volley of shots is heard.*)

JUDGE: Court is adjourned until tomorrow morning at ten. (HE *walks out from behind the bar.*) You see, Mr. Crookshank, two minutes is time enough—time enough. Until tomorrow morning at ten, then. (HE *and the* OTHERS *go.* ROSE *runs to the door leading to the parking lot while* ARCHIE *stands at the center of his place of business, in a daze.*)

ROSE: What are we going to do, Archie?

ARCHIE: Do? What are we going to do? From now until one o'clock in the morning I'm going to run my business—that's what I'm going to do—if anybody'll ever come into the place again.

ROSE: Why wouldn't they come into the place again?

ARCHIE: They'd be scared to death, wouldn't they, excepting maybe one or two who didn't know or didn't care?

ROSE: Or one or two who'd be sent to *spy*, Archie? They'd send one or two to spy, wouldn't they? You *have* fallen into their hands, haven't you? Well, if you have, then so have I. I've never been so proud, though, Archie. I thought you'd tell him I *wasn't* your daughter.

ARCHIE: I couldn't do that. How should I know what he might do? He might put you out there with the others, the poor souls.

ROSE: They were none of them guilty of anything. If they can kill *them*, Archie, God knows they'll get around to me soon enough, but while I'm waiting, I'm ever so proud to be your daughter— and ever so ashamed of being alive while all the others are dead.

ARCHIE: You'd better have your whiskey now.

ROSE: Yes, thanks, Archie. Yes, I need some whiskey all right. (HE *pours for her, and for himself.* SHE *reaches out to touch glasses.*) I don't know what to say, Archie. God help us, I guess. God have mercy on us, I guess. God forgive us, I guess. Jesus, Archie, I've got the shakes and I want to cry. Can I cry? Can I drink this down and cry someplace? I'm afraid to go to my room and cry, and I wouldn't cry in a place of business.

ARCHIE: Drink your whiskey, girl. Drink your whiskey and I'll fill your glass again. (HE *gulps down his drink.* SHE *drinks hers.* HE *fills her glass again.*) Cry anywhere you like. (HE *pours himself another shot quickly and drowns it.* ROSE *takes her glass and goes to a table and sits down.*) They'll nobody decent come in here again. I might as well get up and go, and leave it to them altogether.

ROSE: *Leave*, Archie? You can't be thinking of running away. It would be the same anywhere you went.

ARCHIE: There must be somewhere to go.

ROSE: It's the same everywhere. This is your place. You can't run away from it. All you can do is keep it going from five in the afternoon to one in the morning.

ARCHIE: I can't do anybody any good here any more.

ROSE: You can't do them any harm here, either, and you can't do them any good at all anywhere else.

ARCHIE: Will you please stop talking as if you *were* my daughter?

ROSE: Well, you don't have to shout at me, do you? (SHE *gets up and goes to the door to the kitchen.*)

ARCHIE: Well, now, sit down a minute and let's see if we can talk sense.

ROSE: There's no use talking. I'm going to straighten out the kitchen. You'd better fill out the form for the drinks.

ARCHIE: I don't want any money for the drinks.

ROSE: They won't like that, Archie. You'd better fill out the form, and the one for the food, too. You've got to keep the place going the same as ever if you don't want them to take *you* for an enemy.

ARCHIE: They *know* I'm an enemy. They know everybody is.

ROSE: Well, then they'll expect you to *pretend* you're not, and you'd better do it. I'll straighten out the kitchen. You fill out the forms. You'll need the money to keep supplies in the kitchen, and bottles on your shelves. (SHE *goes.*)

ARCHIE: (*Examining forms*) Merry Christmas. Happy birthday (*Shouting.*) Rose!

ROSE: (*Appears in doorway*) What *is* it, Archie?

ARCHIE: What did he mean?

ROSE: Well, he'd dead now; so I guess we'll never know. The kitchen's a mess. I'm tired just noticing what a mess it is, but for once in my life I'm going to do my work just the same. (*Pause.*) Archie?

ARCHIE: Yes, Rose?

ROSE: You're not sorry you told him I'm your daughter, are you?

ARCHIE: I *had* to tell him that, didn't I?

ROSE: But you're not sorry, are you?

ARCHIE: Well, no, Rose. Why should I be sorry?

ROSE: I mean, you're not ashamed, are you?

ARCHIE: Look here, now. A lot of things have happened today that have all but destroyed my soul and made me ashamed of my whole life—for the stupid way I've gone along with it. If *they* were guilty—any of them—I'm guiltier. But I won't be ashamed. I won't be ashamed of any human being who tries not to hurt another human being. No, I'm not ashamed I told him you're my daughter.

ROSE: Thanks, Archie. I've never had a father, you know. Christ, he was gone before I even *smelled* him.

ARCHIE: And I've never *been* a father, either. Yes, I have children

somewhere in the world. For hating their mother so, I left them
—twenty years ago.

ROSE: I didn't know, Archie. I'm awful sorry.

ARCHIE: God knows what's become of the poor woman, or the boy,
or the two girls.

ROSE: Oh, I'm sorry, Archie. I'm so sorry for your poor babies—father-
less.

ARCHIE: The boy was six, the first girl was four, the baby two. I'd all
but forgotten them until today. I've never been a father.

ROSE: I'll be a good daughter, Archie. I'll never again be tired the way
I've been all my life. (SHE *goes into the kitchen.*)

ARCHIE: If they'd had homes, if they'd had mothers and fathers, they'd
not have ended the way they did, killed for nothing.

ROSE: (*At the door*) Now, what is it you're saying, Archie? I've got
work to do but I can't do it with you saying something I can't
hear. I've got to hear everything you say. What it is, Archie?

ARCHIE: I'm saying they'd not have been murdered if they'd had
mothers and fathers who had *been* mothers and fathers, if they'd
not been orphans from the beginning, that's what I'm saying.

ROSE: Why, that's silly, Archie. Just think what you're *really* saying.
You're saying it's better to be a murderer than to be murdered,
and you know that's not so at all. One's as bad as the other, and
everybody's as much an orphan as anybody else. So if *that's* what's
the matter with us, it's the matter with all of us, and not just the
ones who are being murdered every day. They've all had the same
father and mother—a man and a woman each, some luckier than
others in the *names* of the men and women, or the place of them
in society, or the wealth of them, or something else accidental.
It's all of us, Archie, and not one side on this side, and another
on the other. What about the man who said I was your daughter?
He set the Court up, didn't he, and started the killing? But who
is *he*, Archie? Who is he himself?

ARCHIE: Who is he? I'll tell you who he is. He's a son of a bitch, that's
who he is.

ROSE: Isn't he a man, too, like everybody else, and not altogether unkind or inhuman, although he knows the Court he has set up
must find everybody guilty? Who *is* he, anyway?

ARCHIE: Now, why do you try to confuse me?

ROSE: Oh, I hate him, too, Archie, but what could he do that would
change him from a son of a bitch to something better?

ARCHIE: What could he do? He could—Well, he could—

ROSE: Isn't he carrying out orders?

ARCHIE: I won't have you speaking up for the murderers as though they were every one of them helpless and sorry.

ROSE: But if it's the truth, Archie? If they are all of them helpless, and maybe sorry, too, are we to pretend something else?

ARCHIE: Somebody has got to accept responsibility for the murders. They can't just say they're helpless and sorry and keep killing everybody. Somebody's got to refuse to carry out orders.

ROSE: Archie?

ARCHIE: Now, don't make me angry, Rose. Don't annnoy me. I'm annoyed enough as it is. (HE *takes a drink straight from the bottle.*) What is it?

ROSE: You yourself are carrying out orders. I don't want to annoy you, but isn't it so, Archie?

ARCHIE: Well, it's different with me. I have this little restaurant and saloon. I'm not a politician. I'm not in the Government. They're the ones who've got to refuse to carry out orders.

ROSE: By doing that they'd only condemn themselves to death, wouldn't they, Archie?

ARCHIE: They can get the hell out of the Government, can't they?

ROSE: Do you think so, Archie? Do you think it's as easy as all that?

ARCHIE: Nothing's easy. Why *should* it be easy?

ROSE: Why? Because everybody wants everything to be easy, I guess.

ARCHIE: One of them's got to have the courage to refuse to carry out orders and pay for it with his life.

ROSE: Why should it be one of *them* any more than it should be one of us, Archie?

ARCHIE: You're annoying me, Rose. You're making me feel guilty for every murder that took place here today. If I had spoken up I would have been killed, wouldn't I?

ROSE: Yes, Archie, you would have.

ARCHIE: Well, then, don't annoy me about it. Don't be forever nagging at me for not getting myself killed the first day they turn my place into a slaughter house. Don't tell me I'm to pity the murderers and the murdered alike, and myself, and yourself. Life's not worth living if you've got to pity *everybody*. It doesn't make sense pitying everybody. You've got to love some and hate others.

ROSE: It's easy to love and hate, Archie. Just as easy as it is to breathe, but what does it mean? Does it mean something? I love you, I hate you, you love me, you hate me, we love the murdered ones, we hate the ones who murdered them, what does it mean? And who was it murdered them? Was it the Lawyers, the Judge, the Bailiff with the rubber stamp, the Guards in here, the Captain of the Guards in the parking lot shouting *Guards of the Republic, for the people,* and the Guards shouting back *For the people,* and then killing one of the people. For *which* people is it? Is there two people? There's only one people. It's easy to love and hate, Archie. And by now I'm sick and tired of it.

ARCHIE: Well, now, I've taken you in, I've told them you're my daughter, but it's no good your annoying me with the hopelessness of my position.

ROSE: Not yours alone, Archie. Mine, too. And anybody's. Everybody's. If it is hopeless, it's hopeless for all of us, but is it hopeless? Is there no answer?

ARCHIE: Answer *them?* We'd be shot.

ROSE: Not *them*—ourselves, Archie. Have we no answer for ourselves?

ARCHIE: Are you telling me to get myself killed the first thing tomorrow morning? Are you telling me to speak up for the Accused, to defy the Accusers, to refuse to obey my orders, and get myself killed? Is that it?

ROSE: I don't know, Archie. I don't mean for you, I mean for me, too. I don't know what I'm telling you, or myself.

ARCHIE: Well, for somebody who doesn't know, you're annoying me enough, I'll say that. I've lived sixty-two years, and that's long enough at that. Now, I *will* ask you to help me. Help me find out what my duty is, and I swear to God I'll do it. Is it to kill the Judge, standing here where I now stand?

ROSE: I'm sure it couldn't be that.

ARCHIE: Is it to plead with them to let myself be shot in place of another—in place of—well, one of the younger men, in place of somebody like that last one today? Is that it, Rose?

ROSE: Wouldn't they shoot *him,* too, after they'd shot you?

ARCHIE: I don't know, Rose. I'm asking you.

ROSE: If you pleaded with them to let you take the place of another, they would not let you take his place, but they *would* put you down as an enemy of the Republic, and the next day you would be tried and executed, too.

ARCHIE: Then, would it be to poison their food at lunchtime? The

Judge, the Bailiff, the Lawyers, the Guards, the Firing Squads, and all the others? Would it be that?

ROSE: Oh, they'd die all right, Archie, but that wouldn't stop the trials and the executions. It would only make *us* accuse and kill more of us.

ARCHIE: *Them*, you mean, don't you? It would only make *them* accuse and kill more of us. Is that what you mean?

ROSE: No, we're all together. *We* accuse and kill, and we *are* accused, and we are killed.

ARCHIE: Ah, for God's sake, girl, would you accuse anybody in the whole world and kill him?

ROSE: I *might*, Archie. I might.

ARCHIE: No, you wouldn't. *They* accuse and *they* kill. We just wait, hoping not to be accused, so we can die of old age. It's the end for all of us now, that's all.

ROSE: I guess it is, Archie.

ARCHIE: Now, how did it happen? And what are we to do? That's the question. We just can't stand by with our mouths open, can we?

ROSE: We've got to sing or something.

ARCHIE: Sing? What good would that do?

ROSE: We might just begin to understand that we *don't* have to kill ourselves.

ARCHIE: Ah, there'll never be another soul come in here to keep my poor business going, that's all I know. I give drinks to the dead now, and food to the killers. My customers are the dead, and the whole business is on credit.

ROSE: (*At the door to the parking lot*) There he is, the poor man, lying dead and alone! They'll take him away in the morning. They couldn't wait to get away from their dirty work. It's killing *them*, too, Archie. They're all sick and tired of it, too. (*Suddenly, terrified.*) Jesus Christ, Archie!

ARCHIE: (*At the door*) What is it, girl?

ROSE: For God's sake, Archie, come and look! Is he getting up or is it my imagination? Look, there, Archie!

ARCHIE: God Almighty, have mercy on us, he's on his hands and knees. (*Shouts.*) Don't do it! Lie down, man!

ROSE: Let me go help him!

ARCHIE: (*Grabs her*) Are you mad, girl?

ROSE: Let me go, Archie! He's not dead! He needs help!

ARCHIE: We can't help him! Get inside here, let me bolt the door, he'll fall back again.

ROSE: Let me go, Archie! Let me go! (SHE *breaks free, but* HE *grabs her again.*)

ARCHIE: Now, will you come to your senses?

ROSE: I've got to help him, Archie! If he's got no more than a minute to live I've got to help him.

ARCHIE: (*Ashamed*) All right, girl. *I'll* help him. I'll fetch him here. Stand at the door on the street to see if anyone's about. Hurry, now! (ROSE *runs to the door on the street,* ARCHIE *goes off into the parking lot.* MAY FOLEY *comes in.* ROSE *tries to get her out again.*)

ROSE: You can't come in here. We're closed. The place is closed.

FOLEY: I'm May Foley, girl. Archie and I are old friends. I've been away. I've just come back. (ARCHIE *comes back in, dragging the limp and bloody body of the young man.*)

ARCHIE: Rose! For God's sake, Rose, get him some brandy!

ROSE: (*Runs, followed by* MAY FOLEY, *a woman of fifty or so, dressed to kill.*) The poor man! The poor man!

MAY: (*Helping Archie*) Here, Archie, over here! (SHE *pushes two tables together.*) Get him up here! (THEY *get him up on the tables.*) I'll help the poor dear boy! (SHE *takes the glass of brandy from Rose's hand.* ARCHIE *lifts the young man's head while* MAY *pours a little of the brandy into his mouth. And finally all of it.*) Well, now, who *did* this?

ARCHIE: Wait a minute, will you, May? Rose, bolt the door! (*To the man*) Listen to me, you're with friends! You're with friends, do you hear? May, can you do something for him?

MAY: We can give him some more brandy! Who is the poor boy?

ARCHIE: He was shot a half hour ago. (MAY *gives him more brandy.*)

YOUNG MAN: (*Slowly*) Happy Birthday!

ARCHIE: What do you mean, man? Tell us, will you? What do you mean? (THE YOUNG MAN's *body leaps up suddenly, sags enormously, and then is limp.*) Oh, Christ!

MAY: (*Folds his arms*) What a sin to kill a man like that. Who did it, Archie?

ARCHIE: I've got to get him back. I've got to get him where they left him before somebody steps into the place. (HE *picks the man up again.*)

MAY: Here, let me help you! You're not his age, you know, though he's dead and you're still alive. (THEY *go out together with the young man.*) Now what's all this about happy birthday?

ARCHIE: How should I know? He said it to the Judge, he said it to the Firing Squad, he stayed alive long enough to say it once more to me—and to you, too. (THEY *are gone.* ROSE *comes back into the place, runs after them.*)

SCENE 3

It is ten minutes to one that night. ARCHIE *is behind the bar,* MAY FOLEY *is standing further down the bar,* ROSE *is sweeping toward the door of the kitchen.*

ARCHIE: Well, there it is. The whole eight hours, not one customer, except the poor boy from the grave. Not a soul from the living world.

MAY: Well, I like that! What world do you think *I'm* from?

ARCHIE: Except you, May. (*Pauses, glances at her*) One of the thirty-nine they killed today was not unlike yourself, May.

MAY: Impossible. There *is* no other woman like myself. I've been around a long time and I've never seen another. Where do you find women who wear clothes the way I do? And they're not expensive clothes, either. If I spent my money on clothes I wouldn't be able to drink the way I drink. I've always drunk the best of everything, haven't I? Or travel the way I travel. I bought the car myself and learned to drive. I drove across the country and back. I saw my three sons. Oh, they're strangers in a way, and I suppose I embarrass them, but not one of them turned his back on me, and I'll tell you why, too, Archie. A man's mother is his mother, that's all—even if it's *me*. They were astonished of course. Their father stole them away when the oldest was five and I myself was only twenty-one or twenty-two. But I kept track of them. They're good boys. Married, got kids of their own. Christ, they're unhappy, though. Do you understand what I mean, Archie? For all their success and happiness, they're unhappy. I see it in their eyes, poor dears. Now, I didn't mean to interrupt. What was it you were telling me?

ARCHIE: Ah, you've done nothing but tell me the story of your year of travel all night as if you'd gone and found the Holy Grail or something twice as good. And you don't seem to understand what's happened. They've made a slaughter house out of the place. One of the thirty-nine they killed today was a woman not unlike yourself and when the time came for her to say anything she wanted to say she said, "I've got a son some place. What's going to happen to him?" "How old is your son?" the Judge said, and she said, "Well, I guess he's about thirty by now. What's going to happen to him?" Well, they asked her some more questions and it turned out she'd had a son about thirty years ago who'd died when he was three years ago. I mean, she suddenly remembered that he'd died, and she began to cry because he had. They let them have something to drink and a cigarette. She *was* a drinker. I poured her a double brandy because she was still crying, but just before she tossed it down she stopped crying and said, "Well, here's looking at you." I mean, for an instant there —just before taking the drink—she forgot they were going to shoot her. I mean, there she was at the last minute remembering and forgetting. (*Pause*) Not one customer the whole night. Oh, they're afraid all right, and I can't say I blame them.

MAY: What did she do?

ARCHIE: Who?

MAY: The woman, Archie. The one you were just telling me about. What did she do *wrong*?

ARCHIE: Oh, hell, I've forgotten. None of them did *anything* wrong. Rose? What did that woman do that asked what was going to happen to her son, and then it turned out her son had died almost thirty years ago? What did she do? It was right after lunch, and she reminded me a little of May here.

ROSE: Her name was Margaret Cathcart. She was fifty-five. A long history of shoplifting. She wore a big hat and laces and long gloves. She got into somebody's house and went to the nursery where a small boy was sleeping. She picked the boy up and went through the house to the front door when the boy woke up and began to cry.

ARCHIE: Yes, that was it. There were so many of them I forgot what she had done. Well, now look, the both of you. It's after one now. You'd better get going. (ROSE *looks at him strangely. He looks at her.*)

MAY: Well, it's only around the corner for me, Rose, but I'll walk you to your door.

ROSE: (*She is frightened*) Yes. That's awful nice of you, May.

ARCHIE: Oh, May. You'd better not come around till after five to-morrow.

MAY: Why? Where would I go *until* five? Of course I'll come around.

ARCHIE: But you can't! The place is a Court of Justice from ten to five, I tell you. Don't come by until after five, that's all.

MAY: Well, all right if you say so, Archie.

ARCHIE: Here. Here's one for the road, May. And one for you, Rose.

MAY: (*Lifting her glass*) Well, here's looking at you.

ROSE: Good luck. (THEY ALL *drink.* MAY *and* ROSE *go, saying good-night.* ARCHIE *bolts the door, turns down the light, stands at the center of his place, his head bent forward, thinking.* HE *hears a soft rapping at the door on the parking lot.* HE *turns in terror. The door knob is turned.* HE *backs away. The door opens slowly and the shoplifting woman he has just spoken about, who is in fact not unlike* MAY FOLEY, *steps in.*)

WOMAN: What's going to happen to my son?

ARCHIE: Your son's dead.

WOMAN: He's *not* dead. I saw him. I held him in my arms. When they took me away he cried. What's going to happen to him?

ARCHIE: He'll be all right.

WOMAN: I don't want anything bad to happen to my son.

ARCHIE: He'll be all right. He's with good people.

WOMAN: I'm awful worried about my son and—I need a drink. I need a good stiff shot, so I can sleep. I can't sleep. (ARCHIE *pours her a drink and one for himself, his hands shaking.* SHE *picks up her drink and* HE *picks up his.*) I don't know what's happened to me lately. I'm awful nervous, scared to death of the least little thing. (SHE *looks at the glass in her hand, then at* ARCHIE.) Well, here's looking at you. (THEY *drink.*)

ARCHIE: He'll be all right. You can rest now. You can sleep.

WOMAN: Are you sure? Are you sure he'll be all right? Forever and ever?

ARCHIE: Yes, I'm sure.

WOMAN: I feel better now. I feel much better now. (SHE *moves back-ward and out, closing the door behind her.* ARCHIE *pours himself another drink, tosses it down quickly, goes to the door.* HE *tries the door. It is locked.* HE *goes to the door on the street and stands there pathetically. After a moment there is a soft knock.*)

ARCHIE: Who is it?

ROSE'S VOICE: It's me, Archie . . . Rose. (ARCHIE *unbolts and swings the door open and* ROSE *comes in, carrying a small rattan suitcase.* HE *stands a moment staring at her.*)

ROSE: I had to come back, Archie. I'm sorry. I couldn't stay there. I just couldn't. You're not ashamed of me, are you? Not ashamed of the way I turned out? I didn't mean it to happen that way. I —I was tired. I was very tired. But I'm not tired any more. And I'll make a good home for you. You're not ashamed, are you, Archie? When you told me to go with May you *were* ashamed, but you're not any more, are you?

ARCHIE: No, Rose. No. I'll tell May tomorrow.

ROSE: Tell her what, Archie?

ARCHIE: I'll tell her you're my daughter. I'll tell everybody.

ROSE: No, you couldn't do that, Archie. They know about me. You couldn't do that. I wouldn't let you do it.

ARCHIE: I couldn't tell her tonight, but I'll tell her tomorrow. (*Pause*) I'll tell her because it's the truth . . . in a deep and strange way it *is* the truth. (SHE *walks to him slowly, shyly.* HE *embraces her as a father embraces a daughter, each of them ashamed, hurt, frightened.*) The whole world's haunted now. Haunted by the homeless dead, and haunted by the homeless living, too. Now *I'm* scared, Rose.

ROSE: Don't be scared, Archie. I'll make a good home for you. (SHE *picks up her suitcase and goes up the stairs while* ARCHIE *stands at the bar, watching.*)

ACT TWO

SCENE 1

It is fifteen or twenty minutes to ten the following morning. ARCHIE CROOKSHANK *comes down the steps, goes to the door on the street, opens it, looks up and down, returns, goes behind the bar and examines what he's got on the shelves.* ROSE *steps out of the kitchen.*

She is wearing a new dress, she hasn't put on makeup, and she's combed her hair differently. She looks new and serious, like a little girl playing house. SHE *has two cups of coffee on a tray.*

ARCHIE: You've been up half the night, haven't you?

ROSE: I thought I'd get up early and get things started in the kitchen. (SHE *sets a cup of coffee down in front of* ARCHIE.) I've made bean soup, and I hope they like it.

ARCHIE: Who? The poor souls who happen to be still alive at lunchtime?

ROSE: Yes, Archie.

ARCHIE: They'll like it all right.

ROSE: I used up everything in the kitchen. I *had* to. There was almost nothing left.

ARCHIE: Whatever it is, they'll like it because it's the last eating they're going to do.

ROSE: They don't know that, though.

ARCHIE: They know it, but they won't believe it. They pretend it's just another poor meal they're going to eat until things get better and they get to the wonderful meal they think they're going to eat some day. The *first* supper, so to say.

ROSE: The first supper? Do you have a meal like that, Archie?

ARCHIE: Sure. I've had it all my life, but I've never sat down to it.

ROSE: What is the first supper, Archie?

ARCHIE: Well, to begin with you've got to be ready for it. Everything's got to be in order. You can't have anything troubling your soul. You've got your home and your family and everybody's in good health. It's a fine cold day and you've been out with your wife and your kids for a long walk, and you've come home just before evening. There's some leaves to rake into a pile and burn, and you do that while your wife goes inside to get supper. Some of the kids are out there with you, and you're smelling the smoke of the burning leaves. The kids look fine, and your wife's getting more beautiful every day. She's had a lot of kids—not just one or two, or two or three—she's had seven or eight of them, and she's still a beauty. The kids love her and she loves them, and every kid is different. Every one of them's a lot of trouble, but it's trouble your wife and you enjoy putting up with. The older girls are inside helping her, talking about love and marriage and men, and the older boys are outside talking about the things they want to do before they get married and settle down—a trip around the world, to see the whole thing—an exploration trip, in Brazil maybe—and things like that. Your wife comes out to the fire with a glass of cold wine for you, and one for herself, and you touch glasses and look at each other and smile because you belong to each other, and like it, with all its troubles, and your kids look at you out of the corners of their eyes and smile to themselves because they belong to each other, too, and to you and your wife, and like it, too, with all of *its* troubles. After the drink of cold wine you go inside and everybody sits down at the table. Well, the food's important, but the food's not what counts in *this* meal, it's the other stuff. The way I see it we'd have—well, home-made bread, baked in the morning. Fresh butter. Roast beef. Baked potatoes. Cheese. Tea and coffee and milk. But if it was bean soup, bean soup would be all right, too. That's the meal I've always wanted to have some day. And every one of the poor souls who'll be eating the bean soup at lunchtime today is going to pretend it's just another poor meal until things get better and they get to that wonderful meal they're going to eat before they die. Well, they'll never eat that meal and neither will I. I guess nobody will.

ROSE: But it could happen so *easily*, Archie!

ARCHIE: Yes, it could, I suppose, but it never does. Well, that was good coffee, Rose. (ROSE *goes off with the cups.* ARCHIE *straightens out a chair.* MAY FOLEY *comes in.*)

MAY: (*cheerfully*) Now, Archie, don't you dare scold me, and don't you dare tell me to go. I've got something to tell you.

ARCHIE: You've got to get out of here.

MAY: Not until I tell you.

ARCHIE: They'll be here in a minute, May. Come and tell me after five this evening.

MAY: I've got to tell you now. In the middle of the night somebody knocked at my door and woke me up. I was never so scared in my whole life. I didn't say a word, hoping whoever it was would go away. Well, he didn't go away. Instead, the door opened and a young fellow stood there.

ARCHIE: Ah, you were dreaming.

MAY: I swear to God I wasn't dreaming, Archie. If I was dreaming I would have screamed. The minute I saw him I stopped being scared. He was just a boy, lonely and lost. He came to the bed and knelt there and cried. It was as if he was my own son. "Now, now," I said. "That's all right. That's all right."

ARCHIE: Who was it?

MAY: Well, I don't know, Archie. I'm trying to tell you. He looked a lot like the poor boy who came in here last night and died, though.

ARCHIE: Well, what did he say?

MAY: That's just it. He didn't say a word. Not one word. He just cried, and then after a while he got up and went out and closed the door behind him. (*Pause*) Well, this is the part I can't figure out, Archie. After he was gone, I went to the door to lock it again, but it was *already* locked. I swear it happened, Archie. Now, why should a thing like that happen to me? I was awful scared at first, but after I saw him I wasn't scared, I was proud. Proud that he'd come to *me*—an old bag like me, as if I was his own mother. You believe me, don't you Archie?

ARCHIE: All right, all right, May, I believe you. Now get out of here before it's too late.

MAY: I'm going. (SHE *turns to go just as the* JUDGE *and the* OTHERS *come in.*)

JUDGE: Ah, good morning, Mrs. Crookshank. It *is* Mrs. Crookshank, isn't it, Mr. Crookshank?

ARCHIE: (*Trying not to hestitate*) Yes. Yes, it is.

JUDGE: Well, that's fine. We missed you yesterday, Mrs. Crookshank. We were a little short-handed, especially at lunchtime. You will be a great help, and of course you will be paid for your work. Well, I see everything's in order. Take your places, gentlemen. (ROSE *comes out of the kitchen.*) Miss Crookshank. (ROSE *half-nods.*)

ROSE: (*softly*) Good morning.

JUDGE: Take your place, please. (*To* MAY) Mrs. Crookshank, you may stand beside your husband. (ROSE *watches incredulously.*)

MAY: Yes, sir.

JUDGE: (*Taking his place*) You've prepared a good lunch?

MAY: Well, yes. Yes sir.

ROSE: Bean soup.

MAY: Yes, bean soup.

ROSE: But there's a shopping list to fill.

JUDGE: Very good. Mrs. Crookshank may be excused to attend to the shopping.

ROSE: Here's the list. (SHE *hands* MAY *a list.*) And here's the ration coupons.

ARCHIE: I'm afraid I don't have any money in the cash register. I had no customers last night.

JUDGE: You've filled out Form 333, Mr. Crookshank?

ARCHIE: Yes, it's here. (HE *hands it to the* JUDGE, *who goes over it quickly.*)

JUDGE: Bailiff, this seems to be in order. Will you adjust it, please? (*The* BAILIFF *takes the form, counts out money, hands it to* ARCHIE, *who hands some of it to* MAY.) Very good, then, Mrs. Crookshank, you are excused until the shopping has been attended to.

MAY: Yes, sir. (SHE *goes.*)

JUDGE: Well, I see we have another minute. I'm sorry you had no customers last night, Mr. Crookshank. None at all?

ARCHIE: No, sir.

JUDGE: A healthy sign. Excessive drinking is an offense against the people.

ARCHIE: I served food, too, and my customers don't drink excessively.

JUDGE: Court is open. The first Accused, please. (*The* GUARDS *step out and return instantly with a very distinguished gentleman of sixty-five or so who is smoking a cigarette in a white cardboard cigarette holder.*) Attorney for the People.

ATTORNEY FOR PEOPLE: Jeffrey Johnson. Age sixty-seven. May it please your honor, it says here, Profession—Drama.

JEFFREY: Drama *Critic.* Although my actual profession is no such thing.

PEOPLE'S ATTORNEY: You do not earn your living as a Drama Critic?

JEFFREY: Certainly not. I write drama criticism for pleasure. I have lived on an income from a trust fund since I was eleven years of age.

PEOPLE'S ATTORNEY: If your profession is not Drama Critic, what is it?

JEFFREY: The observation of the human creature.

JUDGE: (*To the* PEOPLE'S ATTORNEY) Proceed, please.

PEOPLE'S ATTORNEY: A life-long history of cynicism, indifference, and irresponsibility.

JEFFREY: Two baths a day, one in the morning and one at night, and I believe you might have added that I despise chicken.

PEOPLE'S ATTORNEY: That does not constitute being an enemy of the people.

JEFFREY: I don't care what it constitutes, I despise chicken. I also despise those who do *not* despise it.

BAILIFF: One moment, please. You are out of order.

JEFFREY: I have never been out of order!

BAILIFF: You are out of order now.

JEFFREY: Don't be silly.

JUDGE: I must ask that a pace be established and maintained. Attorney for the People, will you *please* proceed?

PEOPLE'S ATTORNEY: He is accused of having written favorably of the performance of a beautiful girl in a new play, but the girl actually gave a very bad performance.

JEFFREY: Nonsense: It was excellent.

PEOPLE'S ATTORNEY: Furthermore, the girl was his mistress.

JEFFREY: She *was*. (A GIRL *breaks into the scene.*)

GIRL: Jeffrey! (*Embraces him.*)

JEFFREY: And she still *is*.

GIRL: What have they done to you?

JEFFREY: But where's Bismark? Why haven't you brought Bismark? He might have bitten somebody here for my amusement.

GIRL: He ran away.

JEFFREY: Ran away? Good God, girl, why didn't you go after him?

GIRL: I wanted to find *you*. I couldn't imagine what had happened to you. I've been terribly worried. I couldn't go looking for Bismark when you were lost, too, could I?

JEFFREY: You most certainly could. Where did you see him last?

GIRL: Just outside the hotel.

JEFFREY: (*To the* JUDGE) Would you be good enough to call me a taxi, please? I've lost my dog.

BAILIFF: Just a moment. You can't go anywhere.

JEFFREY: I will speak to you when I have something entertaining to say. Entertaining to *me*, that is. Until then I would rather you occupied your mind with—whatever it is that you—

BAILIFF: Your Honor, the Accused does not seem to understand the nature of his—

JUDGE: Just a moment, Bailiff. Guard, will you call a taxi, please?

JEFFREY: Thank you. (HE *brings out his wallet, hands the* JUDGE *a piece of currency.*) Come along, my dear. You're distraught, but you needn't be. We'll find Bismark. I'm sure he's sitting outside my door. (HE *looks around at everybody and goes off with the girl.*)

JUDGE: Bailiff, this Court is quite capable of *postponing* correction in the interest of the people. You will arrange for the further observation of the Accused, *and* his accomplice. And—please observe, Bailiff, the wisdom of the People's method of finding out its enemies. (HE *tosses the currency to the* BAILIFF.) Be good enough to put that into the People's Fund. Next Accused, please. (*The next* ACCUSED *is a man of about the same age as the* DRAMA CRITIC.)

JUDGE: Attorney for the People, proceed.

PEOPLE'S ATTORNEY: Andrew Abernathy. Age sixty-one. No trade or profession.

ABERNATHY: That's not so. I make money. I've been making money for more than thirty years.

PEOPLE'S ATTORNEYS (*ignoring him*) *Counterfeit* money!

BAILIFF: May I examine some, please? (ABERNATHY *brings thick wads of currency, all new and crisp, from every pocket of his jacket and trousers.*)

BAILIFF: This batch, Your Honor, is thousands, these are five thousands, these are ten thousands, these are twenty thousands.

ABERNATHY: There's close to three hundred *million* dollars there.

JUDGE: The pace, please. Let's not lose the pace we established yesterday. Proceed, please.

ABERNATHY: Can I say something?

BAILIFF: No. You must wait your turn. It is now the turn of your attorney.

ABERNATHY: I would like to speak to him.

BAILIFF: That is not necessary. He is quite able to defend you without any coaching.

ATTORNEY FOR ACCUSED: It's obvious that the accused is not a true counterfeiter. I have here one of his million-dollar bills. The paper and print is quite good. Excellent, in fact. On it, however, is lithographed on this side a picture of someone called My Father, and on *this* side a picture of a house called My Father's House. The situation on *this* bill is much the same, except that the person is called My Mother, and on this side is a picture of a man called My Mother's Brother.

ABERNATHY: He died when he was twenty-seven and my mother was broken-hearted.

BAILIFF: You must wait your turn to speak. The Court will inform you when it's your turn.

ATTORNEY FOR ACCUSED: One question, Your Honor, and I rest. (*To* ABERNATHY) How much of the money that you have made have you spent?

ABERNATHY: About six million dollars, but I had a few debts.

ATTORNEY FOR ACCUSED: I'm afraid I'll have to sacrifice pace in the interest of—Well, I'd like to know what your debts were.

ABERNATHY: Gambling.

ATTORNEY FOR ACCUSED: I'm sorry, Your Honor, I must know who he lost so much money to.

ABERNATHY: My mother. I knew she cheated but it made her happy, so I always paid.

ATTORNEY FOR ACCUSED: What did *your mother* do with the money?

ABERNATHY: She gave most of it away. She was careless with money.

ATTORNEY FOR ACCUSED: Who'd she give it to?

ABERNATHY: Members of the family.

ATTORNEY FOR ACCUSED: What did *they* do with it?

ABERNATHY: The careful ones kept it, the careless ones didn't

ATTORNEY FOR ACCUSED: Did you ever take any of these bills to a store and get merchandise with them?

ABERNATHY: No. We had all the merchandise we wanted.

ATTORNEY FOR ACCUSED: Why did you manufacture this money?

ABERNATHY: I made up my mind as a schoolboy to become the richest man in the world.

ATTORNEY FOR ACCUSED: You shouldn't have said that. (*To the Judge*) Rest.

JUDGE: Do you wish to say anything?

ABERNATHY: What do you mean?

ATTORNEY FOR ACCUSED: (*looking idly at a bill*) This one says *Sonya's* Mother. Who's Sonya?

ABERNATHY: Sonya and her mother were neighbors of ours for a couple of years.

JUDGE: We're losing pace. Guilty.

ABERNATHY: Why? On account of Sonya? She was like a sister.

JUDGE: You may have a drink and a cigarette. What'll you have?

ABERNATHY: Glass of water. (ARCHIE *fills a large glass which* ABER-NATHY *drinks thirstily.*)

JUDGE: Guards. (*The* GUARDS *go to Abernathy.*)

ABERNATHY: I'd like to have my money back.

ATTORNEY FOR ACCUSED: This one says Mike's Mother. Who's Mike?

ABERNATHY: (*almost blowing up*) What do you care who Mike is? Find out for yourself who Mike is. Nobody around here has any feeling for money. I'd like to have all of my money back, please.

ATTORNEY FOR ACCUSED: I'd like to keep this one. Susie's Father.

ABERNATHY: No. Nothing doing.

JUDGE: Bailiff, let him have his money. (*The money is piled up and handed to* ABERNATHY *who is hustled off by the* GUARDS, *as* HE *tries to get the money back into his pockets.*)

JUDGE: We've lost pace and I must insist that we restore it. Attorney for the Accused, it's not advisable to seek to satisfy your personal curiosity about the Accused. Make the routine defense, make it snappy, and sit down.

ATTORNEY FOR ACCUSED: Yes, Your Honor.

VOICE: Guards of the Republic, for the people!

CHORUS OF VOICES: For the people! (*Volley of shots.*)

JUDGE: Next Accused, please. (*The next* ACCUSED *is an old woman who looks like a little smiling girl.*)

OLD WOMAN: Guilty. Can I go?

BAILIFF: Wait your turn to speak, please.

PEOPLE'S ATTORNEY: Elinor Moriarity. Age seventy-two. Unemployed. Begs. Rest.

JUDGE: That's better. (*To the Attorney for Accused*) You, then.

ATTORNEY FOR ACCUSED: Rest.

JUDGE: Excellent. (*To Elinor*) Do you wish to say anything?

ELINOR: Can I go?

JUDGE: Guilty! Guards! (*The* GUARDS *start to go off with* HER.)

ARCHIE: What about her drink?

JUDGE: She *is* entitled to a drink, Mr. Crookshank. You're quite right.

ARCHIE: What'll you have?

ELINOR: (*like a child*) Oh.

ARCHIE: How about a little brandy?

ELINOR: Oh. (ARCHIE *pours one,* SHE *drinks, the* GUARDS *go off with* HER, *the pace is kept up in the usual manner.*)

JUDGE: Next Accused, please. And see that you keep up the pace. (*This time the* ACCUSED *is a* YOUNG MAN.)

PEOPLE'S ATTORNEY: Edward Hawkins. Age twenty-three. Unemployed. Writes poems. Never works. Steals groceries. Rest.

ATTORNEY FOR ACCUSED: Rest.

JUDGE: Do you wish to say anything?

EDWARD: My reason for seeking a Fellowship is to enable me to finish a trilogy of heroic poetry which is to concern itself with man's eternal struggle for truth and meaning. The first book of the trilogy has been started and concerns itself with man's eternal struggle for peace and quiet. The second book is in outline and concerns itself with man's eternal struggle for home and hearth. The third and final book is still in a nebulous stage but will concern itself with man's eternal struggle for food and drink.

ARCHIE: What'll you have?

EDWARD: Brioche and coffee, half and half.

ARCHIE: Better have this brandy and a cigarette. (HE *pours, the* POET *drinks,* HE *offers him a cigarette, lights it for him.*)

EDWARD: If I win the Fellowship, I know I shall produce something memorable.

JUDGE: Guards. (*The* GUARDS *stand on either side of him.*)

EDWARD: I certainly would appreciate the Fellowship. It would certainly be a great help. I've got a mother to support and although I've cracked Poetry Magazine twice everybody knows that that's not enough to support your mother on. (*The* GUARDS *go off with* HIM *and the routine procedure of correction follows.*)

JUDGE: Next Accused, please. (*The* ACCUSED *is a* SMALL BOY.)

PEOPLE'S ATTORNEY: (*Examining papers*) John Delamere. Age three years, nine months. No trade or profession. Father in the Guards of the Republic. Mother in the Women's Land Army, Home Corps. (*Slight pause*) Accused has publicly expressed hatred and contempt for both parents. (HE *looks at the angry, innocent-and-lonely-looking boy, then speaks faintly*) Rest.

ATTORNEY FOR ACCUSED: Rest.

ARCHIE: Now, look here! You've made a bloody slaughter house out of my saloon and I've kept my mouth shut the whole time, out of cowardly fear and eagerness to get to my own silly lunch and sleep, but if you're going to start butchering children, too, as well as the aged and infirm, the eccentric and ill, the homeless and unfortunate, then by God pass your dirty sentence on me, too, for I will not live in the same world with you! (HE *stands beside the small boy, in the place of the Accused.*)

BAILIFF: You're out of order! Get back to your place!

ARCHIE: Don't tell me I'm out of order, you stupid rubber-stamp of a man!

ROSE: Archie, for God's sake, get back in your place before it's too late!

JUDGE: One moment, please, Miss Crookshank. (HE *glances at Archie, as if with charity*) Mr. Crookshank—

ARCHIE: Do you call yourself a Judge in a Court of Justice? Do you think for a minute that you can live in your *own* world, in the fantasy world you have made out of your panic and fear? A world in which you are terrified even of a child—this small boy who would walk out there and be shot and not know such a thing was unusual, like the others you've murdered who, for all their years, weren't much different from him? You yourself haven't any more brains than the child here. Do you think you can survive in your own sick world? Like all the others you've each had a mother and a father, and you may have children, too. Where do you think *you* are going to live in this world you have made?

JUDGE: (*patiently*) Mr. Crookshank—

ARCHIE: I've got no more brains myself than any of you here, but it's no good putting ignorance with power, is it? Power must be put with intelligence and kindness. You know how ignorant you are. How can you allow yourself to have power, too?

ROSE: Archie, for God's sake, stop it!

ARCHIE: If you *must* be ignorant, you must try to be kind, too.

JUDGE: You there! Guard! Stop him! (*One of the* GUARDS *raises his rifle and aims at Archie.*)

ARCHIE: I won't forget the manner in which you have lifted that rifle to your shoulder, young man. And you won't forget it, either.

JUDGE: (*growing angry*) Stop him, Guard!

ROSE: (*standing in the line of fire*) No! He doesn't know what he's saying! He's a father! He's lost his senses!

ARCHIE: Stand aside, girl!

JUDGE: Take her aside, please, Bailiff! (*The* BAILIFF *tries to take* ROSE *aside but* SHE *will not be moved.*)

ROSE: No! You can't take me aside! He's my father! He's a good man! You can't kill him! (MAY FOLEY *comes in lugging two shopping bags loaded with groceries.*)

MAY: Now, what the devil is this, dearies? I've brought all sorts of goodies for a feast, and more's on its way, but what's all the excitement about? (SHE *notices the boy*) Now, there's a boy you *know* is going to be a great man some day. (SHE *plunks the bags down and picks up the boy*) There you are, dearie. You're not alone at all in the world, for every woman who's still half a woman is your own dear mother, so you needn't look at everything with such dark sorrowful eyes. Why, I'll make you cookies, I believe. I'll learn *how*. I'll read a recipe, if it's cookies your blessed little heart desires. Is it cookies you want?

BOY: I don't want anything.

MAY: Now, who is it's annoyed the boy to make him reject everything so bitterly? I'll slap the face of anybody who's twisted the love in this boy around to hatred. (*The* GOVERNMENT MAN *comes in.*)

JUDGE: (*with controlled rage*) Mrs. Crookshank, will you please put the Accused down in his proper place?

MAY: The Accused? This boy? Ah, you make me sick. His proper place, did you say? His proper place is right here on my bosom, with all the distractions of the beads I'm wearing and the scent of the perfume of a woman who *is* a woman. It was not so long ago I had three handsome boys of my own, though they weren't the man this fellow is. If he hates, you know damned well he's got reason to hate. I'll put him down in his proper place, I will. I'll be his mother, and Archie'll be his father, and I'll put him down upstairs in a home where he'll be loved. As for the rest of you—whatever it is you're doing here—why, stop it! (SHE *turns grandly to go. The* BAILIFF *grabs her*) Stop it, I said! (SHE *hauls off and slaps him across the face.*)

BOY: (*delighted*) Do it again!

MAY: Just let him lay another hand on me and I'll do it again, dearie. (SHE *goes off grandly, up the stairs, and slams a door.* EVERYBODY'S *mouth is open with amazement, including* ARCHIE'S. *The* GOVERNMENT MAN *strolls through the silent crowd to the end of the bar,* EVERYBODY'S *eyes on him.* HE *pours himself a drink and tosses it down.*)

GOVERNMENT MAN: I have come with a new directive. You will all be good enough to close your mouths and return to your places.

The wrath of a mother should by now no longer astonish us. (HE *brings a document from his pocket, opens it, and studies it a moment.* HE *notices the* GUARD *with the rifle still pointed at* ARCHIE) My dear fellow, will you please put that rifle down, or press the trigger? (*The* GUARD *puts the rifle down with relief.*)

JUDGE: It was necessary to order the Guard to stop Mr. Crookshank. He was inciting to riot, but the Guard disobeyed his orders.

GUARD: The boy is my son. I was afraid to speak up for him myself. You can't expect me to shoot a man who *wasn't* afraid. Yes, my son does hate me, and he hates his mother, too, but he didn't *always* hate us. It's just these past nine months.

JUDGE: The nine months of the Republic, is that what you mean? Do you realize what you're saying?

GUARD: Yes, the nine months of the Republic. Yes, I realize what I'm saying.

JUDGE: (*to the Government Man who has poured another drink and has lifted it to his lips*) It is Mr. Crookshank who is responsible for the present situation.

GUARD: It is *not* Mr. Crookshank. It's my son.

GOVERNMENT MAN: (*tossing down his drink*) That's two, Mr. Crookshank. Will you enter it on Form 333, please? (HE *looks at the Judge*) I will ask everyone here to keep his big mouth shut while I open my own to read the new directive. (HE READS) To the Servants of the People of the Republic. Instantly upon the reading of this directive, its terms will be put into effect, to the letter. Every Court of Justice, including Judge, Bailiff, Attorney for the People, Attorney for the Accused, and Court Guards will *exchange places* with the six Accused next in line for trial. The first of the Accused will take his place as Judge, the second as Bailiff, the third, fourth, fifth and sixth as Attorney for the People, Attorney for the Accused, and Court Guards respectively. And in that order will the members of the previous Court stand trial. That is all.

GUARD-FATHER: That's O.K. by me. I'd like to embrace my son once again before I'm shot, that's all.

JUDGE: I don't understand.

GOVERMENT MAN: It's not necessary for you to understand. I don't understand any too well myself, and I expect the worst for *myself*—(HE *tosses down another drink*)—that's three, Mr. Crookshank. But that's the directive.

JUDGE: Who is responsible for the directive, may I ask?

GOVERNMENT MAN: You may ask, and I may answer. The directive is from the same source which has issued all of the directives during the nine months of the life of the Republic. I did not question the right of the source to send forth any previous directive. I cannot question its right to send forth this one, and I doubt if you can, either.

JUDGE: But I have served the Republic faithfully, holding high at all times the deep and mysterious interests of the people.

GOVERNMENT MAN: No doubt, and it has been much the same with myself, though I now wish I might have been a saloon-keeper. You and I will both continue to hold high—at *this* time—the same deep and mysterious interests of the people, as set forth in this latest directive. You will take the place of the Accused. (*The* JUDGE *moves around the bar to where Archie has been standing, and stands there*) Bailiff, read off the names of the next six Accused, and let us follow the instructions.

BAILIFF: (*examining papers*) Stephen Lockhead.

GOVERNMENT MAN: Stephen Lockhead, please. (STEPHEN LOCKHEAD is a man of about fifty with a dejected countenance.)

STEPHEN: If it's all the same to you, let's skip the baloney, give me the free drink and the free cigarette, and take me out to the empty lot and shoot me, the way you shot all the others.

GOVERNMENT MAN: Stand there behind the bar, please. You will serve as the Judge of this Court of Justice in the next six cases.

STEPHEN: What about the free drink?

GOVERNMENT MAN: It is not mentioned in the directive, but here. (HE *pours and* STEPHEN *tosses it down.*)

STEPHEN: How about one more? I haven't had a drink in twenty-four hours and I've got the shakes.

GOVERNMENT MAN: Very well. Please keep count, Mr. Crookshank. (HE *pours another and* STEPHEN *tosses it down, too.*)

STEPHEN: Is this where you want me to stand?

GOVERNMENT MAN: Just a little to the right. The second Accused, Bailiff.

BAILIFF: Anthony Beacon. (*The* GUARD *comes in with* BOY *of seventeen or eighteen who might be feeble-minded.*)

GOVERNMENT MAN: Anthony Beacon?

ANTHONY: What?

GOVERNMENT MAN: Are you Anthony Beacon?

ANTHONY: Who?

GOVERNMENT MAN: Stand behind that man at the table there, please.

ANTHONY: What?

GOVERNMENT MAN: (*takes him by the arm gently and places him behind the Bailiff*) He may be deaf. (*He nods to the boy.*)

ANTHONY: (*very swiftly*) What do you want with me? What do you want with me? What do you want with me all the time?

GOVERNMENT MAN: The third Accused, Bailiff.

BAILIFF: Gordon Peecham. (*The* GUARD *brings in a down-in-the-heels intellectual who is smiling contemptuously.* HE *speaks softly.*)

GORDON: Well, I guess I don't even get lunch. I wanted to eat once more. I had forgotten what a strange and wonderful thing it is to eat. I wanted to taste whatever it might be very carefully for the last time. Where do I stand?

GOVERNMENT MAN: There, sir. You will serve as the Attorney for the People.

GORDON: I beg your pardon.

GOVERNMENT MAN: A new directive. I will explain further in a moment.

GORDON: One question, if I may. Am I apt to have lunch, after all?

GOVERNMENT MAN: Yes. Bailiff, the fourth Accused, please.

BAILIFF: Dora Livingston. (*The* GUARD *brings in a woman of twenty-five with a harsh, loud voice.*)

DORA: O.K., shoot me! I'm just a plain ordinary tramp who flopped at everything decent, and I hate your guts, every dirty one of you.

GOVERNMENT MAN: Miss Livingston will be the Attorney for the Accused. Will you stand over there, please, Miss Livingston?

DORA: I've had too many jokes played on me already. Lay off me, will you? Just lay off.

GOVERNMENT MAN: Miss Crookshank, will you tell Miss Livingston no one is playing a joke on her.

ROSE: It's a new directive. You are to defend the Accused.

DORA: The hell I am! I'm going to defend nobody! I never was in this bar before in my life, but if anybody here remembers Joey Turner who had Joey's Joint for so many years, he was a friend of mine, and maybe you could let me have a drink on credit.

GOVERNMENT MAN: Of course. (*He pours one, hands it to her,* SHE *tosses it down*) Will you stand over there, please? (SHE *does so*) The fifth Accused, Bailiff, please.

BAILIFF: Samuel Croffit. (*The* GUARD *brings in a very high-strung man of about twenty-two.*)

GOVERNMENT MAN: Samuel Croffit?

SAMUEL: Yeh, That's me. Yeh. I'm Samuel Croffit, and I wish to God I wasn't.

GOVERNMENT MAN: You will be one of the two Court Guards. Guard, hand him your rifle. (*The* FATHER-GUARD *does so*) Stand there, Mr. Croffit. Guard, stand here. (*The* GUARD *goes and stands near the Judge*) The sixth Accused, Mr. Bailiff.

BAILIFF: Leander Lawford. (*The* GUARD *brings in a fat little man of forty-five or so who is in a panic.*

GOVERNMENT MAN: Leander Lawford.

LEANDER: Yes, sir.

GOVERNMENT MAN: You will be the second Court Guard. Guard, hand Mr. Lawford your rifle. (*The* GUARD *does so, and on his own goes and stands beside the other Guard. The* OTHERS *of the deposed Court go and stand behind the Guards.*)

NEW JUDGE: I'm the Judge. Is that it?

GOVERNMENT MAN: Yes, you are.

NEW BAILIFF: What am I? What am I? What do you want with me all the time?

GOVERNMENT MAN: You are the new Bailiff.

NEW BAILIFF: What?

GOVERNMENT MAN: I will continue reading from the directive. Your attention, please. (HE *reads*) When the New Court is established and the Accused stand where the Accusers stood, the first Accused, formerly the Accuser, will stand trial. His crime against the people will be the same as the crime of his counterpart. (*To the New Attorney for the People*) Will you read the accusation?

NEW ATTORNEY FOR THE PEOPLE: Stephen Lockhead. Age fifty. Divorced. Three children. Profession, actor. Long history of alcoholism and social irresponsibility. Publicly cursed Republic, ridiculed its achievements, and spit in the eye of a high servant of the people.

OLD JUDGE: Am I to stand trial on *these* accusations?

GOVERNMENT MAN: You are. Proceed. Attorney for the People. Your duty, I'm sure you understand, is to impress the court with the guilt of the Accused.

NEW PEOPLE'S ATTORNEY: I understand. That may very well be my duty to the Republic, and I would be a fool not to do my duty,

I suppose, but my duty to myself still comes first. I have no doubt that the accused, like myself, is not a good man, certainly not a *truly* good one. Even so, I do not believe any Republic can punish any individual. It can stop a man's life, which I do not feel improves matters for the people, although it may be of use to the machinery of the Republic. Rather than try this man on the basis of accusations which do not apply to him specifically, I place the entire matter in his own hands. He knows himself best, he will do my work for me, and the people's work for them.

GOVERNMENT MAN: Quite in order.

NEW PEOPLE'S ATTORNEY: You are on trial for your life. Make the most of it.

OLD JUDGE: I was charitable to no Accused. I insisted on speed in the trials and in the executions. Had I permitted a great deal of time to be taken, had we sought to trace to its source the *reason* for any Accused's crime, the Accused would still have been executed. I therefore will not blame anybody or any circumstance for my present position. I am here in the place of the Accused. It must follow that I shall be executed. I am now, for being where I am, not only useless to the people, but dangerous to them. I must be put to an end.

GOVERNMENT MAN: I had imagined you would put up a fight.

OLD JUDGE: No. I never did. I can't now. I am ready.

NEW JUDGE: Whether the Accused likes it or not, his trial will proceed, and at the proper time I will pass judgment on him. Attorney for the Accused, please defend him.

DORA LIVINGSTON: (*new Attorney for the Accused*) Who? Me?

NEW JUDGE: Yes. Defend the Accused.

ATTORNEY FOR ACCUSED: To hell with the bum. He's guilty, like he says.

NEW JUDGE: Guilty of what?

ATTORNEY FOR ACCUSED: Guilty of *what*? Didn't we have all the others shot? That's what he's guilty of.

NEW JUDGE: He was acting on behalf of the Republic, on behalf of the people. The Republic is not on trial, the people are not on trial, *he* is. He did his duty.

ATTORNEY FOR ACCUSED: To hell with his duty. I say kill the dirty son of a bitch for killing all the others.

NEW JUDGE: Very good. Then the responsibility to pass judgment on the Accused must now rest solely on me. I must ask the Accused several questions. First do you want to live?

OLD JUDGE: I would *prefer* to.

NEW JUDGE: Why?

OLD JUDGE: I have a son in the Navy who's been away eight months. I would like to see him again. I have a married daughter who is to become a mother in several months. I would like to see my grandchild. I have a brother who has been farming in the west whom I have not seen in more than twenty years. He was to visit me next spring. I looked forward to seeing him again. There are many other similar reasons, but that's too bad, isn't it?

NEW JUDGE: You have been in the Republic from the beginning?

OLD JUDGE: I was for many years in the underground which *established* the Republic nine months ago.

NEW JUDGE: Why were you in the underground?

OLD JUDGE: It's a long story. To sum it up, in the old Government I was an underpaid clerk. In the Republic I was a Judge. I am guilty. There is no need to waste any more time.

NEW JUDGE: If you were to be set free, how would you live the rest of your life?

OLD JUDGE: The same as ever.

NEW JUDGE: You would become a Judge again?

OLD JUDGE: I would *try*.

NEW JUDGE: Why?

OLD JUDGE: I don't know.

NEW JUDGE: If you were now passing judgment on me, what would the situation be?

OLD JUDGE: You would have been executed long ago. Make your decision. You have no choice but to put me to death. Your conscience need never bother you.

NEW JUDGE: I will pass judgment. (*Slight pause*) I find the accused guilty—

DORA: God damn right he's guilty!

NEW JUDGE: —guilty of being alive, which is the guilt of all of the people, without exception. This is a guilt that cannot be dispelled by measures of external correction or punishment, consequently the decision of the Court will apply to all six of the Accused. I sentence them to live. (*To the Government Man*) What do I do now?

GOVERNMENT MAN: Are you satisfied that the six Accused have been tried?

NEW JUDGE: Yes. They're free to go and live and die. What about me and these others?

GOVERNMENT MAN: I must refer to the directive. (*He does so*) Your attention, please. I read from the directive. Immediately after the trials of the members of the Court of Justice by the six Accused, there will be a recess of two hours, after which the Court of Justice will be re-established on its original basis. If any of the original members of the Court of Justice have not been executed they will return to their places, otherwise their counterparts will remain in their places. (*To everybody*) Do you understand?

DORA: Ah, you dirty son of a bitch! Now we'll get it, just because you let them all go.

GOVERNMENT MAN: That is correct. I continue from the directive. The Six Accused which served as the Court of Justice, with the exceptions hereinbefore noted, will, after the recess, stand trial, by turn.

NEW JUDGE: Well, I guess I cooked my goose—and yours, too, Miss. I'm sorry. If it's recess, perhaps we'd better have a drink, at any rate.

SCENE 2

It is five minutes to five. LEANDER LAWFORD, *the fat man, is standing in the place of the Accused.*

JUDGE: Is there anything you wish to say?

LEANDER: I don't want to be shot.

JUDGE: That's understandable.

LEANDER: All I did was buy more food than I am allowed, but I eat more than most people. That's nothing to kill a man for.

JUDGE: The Court is familiar with the facts of the crime you have committed against the people.

LEANDER: When *we* judged you, we let all six of you go free. You've killed the other five. Why can't you let me go free?

JUDGE: The results of what I shall call the Experimental Trial only prove once again the profound wisdom of the people, by whose wisdom, I may point out, I have been restored to my proper post of service. Had the results been of another order, the wisdom of the people would have been repudiated, and it might very well have followed that the conduct of human affairs would have deteriorated to a military dictatorship. Guards. (*The* GUARDS *push the fat man before them.*)

LEANDER: It's not fair! You talk with words that don't mean anything! You don't talk like a human being, you talk like a machine! It's not fair! It's not fair!

JUDGE: Two matters must be resolved by the Court before adjournment. First, the matter of Mr. Crookshank inciting to riot. Second, the matter of the Accused who impelled Mr. Crookshank's criminal act.

VOICE: Guards of the Republic, for the people!

CHORUS OF VOICES: For the people! (*A* volley of shots. *The* COURT GUARDS *return and take their places.*)

JUDGE: Bailiff, you will prepare a report on Mr. Crookshank's criminal act and hand it this evening to the Chief of the Department of Internal Security for immediate action. That disposes of the first matter for the time being. Now, the second matter. The Accused whose trial was interrupted by Mr. Crookshank—what is his name, Bailiff?

BAILIFF: John Delamere.

JUDGE: At the present time where is the Accused?

BAILIFF: Upstairs.

JUDGE: Ask the Court Guards, Bailiff, to bring the Accused to trial.

BAILIFF: Court Guards, you are ordered to go upstairs and bring Accused John Delamere to trial.

FATHER-GUARD: John Delamere is my son. I have been a poor father, but I will not drag him down here. My life has been spared once today. (HE *and the* GUARD *beside him lift their rifles to their shoulders*) The Guard beside me is my brother. He and I will shoot any man here who harms my son. We know this act is a crime. We have agreed to pay for it with our lives, but my son must live.

JUDGE: Put down those rifles, both of you, immediately!

BROTHER-GUARD: My brother is a father, and so he is more patient than I am. His son John Delamere will be pronounced innocent by you, the Bailiff will put John Delamere's papers in order, and John Delamere will remain alive—somewhere in this world.

JUDGE: Bailiff, I order you to go upstairs and bring the Accused to trial. (*The* BAILIFF *does not move or speak.*)

BROTHER-GUARD: You will say that John Delamere is innocent—you will say it now—or by God—

JUDGE: (*shouting*) The Accused will be tried precisely as all of the other Accused have been tried! (HE *is looking straight at the Guards.* ARCHIE *walks up behind him, slugs him with a blackjack, the* JUDGE *falls limp,* ARCHIE *catches him, sets him down behind the bar out of sight.*)

ARCHIE: Now, look here, all of you! We're all in the same boat. The Judge is unconscious and will remain unconscious for some time, but he is still alive. We stood by when grown men and women, no more guilty than any of us, were brought to trial and murdered. Each of us participated in these murders by not protesting by word or act, and so we are all of us murderers. But when a child was brought before us, we were unable to protest. We protested. We are protesting now, and we are doomed. (*To the* GOVERNMENT MAN, *who is holding a shot of brandy to his lips*) Is that right?

GOVERNMENT MAN: Quite right. Quite right, Mr. Crookshank. (HE *tosses the drink down*) And that's the ninth for me, I believe.

ARCHIE: We shall all of us soon be put to death.

GOVERNMENT MAN: Quite right. No one here, myself included, can now escape, not even the unconscious Judge, for having permitted such a circumstance as this to arise in a Court of Justice.

ARCHIE: There is no use thinking of ourselves any more. The problem is the child. What are we going to do about the child?

FATHER-GUARD: (*brings his rifle down*) He must escape.

GOVERNMENT MAN: There is no place to escape *to*, my dear fellow. This is the world we live in. A home, restaurant, saloon, Court of Justice. It is my duty to telephone the Chief of the Department of Internal Security and inform him, but I assure you I shall not do so. I shall tell you why, also. It wouldn't do *me* any good. Anyone else here who wishes to do so—whether in the hope of saving himself or because he feels it is his duty to do so—may of course do so. Is there anyone who wishes to telephone? (HE *pours a drink and tosses it down while he waits.* NOBODY *speaks up*) Then, that's settled. (HE *goes to the door leading to the parking lot and shouts out*) Court is Adjourned! You may return to your stations, as ordered! (HE *comes back into the saloon, walks to the front door, and shouts out*) Court is Adjourned! You may return to your stations, as ordered! (HE *comes back to his place at the end of the bar, studies the bottle of brandy, smiling*) Then, it's here we are for the rest of our lives, in Mr. Crookshank's world. Under the circumstances I know of no better world in which to spend our last hours.

BAILIFF: How much time do we have?

GOVERNMENT MAN: This night and some of tomorrow's day, I should say.

ATTORNEY FOR PEOPLE: Well, I plan to drink, Mr. Crookshank, and so here's my money in advance. It's all I have.

ARCHIE: The drinks are on the house. The food is on the house. The shelter is on the house. That is, if anybody wants to stay.

ATTORNEY FOR ACCUSED: Everybody's *got* to stay.

ARCHIE: Not here, they don't. This is no prison.

ATTORNEY FOR ACCUSED: Anybody who left here might report us to the Department of Internal Security. We'd be taking an awful chance if we let anybody get out of here. We'd lose the freedom of these last few hours of our lives.

ARCHIE: Quite so, but this is my place of business, and I am in charge here. Anybody who wishes to go—even to report us to the Department—is free to go. At any time.

ATTORNEY FOR ACCUSED: But *why*, Mr. Crookshank?

ARCHIE: Why? Because I want my daughter to go.

ROSE: I don't want to go, Archie.

ARCHIE: This is our last night. It doesn't need to be yours, too. There's no telling what'll happen tomorrow.

ROSE: I want to stay, Archie. I have no place to go. I'm scared. I want to sit down at one of the tables and drink, that's all, Archie.

ARCHIE: Before we begin to spend our last hours the best way we know how, before we begin to eat and drink, anybody who wishes to leave *now* may do so, and everybody must know that he may leave at any time, without explanation or farewell. That is how I have always run my joint, and that is how I shall run it tonight, too. (MAY FOLEY *comes down the steps holding the hand of* JOHN DELAMERE.)

MAY: He doesn't hate his mother and father at all. (FATHER-GUARD

kneels, holds his arms open to the boy. The BOY *runs to him,*
HE *picks the boy up,* THEY *press their faces together, smiling.*)

FATHER: (*to May*) Thank you very much, Mrs. Crookshank.

MAY: Ah, he's a darling boy, and awful bright, and good. It's terrible, almost, how good he is—when you know in your heart
how he's going to have to change and be like all the rest of us.
When he took his nap, I cried the whole time.

FATHER: (*to the* BOY, *who has been whispering in his ear*) What? Say
it again. (*The* BOY *whispers again. The* FATHER *turns to May
and Archie*) He'd like to go home. He'd like to see his mother.

MAY: Well, now, what are you so downhearted about *that* for? Of
course he wants to go home. Of course he wants to see his
mother.

FATHER: I *can't* go home. I can't go home again.

MAY: What's he talking about, Archie?

ARCHIE: We're in trouble, May. We're all in trouble.

MAY: Ah, take the boy home to his mother, man. If a man's in
trouble, his wife had better be in trouble with him, and his son,
too.

FATHER: I'd *like* to take him home. I don't know what else to do for
him, or for anybody else.

ARCHIE: Take him home, man. There's nothing else to do.

FATHER: Is it all right with everybody?

MAY: Will you go on home now, and the three of you have a nice
dinner?

FATHER: Well, I wish you knew what this means to me, Mr. Crookshank. I wish I could tell you what it's going to mean to his
mother. Well. Goodbye. (HE *turns and goes.* HE *stops at the
door.*)

BOY: Goodbye, May Foley!

MAY: Goodbye, John Delamere! (HE *runs to her, gives her a big hug,
then runs back to his father, the* MAN *waves,* EVERYBODY *waves
back, and* THEY *go.*) A darling boy, and so good it's almost terrible, God have mercy on his soul. Well, give me a drink, dearies,
will you?

THE END

THE ADVENTURES
OF WESLEY JACKSON

CHAPTER 1 *Wesley Sings Valencia and Gets an Important Letter*

My name is Wesley Jackson, I'm nineteen years old, and my favorite song is *Valencia*. I guess everybody in the world gets himself a favorite song sometime or other. I know I've got mine because I keep singing it or hearing it all the time, even in my sleep. I like the way the fellow hollers at the top of his voice:

> *Valencia!*
> *In my dreams*
> *It always seems*
> *I hear you softly calling me!*
> *Valencia!*
> *Dat tarrata*
> *Dat tarrata*
> *Dat tarrata, dat ta ta!*

You can't get away from songs in this world because there's always some kind of trouble going on in everybody and trouble goes with singing. My pal Harry Cook sings *If I had my way, dear, you'd never grow old*. He sings it to people he doesn't like, and he means if he had his way they'd be dead, he doesn't mean he wants them to stay young forever. At the same time he sings the song as if he meant it the way the writer of the song meant it—as if he were singing it to his bride and was broken-hearted because he couldn't keep her young and pretty forever. But the man Harry's sore at knows what Harry means, only he can't do anything about it because it's a clean song and nobody could ever prove that Harry wasn't singing it to the girl who is going to be his bride some day. There's no law against singing to your sweetheart.

Nick Cully sings:

O Lord, you know I have no friend like you—
If Heaven's not my home, O Lord, what will I do?
Angels beckon me to Heaven's open door
And I can't feel at home in this world any more.

Nick sings his song two ways too—serious and kidding. From the way Nick sings you know he means, "I don't like this life," but at the same time you know he also means, "I don't like it, but I want to keep it, so if I've *got* to go, for God's sake, let me go to a better place than this place—let me go to Heaven." You know Nick's homesick for some kind of impossible life, and you know he's making fun of his homesickness. Every time I hear Nick sing that song or remember his singing it, I get so sad I wish I was somebody else instead of who I am. I wish I was a Chinaman or an Eskimo or anything except what I am—an American born in San Francisco whose mother came from Dublin, whose father came from London, met in San Francisco, fell in love, got married and had two sons, myself and my brother Virgil. I get sick of my life when I hear Nick Cully asking the Lord what will he do if Heaven isn't his home, either.

Everybody I know has a song that he remembers from somewhere, that means something special to him. I like to wonder what kind of songs famous men sing to themselves when nobody's around. What a man sings in church is one thing and what he sings when he's alone is another.

So far you know my name, my age, and my favorite song, but you don't know the most important thing about me there is to know: I'm ugly. I'm not a *little* ugly like some fellows. I'm *all* ugly. Why this is so I don't know, but it's so and that's the end of it. Every time I go to shave I get a surprise. I can't believe *anybody* could be so ugly, but there he is right in front of my own eyes, and it's *me!* It's Wesley Jackson (39, 339, 993), it's not somebody else. I didn't know how ugly I was until I started to shave three years ago and had to look at myself every two or three days, and that's what I've got against shaving. I don't mind doing it, I don't mind trying to get neat, but I've got to look at myself when I shave and what I see makes me so sick I don't even bother to wish I was an Eskimo, I wish I was dead.

On account of this I took it into my head three years ago to stay out of sight as much as possible. I took long walks and read a lot of books. Walking gets you to thinking and reading puts you in touch with the thoughts of other men—most of them ugly men too, most likely. After you walk a lot and read a lot and think a lot you get to talking to yourself, only it isn't exactly to *yourself*, it's to the fellows you came to meet in the books. Pretty soon you get a hankering to talk to somebody alive, but when you go to do it, well, they don't know what you're talking about because they haven't been reading the books you've been reading or thinking the things you've been thinking, and chances are they think you're crazy. Maybe you are, but who knows who's crazy and who isn't? I wouldn't take it upon myself to say any man was crazy. I might be mistaken.

Next, you go to thinking you ought to write a letter to somebody, and that's what I did. I mean I *thought* I ought to write a letter, only I didn't know who to send it to. Mom had been separated from Pop most of my life, and I'd gotten out of touch with her.

As for Pop—hell, I didn't know where Pop was. As for my brother Virgil—what could you tell a fellow only thirteen years old even if you knew him, which I didn't? If I wrote to the President, wouldn't *he* be surprised?

I didn't know anybody else well enough to write to, so at last I wrote to Mrs. Fawkes who used to teach Sunday School in San Francisco.

Pop made me go to Sunday School because he claimed he'd lost the way to the good life and was afraid I'd lose it too if I didn't get a little assistance from somebody. He said it was up to me to find the way for the two of us, but hell, *Pop* was the drunkard, not me. *He* should have gone to Sunday School.

I wrote to Mrs. Fawkes a long letter and told her some of the things that had happened to me since I had seen her last which was nine years ago. I didn't think she would remember me, but it seemed to me I ought to write to somebody, so I wrote to her. What's the use being in the Army if you don't write a letter once in a while and get one back once in a while? If Mrs. Fawkes wrote back, O.K. If she didn't, O.K.

One night about a month after I had sent my letter to Mrs. Fawkes there was a big commotion at Mail Call because there was a letter for me. Vernon Higbee started the fuss. Instead of throwing the letter to me the way he did for everybody else, he said he wanted to present it to me officially. The boys liked the idea of making it official and I didn't mind particularly, so when they made a path for

me to the platform, I walked down the path and up onto the platform beside Vernon, the way they expected me to do it. I knew
they wanted to have a little fun and when a lot of fellows in the
Army want to have a little fun the best thing to do is let them, because if you don't, they have *more* fun, and you don't have any at
all. But if you let them, then you have a little fun yourself. If people laugh at you, who are they laughing at? I laugh at myself, why
shouldn't a lot of fellows in the Army laugh at me too? Everybody
learns to laugh at himself after the age of eighteen, I guess.

Well, when I got up onto the platform beside Vernon everybody
was laughing and having fun, so Vernon stretched his arm out the
way public speakers do who've got control over their audience.

"Quiet, everybody!" he said. "This is the most important occasion
of my career as Mail Clerk of Company B. I have the honor to announce that a letter has come through the American Postal System
—and I have the further and greater honor to announce that this
letter is addressed to Private Wesley Jackson. Three cheers for Private Jackson please."

The fellows cheered and I kept wondering what Mrs. Fawkes had
to say in the letter. At the same time I kept hearing the fellow hollering *Valencia*.

After the cheers somebody said, "Who's the letter from?" And
somebody else said, "Don't tell us even Wesley's got a girl."

But I didn't care.

"One thing at a time please," Vernon Higbee said. "With Private Jackson's kind permission I will tell you who the letter is from.
As to the matter of whether or not Private Jackson has a girl, the
affirmative or the negative of that circumstance is not involved in
this ceremony which is official. The letter I hold in my hand, which
is the private property of Private Jackson, is very clearly addressed to
him by title, which is Private, by name which is Wesley Jackson,
and by Army Serial Number, which is 39, 339,993—all in accordance
with Army Regulations. Three cheers for Army Regulations."

The fellows cheered the Army Regulations, and then Vernon
said, "Now. Who is the letter from? The letter is from the Seventh
Avenue Presbyterian Church of San Francisco." Here Vernon turned
to me.

"Private Jackson," he said, "I take great pleasure in presenting to
you on behalf of the Nation this letter which has come to you from

the Seventh Avenue Presbyterian Church of San Francisco, a city close to my heart, only nine miles across the bay from my own home in San Leandro, and almost two hundred miles from this Army Post."

Vernon clicked his heels and came to attention. For some reason every one of the fellows standing around waiting for their own mail, about a hundred of them, did the same thing. They didn't follow Vernon's *example*, they clicked their heels and came to attention *with* him, the way a flock of sparrows will fly from a telegraph wire together. It was a game, but I didn't mind at all. I even liked it a little because I never saw those fellows so smart before, not even on parade. If it's for fun, a fellow can do almost anything in a smart way. Besides, Mrs. Fawkes had answered my letter and pretty soon I'd be reading it.

Vernon bowed, handed me my letter, and everybody roared with a kind of laughter you don't hear anywhere except in the Army, or maybe in a penitentiary. I could still hear them laughing as I ran to the woods I used to go to when I was at that Post. When I got to the woods I sat down under a tree and put the letter on the ground in front of me and looked at it.

It was the first letter I had ever gotten in my life, and my name and everything was typed out on the envelope, *oh Valencia!*

After a while I opened the envelope to see what Mrs. Fawkes had to say, but the letter wasn't from Mrs. Fawkes, it was from the preacher of the church. He said he was sorry to tell me that Mrs. Fawkes was dead. She had passed on in her sleep three months ago, aged 71. He said he had taken the liberty of opening my letter, and he said he had read it a half dozen times. I was a fine Christian young man (which was something I never knew until he told me and something Pop would be glad to hear). He said he was going to pray for me and he told me to pray too—but he didn't tell me to pray for *him*. He said a lot of other things that I read while the tears came out of my eyes because Mrs. Fawkes was dead, and then he said, "There is one thing I have decided after careful consideration to tell you, which I hope you will have the courage to accept with dignity and resignation: *You are a writer.* I have been writing for the better part of forty years, and I must say that even though my work has not gone altogether unheeded (I published a small inspirational book fifteen years ago at my own expense called *Smiling Through in Spite of the Tears* which Reverend R. J. Featherwell of Sausalito,

California, used as the subject of a sermon in which he said, 'Here is a book the world has long been waiting for—a book whose gentle light a dark and evil world stands very much in need of')—even though, as I say, my work has not gone altogether unheeded, I must tell you that your writing is better than mine, therefore you must write. Write, my boy!"

Well, I thought the man must be foolish, but after a while I found myself taking his advice, and that's how it happens that I am writing this story which is about myself mainly, since I don't know anybody else very well, but about others too as far as I know them.

I was pretty careful of my language in my letter to Mrs. Fawkes— and my thoughts too, I guess—but I don't have to be careful any more and I mean to say what I think is right at the time, no matter what it comes to.

CHAPTER 2 *Wesley Explains What the Army Does to a Fellow, Says Something He Thinks Is Right, and Can't Sleep*

I said the letter I got from the preacher in answer to my letter to Mrs. Fawkes was the only letter I ever got in my life, but that isn't quite the truth, although it's not a lie either. I got a letter from the President once, but I don't think he knew very much about it, so I didn't count it. It wasn't personal anyway. It didn't seem sincere either. I read the word *Greetings* and wondered why it wasn't *Goodbye*, considering it meant I was going to be in the Army very soon. I'd heard that if you could breathe, the Army wanted you, and I used to breathe just fine. I'd heard a lot of other things about the Army, some of them funny and some of them dirty, but all they ever came to was that I'd soon be in uniform because I had no criminal record, I wasn't insane, I didn't have a weak heart, my blood pressure was fine, and I had all the fingers and toes and eyes and ears and different things I was born with, all of them O.K. It seemed as if I had been cut out to be a soldier all the time and was only hanging around the Beach and the Public Library in San Francisco waiting for the declaration of War. All the same, I wasn't raring to go. I was raring *not* to go.

One or two times I thought I'd hide away in the hills somewhere and wait for the War to end. One time I even got the stuff I'd need for a life like that and tied it up into a bundle and took a street-car as far out of town as I could go. I got out on the Great Highway and a fellow gave me a ride sixty miles south to Gilroy, but when I looked around I was still in the same country and everybody was still excited about the War. Everybody seemed sick with the excitement, and the excitement seemed obscene. I bought a hamburger and a cup of coffee, and then I hitch-hiked home. I didn't tell a soul what I'd done. I didn't even mention how I'd looked over my shoulder at the Coast Range Mountains where I thought I'd go to live during the War and felt so lonely and helpless and ignorant and cheap and disgraceful that I began to to hate the whole world, which is something I don't like to do because the world is people and people are too pathetic to hate. I just moved along with everybody else, and when the time came I went down to 444 Market Street and got took into the Army.

But that's all ancient history now, and I don't propose to fool with any ancient history in this story. Some day this whole War is going to be ancient history and I am going to want to know what the consensus of opinion is going to be about it then. I am going to want to be interested in the outcome. I wouldn't be a bit surprised if this War turned out to be the turning point, as they say on the radio. The trouble is if you think about a turning point three or four minutes you come to the conclusion that there is nothing in the world that *isn't* a turning point, and the only thing that's important about a turning point is what it's a turning point from, and what it's a turning point to. If it's a turning point from nothing to nothing, what good is it? Maybe it might have been ignored even, although I can't see how anybody who isn't lame or mad can ignore a War, considering the mail he gets and the complications that come into his life once he's opened the mail and looked at it.

I remember before the War started that nobody in the whole country knew I was alive or cared much one way or the other. Nobody invited me to pitch in and help solve the problems of peace. And yet I was always the same fellow and always in need of a little ready cash. That's why the big-family spirit that comes over a whole country when there's a War makes me a little suspicious of the people who throw the party because it seems to me they are always smiling and full of hope and too quick to be heroic, whereas the fellows in uniform are confused and miserable most of the time and only begin to smile when there's nothing else to do, and are never terribly hopeful because they don't know very much about what's going on or what it means or what the outcome is likely to be—for themselves, I mean—and never in a hurry to be heroic because with a little bad luck they might be both heroic and dead. And when a fellow knows a thing like that he can't enjoy a party with all his heart and soul. Henry Rhodes used to say when he and I were at the Reception Center together for the first few days of our life in the Army, "This is the bum's rush, Jackson, and you and I are a couple of the bums."

Henry Rhodes was a Certified Public Accountant who worked in an office on Montgomery Street in San Francisco until he was drafted. He was no kid. He was forty-three years old, but in those days they took them all.

I said I was going to say whatever I think is right, no matter what it is. Well, the time has come for me to say something that I think is right, but here I am scared to death to say it. *I'm* scared because I'm in the Army, but what the hell's scaring the people who aren't in the Army? The minute a War starts everybody seems to forget everything he ever knew—everything that's worth a hoot—and shuts his mouth and keeps it shut and just groans with agony about the lies he hears all over the place all the time.

From the beginning they scare you to death in the Army. They begin scaring you with the *Articles of War*. They don't mean to be human about any of the difficulties a fellow is apt to get into, they just naturally threaten to kill you, that's all. They tell you so while you're lifting your arm to take the oath. They tell you before your arm is down, before you're *in* the Army, "—the punishment is Death." They are your own family, the same people who tell you so many other things, so many of them so confusing after you've been told what the punishment is. Of course they hardly ever have to give a fellow that punishment, but the word Death is forever after hanging around in the whole idea of Army law and order, and pretty soon it seeps down into every little irritating rule it's possible for a fellow to break, so that if he goes to get a drink of water in the afternoon they call it Absent Without Leave, which is very serious, and for which the punishment, although called Extra Duty, is actually Death. Or if he lets the tap water run while he's washing instead of filling the basin, again the punishment is Extra Duty, but that's just another term for Murder as far as I'm concerned. You get six or seven months of that kind of law and order and if you aren't scared to death, or full of confusion and anger, you're a better man than I am because even though I'm easy-going about all things, and by rights shouldn't be scared or confused or angry, I am scared, I am confused, I am angry. I don't like it, but I just can't help it.

Anyway, I was talking about Henry Rhodes and the thing I felt I ought to say about him because I felt it was right but was afraid to say because I am in the Army was this: Henry Rhodes was sore at the government for drafting him into the Army.

I was afraid to say a little thing like that.

I'm ashamed of myself.

I can't sleep from thinking about these things, but sometimes when I can't sleep it's on account of the noise the fellows make in the barracks all night, talking, telling dirty stories, singing, or playing games on each other, like the game Dominic Tosca and Lou Marriacci play on Dominic's brother Victor who sleeps in the bunk between them.

As soon as Victor falls asleep Dominic on one side and Lou on the other start whispering in his ear: "I don't want to be in the Army. Why did this happen to me? I was minding my own business. I don't want to be a soldier. I don't want to kill anybody. I want to go home. I don't want to die." They whisper louder and louder until poor Victor wakes up and says, "Ah cut it out, will you? I'm going to tell Mama on you Dominic." All the fellows in the barracks roar with laughter, even me, and I don't think it's funny at all.

CHAPTER 3 *Jim Kirby of the U. P. Teaches Harry Cook and Wesley the Art of War and Sends Them Flying to the North*

I think Harry Cook's a funny fellow, though.

One evening I was sitting on the pile of timber in front of our barracks reading around in a book I'd found in town called *The Art of*

War, and Harry was over at the other end of the pile of timber lying on his back. The timber was a good place to sit or stretch out, but what it was for nobody ever knew. From the color it had turned you could see it had been there a long time. Well, Harry kept saying just loud enough for me to hear, "Private Cook reporting as ordered, sir. You can take the Army, Colonel, and I think you know what you can do with it."

So after a while I said:

"Who you talking to?"

"I'm talking to the Colonel," Harry said. "The son of a bitch."

"*What?*"

"You heard me."

"You can get court-martialed for that."

"You heard me," Harry said again.

"What have you got against the Colonel?"

"He used to be the credit manager of a department store."

"How do you know?"

"His stenographer told me. She looked it up."

"What did you have to see him for?"

"The Captain sent me."

"Why?"

"The Lieutenant."

"What'd you do?"

"The Sergeant told the Lieutenant I had made derogatory remarks about the Army."

"What'd the Colonel say?"

"Said I ought to be ashamed of myself. Said the only reason he wasn't having me court-martialed was that he didn't want to give the Post a bad name. So I gave him a bad name, and you know what it is."

Harry rolled down onto the next layer of timber, out of sight, so I went back to the book I was reading, but just then I saw a handful of Army men with one civilian among them come around the corner from the Post Exchange, headed straight for the timber. From the way they moved, I could tell they were important. You can tell an officer from a Private from the way he walks. It's not that the officer walks any better than the Private, it's something else. Even from a distance you can see that an officer feels he is being watched, either by superior officers or by the rank and file, and you can see that he thinks he is a pretty important man in this man's world, as he puts it—not as important as a Captain if he's a Lieutenant, but more important than the great majority of men in the Army, or in the world for that matter. I didn't have to see the tin chicken on the shoulder of the Colonel to know he was a big man, I knew it from the way he occupied his space among the other men in the group. He occupied his space a little more importantly than the Major beside him did, and the Major occupied his space a little more importantly than the two Captains beside him occupied theirs. The First Lieutenant was just a little trashy in that company, but the man who was most important of all was the civilian. He was the youngest of the lot too, probably no more than twenty-six or twenty-seven.

I got a little panic-stricken when I saw so many important men because I was out there in the open where I could be seen. I didn't know whether to scramble down from the timber and throw the lot of them a salute, or duck down a layer or two and hide. I didn't like saluting in those days and I didn't like needing to think about it all the time, but nowadays it doesn't bother me at all because I go according to the way I feel. If I see a little old Colonel coming down the street who seems to be lonely and confused, almost as if he were no better than a Private, well, I catch his eye and give him a smart salute and move on down the street. But if I see some rollicking young fool charging up the street, on the verge of changing the history of the world from something sad to something hideous, I just naturally get lost in thought, or turn to look into a shop window, or lift my eyes to the sky, and move past the imbecile. I'll salute if the spirit moves me. I've saluted old beggars, children in the streets, beautiful girls, drunkards hanging onto lampposts, elevator operators in uniform, and all the fellows in the Army I like, regardless of rank, but I didn't like the group coming down the company street, so I ducked down, around, and out of sight. I crawled over to Harry Cook.

"What's the matter with *you*?" Harry said.

"The Colonel," I whispered. "Four other officers and a civilian."

We heard their voices now, and Harry made a face.

"Let's listen to 'em," I said.

But they didn't say anything worth listening to, so I started reading again, and Harry started singing very softly *If I had my way, dear, you'd never grow old*. I knew he was thinking of the Colonel.

The men were very cheery with one another in that special way that Army men have, but at the same time they were very careful too—not so much of what they said as of the tone of voice they permitted themselves to use. Every once in a while I'd hear the Major talking too brilliantly for his rank, and then I'd hear him change his tone of voice out of deference to the Colonel. It was that way with every one of them excepting the Colonel himself and the civilian. The Colonel was quite brilliant for a man who had only recently left the credit department of a big department store, but the stuff he said sounded pretty silly to me. I gathered that the civilian was a newspaperman who'd been sent by his paper to write a series of stories on how men in the Army live. Then I heard him say:

"Colonel Remington, I wonder if I might have a word with one or two of your men—anybody at all."

Then I heard the Colonel say:

"By all means, Jim. Lieutenant Coburn, will you fetch our friend Jim here a couple of our men? Use your own judgment, Lieutenant."

I heard the Lieutenant make the usual reply and hurry away. The men went back to being cheery, but of course not too cheery. Pretty soon the voices got too close to be comfortable and the first thing I knew the whole bunch of them were all the way around the pile of timber, right where they could see Harry Cook and me. Before I could decide what to do, they saw us! Every one of them saw us, but the Colonel especially. Harry pretended that he didn't know they were there and began to sing louder than he needed to in order to sound as if he didn't know somebody was near by. So it was up to me to do the right thing, only I didn't know what the right thing was. I jumped to my feet and discovered that I was standing a little over the heads of the men which made me feel foolish. Even so, I took the book from my right hand, so I'd be free to salute, and I saluted. Everybody excepting the civilian returned the salute, and the Colonel said, "At ease, son," so I knew he wanted to impress the newspaperman. He wanted the newspaperman to get the impression that he was a regular fellow. So, noticing the book, he said, "Catching up on your home-work?"

By this time Harry had stopped singing. He had spent some time looking up at me and then around at the group. He got to his feet, and when it was absolutely silly to do so, he saluted, but he did it as if he had all the time in the world. Well, there was an awful awkward moment there because Harry had saluted so slowly that the automatic reaction that takes place in Army men when they see a smart salute was upset. Nobody moved to return Harry's salute, and Harry wouldn't give in. He just stood there on the timber and held the salute. After a lot of fidgeting the Colonel returned the salute in a very irritated way, and all the other officers followed his example. By now they were all rattled and wished they hadn't run into us, I guess. It was so long since the Colonel had asked me if I was catching up on my home-work I didn't think a reply was in order, so I just stood there too. The newspaperman broke the tension by saying, "Colonel Remington, have I your permission to speak to these men?"

This time the Colonel didn't feel so cheery.

"I want you to speak to any man you please," he said. "Any man at all."

The newspaperman looked at Harry, smiled, and said, "How do you like the Army, Mac?"

Harry didn't smile.

"I don't like it," he said, "and my name's not Mac, it's Harry."

"What's your last name?"

"Cook."

Harry stepped down from the timber. I thought he was going to stand with the newspaperman and the officers and answer some more questions, but without another word he turned and walked away. I guess he went to the Post Exchange or to the movie. So that left me. I could see the Colonel was sore as hell at Harry for saying what he'd said and for doing what he'd done, so I decided to try to improve matters a little—first for Harry, and then for the Colonel himself, because I hate to see a man upset that way, no matter who he is.

"Harry got a letter from his father this afternoon," I said. "His mother's very sick, and his father thinks she's going to die. He's been crying all afternoon."

I got down from the timber as I spoke. I kept my eye on the Colonel to see how he was taking it, and sure enough he was taking it the right way. He was relieved, for one thing, and I got the feeling that he was thankful to me for getting him out of a tough spot. Newspapermen are a nuisance to Army men. They can make a lot of trouble for a Colonel who's bucking for a B.G. Men out of uniform, especially newspapermen, take Colonels and even Generals with a grain of salt—their hero is the little man. The Colonel was smart enough to see that his best chance to keep the good name of the Post, and his own good name, was to be unhappy about Harry's unhappiness. But at the same time I could see how happy he was that Harry's mother was about to die because that meant that Harry didn't really dislike the Army, he didn't like the idea of his mother dying, which was something else again.

"Yes," the Colonel said looking at the newspaperman, "I thought that poor boy was going through some sort of emotional crisis. Major Goldring, will you please see that Private Cook is given a special furlough home? I want that boy to get on the next train out of town and go home for a few days. I want every man on this Post to understand that we—the Commanding Officers—are their friends. Get Private Cook home immediately, Major."

"Yes, sir," the Major said. "I'll attend to everything the first thing in the morning."

"The first thing in the morning be damned!" the Colonel said. "*Now!* Immediately!"

The Colonel turned to me.

"Where is Private Cook's home?" he said.

Well, I knew Harry's home was in the Sunset District of San Francisco, not far from where Pop and I used to live. But I didn't want to make any trouble because I knew there were two or three trains to San Francisco every night. I thought if I told the Colonel where Harry's home was, and the Major got Harry on the next train, pretty soon everybody would find out that Harry's mother wasn't sick at all, and Harry and me would both be in trouble. So I thought I'd say Harry's home was far away—so far away that the Colonel would drop the idea of getting Harry home on the next train and be satisfied to let him go on being unhappy.

"His home's in Alaska, sir," I said. I said that because when I saw the trouble coming I got to wishing I was somebody else instead of who I am, and that made me think of Eskimos, and Eskimos made me think of Alaska.

"Alaska?" the Colonel said.

"Yes, sir," I said. "He's an Alaskan."

I could see the Colonel had a problem on his hands now, and I was ready to believe the whole matter would be dropped and forgotten. Now, if the Lieutenant would only show up with two men his own judgment told him were appropriate for an interview with a newspaperman everything would be fine, and I'd go look for Harry. The Colonel looked over at the newspaperman, and if I ever saw a face you couldn't figure out it was the face of that newspaperman. It was a real honest-to-God poker face. The Colonel smiled at the newspaperman, but the newspaperman didn't change his expression, so the Colonel knew he was still on the spot.

"What city in Alaska?" he said.

"Fairbanks."

"Major Goldring," the Colonel said, "find out what planes are scheduled to go to Fairbanks, and get Private Cook on the next one—give him a special priority, and if he needs any money, attend to it for me personally."

"Yes sir," the Major said and went off.

"Young man," the Colonel said to me, "go find your friend. He's going home."

"Yes, sir," I said and turned to go, but the newspaperman said, "Excuse me—what's that book you have?"

"*The Art of War*," I said. "By Clausewitz."

"May I ask how it happens that you are reading that book?" the newspaperman said.

"The intelligence of the average enlisted man in this Army," the Colonel began to say, but the newspaperman cut him short.

"Sherman said War is hell," the newspaperman said. "Clausewitz says it's an art. What do you think it is?"

"I don't know very much about it," I said.

"What do you think of Clausewitz?"

"He's easy to read."

"What do you think of his ideas?"

"I think they stink."

"What's your name?"

"Wesley Jackson."

The newspaperman wrote my name on a little pad that he got out of his coat pocket. For a while the Colonel had been pleased with me, but when I got to talking freely—even though I didn't mean to—I saw that he didn't like it at all. It seemed to him that this fool newspaperman was going to go to work and write about a Private instead of about *him*.

"Where you from?" the newspaperman said.

"San Francisco."

"What'd you do as a civilian?"

"Nothing."

"Nothing?"

"I spent some time looking for work, I worked once in a while, but most of the time I loafed. My father was in the last War. He got a pension because he'd been wounded, so he and I always had enough to get by on."

"What's your father do?"

"Nothing."

"What's his trade or profession?"

"Hasn't got any. He was at college when he got drafted, but when he came back he didn't feel like studying any more."

"How do you know all that?"

"He told me. We were good pals until this War started."

"What happened then?"

"Well, Pop always liked to drink, but when they started drafting everybody again he didn't do anything *else*. He wouldn't even eat."

"What was your father's injury?"

"Gas, shrapnel, and shock. He's got some metal on the top of his head where some shrapnel almost scalped him."

"Do you like your father?"

"Sure."

"What'd you fight about?"

"We didn't fight. I tried to get him to stop drinking for a while, but he couldn't stop. He wanted to, but he couldn't. He'd go off on a drunk for three or four days, and when I'd ask him where he'd been he wouldn't be able to remember."

"If you didn't fight, how'd you happen to stop being pals?"

"He didn't come back."

"What'd you live on, then?"

"I found myself a Saturday job—three dollars. I lived on that."

"Where's your father now?"

"I don't know."

"Anybody else in the family?"

"My mother and my brother."

"Where are they?"

"They're in El Paso. My mother's brother—my uncle Neal—he's got a farm-implement business in El Paso, and my mother and my brother have been staying with him about ten years now, I guess."

"But you stayed with your father?"

"Yes. We've been together since I was nine."

Well, the newspaperman kept asking questions and I kept answering them, telling the truth every time and feling more and more like a fool, hoping the Lieutenant would show up with the two men who would give the Post a good name instead of the miserable name Harry and I were giving it. But the Lieutenant didn't show up, and my hands kept sweating and I kept wishing I was an Eskimo, and the fellow kept hollering *Valencia!* because that was the song Pop used to sing when Mom first went off to El Paso with my brother Virgil, and Pop and me were dying of loneliness. After Pop and I got over the loneliness, Pop stopped singing *Valencia*, and I forgot all about it, but I remembered it again when Pop didn't come back, and by the time I was in the Army I kept hearing it all the time.

I thought I didn't like the newspaperman, but once we got to talking I could see he was straight, so I got over not liking him. For some reason the Colonel and the other officers just let us go on talking, but I'll be damned if I know why. Maybe they thought it was interesting.

"One more question," the newspaperman said. He looked at the Colonel out of the corner of his eye. Then he said, "How do you like the Army?"

Well, hell there it was. Harry Cook had told him, so now he wanted me to tell him too. If I told him the truth the Colonel would be more unhappy than ever, and if I didn't tell him the truth I'd be a coward. I don't know why I didn't want the Colonel to be unhappy, considering I didn't like him any more than Harry did, but I know I didn't want the Colonel to be unhappy. It just seemed wrong to make the Colonel unhappy. I don't know how to explain this, but it seemed worse for me to make the Colonel unhappy than to be a coward. So then I got to thinking of the things I liked in the Army, but there were so few of them I knew I couldn't make them an excuse for saying I liked it, and the more I thought about it the more confused I got. I got to feeling sick too, but I had to make a decision real soon, so I tried to seem cheerful and earnest at the same time and I said, "I like it fine."

Just then the Lieutenant came up with the two men he'd selected, so I turned to go, but the newspaperman took me by the arm. The Lieutenant introduced the two men he'd selected. They were a couple of fellows who were permanently stationed at that Post. They did office work. I'd seen them around but I didn't know them. The newspaperman asked them how old they were and where they were from and what kind of work their fathers did, but he didn't write down any of the answers they made. The whole atmosphere got nicer and nicer, and the Colonel got to being cheery again, and then the Major came back and said, "There's a plane leaving for a field about a hundred miles from Fairbanks in three hours, sir. I've got Private Cook's furlough, travel orders, and money in this envelope."

I guess I must have looked pretty sick when I heard that, and I guess the newspaperman caught on to how I felt because he turned to the Colonel and said, "A fellow going all that distance on an airplane alone—" He turned to me. "Don't you think you ought to go along with your pal, considering his mother's so sick, and he's so unhappy?"

"I guess so," I said. "I guess I'd like to see Alaska all right."

By this time the two fellows who did office work were feeling cheery too, so one of them said, "Alaska? Who's going to Alaska?"

"Private Cook," the Major said. "We're sending him home. His mother's very sick."

Well, hell, I knew I was in for it now.

"Private Cook?" the office fellow said. "What Private Cook is that?"

"Private *Harry* Cook," the Major said.

Well, that newspaperman, he was O.K.

"Colonel," he said, "I'd like a word with you alone. Don't go anywhere," he said to me.

"By all means," the Colonel said to the newspaperman.

The Colonel and the newspaperman went around to the other side of the pile of timber and the rest of us stayed where we were and kept looking at one another. The two fellows from the offices knew something was fishy, but they didn't want to go too far with what they knew because in the Army they teach you not to go too far with anything no matter how right it is, just in case it might make trouble for somebody higher up because then he might thank you very much for informing him but after a week or two you might find yourself in some God-forsaken part of the country that you don't want to be in at all, so the fellows from the offices didn't say anything more about where Harry Cook's home was, even though they were sure it wasn't in Alaska.

The Major, he knew what was going on too, and every once in a while he'd sneak a look at me. I'd sort of smile at him, but he'd turn away quickly as if to say, "Steady now—don't weaken—don't say anything. The Colonel's in charge here. This is his show. Let's not embarrass the Colonel. He's talking to the newspaperman now. He'll make a decision for himself and give his orders. And we'll carry them out, too."

The two Captains and the Lieutenant, they all got the idea too, so the only thing we could do was stand there and wait. We couldn't talk because if we did we might make a lot of trouble for the Colonel. Well, I wanted to go to Alaska all right, but I wasn't sure Harry Cook wanted to go. I wanted to go anywhere, just so I could get away from the Army for a while. I was fed-up with the Army, and if they flew Harry and me to Alaska that would be just fine because besides the change maybe I'd see an Eskimo at last.

Pretty soon the newspaperman and the Colonel came back. I could see they were on excellent terms now, so I felt pretty sure the newspaperman had promised to write a fine piece about the Colonel and help get him his B.G. Even though neither of them was smiling I knew everything was O.K., no matter where Harry Cook's home was, no matter who knew it.

The Colonel looked his men over, and they all acknowledged that he was Chief. Then he said, "Major Goldring, I want Private Jackson here to go along with Private Cook to Fairbanks, so please attend to the necessary details. Private Jackson will go as a courier." The Colonel turned to me and said, "Go find your friend and tell him the good news. Then I think the two of you had better hurry and pack your duffle bags. Lieutenant Coburn, will you arrange for transportation to the airfield?"

Everybody stood at attention and saluted the Colonel. He returned the salute, and the group broke up. I went straight to the barracks on the chance that Harry might be lying on his bunk, and sure enough he was. He was asleep. I shook him and when he opened his eyes I said, "Get up—you and I are going to Alaska in an airplane in three hours."

Harry said he and I were going to do something that I won't mention here. He turned over to go back to sleep. I was trying to get him to understand that what I was telling him was the truth when the newspaperman came into the barracks.

Lucky for Harry and me the only other fellow in the barracks was Victor Tosca and he was asleep on his bunk away over at the other end of the big room. The newspaperman looked at Harry and said, "I'm sorry I called you Mac. I didn't mean anything by it. How about shaking hands?"

"Sure," Harry said.

"Where's your home?" the newspaperman said, but I didn't care.

"San Francisco," Harry said. "I live in the Sunset District, just below Red Rock Hill."

"How's the family?"

"O.K."

"Any letters from home lately?"

"I got one this afternoon from my mother. She's made a cake and she's going to send it to me."

"Do you like cake?"

"Hell yes—but this is a special cake," Harry said. "Dates and raisins and walnuts and rum and stuff like that in it. Don't you like cake?"

"I like cake too," the newspaperman said. He looked at the two of us. "I know *your* names," he said, "so I think you ought to know mine. Jim Kirby. I write for U.P."

"Union Pacific?" Harry said.

"United Press," Jim said.

"What do you write?"

"Well, the boss wants me to write about soldiers. *You* fellows. Not the big shots, the *little* shots, you might say. I'm supposed to start out with a series of articles on life in Army Camps at home, and then move along with the mob."

Harry looked over at me and said, "Jackson claims we're going to take an airplane ride to Alaska in three hours."

"That's right," Jim said. "How do you like the idea?"

"I like it fine," Harry said. "Always did want to see the Klondike. But how come?"

"Well, your friend here," Jim said, "he and I went to work on the Colonel, and between the two of us we fixed it."

"No fooling?" Harry said.

"No fooling," Jim said. "And don't worry about anything. It's O.K. Well, you've got to pack your bags, so I'll say so long. Hope I'll be seeing you again."

We said so long to Jim Kirby and he turned and walked out of the barracks. Harry and I started packing our bags and Harry kept saying, "For God's sake, what did you tell the Colonel?"

It was a fine journey, going and coming, and it was a pretty nice place to be for a change, but the only Eskimo I saw worked in a saloon in Fairbanks. His name was Dan Collins, he was a Christian, and he looked more like an American than an Eskimo. I don't suppose the trip was a waste of time and money for the government because the Colonel had me carry some parcels and do a few things for him while we were up there. I went around to a half dozen Army Posts with the Colonel's stuff, and I took stuff back with me from every place I went to.

When Harry found out how and why we had got sent to Alaska he said, "Well, what do you know? The world sure is crooked, isn't it, Jackson?"

We were gone five days all told, and the minute we got back we went right on with our Basic Training, and every night Dominic Tosca and Lou Marriacci played games on Dominic's kid brother.

CHAPTER 4 *Wesley Sees His Name in Print for the First Time and Doesn't Know What to Make of It*

I went back up the hill to tell the writer. He was sitting at his desk looking at some new magazines that had just come for him.

"I think we'll be going back to New York in about a week," I said. "Joe Foxhall and you and me."

"If you say so," the writer said, "it must be so."

He handed me the magazine he was reading—*The New Republic*. He didn't say anything but I knew he wanted me to see something in it. What I saw across the top of the left hand page made me sweat: *A Letter to My Father*. I read the first eight or nine words of the letter and knew it was the letter I had written to Pop when he had gone off—that I'd dropped in the writer's waste basket. At the end of the letter was my name.

"I had no right to do it," the writer said, "but I had no right *not* to do it, either. I happened to look in the waste-basket for an envelope on which I'd written a title for a story, and I found your letter to your father. I didn't tell you I'd sent it along to the magazine because I wasn't sure the editors would agree with me about it.

If it came back, I had planned to try it out on one or two other magazines, but as you see it didn't come back—the editors agreed with me. I have a letter from them asking about you and wanting to see anything else you've written or happen to write in the future. I told them not to say anything about you in the column about contributors because I thought you ought to tell them about yourself the next time they print something of yours. I hope you're not unhappy about any of this."

"I'm not exactly unhappy," I said. "But what about Pop? That letter was written to *him*—I decided not to mail it because—well, I didn't want to hurt him."

"I think your father will understand," the writer said. "That letter isn't to him alone, you know. It isn't from *you* alone, either. That's the way it is when a man's a writer. It's a good way but it's also a bad way—good or bad, though, anything *you* write is for reading. I feel as sure of that as I feel that anything *I* write is for reading. I know I took a hell of a liberty, but I think I did right, and after you read the letter I hope you will think I did right too."

I took the magazine to my desk and read the letter, every word of it—and then I read it again because I was so confused. It was exactly what I had written, word for word, but I had forgotten it— I had been tired and angry when I had written it—and when I read it in *The New Republic*—something I had never expected to see again as long as I lived—well, then, it was like the writer said: It wasn't as if *I* had written a letter to Pop, it was as if somebody had had to say something and had said it. I kept sweating and smoking cigarettes and feeling half-sick and half-crazy—and every time I saw my name at the end of the letter, at the bottom of the page, I couldn't understand what had happened.

I felt funny—lonely in a new kind of way—and a lot of other things. Who was I to write? What right did I have to write? If I could write things like that, I could write a lot of other things too. Did I want to be a writer? Did I want to go around being different from everybody else and see things differently and remember what I saw and write about them all the time? Would that be a good way to be or would it take all the fun out of everything? Was I different from everybody else? The writer didn't seem to be different from anybody else. He didn't seem to be watching and remembering all the time. Being a writer didn't seem to bother *him*.

Well, then, I don't know what happened because I began to cry.

I didn't cry only on the inside the way you do when you won't let yourself cry. I didn't cry the way you do when you keep everything in except the water that gets your eyes to swimming. I really cried —but I got out of the building first and went out to a field where there were some trees and nobody could see me.

CHAPTER 5   *Wesley Reads in the New Republic the Letter He Wrote to His Father*

This is what I wrote to Pop that night in the lobby of the little hotel, and this is what I read in *The New Republic*:

"Bernard Jackson: Even though I don't know where you are or whether this will ever reach you, I've got to write to you because if you're in trouble, then so am I. I have never felt that I had to be loyal to you or that I had to feel proud of you or any of the other things good sons are supposed to feel about their fathers. You're my father and I'm your son and that's the end of it—good or bad's got nothing to do with it. I suppose some people would think yu're a weak man because every now and then you've got to go off the way you do—the way you've just done again—and drink yourself through whatever it is that made you go off. But I don't think you're weak to do that at all. I think it's just naturally necessary for you to do everything you do.

"Then why am I writing to you? I'm writing to you because I think the time has come for me to try to straighten you out in myself, like you told me not so long ago you were counting on me to do. A lot of things happened to you in the last War that I can't even guess about because no man can guess what another man knows, not even if one is the son of the other. From what you've told me, though, I know the worst didn't happen to your body. Your body is still stronger than the bodies of most men. The worst happened to You—all of you, not your body, not your nerves, not your mind, not your heart, not your spirit, but to You Yourself. I know you felt outraged by the War, and that you still do—*personally*. And I know the notion of my going through the same thing scares you because you have been counting on me to turn out all right—for the two of us. You are counting on me to have a son to pick up where I leave off—and I'm counting on it too. You told me you kept yourself alive through the whole War for one reason: to see me. Well, I want you to know that I have decided to do everything I can to keep myself alive so that I can see *my* son. I know you will not be shocked when I tell you that this decision is making a physical coward out of me, because that is the truth. In order to see my own son someday I am willing to be such a coward. The idea of physical cowardice scares the hell out of most fellows in the Army, but it doesn't scare me. I'd really begin to be scared if I found myself unwilling or unable to understand very clearly that under some circumstances and for certain reasons I am willing to be unwilling to die. I absolutely do not want to get killed—for any reason. I honestly don't think I would care if civilization itself (as they are always saying) ended, just so I stayed alive. I swear to God I think I *am* civilization. What the hell do I care what collapses as long as I don't? I don't believe any other honest fellow in the Army doesn't feel in his heart as I do. I know that I might get myself killed (without thinking about it) out of anger about what's true or right, for instance—but I don't think if that happened I'd have helped save civilization. I think it would be damned foolishness. If I've got to get killed in order to keep civilization going, then everybody's got to get killed with me. Since that cannot be, I've got to stay alive or civilization has got to collapse or it's got to be put on the sort of operating basis that will not ask you, then me, then my son to go out and get killed.

"Your good time has come—you can run out on all these things, and I'm glad you can. My bad time has come because I'm caught. The same old machine that caught you and squeezed the bajesus out of you and then let you drop, has caught me and it means to do the same to me, or worse—and I mean not to let it, if I can manage. You've got me, which I guess is something, but I haven't got mine, and I need it badly. You said there's no place in the world for a man to live and watch his children grow—the whole place is caught by the machine and can't get free. I think you're right, Pop. You and I haven't got enough money to buy our own world and put a fence around it and live in it. If we had enough money to do it I think we could make a nation of our own and establish a government of our own and be satisfied with our two acres and our two cents' worth of culture, but I think it's a good thing we haven't got enough money to do it, because nobody's got enough money to do it, and if everybody can't do it, its no use for us to do it. So then what are we going to do? How are we going to get along with ourselves? I mean, how are we going to get to be human beings, as you put it, if the situation simply will not permit it? Well, I don't know about you, but if you really meant for me to be an improvement of you, then I think I've got to find out how to get free of the machine and how to become human—no matter what the situation happens to be.

"I wish you were here now, so instead of writing all this stuff we could have a couple of drinks together. Now, I know why—"

And that's as far as I got in the letter, and that's where it stopped in *The New Republic.*

CHAPTER 6 *Wesley Finds His Girl, Jill Moore of Gloucester*

As often as possible I made Victor Tosca go out walking with me. One Sunday we walked all the way to Limehouse, down East India Dock Road and through Pennyfields, which is the Chinatown of London. I told Victor Pop had been born somewhere in the East End of London. I looked at everything carefully because hell, maybe Pop had looked at the same things. If there was an old church, I'd know Pop had seen that all right, so I'd look at it a long time. There were a lot of bombed places—that part of London got it bad in the Big Blitz—the poor people always get it worst.

Victor and I did a lot of walking in London. We'd walk to Regents Park one evening, down the Strand the next. Down Whitehall or up to Hyde Park. Past St. Paul's and down Threadneedle Street. Past Old Bailey to the Liverpool Street Station. Across the bridges: Waterloo, Westminster, London, Blackfriars, Tower—all of them. Because it was the best city I ever saw to walk around in.

But hell, I hadn't found my girl, and that's what I wanted to do. I'd gone to Piccadilly Circus a lot of times to see the girls trying to make profitable deals with the boys, and I made a few myself, but the girls made me so sad I didn't want them any more.

One night while I was hanging around Piccadilly Circus watching the show a little girl came up to me. She was so young I couldn't

believe my eyes, and I didn't like it at all. I thought she must be
fourteen or fifteen. She didn't have the manner of somebody who
knew what she was doing, so I told her to take a walk with me. We
went down to St. James's Park and sat on a bench and talked. Pretty
soon I got to feeling that this might be *my* girl—but I hated the idea
that she had been in Piccadilly Circus and had come up to me that
way because if that was a true thing, she *couldn't* be my girl—even
if she had been meant to be—because I wouldn't allow it.

I told her to tell me the truth—not to lie to me for any reason
because I hated lying. I told her I liked her, and if it was true, well,
I'd be broken-hearted but I'd still like her. She said she had come
from Gloucester to London that afternoon—she had run away from
home. She was hungry and didn't have any money. One of the girls
of the street advised her to do what she had tried to do. She said the
girl had promised to let her use her place if she had had any luck. I
told her to take me to the place.

We walked half a mile to a doorway, and the girl rang the bell, but
there was no answer. We went to a fish-and-chips place and ate some,
and then went back to the doorway and rang the bell again and a
woman came to the door. I gave the woman a pound note and stepped
into the hall with her. I told her to tell me about the girl. She said
she hadn't seen the girl until a few hours ago. She said the girl was
in London without any money, a little fool like so many others these
days—so she'd taken pity on her and told her she could stay with her
overnight, and maybe make a pound or two for herself if she had any
talent for it.

I thanked the woman and took the girl back to St. James's Park
to think things over. Well, I liked her. I wasn't sure I liked her as
much as I thought I'd like *my* girl, but I knew I liked her a lot. She
said she was almost seventeen, but looked younger because her family
was poor and they never ate very much—it was because she had
always been a little hungry.

I took her home. The writer was sitting in the parlor reading. Joe
and Victor had gone to bed. I asked the writer what I ought to do
about her. He said she ought to take a bath and go to bed—sleep on
the couch in the parlor. I told her to take a bath and I gave her a
pair of my pajamas. The writer and I fixed the couch up into a bed.
Pretty soon she came out of the bathroom in the pajamas and got in
bed.

She had a sweet little face with the upper lip lifted away from the lower in a kind of child-like perplexity, and all sorts of soft thick yellow hair tumbling down. She was all small and white, with the hands of a baby, and little baby legs and feet. But what she had that broke my heart were big staring blue eyes—the amazed eyes of a scared little girl in a crazy and ferocious world. The writer closed the parlor door, and I asked him to go for a walk with me because I wanted to talk to him about her. He went to the bathroom first, and called me over, because she had washed all her clothes and hung them up to dry, and he wanted me to see that.

We went out into the street and I told the writer about her.

"She came up to me in Piccadilly Circus just as if she were a street-walker. Well, I couldn't believe that, so I took her to St. James's Park and we talked a long time. She's almost seventeen, but she looks younger. She's run away from home because the family's poor and she can't get along with her mother—her father's dead. Do you think she's lied to me?"

"All you've got to do is look at her," the writer said. "She hasn't lied to you."

"Well, what shall I do about her?"

"Marry her."

We walked along and I kept remembering the girl and the things she'd told me and her eyes staring at me and her little clean hands after her bath, and her feet, and hell, I didn't know for sure—but she *seemed* to be my girl. It seemed to me I'd found her at last, and all I had to do now was make sure. She was everything she ought to be that I could tell about so far, so all I had to do was find out about everything.

And I had to find out if *she* liked *me*.

I reminded the writer of the Army's ruling about soldiers marrying English girls—how your Commanding Officer had to investigate the matter, which took two or three months because they liked to discourage English-American marriages, and had to give his approval, and all the other red-tape.

"Just marry her," the writer said.

"What do you mean?"

"Find out if she's the girl for you. Find out if she thinks you're the man for her. Find out if you love each other enough to want to get married and have children and live together for the rest of your lives. Forget the Commanding Officer. Let me know what you decide and I'll figure something out."

"What do you *really* think of her?"

"I think she's wonderful. From what I've seen of her, I think she's your wife. I think you're both very lucky."

CHAPTER 7   *The Invasion of Europe Begins*

Well, April and May went along, and the days of June began, and they were bright sweet days—but then one morning—Saturday, June 3rd—Joe Foxhall and Victor Tosca and Duncan Olson and three other Privates and a Lieutenant and a Captain went off, and everybody knew the Invasion would begin very soon. I asked the Captain why I wasn't in Victor's unit, because I wanted to be with him, but he said the rest of us would follow soon. Victor's unit was going over on a special assignment. They'd return to London soon after we'd gone over. Then they'd go over again, and we'd all be over together, till the end of the War in Europe.

Three days later we knew the Invasion had started. It was all over London, but there was no noise or excitement. There was a kind of holding of the breath. Everybody seemed to be praying, even the people in the streets. You could see it in their faces and the way every man went about his business. Would the damn thing work? That was the question. After all that preparing would it work?

I went home early in the afternoon of that day and took Jill to walk through the streets with me once more. We went past St. James's to Green Park, out to Piccadilly, and there we heard the clarinet and banjo team wailing away on *Whispering Grass*. I went up to them and gave them half a crown and asked them to play *Valencia* for me, so they did. But I couldn't go away, I wanted to hear my song again, so pretty soon, after they'd played two other songs and moved a block down the street, I gave them two half crowns and asked them to play it again. They played it three times, and then Jill and I went home and sat down and couldn't talk and I kept wondering "How's Victor and Joe and Olson, for God's sake? Where are they now?"

The next day it was our turn, so we went off, and I didn't even get a chance to say good-bye to Jill. I'd told her it would be that way, so be sure not to worry. I'd be O.K.

So we went to the War, but what the hell is a War? It's the same thing, and I couldn't understand why we weren't getting killed. I expected the War to come tearing at us the minute we set out for it, but it wasn't that way at all. We got on trucks and got off trucks, we got on boats and got off boats, we got on trucks again and got off trucks again, we walked and stopped—and all the time I expected the War to come out of the sky like a hurricane and have at us, but it didn't. Once we got into France and out along the country roads every man thought he was near home because the countryside looks like home wherever home happens to be. France seemed like California to me. There were fellows in our unit from Virginia and Nebraska and Louisiana and Oregon, and they all thought France was like home. Europe seemed sweet and peaceful in the countryside of northern France. There were birds around, and insects, and all the sweet smells of things growing, and French children, and girls, and old women, and young men of one sort or another, and cattle and horses and dogs—it was the same, there was nothing different about it.

"Where's the War?" everybody wanted to know. "We're all O.K. Where's the War?"

Well, the War was down the road a piece. Death was down there, too. Down the road was the same kind of place we were in, but the War was there, and we weren't. We passed through a village, and then another, and then a pretty good-sized town, but everybody was busy living. Nobody was busy dying.

It was the same the next day, except that we took moving pictures of some enemy dead, and some prisoners, and some stuff in town. We took pictures of troops hurrying by in trucks, or walking, or people coming back to their homes, or anything that seemed interesting and worth having on film.

The next night we were closer to the War. We began to dig in, in case we needed cover during the night, and then at last the War came to us. Everybody threw himself on the ground and expected the worse, but it was only one shell—a big one that wheezed and howled from a good way off. It scared us plenty. We didn't get up from the grass and dirt for a long time. I studied the grass and ate some of it. The shell hit the slope of the hill behind us and sent a lot of the earth flying all over, but none of the stuff hit any of us, so after that we had been in the War. We had been in it for sure—a shell had come close to us—but it wasn't much worse than London being bombed, except that it was out in the open. We all felt better after that because we had tasted enough War to let us know how it was and we had come through O.K., every one of us—nobody even a little hurt—but we didn't like it, and everybody calculated that if we had been on the slope of the hill, instead of down in the valley, well, then, some of us would have been hurt and some of us would have been killed.

We finished digging out slit-trenches and practiced diving into them and tried them out for comfort, and then it was night. We had eaten our field rations and they had tasted good because we hadn't eaten them very often and we had been very hungry, but they weren't home cooking—they weren't food at all. They were scientific stuff based on energy units, and they didn't care to be anything else.

We didn't run into anybody we knew, but we saw a lot of different outfits. I got to believing Victor and Joe and Olson were O.K. because we were so O.K., but the next night we weren't so very O.K. Our own planes came over to bomb the enemy, only they went to work and dropped the bombs on us. We hit the dirt again—we didn't have any slit-trenches that night—so we just hit the dirt and waited. The noise and nonsense were awful, but I couldn't believe stuff like that was ever going to kill me or anybody like me—any man in the world—but I was mistaken. Not far from us some fellows in another outfit had two dead and five wounded. I didn't know those fellows and I didn't go over to see them like some of the fellows in our outfit did because I don't like looking at a man in terrible pain, or a fellow about to die and nobody to talk to worth talking to.

But I knew it could happen as easy as anything. It might not be the way you thought it would be—it might be a silly surprise—but it could happen like nothing. A lot of fellows die in a War from things that go on all the time—all kinds of accidents, all kinds of mistakes, all kinds of miserable happenings on account of stupidity. We'd heard stories about such things ever since we'd gotten over. The countryside was full of fellows who'd gotten theirs for no good reason. In the first landings a lot of fellows got washed overboard and were drowned. A lot of fellows who weren't tall stepped off the landing boats all loaded down with their junk and didn't come up again—there wasn't time to fish for them—everybody just kept piling off and hoping he wouldn't sink so deep he wouldn't come up again. You move fast when it's time to move and the miserable and horrible things that haunt your sleep come to seem like nothing. You keep moving, and pretty soon you're walking in Europe.

CHAPTER 8   *Wesley Studies the Various Groups in the German Prison Camp*

Victor and I stayed captured by the Germans until the last day of August when they went off and left us. We saw a lot of stuff in that Prison Camp—some of it funny and wonderful and beautiful, and some of it terrible and ugly. The Germans didn't say anything to us when they left. They just packed up in the night and went off, and the next day we waited and waited, but the Germans were gone. There were over a thousand of us cooped up inside barbed-wire, and we'd been there a long time, so when it got around that the Germans had gone and left us—well, we turned into a mob.

Victor and I had met in that Prison Camp the day before the Fourth of July, so we had been there together almost two months. The Fourth of July was celebrated, but not very successfully. Somebody tried to put on a show, but it didn't work. When a fellow got up to make a speech everybody told him to skip it. They were rude to the fellow, who had only meant to do something right. The show was supposed to be a kind of stage show—a little vaudeville— but nobody wanted to bother with it, so after a half hour it fell to pieces and everybody went back to waiting.

I'll mention the terrible things first and get them out of the way.

One night a boy cut his wrists and was found dead in the morning.

And one afternoon two paratroopers who had been pals got irritated with one another because one of them said a certain girl they both knew had been had by six of their friends (not counting themselves) and the other said she had been had by only five. The sixth was also a paratrooper but a fellow one of them hated, so he didn't want that paratrooper to have had the girl too. His pal kept saying that he *knew* he had had her too, so the fellow who said the girl had been had by only five took his pal by the throat and began to choke him. But his pal had been taught a few things about hand-to-hand fighting too, so they almost killed each other. When they had been separated they agreed through the fellows speaking for them that one of them would stay on one side of the stockade and the other on the other, because they insisted that if they ever met again they would kill each other

—and they meant it too, although they had been pals and had been through a lot of campaigns together. They kept their word, and each of them stayed on his side of the stockade. They never spoke to each other again.

There were a half dozen little fights every day because everybody was so tense, but the fight between the paratroopers was the only serious one.

The fellows divided up into little groups which were held together by the ties that have always made men feel related.

For the most part, fellows who had been in the same outfit stuck together because they had the same things to remember and talk about.

Then there were little groups that were held together because the fellows came from the same city and liked to talk about home or people they remembered.

Then there were groups that were formed because the fellows had had the same trades or professions in civilian life and liked to talk over the circumstances of their work in the past and prospects for the future.

Then there were regional groups. Southerners liked to stay together because they felt the same way about Negroes—and Negroes liked to stay together because they knew how the Southerners felt, or didn't want to be bothered. There were only nine Negroes in the stockade. Only three of them were Southern and weren't college graduates—but the other six were fond of the three who weren't as educated as they were.

Fellows from the Far West—California, Oregon and Washington—felt close together.

Then there were fellows who happened to have the same last name. Sometimes there would be only two and the name would be unusual and they would try to understand how they had come to have that name—Menadue—and yet weren't related and didn't know the same people.

Or there would be two fellows—one from Tennessee and the other from North Dakota—whose last name was Rosevar. They would take up with one another and talk about their families and get to be pals because their names were so unusual, and yet they weren't related.

There were seven Smiths, and they called each other Smithy, and so did everybody else. The four or five Browns got along nicely and were often together.

Then, fellows with the same temperament seemed to like hanging around together—comedians especially, but a lot of fellows who were serious-minded stayed together too.

Fellows feeling homesick would hang around a lot, but as soon as the feeling was gone they'd go back to another group. As soon as they weren't quite as homesick as they'd been, they'd take up with the sporting crowd, for instance, which was always busy with little athletics that didn't require running or a lot of space: Indian wrestling, standing broad jump, distance spitting, and stuff like that.

Or they'd take up with the prophesying group and prophesy this and that.

Or they'd take up with the dreamers—fellows who lived to discuss what romantic things they were going to do after the War.

As soon as a fellow with a cold got over his cold he'd leave his pals with colds and go along to one or another of the other groups, such as the discussers of current events, politics, religion, Communism, or philosophy.

Then there were size groups: little men, medium-sized men, and big men.

Or appearance groups: handsome men, not quite handsome men, plain men, or strange-looking men.

Then there were personality groups.

Fellows with a long record of conquests liked to hang around together and compare notes and go over each success in detail.

Fellows with the attitude that women are meant to be stalked and taken like any other animal not easy to stalk and take enjoyed one another's company.

Fellows who believed their wives were lonely worried about them and stayed together.

Fellows who felt sure their wives hadn't been true to them after so much separation spent a lot of time together wondering whether they ought to get divorced, forgive and forget, or catch the son of a bitch (or the several of them) who took their wives away from them while their backs were turned and they were fighting the War. But even among themselves these fellows were divided because some of them sympathized with their wives. The fellows who didn't sympathize with their wives would be irritated with the fellows who did and would consider them poor specimens of manhood, and the talk would get pretty heated and confused sometimes.

Then there were the fellows who had had very few women.

And the ones who had had none—but this group was very small because they were shy about it.

Then there were those who probably hadn't had any women, but liked to say they had, and understood one another and got along all right.

Then there were the men with one child, and the men with two, and the handful with three or more. The man with seven children —Orin Oakley, of Kentucky—belonged to no group at all. He just sat and invented names for famous men. One of the best was Rearview Mirror.

Then there were the men who went after women a lot but admitted they hated them and only liked to bring them down a peg, especially the proud ones—make them fall in love and then let them suffer. These men liked to discuss the pitiable conditions to which they had reduced many a vain hussy—made them humiliate themselves; made them write letters, send telegrams, telephone all the time; made them leave their husbands; made whores out of them; made them beg to be loved; made them go mad, and so on and so forth.

Then there were groups made up of cynics—fellows who were sure the world was shot to hell for good, and hated humanity because it stank.

Then there were the laughers; the moaners; the travelers; the stay-at-homes; the foolish; the wise, the gamblers; the readers; the chess crowd; the dice boys.

There were all kinds, but no matter how they broke themselves up, they were all one thing; prisoners.

They were captured by the Germans, and they were captured by the Americans—and they didn't like being captured by anybody.

CHAPTER 9 *John Wynstanley of Cincinnati,
Ohio, Puts on a Straw Hat and Plays
the Trombone, Enchanting Enemy and
Friend Alike*

There was a fellow in the stockade named John Wynstanley who
had a trombone. He'd carried it with him from his home in Cincinnati, and he'd kept it in the War two years. He was a little bit
of a fellow with a grave preoccupied expression on his face. He didn't
look more than sixteen or seventeen years old, although he was past
twenty.

Everybody knew he had a trombone, but Wynstanley wouldn't
bring it out of the case and play it because he said he couldn't play
it unless he had a strawhat on his head. He had always had a strawhat,
and he'd brought it to France with him, but somebody had stolen it.

If somebody would get him a strawhat, he'd play the trombone.

Well, nobody had a strawhat, so the only thing to do was take the
matter up with the Germans. There were three or four of our fellows
who could speak German, so one of them told the Guards what was
needed, but the Guards said they didn't have a strawhat. They said
they'd like to hear somebody play the trombone all right, but where
would they be able to get a strawhat?

The Guards were told to scout around, and tell their friends, and
see if they couldn't find a strawhat somewhere because Wynstanley
couldn't play the trombone until he had a strawhat on his head.
Maybe he really knew how to play the trombone, and if he did, it
would be worth it.

The Guards said they would look into the matter.

After a while everybody decided Wynstanley couldn't play the
trombone. They decided he had invented the story about the strawhat, so he could get out of being exposed.

Wynstanley prided himself on being a good trombone-player, and
he didn't like the slur, so on the evening of Sunday, July 9th, he
brought the trombone out of the case and put it together. Everybody gathered around and waited—at least three hundred fellows.

Wynstanley wet his lips and pressed them against the mouthpiece and slided the trombone back and forth a couple of times to get it moving smoothly.

Then he began to play something that just about brought heaven into that miserable place. But, sure enough, he stopped playing and said, "Got to have a strawhat on my head—can't play worth a damn without a strawhat."

So then everybody knew he wasn't kidding. They ran over to the Guards and told them for God's sake, send to Paris for a strawhat because this boy knows how to blow the trombone, so the Guards said yes, they had heard him and would try their best.

Nobody badgered Wynstanley to play the trombone without a strawhat on his head after that because there is something almost religious about a man who knows how to cope with a horn, especially a trombone, and is able to bring music out of it. Everybody had a lot of respect for Wynstanley for having lugged the trombone half across the world, and after he had played enough to let everybody know he wasn't bluffing, they knew this wasn't any ordinary fellow, this was somebody special, and the only thing to do was get him a strawhat.

Wynstanley showed some of the fellows a snapshot of himself when he was nine years old. He had a trombone to his lips and a strawhat on his head.

"Always wore a strawhat when I played," he said.

Well, the song Wynstanley had started to play that night was *You'll never know just how much I love you*, and hell, it was wonderful—it was just naturally out of the world—and he went on to *You'll never know just how much I care*—just as easy and heartbreaking as anything could be, but when he came to the next few bars, well, he just couldn't go on.

Instead of being impatient with him—instead of thinking he was affected or silly—everybody took to feeling sympathetic. They tried to comfort him, and they said, "That's all right, Johnny—you'll get your strawhat, and then you can really play." Everybody could see he *wanted* to play, but was too good to let himself play poorly.

Well, the days and nights dragged along and the groups formed and broke up and re-formed and changed and were abandoned and new groups came along. But everybody had all kinds of stuff going on inside himself that was all his own, and there was no grouping of that stuff at all.

And everybody knew John Wynstanley was there with his trombone. Everybody had heard enough of the song he had started to play to want him to finish it, but nobody tried to rush him into doing a poor job.

One day one of the Guards told one of our fellows who knew German that according to some gossip he'd heard another Guard was returning from leave in Paris, and he was bringing a strawhat with him.

So everybody got happy about that and the news was carried to Wynstanley.

"When's he coming with it?" Wynstanley said.

"Any day now," somebody said. "Does it have to be any particular size?"

"It ought to fit," Wynstanley said, "but if it's straw and I can get it on my head, it'll do."

So then along with all the other waiting—waiting for the War to end, waiting to be captured back by the Americans, waiting to get to some place where we could get our mail—we started waiting for Wynstanley's strawhat to arrive.

Waiting's waiting and it's no trouble at all while you're waiting for a lot of important things to wait for a few unimportant ones too.

At last the fellow who'd been to Paris came back and sure enough, he'd brought a strawhat with him. He said he wanted to give it to Wynstanley himself. He came inside the stockade, and the fellows who spoke German walked along with him to Wynstanley who was sitting on the trombone case, the way he always sat. If he got up to walk, he carried the case with him by the handle. He took the thing with him wherever he went. Well, Wynstanley looked up at the German who'd been to Paris because the German was carrying a package and maybe there was a strawhat in it.

The interpreter said to Wynstanley, "He's brought you a strawhat from Paris—his name's Trott von Essen."

"Ask him," Wynstanley said, "can I keep the hat? I'll pay him what it cost and something for his trouble."

So the interpreter talked to Trott and then said to Wynstanley, "He says it's a pleasure—you can have the hat—glad to do it."

"Ask him," Wynstanley said, "what he'd like me to play because the first song I play has got to be for him—for getting me the hat."

So then the interpreter talked to Trott again, and then said to Wynstanley, "He says finish the song you started to play about two weeks ago."

"Tell him," Wynstanley said, "it's a deal and let's have a look at the hat."

So the interpreter told Trott, and Trott broke the string of the package and brought out a brand new strawhat with a red band on it, and a little cluster of red and green and purple feathers stuck in the band.

Trott handed Wynstanley the hat, and Wynstanley just held it and looked at it a long time.

Then he put it on his head.

It looked very good on him. He looked like a civilian all of a sudden.

Then very slowly Wynstanley opened the case and put the trombone together and slided it back and forth a couple of times. Then he went to work and played the song like nobody in the whole world had ever played it before.

It was the most magnificent thing anybody ever heard. He played it through three times, each time just a little better than the time before.

Wynstanley had been hungry to play and nobody needed to tell him to go on—he just *wanted* to play, and he did. It was the finest thing that happened in the whole War. Trott von Essen was so proud of his share in the event he would hardly talk to the interpreters.

Everybody had a favorite song he wanted to hear, and Wynstanley promised to play them all one after another—if he couldn't play them tonight, he'd play them tomorrow. If you could whistle or hum the tune, he'd pick it up and play it for you, he said. He didn't care what the tune was or whether he'd heard it before, just whistle it or hum it and he'd listen, and play it for you. He told the interpreter to ask Trott if there was any other song he'd like to hear, so Trott thought a minute, and remembered one, but didn't know the name of it. He'd heard one of our fellows singing it one night and he'd liked it, so Wynstanley told the interpreter to ask Trott to hum the song, or whistle it.

Trott hummed a few bars, and Wynstanley smiled and said, "Hell, that's *I'm thinking tonight of my blue eyes*. That's one of my own favorites."

Wynstanley played that song too, and if he was good on the first one, he was better on the second. The German was just as happy and proud as he could be. He wanted to know from the interpreter what the song was about, so the interpreter told him. He asked the interpreter to teach him to say *blue eyes* in English, so the interpreter did, and he went off saying the two words over and over again.

After *Blue Eyes*, Wynstanley played *Oh the moonlight's fair tonight along the Wabash, from the fields there comes the scent of newmown hay*, and damned if every fellow listening didn't have tears in his eyes and go to work and blow his nose and wonder how so much beauty could come out of a little old battered-up piece of plumbing like John Wynstanley's trombone.

I don't know what the fellows in the American Army are fighting for, or what they think they're fighting for, because I haven't asked every one of them, but I think I know what they love—every last one of them, no matter who they are or what group they belong to —they love truth and beauty. They love it and need it and want it and tears come to their eyes when they get it.

And they got it when John Wynstanley of Cincinnati, Ohio, played the trombone. They got it when that great American—that great man of the world—put the strawhat on his head and let them hear the message of love and truth and beauty.

And I don't know what's American as against what's something else, but I know there is no man in the world capable of resisting truth and beauty like the truth and beauty that came out of Wynstanley's trombone on the evening and night of Saturday, July 22, 1944.

I know the German Guards couldn't resist that truth and beauty, because, having got a hint of its enormity one of them had fetched Wynstanley his strawhat. And I know the men named Rosevar and Menadue couldn't resist it; or the men named Smith or Jones; or the men who came from the South and had a special attitude toward Negroes; or the Negroes; or the fellows from the Far West; or the men who were cynics; or the ones who hated women; or the ones with toothaches; or those with colds; or the athletic ones; or the ones who despised the world; or those who had no religion; or the paratroopers. I know everybody in that Prison Camp and everybody outside of it who heard Wynstanley could not resist the truth and beauty he brought out of his trombone—and they were all the same in the presence of that truth and beauty, so what's all this talk about some people being no good by birth, and others being very good by birth, and others being fair to middling by birth? What kind of talk is that?

CHAPTER 10   *Wesley Comes to the End of His Story*

At last we came to Waterloo Station in London, but there were no taxis, so I said, "Come on, let's walk—or run—or something. Let's not just stand here." We started to walk and run, because, oh Jesus, I wanted to see Jill again. We walked and ran across Waterloo Bridge and up the Strand, so then Victor said, "You go ahead—I can't run any more."

I ran on and Victor walked, and pretty soon I was almost home. Pretty soon I'd see my girl again and take her in my arms and see how my son was getting along—but when I turned into Charles II Street I began to die because it was all in ruins. The building Jill and I had lived in—it wasn't there any more.

I guess I went crazy because I kept walking back and forth across the street from where our building used to be—where we used to live—because I was afraid—I was afraid to ask anybody about it. I was afraid to even *think* about it. I guess I must have stayed there a long time because pretty soon it was night. But I couldn't go away and the song was sick with agony in me. It was fierce with aching, and I didn't know what to do.

But I knew I was dead if Jill was dead—and I didn't want to be dead. I began to cry because hell, suppose we were both dead now? Suppose we had both died while I was gone? So where was the star that had come out for me to tell me that I would be spared? What good was the star to me now?

Pretty soon an old man who was begging came to me. I gave him a pound, and then changed my mind and gave him two pounds because I didn't want to be dead.

"Why are you crying?" he said.

"I used to live in the building that used to be across the street," I said. "I used to live there, but it's been bombed. I don't know what's happened to my wife, and I'm afraid to go and find out. I'm afraid. Do you want another pound?"

He said if I gave him another pound my wife was all right—not to worry—so I gave him two more, which was all I had, not counting the change I had in my pocket.

"Your wife's all right," he said. "Don't worry about it. Have you any more money?"

"Only these coins," I said. I gave him the coins because if Jill was all right, I didn't want any money. The beggar went scraping on down Charles II Street. He turned every once in a while to look back at me as if he wasn't sure he hadn't tricked me in order to get a little money, so I said to God, "Please don't let the old man be a liar—please let Jill be alive. I forgot to ask you to keep Jill alive when I made the bargain about the star because I hadn't met Jill then, but if Jill isn't alive, it's no good my being alive, so please keep the bargain, even though I didn't know how things were going to turn out. Please keep the true bargain."

Well, then a taxi came up like thunder and lightning and the writer jumped out and grabbed me and said, "Your wife's in Gloucester."

Well, what do you do when God keeps a bargain? What do you do when He keeps a bigger bargain than you thought you had made? What do you do when you know He will always know what you mean, even if *you* don't, and will stick to His agreement? You thank Him, don't you? I wasn't even polite to the writer—I just got down on my knees on Charles II Street, and I said to God, "I thank You, and I'll go on thanking You as long as I live."

I jumped up and got into the taxi with the writer, and he told the driver to take us to Paddington.

"Why?" I said. "I want my mail. I've got to see my mail."

"Here's your mail," the writer said. "The last train for Gloucester leaves in twenty minutes. When Victor told me you'd gone home, I thought you'd hurry along to find out what had happened, so I sat there and waited. Then I had a hunch what had happened to you, so I got a taxi to get you home. The gossip was that you and Victor were dead. I kept writing to your father and I kept telling Jill whenever she came to London that you were O.K., so now it's O.K. I sure am glad to see you. Our whole unit is being shipped back to New York. Jill was visiting her mother when your house was hit."

"When did it happen?"

"The night you left London. She had planned to stay home all the time you were gone, but she kept crying because she just couldn't be there without you. She came over to our old place on Pall Mall and told me everything—so I got her into a taxi and took her to the station and put her on the train. The next morning your whole street was a shambles."

We got to Paddington just in time for the writer to buy a ticket and get me on the train, so then I was on my way to Jill at last, but I just had to thank God all the way.

I just kept thanking God with all, all, all, all, all my heart, all my soul, all my blood and bone, and all the juices in me for getting Jill out of our house the way He did—for making her love me so much that she couldn't stay in our house one night without me. I thanked Him for putting people in the world like the writer to know what to do and how to do it right away and not fool around—somebody else might have told Jill to go back home and not be afraid. I thanked God for putting fellows like Joe Foxhall into the world—even if it was only for such a short time—and fellows like Dominic Tosca. I had so much to thank God for I just couldn't do anything else.

And then the train stopped in Gloucester, and I went walking to my life, which God had so carefully kept for me.

It was one o'clock in the morning when I got off the train, and I adored the city that gave me my bride and my life—I loved Gloucester —and when I came to the door which would be opened to me, I kissed it, and then knocked softly, and then Jill came to the door and opened it to me.

I held her in my arms and kissed her and bumped upon my son in her because he was pushing out so far now.

And Jill laughed and cried, and her mother came out in her old-fashioned nightgown, in her bare-feet, which were just like Jill's, and she cried and laughed too, and Jill's little brothers and sisters came out in their nightgowns and we all laughed and cried, but pretty soon we stopped laughing and just cried because all of a sudden I knew the soldier—the big brother—had been killed and would never come home again. Nobody said anything about it, but all of a sudden I knew he was dead. I'd only seen him once, but I cried and cried because a fellow like that had been killed.

Jill made tea and her mother and her brothers and sisters set the table and put all kinds of things on it. We all sat down and tried to eat, and tried to talk but couldn't. Every once in a while somebody would break out sobbing and run away from the table and come back after a few minutes, and then somebody else would go, and come back, and I was out of my head with happiness and thankfulness and agony and anger—all together—because if so many things could be right, why couldn't just a few more be right too? Why couldn't the big brother come home too? Why couldn't Joe Foxhall come home too? Why couldn't Dominic Tosca come home too? Why did some have all the luck—like me—and others none?

Pretty soon the brothers and sisters wandered off to bed, and Jill and I sat and talked a long time with her mother, and oh she was a beautiful woman—she was a Queen like her daughter Jill. She didn't cry any more. She talked about her darling son Mike, but she cried no more. She told us about her lovely life—patient, patient, patient—and the child she lost in childbirth before Mike was born— and the one she lost before Jill was born, but after that lost no more, but lost her man, and now her darling Michael—and for what? To make a good home for her man and her children and watch them grow and be good people. So then she kissed us both and went to bed.

I took my wife and held her in my arms a long time, and then I said, "Jill, I died tonight when I saw our house in London gone, because I was afraid you were gone too, and that killed me—and Joe's dead—yes, he's dead, Jill—and your brother Mike's dead—all these things killed me."

But my lovely Jill said, "Mama says it's a boy. She felt him, and she knows. She says he'll be born on Christmas Eve or Christmas Morn."

"I'll be alive again when he's born," I said.

We were too excited to go to sleep, so Jill put on her clothes, and we went out to walk and watch the break of day in Gloucester, and oh the world's too lovely for death. The world's too sweet for murder. Breathing's too good and seeing's too wonderful. Human beings must not murder one another. They must wait for God to take them in His own good time.

THE MAN WITH THE HEART
IN THE HIGHLANDS

In 1914, when I was not quite six years old, an old man came down San Benito Avenue on his way to the old people's home playing a solo on a bugle and stopped in front of our house. I ran out of the yard and stood at the curb waiting for him to start playing again, but he wouldn't do it. I said, I sure would like to hear you play another tune, and he said, Young man, could you get a glass of water for an old man whose heart is not here, but in the highlands?

What highlands? I said.

The Scotch highlands, said the old man. Could you?

What's your heart doing in the Scotch highlands? I said.

My heart is grieving there, said the old man. Could you bring me a glass of cool water?

Where's your mother? I said.

My mother's in Tulsa, Oklahoma, said the old man, but her heart isn't.

Where *is* her heart? I said.

In the Scotch highlands, said the old man. I am very thirsty, young man.

How come the members of your family are always leaving their hearts in the highlands? I said.

That's the way we are, said the old man. Here today and gone to-morrow.

Here to-day and gone to-morrow? I said. How do you figure?

Alive one minute and dead the next, said the old man.

Where is your mother's *mother*? I said.

She's up in Vermont, in a little town called White River, but her heart isn't, said the old man.

Is her poor old withered heart in the highlands too? I said.

Right smack in the highlands, said the old man. Son, I'm dying of thirst.

My father came out on the porch and roared like a lion that has just awakened from evil dreams.

Johnny, he roared, get the hell away from that poor old man. Get

him a pitcher of water before he falls down and dies. Where in hell
are your manners?

Can't a fellow try to find out something from a traveller once in
a while? I said.

Get the old gentleman some water, said my father. God damn it,
don't stand there like a dummy. Get him a drink before he falls down
and dies.

You get him a drink, I said. You ain't doing nothing.

Ain't doing nothing? said my father. Why, Johnny, you know God
damn well I'm getting a new poem arranged in my mind.

How do you figure I know? I said. You're just standing there on
the porch with your sleeves rolled up. How do you figure I know?

Well, you ought to know, said my father.

Good afternoon, said the old man to my father. Your son has been
telling me how clear and cool the climate is in these parts.

(Jesus Christ, I said, I never did tell this old man anything about
the climate. Where's he getting that stuff from?)

Good afternoon, said my father. Won't you come in for a little rest?
We should be honored to have you at our table for a bit of lunch.

Sir, said the old man, I am starving. I shall come right in.

Can you play *Drink to Me Only with Thine Eyes?* I said to the
old man. I sure would like to hear you play that song on the bugle.
That song is my favorite. I guess I like that song better than any
other song in the world.

Son, said the old man, when you get to be my age you'll know songs
aren't very important, bread is the thing.

Anyway, I said, I sure would like to hear you play that song.

The old man went up on the porch and shook hands with my
father.

My name is Jasper MacGregor, he said. I am an actor.

I am mighty glad to make your acquaintance, said my father.
Johnny, get Mr. MacGregor a pitcher of water.

I went around to the well and poured some cool water into a pitcher
and took it to the old man. He drank the whole pitcher full in one
long swig. Then he looked around at the landscape and up at the sky
and away up San Benito Avenue where the evening sun was beginning
to go down.

I reckon I'm five thousand miles from home, he said. Do you think
we could eat a little bread and cheese to keep my body and spirit
together?

Johnny, said my father, run down to the grocer's and get a loaf of French bread and a pound of cheese.

Give me the money, I said.

Tell Mr. Kosak to give us credit, said my father. I ain't got a penny, Johnny.

He won't give us credit, I said. Mr. Kosak is tired of giving us credit. He's sore at us. He says we don't work and never pay our bills. We owe him forty cents.

Go on down there and argue it out with him, said my father. You know that's your job.

He won't listen to reason, I said. Mr. Kosak says he doesn't know anything about anything, all he wants is the forty cents.

Go on down there and make him give you a loaf of bread and a pound of cheese, said my father. You can do it, Johnny.

Go on down there, said the old man, and tell Mr. Kosak to give you a loaf of bread and a pound of cheese, son.

Go ahead, Johnny, said my father. You haven't yet failed to leave that store with provender, and you'll be back here in ten minutes with food fit for a king.

I don't know, I said. Mr. Kosak says we are trying to give him the merry run around. He wants to know what kind of work you are doing.

Well, go ahead and tell him, said my father. I have nothing to conceal. I am writing poetry. Tell Mr. Kosak I am writing poetry night and day.

Well, all right, I said, but I don't think he'll be much impressed. He says you never go out like other unemployed men and look for work. He says you're lazy and no good.

You go down there and tell him he's crazy, Johnny, said my father. You go on down there and tell that fellow your father is one of the greatest unknown poets living.

He might not care, I said, but I'll go. I'll do my best. Ain't we got nothing in the house?

Only popcorn, said my father. We been eating popcorn four days in a row now, Johnny. You got to get bread and cheese if you expect me to finish that long poem.

I'll do my best, I said.

Don't take too long, said Mr. MacGregor. I'm five thousand miles from home.

I'll run all the way, I said.

If you find any money on the way, said my father, remember we go fifty-fifty.

All right, I said.

I ran all the way to Mr. Kosak's store, but I didn't find any money on the way, not even a penny.

I went into the store and Mr. Kosak opened his eyes.

Mr. Kosak, I said, if you were in China and didn't have a friend in the world and no money, you'd expect some Christian over there to give you a pound of rice, wouldn't you?

What do you want? said Mr. Kosak.

I just want to talk a little, I said. You'd expect some member of the Aryan race to help you out a little, wouldn't you, Mr. Kosak?

How much money you got? said Mr. Kosak.

It ain't a question of money, Mr. Kosak, I said. I'm talking about being in China and needing the help of the white race.

I don't know nothing about nothing, said Mr. Kosak.

How would you feel in China that way? I said.

I don't know, said Mr. Kosak. What would I be doing in China?

Well, I said, you'd be visiting there, and you'd be hungry, and not a friend in the world. You wouldn't expect a good Christian to turn you away without even a pound of rice, would you, Mr. Kosak?

I guess not, said Mr. Kosak, but you ain't in China, Johnny, and neither is your Pa. You or your Pa's got to go out and work sometime in your lives, so you might as well start now. I ain't going to give you no more groceries on credit because I know you won't pay me.

Mr. Kosak, I said, you misunderstand me: I'm not talking about a few groceries. I'm talking about all them heathen people around you in China, and you hungry and dying.

This ain't China, said Mr. Kosak. You got to go out and make your living in this country. Everybody works in America.

Mr. Kosak, I said, suppose it was a loaf of French bread and a pound of cheese you needed to keep you alive in the world, would you hesitate to ask a Christian missionary for these things?

Yes, I would, said Mr. Kosak. I would be ashamed to ask.

Even if you knew you would give him back two loaves of bread and two pounds of cheese? I said. Even then?

Even then, said Mr. Kosak.

Don't be that way, Mr. Kosak, I said. That's defeatist talk, and you know it. Why, the only thing that would happen to you would be death. You would die out there in China, Mr. Kosak.

I wouldn't care if I would, said Mr. Kosak, you and your Pa have got to pay for bread and cheese. Why don't your Pa go out and get a job?

Mr. Kosak, I said, how are you, anyway?

I'm fine, Johnny, said Mr. Kosak. How are you?

Couldn't be better, Mr. Kosak, I said. How are the children?

Fine, said Mr. Kosak. Stepan is beginning to walk now.

That's great, I said. How is Angela?

Angela is beginning to sing, said Mr. Kosak. How is your grandmother?

She's feeling fine, I said. She's beginning to sing too. She says she would rather be an opera star than queen. How's Marta, your wife, Mr. Kosak?

Oh, swell, said Mr. Kosak.

I cannot tell you how glad I am to hear that all is well at your house, I said. I know Stepan is going to be a great man some day.

I hope so, said Mr. Kosak. I am going to send him straight through high school and see that he gets every chance I didn't get. I don't want him to open a grocery store.

I have great faith in Stepan, I said.

What do you want, Johnny? said Mr. Kosak. And how much money you got?

Mr. Kosak, I said, you know I didn't come here to buy anything. You know I enjoy a quiet philosophical chat with you every now and then. Let me have a loaf of French bread and a pound of cheese.

You got to pay cash, Johnny, said Mr. Kosak.

And Esther, I said. How is your beautiful daughter Esther?

Esther is all right, Johnny, said Mr. Kosak, but you got to pay cash. You and your Pa are the worst citizens in this whole country.

I'm glad Esther is all right, Mr. Kosak, I said. Jasper MacGregor is visiting our house. He is a great actor.

I never heard of him, said Mr. Kosak.

And a bottle of beer for Mr. MacGregor, I said.

I can't give you a bottle of beer, said Mr. Kosak.

Certainly you can, I said.

I can't, said Mr. Kosak. I'll let you have one loaf of stale bread, and one pound of cheese, but that's all. What kind of work does your Pa do when he works, Johnny?

My father writes poetry, Mr. Kosak, I said. That's the only work my father does. He is one of the greatest writers of poetry in the world.

When does he get any money? said Mr. Kosak.

He never gets any money, I said. You can't have your cake and eat it.

I don't like that kind of a job, said Mr. Kosak. Why doesn't your Pa work like everybody else, Johnny?

He works harder than everybody else, I said. My father works twice as hard as the average man.

Well, that's forty-five cents you owe me, Johnny, said Mr. Kosak. I'll let you have some stuff this time, but never again.

Tell Esther I love her, I said.

All right, said Mr. Kosak.

Goodbye, Mr. Kosak, I said.

Goodbye, Johnny, said Mr. Kosak.

I ran back to the house with the loaf of French bread and the pound of cheese.

My father and Mr. MacGregor were in the street waiting to see if I would come back with food. They ran half a block toward me and when they saw that it was food, they waved back to the house where my grandmother was waiting. She ran into the house to set the table.

I knew you'd do it, said my father.

So did I, said Mr. MacGregor.

He says we got to pay him fifty-five cents, I said. He says he ain't going to give us no more stuff on credit.

That's his opinion, said my father. What did you talk about, Johnny?

First I talked about being hungry and at death's door in China, I said, and then I inquired about the family.

How is everyone? said my father.

Fine, I said.

So we all went inside and ate the loaf of bread and the pound of cheese, and each of us drank two or three quarts of water, and after every crumb of bread had disappeared, Mr. MacGregor began to look around the kitchen to see if there wasn't something else to eat.

That green can up there, he said. What's in there, Johnny?

Marbles, I said.

That cupboard, he said. Anything edible in there, Johnny?

Crickets, I said.

That big jar in the corner there, Johnny, he said. What's good in there?

I got a gopher snake in that jar, I said.

Well, said Mr. MacGregor, I could go for a bit of boiled gopher snake in a big way, Johnny.

You can't have that snake, I said.

Why not, Johnny? said Mr. MacGregor. Why the hell not, son? I hear of fine Borneo natives eating snakes and grasshoppers. You ain't got half a dozen fat grasshoppers around, have you, Johnny?

Only four, I said.

Well, trot them out, Johnny, said Mr. MacGregor, and after we have had our fill, I'll play *Drink to Me Only with Thine Eyes* on the bugle for you. I'm mighty hungry, Johnny.

So am I, I said, but you ain't going to kill that snake.

My father sat at the table with his head in his hands, dreaming. My grandmother paced through the house, singing arias from Puccini. As through the streets I wander, she roared in Italian.

How about a little music? said my father. I think the boy would be delighted.

I sure would, Mr. MacGregor, I said.

All right, Johnny, said Mr. MacGregor.

So he got up and began to blow into the bugle and he blew louder than any man ever blew into a bugle and people for miles around heard him and got excited. Eighteen neighbours gathered in front of our house and applauded when Mr. MacGregor finished the solo. My father led Mr. MacGregor out on the porch and said, Good neighbours and friends, I want you to meet Jasper MacGregor, the greatest Shakespearean actor of our day.

The good neighbours and friends said nothing and Mr. MacGregor said, I remember my first appearance in London in 1867 as if it was yesterday, and he went on with the story of his career. Rufe Apley the carpenter said, How about some more music, Mr. MacGregor? and Mr. MacGregor said, Have you got an egg at your house?

I sure have, said Rufe. I got a dozen eggs at my house.

Would it be convenient for you to go and get one of them dozen eggs? said Mr. MacGregor. When you return I'll play a song that will make your heart leap with joy and grief.

I'm on my way already, said Rufe, and he went home to get an egg.

Mr. MacGregor asked Tom Baker if he had a bit of sausage at his house and Tom said he did, and Mr. MacGregor asked Tom if it would be convenient for Tom to go and get that little bit of sausage and come back with it and when Tom returned Mr. MacGregor would play a song on the bugle that would change the whole history of Tom's life. And Tom went home for the sausage, and Mr. MacGregor asked each of the eighteen good neighbours and friends if he had something small and nice to eat at his home, and each man said he did, and each man went to his home to get the small and nice thing to eat, so Mr. MacGregor would play the song he said would be so wonderful to hear, and when all the good neighbours and friends had returned to our house with all the small and nice things to eat, Mr. MacGregor lifted the bugle to his lips and played *My Heart's in the Highlands, My Heart is not Here*, and each of the good neighbours and friends wept and returned to his home, and Mr. MacGregor took all the good things into the kitchen and our family feasted and drank and was merry: an egg, a sausage, a dozen green onions, two kinds of cheese, butter, two kinds of bread, boiled potatoes, fresh tomatoes, a melon, tea, and many other good things to eat, and we ate and our bellies tightened, and Mr. MacGregor said, Sir, if it is all the same to you I should like to dwell in your house for some days to come, and my father said, Sir, my house is your house, and Mr. MacGregor stayed at our house seventeen days and seventeen nights, and on the afternoon of the eighteenth day a man from the Old People's Home came to our house and said, I am looking for Jasper MacGregor, the actor, and my father said, What do you want?

I am from the Old People's Home, said the young man, and I want Mr. MacGregor to come back to our place because we are putting on our annual show in two weeks and need an actor.

Mr. MacGregor got up from the floor where he had been dreaming and went away with the young man, and the following afternoon, when he was very hungry, my father said, Johnny, go down to Mr. Kosak's store and get a little something to eat. I know you can do it, Johnny. Get anything you can.

Mr. Kosak wants fifty-five cents, I said. He won't give us anything more without money.

Go on down there, Johnny, said my father. You know you can get that fine Slovak gentleman to give you a bit of something to eat.

So I went down to Mr. Kosak's store and took up the Chinese problem where I had dropped it, and it was quite a job for me to go away from the store with a box of bird seed and half a can of maple syrup, but I did it, and my father said, Johnny, this sort of fare is going to be pretty dangerous for the old lady, and sure enough in the morning we heard my grandmother singing like a canary, and my father said, How the hell can I write great poetry on bird seed?

THE LA SALLE HOTEL
IN CHICAGO

THE philosophers were standing around the steps of the Public Library, talking about everything. It was a clear dreamy April day and the men were glad. There was much good will among them and no hard feelings. The soapboxers were not supercilious towards the uninformed ones as they ordinarily were. The Slovak whose face was always smoothly shaven and whose teeth were very bad and who was usually loud and bitter and always in favor of revolution, riot and fire and cruelty and justice, spoke very quietly with a melancholy and gentle intonation, his bitterness and sadness still valid, but gayety valid too.

I don't know, he said with an accent. Sometimes I see them in their big cars and instead of hating them I feel sorry for them. They got money and big houses and servants, but sometimes when I see them, all that stuff don't mean anything, and I don't hate them.

The listeners listened and smiled. The eccentric one, who was religious in an extraordinary way, and old, who hated three kinds of people of the world, Catholics, Irishmen, and Italians, scratched his beard and didn't make an argument. He hated Catholics because he had once been a Catholic; he hated Irishmen because Irishmen were cops and cops had hit him over the head with clubs several times and pushed him around and knocked him down and taken him to jail; and he hated Italians because Mussolini was an Italian and because an Italian in New York had cheated him thirty years ago.

Now he listened to the Slovak and didn't make an argument.

The young men, who were always present but never joined the meetings, stood among the old men and smoked cigarettes. One of them, who was in love with a waitress and wanted to get married, said to the small anarchist who was violently opposed to everything in the world, A lot of people that are married—both of them work.

The anarchist was usually high-strung, impatient, and sarcastic, but on this day he did not mock the young man or laugh out loud in the peculiar way he had that was neither natural nor artificial.

That's true, he said. And the young man was glad to have someone to talk to.

The anarchist was a man of forty-five or so. He had a well-shaped head, thick brown hair, and his teeth were good. He thought Communists were dopes. You God damn day-dreamers, he said to them one day. I know all about your Karl Marx. What was he? He was a lousy Jew who was scared to death by the world. (The anarchist himself was a Jew, but his love of Jews was so great that it had turned to hate and mockery.) You think you've got a chance, he said, but you've got no more chance than anybody else. Nobody's got a chance. Even after you have your lousy revolution you won't have a chance. What will you do? Do you think anything will be different?

Then he became very vulgar and the Slovak said, What's the use talking to you? You've got your mind made up.

On this day, though, the anarchist was very kindly and allowed the young man who was in love to tell his story.

I only had a quarter, the young man said, so I walked into that cheap hamburger joint—Pete's on Mason Street, right around the corner from the Day and Night Bank—because I figured I could get a lot for my money. It was around midnight and I hadn't had anything to eat since breakfast. That was last week, Friday. I ain't been working lately and on top of everything else I got kicked out of my room. The landlady kept my stuff because I owed her two dollars. I got the quarter from a rummy-player on Third Street who'd been lucky. Well, my insides were groaning and I felt sick, but all I wanted was a big sandwich and a cup of coffee. It's funny the way things go. I didn't have any place to sleep either, and when I sat down on the stool at the counter and she came up to take my order I didn't even look at her. She put a glass of water down and I said, A hamburger with onions and everything else and a cup of coffee. The Greek started to make the hamburger and she brought the coffee. I took two sips and looked up. I had been looking down at the spoon and fork and knife. She was standing to one side looking at me and when I looked up she smiled, only it was different. It looked like she had known me all her life and I had known her all my life and we hadn't seen one another for maybe ten or fifteen years. I guess I fell in love. We started talking and I didn't try to make her or anything because I was so hungry and tired I guess, and maybe that's why she liked me. Any other time I guess I would have tried to make her and just have a little fun. She took me up to her room that night and I been staying there ever since, five nights now.

Here the young man began to be confused. The anarchist was very kind, however, and the young man explained.

I haven't touched her or anything, but I really love her and she really loves me. I kissed her last night because she looked so tired and beautiful, and she cried. She's a girl from Oklahoma. I guess she's had a few men, but it's different now. It's different with me too. I used to do office work, but I ain't got a job any more. I been going around to the agencies, but it don't look very good. If I could get a job we could get married and move into a small comfortable apartment.

A lot of people that are married—both of them work, he said. But I ain't got a job. When one of them works, he said, it's usually the man. I don't know what to do.

That's true, the anarchist said. Maybe you'll get a job tomorrow.

Where? the young man said. I wish I knew where. Everything's different with me now. My clothes are all worn out. I saw some swell shirts in the window of a store on Market Street for sixty-five cents; I saw a blue-serge suit for twelve fifty; and I know where I can get a good pair of shoes for three dollars. I'd like to throw away these old clothes and begin all over again. I'd like to marry her and get rid of everything old and move into a small comfortable apartment.

The anarchist was very sympathetic. He didn't care about the young man himself, who was miserable-looking and worried and undernourished and yet rather handsome because of this new thing in his life, this love of the waitress. He was delighted with the abstract purity and holiness of the event itself, in the crazy world, the boy starving and going into the dump for a hamburger and running headlong into love.

Maybe you'll get a job tomorrow, the anarchist said. Why don't you try a hotel?

The young man didn't quite understand.

No, he said, I don't think we'd care to live in a hotel. What we'd like to get is a small comfortable apartment with a bathroom and a little kitchen. We'd like to have a neat little place with some good chairs and a table and a bathroom and a little kitchen. I don't like these rooms that ain't got no bath in them, and you've got to do down the hall to take a bath and nine times out of ten there ain't no hot water. I'd like to fill a tub with warm water and sit in it a long time and then clean off all the dirt and get out and put on new clothes.

I don't mean to live in, the anarchist said. I mean to get a job at. I was thinking of these fine hotels that I'm accustomed to visiting the lobbies of.

Oh, the young man said. You mean to go to the hotels and ask for work?

Sure, the anarchist said. If you could get a job they'd give you a regular weekly salary and on top of that you'd make a little on tips.

I ain't had no experience being a bell-boy, the young man said.

That don't make no difference, the anarchist said.

Some of his old impatience began to return to him, and he believed nothing in the world should stop this boy from getting a job in a hotel and earning a regular weekly salary and making a little more on tips and marrying the waitress and moving into a small comfortable apartment with a bath and filling the tub with warm water and cleaning off all the dirt and getting out and putting on new clothes, the sixty-five cent shirts and the twelve fifty blue-serge suit.

That don't make a God damn bit of difference, the anarchist said. What does a bell-boy have to know? If they ask you have you had any experience, tell them sure, you were bell-boy at the La Salle Hotel in Chicago five years.

The La Salle Hotel in Chicago? the young man said.

Sure, the anarchist shouted. Why the hell not?

Maybe they'll be able to tell I ain't had no experience being a bell-boy, the young man said. Suppose they find out I ain't never been in Chicago?

Listen, the anarchist said. What if they do find out you ain't never been in Chicago? Do you think the world will end? (The anarchist himself was beginning to think the world would end if the young man didn't go out and get a job and move into an apartment with the girl.) Do you have to tell the truth, he said, when it doesn't make any difference one way or another if you've had any experience as a bell-boy or not or if you've ever been in Chicago or not, except that they *won't* give you a job if you *do* tell the truth and *might* if you don't?

The young man was a little bewildered and couldn't speak. The anarchist was so angry with the world and so delighted about this remarkable love affair that he himself didn't know what to say, or how to put what he meant.

He became a little unreasonable.

How the hell do you *know* you've never been in Chicago? he shouted.

The Slovak heard him shouting and stopped talking to listen. The eccentric one, the man of God, whose God was unlike anybody else's, moved closer to the anarchist and the young man, and little by little all the men gathered around the two.

What? said the young man.

He was beginning to wake up, and at the same time he was beginning to be embarrassed. He had been telling secrets, and now everybody was near him, near the secret, and everybody was listening and wanting to know what it was all about; why, on such a day as this, when everybody was glad and without ill will, and quiet, the anarchist was shouting.

How the hell do you know it? the anarchist shouted. Catch on? he said. You were *born* in Chicago. You lived there all your life until three months ago. Your father was born in Chicago. Your mother was born in Chicago. Your father worked in the La Salle Hotel in Chicago. Your mother worked in the La Salle Hotel in Chicago. *You* worked in the La Salle Hotel in Chicago.

The listeners didn't understand. They looked around at one another, smiling and asking what it was all about, and then they looked again at the anarchist who was suddenly so different and yet so much the same, and then they looked at the young man. It was all very confusing. But they knew it would be dangerous to interrupt the anarchist and ask a question or say something witty. They listened religiously.

There are a lot of good hotels in this town, the anarchist said. Begin at the beginning and go right on down the line and don't stop until they give you a job. Get up in the morning and shave cleanly and go down and talk to them and don't be afraid. Them hotels are full of people that got plenty of money and not one of them in the whole city has got better use for a little money than you have. Not a lousy one of them, he shouted. What the hell makes you think you ain't never been in Chicago? Start with the St. Francis Hotel on Powell Street. Then the Palace on Market Street. Then the Mark Hopkins. Then the Clift. Then the Fairmont. What the hell do you mean you ain't been in Chicago? What the hell kind of talk do you call that?

Now the young man was completely awake, as the anarchist was awake. He seemed to understand what the anarchist was trying to tell him and he was ashamed because the men were near him and could feel, even though they didn't *know* what it was all about, what it was all about.

The anarchist took the young man by the arm. His grip was very strong and the young man felt as if the man might be an elder brother or a father.

You understand what I'm telling you, don't you? he said.

Yes, the young man said.

He moved to go.

Thanks, he said.

He hurried down the street, and the anarchist stamped into the Public Library.

The men were very silent. Then one of them said, What the hell was he shouting about anyway? What the hell was all that stuff about the La Salle Hotel in Chicago? What *about* the La Salle Hotel in Chicago?

THE ORANGES

THEY told him, Stand on the corner with two of the biggest oranges in your hand and when an automobile goes by, smile and wave the oranges at them. Five cents each if they want one, his uncle Jake said, three for ten cents, thirty-five cents a dozen. Smile big, he said. You *can* smile, can't you, Luke? You got it in you to smile once in a while, ain't you?

He tried very hard to smile and his uncle Jake made a terrible face, so he knew it was a bad smile. He wished he could laugh out loud the way some people laughed, only they weren't scared the way he was, and all mixed-up.

I never did see such a serious boy in all my life, his uncle Jake said. Luke, he said.

His uncle squatted down, so his head would be level with his, so he could look into his eyes, and talked to him.

Luke, he said, they won't buy oranges if you don't smile. People like to see a little boy smiling, selling oranges. It makes them happy.

He listened to his uncle talking to him, looking into his uncle's eyes, and he understood the words. What he felt, though, was: Jake is mixed-up, too. He saw the man stand up and heard him groan, just as his father used to groan.

Luke, his uncle Jake said. Sometimes you can laugh, can't you?

Not him, said Jake's wife. If you weren't such a coward, you would be out selling them oranges yourself. You belong the same place your brother is, she said. In the ground. Dead, she said.

It was this that made it hard for him to smile: the way this woman was always talking, not the words only, but the meanness in her voice, always picking on his uncle Jake. How did she expect him to smile or feel all right when she was always telling them they were no good, the whole family no good?

Jake was his father's younger brother, and Jake looked like his father. Of course she always had to say his father was better off dead just because he was no good selling stuff. She was always telling Jake,

This is America. You got to get around and meet people and make them like you. And Jake was always saying, Make them like me? How can I make them like me? And she was always getting sore at him and saying, Oh, you fool. If I didn't have this baby in my belly, I'd go out and work in Rosenberg's and keep you like a child.

Jake had that same desperate look his father had, and he was always getting sore at himself and wanting other people to be happy. Jake was always asking him to smile.

All right, Jake said. All right, all right, all right, kill me, drive me crazy. Sure. I should be dead. Ten boxes of oranges and not a penny in the house and nothing to eat. I should be dead. Should I stand in the street, holding oranges? Should I get a wagon maybe and go through the streets? I should be dead, he said.

Then Jake made a face, so sad it looked, as if nobody was ever that sad in the world, not even he, and wished he didn't want to cry because Jake was so sad. On top of that Jake's wife got sorer than ever and began to cry the way she cried when she got real sore and you could just feel how terrible everything was because she didn't cry sad, she cried sore, reminding Jake of all the bills and all the hard times she had had with him and all about the baby in her belly, to come out, she said, Why, what good is another fool in the world?

There was a box of oranges on the floor, and she picked up two of them, crying, and she said, No fire in the stove, in November, all of us freezing. The house should be full of the smell of meat. Here, she cried, eat. Eat your oranges. Eat them until you die, and she cried and cried.

Jake was too sad to talk. He sat down and began to wave back and forth, looking crazy. And they asked *him* to laugh. And Jake's wife kept walking in and out of the room, holding the oranges, crying and talking about the baby in her belly.

After a while she stopped crying.

Now take him to the corner, she said, and see if he can't get a little money.

Jake was just about deaf, it looked like. He didn't even lift his head. So she shouted.

Take him to the corner. Ask him to smile at the people. We got to eat.

What's the use to be alive when everything is rotten and nobody knows what to do? What's the use to go to school and learn arithmetic and read poems and paint eggplants and all that stuff? What's the use to sit in a cold room until it is time to go to bed and hear Jake and his wife fighting all the time and go to sleep and cry and wake up and see the sad sky and feel the cold air and shiver and walk to school and eat oranges for lunch instead of bread?

Jake jumped up and began to shout at his wife. He said he would kill her and then stick a knife in his heart, so she cried more than ever and tore her dress and she was naked to the waist and she said, All right, better all of us were dead, kill me, but Jake put his arms around her and walked into the other room with her, and he could hear her crying and kissing him and telling him he was just a baby, a great big baby, he needed her like a mother.

He had been standing in the corner and it all happened so swiftly he hadn't noticed how tired he had become, but he was very tired, and hungry, so he sat down. What's the use to be alive if you're all alone in the world and no mother and father and nobody to love you? He wanted to cry but what's the use to cry when it don't do any good anyhow?

After a while Jake came out of the room and he was trying to smile.

All you got to do, Luke, he said, is hold two big oranges in your hand and wave them at the people when they go by in their automobiles, and smile. You'll sell a box of oranges in no time, Luke.

I'll smile, he said. One for five cents, three for ten cents, thirty-five cents a dozen.

That's it, said Jake.

Jake lifted the box of oranges from the floor and began walking to the back door.

It was very sad in the street, Jake holding the box of oranges, and him walking beside Jake, listening to Jake telling him to smile big, and the sky was sad, and there were no leaves on the trees, and the street was sad, and it was very funny, the smell of the oranges was clean and good and they looked so nice it was very funny. The oranges looked so nice and they were so sad.

It was Ventura corner, where all the automobiles went by, and Jake put the box on the sidewalk.

It looks best with only a small boy, he said. I'll go back to the house, Luke.

Jake squatted again and looked into his eyes. You ain't afraid, are you, Luke? I'll come back before it gets dark. It won't be dark for two hours yet. Just feel happy and smile at the people.

I'll smile, he said.

Then Jake jumped up, like maybe he couldn't get up at all unless he jumped up, and he went hurrying down the street, walking away swiftly, making it a sad world: five cents for one, three for ten cents, thirty-five cents a dozen.

He picked out two of the biggest oranges and held them in his right hand, and lifted his arm over his head. It didn't seem right. It seemed sad. What's the use to hold two big oranges in your hand and lift your arm over your head and get ready to smile at people going by in automobiles?

It seemed a long time before he saw an automobile coming up the street from town, right on his side, and when it got closer he saw there was a man driving and a lady in the back with two kids. He smiled very big when they got right close, but it didn't look as if they were going to stop, so he waved the oranges at them and moved closer to the street. He saw their faces very close, and smiled just a little bigger. He couldn't smile much bigger because it was making his cheeks tired. The people didn't stop and didn't even smile back at him. The little girl in the automobile made a face at him as if she thought he looked cheap. What's the use to stand on a corner and try to sell oranges to people who make faces at you because you are smiling and want them to like you?

What's the use to have your muscles aching just because some people are rich and some people are poor and the rich ones eat and laugh and the poor ones don't eat and always fight and ask each other to kill them?

He brought his arm down and stopped smiling and looked at the fire hydrant and beyond the fire hydrant the gutter and beyond the gutter the street, Ventura, and on both sides of the street houses and in the houses people and at the end of the street the country where the vineyards and orchards were and streams and meadows and then mountains and beyond the mountains more cities and more houses and streets and people. What's the use to be in the world when you can't even look at a fire hydrant without wanting to cry?

Another automobile was coming up the street, so he lifted his arm and began to smile again, but when the automobile went by he saw that the man wasn't even looking at him. Five cents for one. They could eat oranges. After bread and meat they could eat an orange. Peel it and smell the nice smell and eat it. They could stop their automobiles and buy three for ten cents. Then another automobile went by while he smiled and waved his arm, but the people just looked at him and that was all. If they would just smile back it wouldn't be so bad, but just going by and not even smiling back. A lot of automobiles went by and it looked as if he ought to sit down and stop smiling and cry because it was terrible. They didn't want any oranges and they didn't like to see him smile the way his uncle Jake said they would. They just saw him and didn't do anything else.

It began to be pretty dark and for all he cared the whole world could end. He just guessed he would be standing there holding up his arm and smiling until the end of the world.

He just guessed that's all he was born to do, just stand on the corner and wave oranges at the people and smile at them with great big tears coming down his cheeks till the end of the world, everything black and empty and him standing there smiling until his cheeks hurt and crying because they wouldn't even smile back at him and for all he cared the whole world could just fall into the darkness and end and Jake could be dead and his wife could be dead and all the streets and houses and people and rivers and meadows and sky could end and there could be nobody anywhere, not even one man anywhere or one empty street or one dark window or one shut door because they didn't want to buy oranges and they wouldn't smile at him, and the whole world could end.

A VISITOR IN THE
PIANO WAREHOUSE

I WORK in the warehouse of Sligo, Baylie on Bryant Street between First and Second, directly under the curve of the Fremont
Street ramp of the Bay Bridge in San Francisco. The warehouse is
one block long, and half a block wide. It is full of pianos.

Sligo, Baylie is an old San Francisco music store located at the
corner of Grant Avenue and Geary Street, about two miles from the
warehouse. It has been in business one hundred and eleven years. The
company occupies its own building of six floors. It deals in everything
pertaining to music, as well as in radios, televisions, refrigerators,
deep-freeze boxes, stoves, sporting goods, and many other things. I
have never met Lucander Sligo III, who owns and operates the
business.

The first Lucander Sligo founded the company with Elton Baylie
The business was a piano business exclusively for quite a number of
years. Baylie had no sons, but his daughter Eltonia went into the
company. Baylie hoped she would marry the first Lucander's son, but
Eltonia married a man named Spezzafly when she was forty-four and
he was ten or eleven years younger. Eltonia's husband wasn't interested
in pianos, if in fact he was interested in Eltonia. He certainly wasn't
interested in their son. He left Eltonia before the boy was born.

The staff at the warehouse of Sligo, Baylie consists of Eltonia's son,
Oliver Morgan, Spezzafly, now sixty-nine, and myself, Ashland Clewpor, twenty-four.

I have been at the warehouse a year and a half.

I applied for work at the personnel department of Sligo, Baylie,
on the sixth floor. The girl in charge was quite impressed with the
facts of my background, but she regretted very much that there was
no opening.

"Unless," she said, "you wouldn't mind working at the warehouse."

"What kind of work is it?"

She then told me about O. M. Spezzafly. She warned me that over the past twenty-five years nobody had worked for him for longer than a month.

"Why not?"

She tried to tell me as nicely as possible that O. M., as she called him, was certainly entitled to an important position with the firm, with an important yearly salary, but that it had been absolutely necessary twenty-five years ago to make him manager of the warehouse— or, to put it bluntly, to get him out of the way.

As manager of the warehouse, O.M. had asked for a staff, she said, and Lucander Sligo III had insisted on letting O.M. have a secretary, a bookkeeper, a janitor, and an all-around piano man, one who could tune and repair pianos. The secretary quit after a week, though, and the others within a month. Little by little O.M. became adjusted to the idea of having a staff of only one.

"What does the job pay?" I said.

"Sixty-five dollars a week to start. There is a five-dollar raise every month, however."

"For how long?"

"For as long as you keep the job."

"Suppose I keep it three years?"

"You will get a raise of five dollars every month."

"What are my duties?"

"O.M. will let you know."

"Can you give me an idea what they *might* be?"

"I'm afraid not," the girl said. "All I know is that you will be at the warehouse eight hours a day Monday through Friday. I'm afraid I can't urge you to take the job."

Half an hour later I was at the warehouse, knocking at the front door. I knocked because the door was locked. At last I heard footsteps, light and swift, and the door was swung open. I saw a tall man who wore a dark business suit. I introduced myself, and he asked me to come to his office, the door of which was only a few feet from the entrance to the warehouse.

Mr. Spezzafly's office was large and handsomely furnished. His desk was enormous and expensive. His chair was made of black leather. Behind his chair was a large portrait in oils of his grandfather Elton Baylie, and beside it a portrait of his mother Eltonia.

The interview was short, although Mr. Spezzafly examined the form I had filled out at the personnel department.

"Ashland Clewpor?"

"Yes, sir."

"Let me show you your office, Mr. Clewpor."

We walked through pianos of all kinds, but not through a path of any kind, to the far end of the warehouse where a fence had been put around a small area. The fence began two feet from the floor and stopped at five feet. We entered through swinging doors and I saw a small area entirely bare of anything except a plain flat-top desk and a plain unvarnished chair. There was a telephone on the desk. Nothing else.

"Sit down, please, Mr. Clewpor."

I sat at the desk.

"Very good," Mr. Spezzafly said, and left.

I sat at the desk without moving for about ten minutes, and then I drew open the drawers of the desk and found all six of them empty. The whole office was a desk and a chair, surrounded by a fence.

At a quarter to five I decided to use the telephone, more for something to do than somebody to talk to. I thought I would call Newbegin's and ask if they could recommend a good book on pianos. I began to dial Information for the number, but while I was doing so I heard somebody say, "Yes?"

It was Mr. Spezzafly.

"I thought I would telephone Newbegin's to see if they have a good history of the piano."

"O.M. Spezzafly speaking."

"Yes, sir."

"May I ask who's calling?"

"There must be something the matter with the phone, Mr. Spezzafly," I said. "This is Ashland Clewpor."

"What is it, Mr. Clewpor?"

"I was wondering if I might telephone Newbegin's."

"What is Newbegin's?"

"It's a bookstore, sir."

"I'll call you back," Mr. Spezzafly said.

I thought he meant in a few minutes.

He called me back on Friday at five minutes to five.

"Mr. Clewpor," he said, "on your way out please stop at my desk and pick up your check."

"Yes, sir."

The check was in a green plate that might have served as an ash tray.

"You'll find it there every Friday," Mr. Spezzafly said.

"Yes, sir. Thank you."

I took the check and folded it, so that if there was anything he might wish to tell me there would be time for him to do so.

"Well done," he said. "That was a perfect fold."

I waited a moment in the hope that he would say something about what I might expect next week, but he said nothing.

Saturday morning I visited the personnel department of Sligo, Baylie, and the girl there said, "Well?"

"I was wondering if there is anything you might care to tell me about Mr. Spezzafly."

"You haven't come to quit?"

"No, I don't think I have."

"What did you do all week?"

"Nothing."

"What did he do?"

"I don't know."

"Do you think him odd?"

"He doesn't *look* odd."

"You plan to stay, then?"

"Is there an opening here?"

"Well," the girl said, "to be perfectly honest, there *is*, but it's in the stove department, and it's sixty-five a week, with no raises at all. Certainly not for a year or two. Would you like to meet the manager of the stove department?"

"Well, if I kept my job with Mr. Spezzafly for a year I'd be getting a salary of one hundred and twenty five dollars a week, wouldn't I?"

"Yes, that's right," the girl said.

"That's pretty good, isn't it?"

"Yes, it is."

"Well, I'm not married."

"Yes, I noticed that you're not when I read your application last Monday."

"Well, after a year with Mr. Spezzafly if I said to you will you be my wife, what would you say?"

"I'm married," the girl said. "Do you want to meet the manager of the stove department?"

"No," I said. "Is there anything you can tell me about Mr. Spezzafly? I mean, what are my duties?"

"Well," the girl said, "if you've decided to stay with Mr. Spezzafly another week, why not ask him Monday morning?"

Mr. Spezzafly was standing outside the door of his office at eight o'clock Monday morning.

"I appreciate punctuality," he said. "The time is one minute to eight. I am apt to be here at *ten* minutes to eight, but it is quite all right for you to be here at one minute to eight."

"Yes, sir."

"I also appreciate a good appearance. A man who comes to work Monday morning looking fit is a man who is going to look fit all week."

"Mr. Spezzafly, what are my duties?"

"My boy," Mr. Spezzafly said, "your work is waiting for you in your office."

He nodded courteously and went into his office. I walked through the pianos and went into my office. I expected to see a stack of papers on my desk, but there wasn't anything there. I sat down and tried to guess who she had married, but I couldn't. A girl who is married is married, that's all.

The second week went by exactly like the first. Friday afternoon at five I picked up my check and went home. Saturday morning I went back to the personnel department, because I had to see her again.

"There's an opening in the refrigerator department," she said. "Would you like to meet the manager of the refrigerator department?"

"Who is he?"

"Mr. Stavros."

"How much is the salary?"

"Sixty-five, but there's no promise of a raise. Aren't you happy at the warehouse?"

"I don't know what I'm supposed to do."

"Yes, that's how it goes."

"I made a path through the pianos."

"Did Mr. Spezzafly approve?"

"He didn't say."

"Did he *use* the path?"

"No, but the day I made the path he phoned at a quarter to five and said that whenever I answer the phone in the future I should say, 'Ashland speaking.' I *had* been saying 'Hello.' "

"I believe he likes the path you made."

"Do you mean I should go ahead and do things like that?"

"Yes, I think so."

"Shouldn't I try to *sell* a piano?"

"Has anybody asked for one?"

"No, but he keeps the front door locked."

"Well, it *is* a warehouse, not a salesroom."

"What are the pianos for?"

"People trade in old pianos for various modern things, and we put the old pianos in the warehouse, that's all."

"Do you ever take them out?"

"There isn't much demand for old pianos."

"We've got a hundred and twenty-three of them. I counted them."

"Do you like being among a lot of pianos?"

"Yes, I *do.* I like to see those pianos every morning. Of course, I see them all day, too, but I mean when I go in there every morning I *especially* enjoy seeing them. There they are, I mean. *All* of them. All kinds of them. Who did you marry?"

"My husband is an accountant at Wells, Fargo. The refrigerator department is full of laughter and jokes all day long, because Mr. Stavros is such a humorous man. Would you like to meet him?"

"No, but if you have a sister, I'd like to meet her."

"I don't have a sister. There are three rather attractive girls in the refrigerator department, though. Perhaps you ought to leave the warehouse."

"I never *expected* to work in a warehouse. My ambition has always been to be famous."

"A lot of people think Mr. Stavros would have been famous if he had gone on the stage." She scribbled something on a piece of paper with some mimeographed typing on it. She folded the piece of paper and held it out to me.

"What is it?"

"An introduction to Mr. Stavros."

"I don't think I want to leave the warehouse just yet."

Monday morning at one minute to eight Mr. Spezzafly was standing outside the door of his office.

"Ash," he said, "if you go straight to your office and sit at your desk, I'm going to try something."

I went to my office and sat at my desk, and after two or three minutes the telephone buzzed and I lifted the receiver.

"Ashland speaking," I said.

"Ash," Mr. Spezzafly said, "I'm thinking of leaving the front door unlatched, so that it can be opened from the street without a key. I thought I'd try that this morning, and possibly this afternoon."

"Yes, sir."

"If somebody comes in, I'll let you know by telephone."

"Yes, sir."

"In case I don't happen to notice, though, and you *do*—"

Mr. Spezzafly stopped. I waited a moment, and then I said, "Yes, sir?"

"Well, Ash, what I mean is, find out who it is."

"Yes, sir. Shall I let you know?"

"I don't think so, Ash. This is only an experiment."

"Yes, sir."

Nobody came in all day Monday. Tuesday morning at half past ten my telephone buzzed and Mr. Spezzafly said, "I just want you to know, Ash, that I've left the door unlatched again."

"Yes, sir."

"On second thought, if somebody comes in, give me a ring. Just say, 'Visitor in the warehouse.' I'll understand."

"Yes, sir. Visitor in the warehouse."

"Precisely."

Nobody came in, but at a quarter to five I thought I'd phone him to ask if he wanted me to try to sell a piano.

When he lifted the receiver he said, "Visitor in the warehouse, Ash?"

"No, sir."

"Dang."

"I called to ask if you'd like me to try to sell a piano."

"Ash," Mr. Spezzafly said, "let's just call when there's a visitor in the warehouse."

"Yes, sir."

There wasn't a visitor all week. Friday afternoon I picked up my check and went home, and Saturday morning I went up to the personnel department again, and the girl there said, "I've got a rather exciting position to offer you in the sporting goods department. Mr. Plattock wants a likely-looking man to demonstrate the rowing machine and the limbering-up bicycle. Would you like to meet Mr. Plattock?"

"I don't know."

"You will be permitted to wear sports clothing supplied by Sligo, Baylie, and I have an idea you will make an excellent impression."

She began to scribble on the small piece of paper again, but I just wasn't thinking about demonstrating a rowing machine or a limbering-up bicycle, I was thinking about having a visitor in the warehouse.

"Could you come to the warehouse next Monday during your lunch hour?"

"I *could*—of course," the girl said. "Is there a particular reason why I *should*, however?"

"Well, Mr. Spezzafly is trying out something new. He's leaving the front door unlatched, so that anybody who wants to come into the warehouse from Bryant Street can do so, but all last week nobody came in. I thought if you were to come in, I could telephone Mr. Spezzafly."

"I see."

"Afterwards, we could go to lunch at the place next to the S.P. depot."

"I generally have lunch with my husband at a little place next door to Wells, Fargo."

"Could you skip lunch with your husband on Monday?"

"You'd rather not meet Mr. Plattock, then?"

"I don't think so. You see, when I start something, I like to try to see it through."

"Oh? You feel you've started something, do you?"

"Yes, I do."

"What is it that you feel you've started?"

"I've started to understand Mr. Spezzafly."

"Really?"

"Yes, and a few other things, too."

"What else have you started to understand?"

"Well, being famous, for instance. Now, being famous the way famous people are famous is not *really* being famous, but being famous the way Mr. Spezzafly's famous, that's really being famous And a few others I know."

"Everybody at Sligo, Baylie has known about Mr. Spezzafly's fame for years. Who are the others?"

"Well, the way *you're* famous seems to me to be a way that's more famous than the way the famous movie actresses are famous."

"Well, that's very nice of you, but hardly anybody in the whole world knows me."

"That's the part I'm beginning to understand. You're famous without very many people knowing you, but the ones who *do* know you, *they* know you're famous."

"How do you know they do?"

"Well, I hardly know you, and I know you're famous, so just imagine how it is with those who really know you, like your husband, or your children, if you've got any."

"I haven't got any."

"But if you had some, wouldn't they know how famous you are, though?"

"Yes, I suppose they would, at that."

"Will you visit the warehouse?"

"Well, perhaps not Monday, but perhaps Tuesday or Wednesday."

"You'll find the door unlatched. My office is in the back, on the right."

Monday I took my lunch and ate it under the Fremont Street ramp of the Bay Bridge, while Mr. Spezzafly ate his at his desk. I don't know why he eats his sandwiches in his office. I eat mine in the streets because I enjoy walking during my lunch hour.

I walk down First Street to Pier 38 or down Bryant Street to Pier 28 and I look at the ships down there, and think.

I think about the past, the present, and the future, but mainly about the future, although I can't forget the past, especially where I spent so many years in the homes of people who wanted to find out if they wanted to adopt me, and decided they didn't—about when I was fifteen, and ran away because I wanted to live my own life, and when I was eighteen and got in the Marines and went to Korea and got wounded but didn't get killed, the way three of my pals did, just spent a year in different hospitals, and got discharged in San Francisco when I was twenty-two.

Mostly, though, on the lunch-hour walks I think about the future.

At twelve o'clock on Tuesday I didn't leave my office, even though I had no lunch to eat. I just sat at my desk, listening. There wasn't anything to listen to, but there *might* be pretty soon, and I wanted to be ready for it. At a quarter after twelve I heard it.

It was a visitor in the warehouse.

The footsteps came closer, and then the swinging doors of my office opened.

I got on the phone.

"Visitor in the warehouse, Mr. Spezzafly."

"Who is it, Ash?"

"Girl here in a blue dress."

"Thank you, Ash."

Mr. Spezzafly hung up, I hung up, and the girl in the blue dress stepped up to my desk and held out a piece of folded paper to me. It was the introduction form of the personnel department of Sligo, Baylie, and it said: *Introducing Miss Stella Mayhew to Mr. Ashland Clewpor. P.S. Good luck.*

I walked around the desk and put my hand out, and Stella Mayhew and I shook hands.

"I'm happy to make your acquaintance," I said.

Stella seemed awful scared, but I was awful scared myself, because in the first place I had expected the visitor to be the girl in the personnel department, a married girl, and in the second place Stella was the first visitor in the warehouse, and in the third place I had never seen a girl I liked so much.

Stella opened her handbag quickly and brought out a folded application. I unfolded it and started reading the answers she had given to the questions.

I wanted to be as businesslike as possible, so after I had read a few answers I said, "I see." I read a few more answers and again I said, "I see."

And then—well, I just took her in my arms and kissed her, I knew I ought to try to be a little more businesslike, but I kept thinking about the past and the future. I kept seeing the past all smoothed out on account of her, and I kept seeing the future just the way I'd always wanted to see it—a little house of our own, both of us famous, and a famous son, and a little later on a famous daughter.

I was kissing Stella when the telephone buzzed.

"Ashland speaking."

"What's the visitor want, Ash?"

"I don't know, sir."

"Everything in order?"

"Yes, sir."

"All right, Ash. I'll have my lunch, then."

"Yes, sir."

Again Mr. Spezzafly hung up and I hung up.

I took my chair around the desk and asked Stella Mayhew to please sit down, because I wanted to talk to her. She sat down, and I told her about my whole life, past, present, and future, and then I said, "I mean, I'm not really a business executive or anything like that. I don't have a job to offer, but I've got a job myself, and I plan to keep it, especially if there's something nice and sensible I can do with the money I earn. I'd like to make a down payment on a new house somewhere, but I wouldn't care to do that unless I had somebody to move in there with, to be my wife. That's the only job I can offer you—if it's all right. I've read the application and I like everything in it. And of course I can *see* you. I mean, I'm glad you've been in San Francisco only a week, and I'm glad you don't have any people, either, because I don't, either, and people who don't have any people—well, when they have one another, I guess it means something. Is it all right?"

"Yes, sir," Stella Mayhew said.

I was kissing her again when I heard Mr. Spezzafly coming down the path I had made through the pianos, but I just couldn't stop. Mr. Spezzafly pushed the swinging doors open, and I said, "Mr. Spezzafly, may I present Miss Stella Mayhew?"

"How do you do, Miss Mayhew," Mr. Spezzafly said.

"Miss Mayhew," I said, "is the future Mrs. Ashland Clewpor."

"Well, Ash," Mr. Spezzafly said, "I think that's very nice. You couldn't have found a nicer girl if you had looked all over the world." He smiled at Stella. "And you couldn't find a nicer boy," he said.

"Thank you, sir," Stella said.

"Not at all," Mr. Spezzafly said. He left the office, and Stella and I listened to him walking up the path back to his office.

Then Stella told me everything she knew about her own life, past, present, and future. She tried not to cry a couple of times, and made it, too, but one time she didn't. I didn't, either.

The year and a half that I've been employed in the warehouse of Sligo, Baylie has been the happiest time of my whole life. I don't ever expect to quit, although I've asked the girl in the personnel department to stop giving me the five-dollar raise every month.

"Not yet," she says. "Plenty of time to stop the raises. How is Mr. Spezzafly?"

"Just famous, the same as ever."

"And how is your wife Stella?"

"Just famous, too, thank you."

"And how is your son?"

"My son is the most famous man in the world."

"I've got a rather attractive position in the television department I can offer you," the girl in the personnel department says, but she just says that for the fun of it, because she knows I don't want to leave the warehouse.

She knows that when I start something I like to see it through

DEAR GRETA GARBO

D EAR Miss Garbo:

I hope you noticed me in the newsreel of the recent Detroit Riot in which my head was broken. I never worked for Ford but a friend of mine told me about the strike and as I had nothing to do that day I went over with him to the scene of the riot and we were standing around in small groups chewing the rag about this and that and there was a lot of radical talk, but I didn't pay any attention to it.

I didn't think anything was going to happen but when I saw the newsreel automobiles drive up, I figured, well, here's a chance for me to get into the movies like I always wanted to, so I stuck around waiting for my chance. I always knew I had the sort of face that would film well and look good on the screen and I was greatly pleased with my performance, although the little accident kept me in the hospital a week.

Just as soon as I got out, though, I went around to a little theatre in my neighborhood where I found out they were showing the newsreel in which I played a part, and I went into the theatre to see myself on the screen. It sure looked great, and if you noticed the newsreel carefully you couldn't have missed me because I am the young man in the blue-serge suit whose hat fell off when the running began. Remember? I turned around on purpose three or four times to have my face filmed and I guess you saw me smile. I wanted to see how my smile looked in the moving pictures and even if I do say so I think it looked pretty good.

My name is Felix Otria and I come from Italian people. I am a high-school graduate and speak the language like a native as well as Italian. I look a little like Rudolph Valentino and Ronald Colman, and I sure would like to hear that Cecil B. De Mille or one of those other big shots noticed me and saw what good material I am for the movies.

The part of the riot that I missed because they knocked me out

I saw in the newsreel and I mean to say it must have got to be a regular affair, what with the water hoses and the tear-gas bombs, and the rest of it. But I saw the newsreel eleven times in three days, and I can safely say no other man, civilian or police, stood out from the crowd the way I did, and I wonder if you will take this matter up with the company you work for and see if they won't send for me and give me a trial. I know I'll make good and I'll thank you to my dying day, Miss Garbo. I have a strong voice, and I can play the part of a lover very nicely, so I hope you will do me a little favor. Who knows, maybe some day in the near future I will be playing the hero in a picture with you.

Yours very truly,

Felix Otria.

THE LIVING AND THE DEAD

I WAS in my room fast asleep at three in the afternoon when Pete the writer came in without knocking. I knew it was Pete from the extra nervous way the door opened and I didn't even need to open my eyes to make sure who it was *after* he was in because I could smell it was somebody who needed a bath and I couldn't remember anyone I knew who needed one, except Pete, so I tried to stay asleep. I knew he wanted to talk and if there was anything I didn't want to be bothered with at that hour of the day it was talk.

When you are asleep at an hour when everybody but a loafer is supposed to be awake you understand how foolish all the activity and talk of the world is and you have an idea the world would be a better place in which to suffer if everybody would stop talking a while and go to sleep, especially at three in the afternoon when sleeping is supposed to be immoral and an indication of the spiritual disintegration of modern man. You figure speech is one of the extra special privileges of the mortal. You figure not being able to sleep is the basic cause of man's jumping around in the world, trying to do stuff.

It was a warm day and the light of the sun was on my face, going through my shut eyes to the measureless depths of the rest of it, the past of my life, the place where the past is assembled, lighting up this vast area, inside, and I was feeling quiet as a rock and very truthful. Try it sometime. Maybe you have no idea how far away you've been from where you are now, within your skull and skin, but if you are alive and know it, chances are you've been everywhere and seen everything and have just reached home, and my slogan is this: What this world needs is a better understanding of how and when to sleep. Anybody can be awake, but it takes a lot of quiet oriental wisdom to be able to lay your weary body in the light of the sun and remember the beginning of the earth.

Pete isn't a bad guy and in his own way he can write a simple sentence that sometimes means what he wants it to mean. Ordinarily, in spite of the smell, he is good company. He is excited, but that's because he is trying hard to say something that will straighten out everything and make everybody get up tomorrow morning with a clean heart and a face all furrowed with smiles.

Asleep, I am a pretty profound thinker. Consequently I get sore at people who have no consideration for the sanctity of prayer and the holiness of comfort. Awake, however, I am a picture of good breeding.

There were two quart bottles of cheap beer on the table, a bottle-opener, a glass, and a package of Chesterfields. Pete opened a bottle, poured himself a glass, took a gulp, lit a cigarette, inhaled, and I sat up and yawned, my only form of exercise.

God Almighty, Pete said, how can you sleep at a time like this? Don't you realize the world is going mad? The poor are perishing like flies. Starving to death. Freezing to death. And you stretch out here in this hole in the wall and act as if everything were jake. Do you mind if I have a drink?

I told him anything I had was his, and he said: The true bourgeois, all kindness, but you can't fool me. That sort of charity isn't going to stand in the way of the revolution. They are trying to buy us off with their cheap groceries and their free rent, but we'll rise up and crush them.

I yawned and opened the window. A little clean air moved past the curtain and I breathed it and yawned again. Who do you want to crush? I said.

Don't be funny, said Pete. This tyranny's got to end. They're trying to cram Fascism down our throats, but they won't get away with it.

Who are you talking about? I said.

The bosses, said Pete, the lousy bosses.

You haven't done an honest day's work in ten years, I said. What bosses?

The rats, said Pete. The blood-sucking Capitalists. Morgan and Mellon and them big pricks.

Them guys are just as pathetic as you are, I said. I'll bet ten to one if you could meet Morgan you'd appreciate how close to death he is. He'd give two or three million dollars to be in your boots, just so he wouldn't have to be a writer. He'd give every penny he has to be as young as you are. Morgan's an old man. He isn't long for this world. He'll be dead any minute now. You've got a good forty years ahead of you if you don't fall down somewhere and bust your head against a fire hydrant.

That's all bourgeois talk, said Pete. I'm talking about *twenty-five million hungry men, women and children in America.*

Everybody gets hungry, I said. Even the rich get hungry between meals.

Don't get funny, said Pete. I'm talking about getting hungry and not having anything to eat.

He poured himself another glass of beer and spilled some of the foam onto his vest and wiped it off and said he wished to Christ I wouldn't be a Fascist and be an honest Communist and work toward international good will among men.

I'm no Fascist, I said. I don't even know what the word means.

Means? said Pete. (Very nervous writer: he spilled more beer on his vest and began to shout.) You don't know what Fascism means? I'll tell you what it means. It means muzzling the press. It means the end of free speech. The end of free thinking.

Well, that isn't so bad, I said. A man can always get by without free speech. There isn't much to say anyway. Living won't stop when free speech does. Everybody except a few public debaters will go right on living the same as ever. Wait and see. We won't miss the debaters.

That's a lot of hooey, said Pete. Do you mind if I have another cigarette?

You're excited, I said. What's on your mind?

Confidentially, said Pete, I've been sent out by the local chapter of the Party to get a dollar from you.

Oh, I said. I thought you were really upset about the poor.

I *am* upset about them, said Pete.

What do they want a dollar for? I said.

To help get out the next number of the *Young Worker*, said Pete.

Young Worker, my eye, I said. *Young Loafer.* You punks never worked in your lives, and what's more you don't even know how to loaf.

I got a story in the next number, said Pete.

That clinches it, I said. I hope they never raise the money to get the paper out.

It's the best story I ever wrote, said Pete.

And that's none too good, I said.

It's the sort of story that will tear out their rotten hearts, said Pete.

Have another beer, I said. Open the other bottle. That's what you think. You've got twenty or thirty dopes down there who want to be writers and not one of you knows where the hell to begin and what to say. Communism is a school of writing to you guys.

I say plenty in this story, said Pete. I talk right out in this one.

What do you say? I said.

I say plenty, said Pete. Wait till you read it. It's called *No More Hunger Marches*.

I'll wait, I said, gladly.

You've got to let me have a dollar, said Pete. I haven't collected a dollar in six weeks and they're checking up on me.

Suppose you never collect a dollar? I said.

I'm supposed to be an active member, said Pete.

A militant member, I said.

Yeah, said Pete.

You boys are fighting *some* war, I said. I'm lousy with money. I'm the guy to go to for a dollar. Why don't you visit Montgomery Street? Why don't you be a militant Communist and try to get a dollar from Fleishacker or Spreckels?

They're our enemies, said Pete. They hate our guts.

And you just love them, don't you? I said.

We hate their guts, too, said Pete.

One big happy family, I said. Here's a dollar. Get the hell out of here. Bring me a copy of your story when it's printed. You may be Dostoyevsky in disguise. You smell bad enough to be somebody great. When you are going to take another bath?

Day after tomorrow, said Pete. Thanks for the dollar. Do you think I like going around this way, dirty clothes, no money, no baths? Under Communism we'll have bathtubs all over the place.

Under Communism, I said, you'll be exactly the way you are now, only you'll be just a little worse as a writer because there won't be anything to tear out their rotten hearts with and there won't be any rotten hearts to tear out. I was sleeping when you busted into this place. Why don't you guys send out circular letters instead of making personal calls?

Can't pay the postage, said Pete. Do you mind if I take three or four cigarettes?

Take the package, I said.

He went to the door and then turned around a little more excited than before.

They want you to come to the meeting tonight, he said. They
asked me to extend a special invitation to you to attend tonight's
meeting.

You guys make me laugh, I said.

This isn't one of those boring meetings, said Pete. This is going
to be better than a movie. We've got a very witty talker tonight.

I'm going to be playing poker tonight, I said. I can learn more
about contemporary economics playing poker.

I'll be expecting you at the meeting, said Pete.

I may drop around, I said. If I lose at poker, I'll *be sure* to drop
around. If I win, I'll want to stay in the game and see if I can't win
enough to get out of town.

Everybody wants you to join the Party, said Pete, because they
claim Communism is in need of guys who have a sense of humor.

They want dues, I said.

Well, you could do at least that much for your fellowman,
couldn't you?

I always tip the barber and the bootblack and the waitress, I said.
Once a week I give a newsboy half a dollar for a paper. I'm doing my
little bit.

That's bourgeois talk, said Pete. I'll see you at the meeting.

If I lose at poker, I said.

You'll lose, said Pete.

He closed the door behind him and hurried down the hall. I
opened all three windows of the room and breathed deeply. The
sun was still shining and I stretched out again and began to sleep
again.

II

Then my grandmother came into the room and stared bitterly at
everything, grumbling to herself and lifting a book off the table,
opening it, studying the strange print and closing it with an angry
and impatient bang, as if nothing in the world could be more
ridiculous than a book.

I knew she wanted to talk, so I pretended to be asleep.

My grandmother is a greater lady than any lady I have ever had
the honor of meeting, and she may even be the greatest lady alive
in the past-seventy class for all I know, but I always say there is a

time and place for everything. They are always having a baby contests in this crazy country, but I never heard of a grandmother contest. My old grandmother would walk away with every silver loving cup and gold or blue ribbon in the world in a grandmother contest, and I like her very much, but I wanted to sleep. She can't read or write, but what of it? She knows more about life than John Dewey and George Santayana put together, and that's plenty. You could ask her what's two times two and she'd fly off the handle and tell you not to irritate her with childish questions, but she's a genius just the same.

Forty years ago, she said, they asked this silly woman Oskan to tell about her visit to the village of Gultik and she got up and said, They have chickens there, and in calling the chickens they say, *Chik chik chik.* They have cows also, and very often the cows holler, *Moo moo moo.*

She was very angry about these remarks of the silly woman. She was remembering the old country and the old life, and I knew she would take up the story of her husband Melik in no time and begin to shout, so I sat up and smiled at her.

Is that all she had to say? I said. *Chik chik chik* and *moo moo moo?*

She was foolish, said my grandmother. I guess that's why they sent her to school and taught her to read and write. Finally she married a man who was crippled in the left leg. One cripple deserves another, she said. Why aren't you walking in the park on a day like this?

I thought I'd have a little afternoon nap, I said.

For the love of God, said my grandmother, my husband Melik was a man who rode a black horse through the hills and forests all day and half the night, drinking and singing. When the townspeople saw him coming they would run and hide. The wild Kourds of the desert trembled in his presence. I am ashamed of you, she said, lolling around among these silly books.

She lifted the first book that came to her hand, opened it, and stared with disgust at the print.

What is all this language here? she said.

That's a very great book by a very great man, I said. Dostoyevsky he was called. He was a Russian.

Don't tell me about the Russians, said my grandmother. What tricks they played on us. What does he say here?

Everything, I said. He says we must love our neighbors and be kind to the weak.

More lies, said my grandmother. Which tribe of the earth was kind to our tribe? In the dead of winter he went to Stamboul.

Who? I said.

Melik, she shouted. My own husband, she said bitterly. Who else? Who else would dare to go that far in the dead of winter? I will bring you a bright shawl from Stamboul, he said. I will bring you a bracelet and a necklace. He was drunk of course, but he was my husband. I bore him seven children before he was killed. There would have been more if he hadn't been killed, she groaned.

I have heard he was a cruel man, I said.

Who said such an unkind thing about my husband? said my grandmother. He was impatient with fools and weaklings, she said. You should try to be like this man.

I could use a horse all right, I said. I like drinking and singing, too.

In this country? said my grandmother. Where could you go with a horse in this country?

I could go to the public library with a horse, I said.

And they'd lock you up in jail, she said. Where would you tie the horse?

I would tie the horse to a tree, I said. There are six small trees in front of the public library.

Ride a horse in this country, she said, and they will put you down for a maniac.

They have already, I said. The libel is spreading like wildfire.

You don't care? she said.

Not at all, I said. Why should I?

Is it true, perhaps? she said.

It is a foul lie, I said.

It is healthful to be disliked, said my grandmother. My husband Melik was hated by friend and enemy alike. *Bitterly* hated, and he knew it, and yet everybody pretended to like him. They were afraid of him, so they pretended to like him. Will you play a game of *scambile*? I have the cards.

She was lonely again, like a young girl.

I got up and sat across the table from her and lit a cigarette for her and one for myself. She shuffled and dealt three cards to me and three to herself and turned over the next card, and the game began.

Ten cents? she said.

Ten or fifteen, I said.

Fifteen then, but I play a much better game than you, she said.

I may be lucky, I said.

I do not believe in luck she said, not even in card games. I believe in thinking and knowing what you are doing.

We talked and played and I lost three games to my grandmother. I paid her, only I gave her a half dollar.

Is that what it comes to? she said.

It comes to a little less, I said.

You are not lying? she said.

I never lie, I said. It comes to forty-five cents. You owe me five cents.

Five pennies? she said.

Or one nickel, I said.

I have three pennies, she said. I will pay you three pennies now and owe you two.

Your arithmetic is improving, I said.

American money confuses me, she said, but you never heard of anyone cheating me, did you?

Never, I admitted.

They don't dare, she said. I count the money piece by piece, and if someone is near by I have him count it for me, too. There was this thief of a grocer in Hanford, she said. Dikranian. Three cents more he took. Six pounds of cheese. And I had five different people count for me. Three cents more he has taken, they said. I waited a week and then went to his store again. For those three cents I took three packages of cigarettes. From a thief thieve and God will smile on you. I never enjoyed cigarettes as much as those I took from Dikranian. Five people counted for me. He thought I was an old woman. He thought he could do such a thing. I went back to the store and said not a word. Good morning, good morning. Lovely day, lovely day. A pound of rice, a pound of rice. He turned to get the rice, I took three packages of cigarettes.

Ha ha, said my grandmother. From thief thieve, and from above God will smile.

But you took too much, I said. You took fifteen times too much.

Fifteen times too much? said my grandmother. He took three pennies, I took three packages of cigarettes, no more, no less.

Well, I said, it probably comes to the same thing anyway, but

you don't really believe God smiles when you steal from a thief,
do you?

Of course I believe, said my grandmother. Isn't it said in three
different languages, Armenian, Kourdish, and Turkish?

She said the words in Kourdish and Turkish.

I wish I knew how to talk those languages, I said.

Kourdish, said my grandmother, is the language of the heart.
Turkish is music. Turkish flows like a stream of wine, smooth and
sweet and bright in color. Our tongue, she shouted, is a tongue of
bitterness. We have tasted much of death and our tongue is heavy
with hatred and anger. I have heard only one man who could speak
our language as if it were the tongue of a God-like people.

Who was that man? I asked.

Melik, said my grandmother. My husband Melik. If he was
sober, he spoke quietly, his voice rich and deep and gentle, and if
he was drunk, he roared like a lion and you'd think God in Heaven
was crying lamentations and oaths upon the tribes of the earth. No
other man have I heard who could speak in this way, drunk or sober,
not one, here or in the old country.

And when he laughed? I said.

When Melik laughed, said my grandmother, it was like an ocean
of clear water leaping at the moon with delight.

I tell you, my grandmother would walk away with every silver
loving cup and gold ribbon in the world.

Now she was angry, ferocious with the tragic poetry of her race.

And not one of you *opegh-tsapegh* brats are like him, she shouted.
Only my son Vahan is a little like him, and after Vahan all the rest
of you are strangers to me. This is my greatest grief.

Opegh-tsapegh is untranslatable. It means, somewhat, *very haphazardly assembled,* and when said of someone, it means he is no
particular credit to the race of man. On the contrary, only another
fool, someone to include in the census and forget. In short, everybody.

And when he cried? I said.

My husband was never known to weep, said my grandmother.
When other men hid themselves in their houses and frightened their
wives and children by weeping, my husband rode into the hills, drunk
and cursing. If he wept in the hills, he wept alone, with only God to
witness his weakness. He always came back, though, swearing louder

than ever, and then I would put him to bed and sit over him,
watching his face.

She sat down with a sigh and again stared bitterly around the
room.

These books, she said. I don't know what you expect to learn
from books. What is in them? What do you expect to learn from
reading?

I myself sometimes wonder, I said.

You have read them all? she said.

Some twice, some three times, I said. Some only a page here
and there.

And what is their message?

Nothing much, I said. Sometimes there is brightness and laughter,
or maybe the opposite, gloom and anger. Not often, though.

Well, said my grandmother, the ones who were taught to read
and write were always the silliest and they made the worst wives.
This soft-brained Oskan went to school, and when she got up to speak
all she could say was, They have chickens there, and in calling the
chickens they say, *Chik chik chik.* Is that wisdom?

That's innocence, I said in English.

I cannot understand such an absurd language, she said.

It is a splendid language, I said.

That is because you were born here and can speak no other
language, no Turkish, no Kourdish, not one word of Arabic.

No, I said, it is because this is the language Shakespeare spoke
and wrote.

Shakespeare? said my grandmother. Who is he?

He is the greatest poet the world has ever known, I said.

Nonsense, said my grandmother. There was a traveling minstrel
who came to our city when I was a girl of twelve. This man was
ugly as satan, but he could recite poetry in six different languages,
all day and all night, and not one word of it written, not one word
of it memorized, every line of it made up while he stood before the
people, reciting. They called him Crazy Markos and people gave him
small coins for reciting and the more coins they gave him the drunker
he got and the drunker he got the more beautiful the poems he
recited.

Well, I said, each country and race and time has its own kind of
poet and its own understanding of poetry. The English poets wrote
and your poets recited.

But if they were poets, said my grandmother, why did they write?
A poet lives to sing. Were they afraid a good thing would be lost and
forgotten? Why do they write each of their thoughts? Are they
afraid something will be lost?

I guess so, I said.

Do you want something to eat? said my grandmother. I have cab-
bage soup and bread.

I'm not hungry, I said.

Are you going out again tonight? she said.

Yes, I said. There is an important meeting of philosophers in the
city tonight. I have been invited to listen and learn.

Why don't you stop all this nonsense, she said.

This isn't nonsense, I said. These philosophers are going to explain
how we can make this world a better place, a heaven on earth.

It *is* nonsense, said my grandmother. This place is the same place
all men have known, and it is anything you like.

That's bourgeois talk, I said in English.

These philosophers, I said in Armenian, are worrying about the
poor. They want the wealth of the rich to be shared with the
poor. That way they claim everything will be straightened out and
everybody will be happy.

Everybody is poor, said my grandmother. The richest man in the
world is no less poor than the poorest. All over the world there is
poverty of spirit. I never saw such miserliness in people. Give them
all the money in the world and they'll still be poor. That's something between themselves and God.

They don't believe in God, I said.

Whether they believe or not, said my grandmother, it is still a
matter between themselves and God. I don't believe in evil, but does
that mean evil does not exist?

Well said, I'm going anyway, just to hear what they have to say.

Then I must be in the house alone? she said.

Go to a movie, I said. You know how to get to the neighborhood
theatre. It's not far. There is a nice picture tonight.

Alone? said my grandmother. I wouldn't think of it.

Tomorrow, I said, we will go together. Tonight you can listen to
the radio. I will come home early.

Have you no books with pictures?

Of course, I said.

I handed her a book called *The Life of Queen Victoria*, full of pictures of that nice old lady.

You will like this lady, I said. She was Queen of England, but she is now dead. The book is full of pictures, from birth to death.

Ah, said my grandmother looking at an early picture of the Queen. She was a beautiful girl. Ahkh, ahkh, alas, alas, for the good who are dead, and my grandmother went down the hall to the kitchen.

I got out of my old clothes and jumped under a warm shower. The water was refreshing to the skin and I began to sing.

I put on fresh clothes and a dark suit. I went into the kitchen and kissed my grandmother's hand, then left the house. She stood at the front window, looking down at me.

Then she lifted the window and stuck her head out.

Boy, she shouted. Get a little drunk. Don't be so serious. A blue-ribbon old lady.

O.K., I said.

III

Now, a man's life begins from the beginning, every moment he is alive, wakeful or not, conscious or not, and the beginning is as distant in the past as the ending is in the future, and walking to town, alive and miraculously out of pain, I looked upon the world and remembered. Sometimes, even in the artificial and fantastic world we have made, we are able somehow to reach a state of *being* in which pain does not exist, and for the moment seems forever an unreality. Miraculously out of pain, I say, because in this place, in this configuration of objects and ideas which we call the world, pain in the living seems more reasonable than the absence of pain, and the reason is this: that *stress* (and not ease) is the basic scheme of function in our life, in this world. All things, even the most simple, require effort in order to be performed, and to me this is an unnatural state of affairs.

And I do not mean sloth which leads inevitably to degeneracy: I mean only ease and effortlessness. Grace which all living creatures, save man, naturally possess, the bird, the fish, the cat, the reptile. I mean inward grace, inherent freedom of form, inherent truthfulness of being.

I mean, *being*, but in this world ease and truthfulness are difficult because of the multitude of encumbrances halting the body and spirit of man on all sides: the heavy and tortuous ideas of civilization, the entanglement of the actual world in which we are born and from which we seem never to be able to emerge, and, above all things, our imprisonment in the million errors of the past, some noble, some half-glorious, some half-godly, but most of them vicious and weak and sorrowful.

We know we are caught in this tragic entanglement, and all that we do is full of the unholiness of this heritage of errors, and all that we do is painful and difficult, even unto the simplest functions of living creatures, even unto mere being, mere breathing, mere growing, and our suffering is eternally intensified by impatience, dissatisfaction, and that dreadful hope which is all but maddening in that its fulfillment seems unlikely, our hope for liberation, for sudden innocent and unencumbered reality, sudden and unending naturalness of movement, sudden godliness.

So we turn, somewhat in despair, to the visible in our problem, to matter, and we say if all men had food enough to eat, shelter and comfort, once again all would be well in the world and man would regain the truthfulness of his nature and be joyous.

Anyway, I was walking to town, whistling a comical American song, at five in the afternoon, feeling for a moment altogether truthful and unencumbered, feeling, in short, somewhat happy, personally, when suddenly and apparently for no reason, at least no new reason, the whole world, caught in time and space, seemed to me an absurdity, an insanity, and instead of being amused, which would have been philosophical, I was miserable and began to ridicule all the tragic straining of man, living and dead.

Worse still, I saw a child staring out at the world from a window and crying, and this too, brought to me the essential error of our effort, since if a child, who is innocent, cannot see good in this world, then certainly there must be little good in it, and we do no more than grow and accept, since acceptance is easier than denial, and we deceive ourselves into believing all is well, though, actually, we suffer pain enough from day to day to know that all is not well.

I guess I'd better get drunk at that, I said, but this, of all evasions, is the most ignoble, since one escapes to nowhere, or at any rate to a universe even more disorderly, if more magnificent, than our own, and then returns with sickened senses and a stunned spirit to the place only recently forsaken.

The drunkard is the most absurd of the individualists, the ultimate egoist, who rises and falls in no domain other than that of his own senses, though drunkards have been, and will long be, most nearly the children of God, most truthfully worshippers of the universal.

Insanity, I said, idiocy and waste and error, cruelty and filth and dreadfulness, pride and pomposity, pain and poverty, and birth, and the children of the world eternally at the window, weeping at the strangeness of this place. Sure. Teach them the gospel of Marx and have them born in Russia and they will not stare from the window, they will run through the streets of Moscow like mountain goats and laugh and never after will they know grief, because Marx is a nobler father than God, amen.

I began to feel down in the mouth. I began to feel lousy, or, as my grandmother would say in Armenian, melancholy, which is my natural state, except when I am among others and then my natural state is this: to oppose possible error with possible laughter, since laughter, though largely pointless, is at least less damaging than error, and less pompous than blind sincerity, which is infinitely more dangerous than utter irresponsibility. In fact, I admire most those men of wisdom who accept the tragic obligation to be irresponsible until the time when sincerity will have become natural and noble and not artificial and vicious as it is now.

I walked to The Barrel House on Third Street, the street in San Francisco where the misery of man stalks back and forth in the nightmare images of creatures once mortal and now dispersed, as a large seeded flower is dispersed by a strong wind, or mangled as a crushed insect is mangled, yet crawls, impelled by life in itself to move, these broken bodies, these slain souls, passing in the street, going nowhere, and returning nowhere.

And I stood in the street, clean and comfortable and secure and out of danger, and angry with myself and with the world that had done these things to these men, asking myself what I intended to do about it. The thick smell of fear in the air, of decay, the decay of flesh, of spirit, the waste of animal energy mingling with the rotten smells pouring out of the doorways and windows of the cheap restaurants, and I said, Breathe deeply, draw deeply into your lungs the odor of the death of man, of man alive, yet dead, most filthily dead, yet alive, and let the foul air of this death feed your blood, and let this death be your death, for these men are your brothers, each of these men is yourself, and when they die, you die, and if they cannot live, you cannot live, though you forsake the world and enter a world of your own, you die.

And what will you do about this? Here is one who may be saved. A boy, years younger than yourself, torn by the cruelty of the world, yet young enough to be saved, and what are you going to do about him? And the boy walked by, blind and deaf and dumb, yet alive, crawling like the crushed insect, pulling himself to another, one more moment of life, of misery, of fear.

And this old man who is crippled, whose legs are tied by the tightening pains of years of agony, whose face is the mask of one in hell, yet on earth, what are you going to do about him?

Be a gentleman and give him a dime for coffee and doughnuts. Humiliate him again and let his trembling hand close upon the small coin, his rotted heart close upon the cheap charity of the strong and secure, and the old man went by, and across the street the shabby saints of the Salvation Army preached and prayed and sang and asked the hungry men for alms with which to spread the holy gospel of truth, and the men gave no alms.

When the revolution comes, these men will be like gods, and their sons will come into the earth innocent and whole, and within them will be no germ of sin, no germ of greed or envy or cruelty or hatred, and they will grow to be greater gods than their fathers, and the daughters of these dead men will move upon the earth with the feline power and grace and poise of jungle cats, and when the revolution comes all misery on earth will end, and all error will end.

Indeed. And the thing to do is to get cockeyed, to be blind and deaf, to go stumbling through the filth of the world, laughing and singing.

I walked into The Barrel House and sat at a table.

Nicora, the waiter, came over and wiped the table clean, leaving the wood moist, standing sullenly, a little drunk, his dark Italian face weary and worried, yet indifferent, lots of trouble in the world, *paesano*, but I got a good job: all day I drink, what do I care about trouble? Wife, two kids, and himself, and when the revolution comes Nicora will serve drinks to his brothers in a big garden in the sun.

Hi-ya, Nick, I said.

O.K., kid, he said. Little shot, maybe?

Yeah, I said. How's your wife?

Oh fine, he said. She's very sick, another kid coming.

Congratulations, I said, and he went to the bar and got a drink.
He put it down in front of me, talking.

I tell you, kid, he said, take my advice, don't get married, first
the wife, then the kids, then the rent, then the bread, then the kid
falls down and breaks the arm, then the wife cries, then you get drunk
and break the window and the dishes, then the wife's brother comes
and makes trouble, then you fight him, then the jail, then you sit inside the jail and think, and Jesus Christ, kid, don't be crazy and get
married, I know, and I don't want to see another guy in trouble.

All right, Nick, I said.

I swallowed the whiskey and it burned all the way down and I
began to feel all right, like a big gesture in the world, all right, and
I began to feel gay and at the same time very proud, like, *who me?*

Don't worry about me, pals, just worry about yourselves, pals: I'm
doing all right, pals, and I told Nick to get me another because I
figured I'd get good and drunk and laugh the way my grandfather
Melik used to laugh when he got drunk in the old country, and
Nick brought another and I swallowed it, everything's jake, pals, and
I told him to get another and he did and I swallowed this one, everything's O.K., pals, and another, and then I started to laugh, but not
out loud, only inside, away back in the old country, on the black
horse, riding through the hills, in the beginning, cussing and singing.

IV

Drink expands the eye, enlarges the inward vision, elevates the ego.
The eye perceives less and less the objects of this world and more and
more the objects and patterns and rhythms of the other: the large
and limitless and magnificent universe of remembrance, the real
and timeless earth of history, of man's legend in this place. Until, of
course, one is under the table. Then the magnificence is succeeded
by sensory riot and lawlessness, and the law of gravity comes to an
end, amid comedy and tragedy. Distance is unreal, and flesh and
spirit exist not alone in one place and in one time but in all places
and during all times, including the future. In short, one achieves the
ridiculous and glorious state of fool.

The gesture blossoms in the universe, dramatic and significant,
saying *I know*, the language of limb in motion, artfully. The head
wags yea and nay. The tongue loosens with the chaos of a million

languages. The spirit laughs and the flesh leaps, and sitting at a small table in a dark saloon, one travels somehow to all the places of the world, returns, and goes again, gesturing and reciting, wagging the head and laughing, singing and leaping.

I got a little drunk, sitting at the small table, and Nicora came and went, telling me what to do and what not to do in order to be happy in the world, my spiritual adviser.

I wished Paula were getting drunk with me, sitting across the table from me, so I could see her round white face with the deep melancholy eyes and the full melancholy lips and the pert melancholy nose and the small melancholy ears and the brown melancholy hair, and I wished I could take her warm melancholy hand and walk with her over the hard melancholy streets of our dark melancholy city and reach a large melancholy room with a good melancholy bed and lie with her beautiful melancholy body, and all during the night have a quiet melancholy conversation between long melancholy embraces and in the morning waken from deep melancholy sleep and hide our melancholy nakedness with cheap melancholy clothes and go out for a big cheerful breakfast.

So I went to the telephone booth and dropped a nickel in the slot and dialed the number. I guess I dialed the wrong number or forgot the right one because the girl who answered wasn't Paula. She didn't have Paula's quiet melancholy voice: she had a loud melancholy voice.

This is fate, I said, or something like it, so I talked to the girl. The telephone is a great invention. If you get a wrong number, it doesn't make much difference because you get a girl anyway, even if it isn't the one you had in mind, and the whole thing amounts to fate, slightly assisted by the noble mechanics of our age.

What's the good of getting a wrong number if you don't talk a little? Where's the Christian kindliness and love of neighbor in hanging up on a girl with a loud melancholy voice just because you've never seen her?

Young lady, I said, I'm getting drunk on rotten whiskey at The Barrel House on Third Street. Jump into the first street car and come right down and have a drink. After a while we will take a taxi to The Universe Restaurant on Columbus Avenue and have a dinner of spaghetti and roast chicken. We will sit at the table and talk and then we will go through the city and see the sights. When we are tired we will go to a movie or if you prefer we will go to a Com-

munist meeting and join our comrades in singing the Internationale
and in hating the guts of the rich.

The girl hung up with a fierce melancholy bang. I dialed the number again and the bell rang once, twice, three times, four times, and
then it was Paula.

We talked, over the wires, by electricity, our voices passing under
the city and over it, each of us unseen by the other, while a thousand
others talked with one another.

Hello, said Paula.

Hello, I said.

How are you? said Paula.

I'm fine, I said. How are you?

Fine, said Paula. What's the matter?

Nothing, I said. Something the matter?

You sound serious, said Paula.

Wait a minute, I said. I want to light a cigarette.

All right, said Paula. I want to light one too.

I inhaled smoke and began to feel less and less gay.

Hello, I said.

Hello, said Paula.

I heard her exhale smoke, and even this sounded melancholy. I
could see her round melancholy face.

How are you, Paula? I said.

I'm fine, Mike, she said. How are you, Mike?

I'm fine, too, I said.

I guess we both feel lousy, said Paula.

No, I said. I feel great.

I went to a movie last night, said Paula.

Swell, I said. How was it?

Great, said Paula. It was just like life.

Did you cry? I said.

No, said Paula, I laughed. It was about a boy and a girl in love.
A new idea in the movies. They had a lot of trouble at first, but in
the end they were married.

Then what happened? I said.

The movie ended, said Paula.

That's bourgeois propaganda, I said. I saw a movie like that once.
They got married, too.

Must have been the same boy and girl, said Paula.

The universal male and female, I said.

Then I got sore at myself for being smart again. I wasn't saying what I wanted to say, the way I wanted to say it, and I got sore.

Listen, Paula, I said, to hell with that stuff.

Sure, said Paula. To hell with it.

Paula, I said, come to town and have dinner with me.

Can't, said Paula. I'm going out.

Who with? I said.

Friend of mine, said Paula.

Sure, but who? I said.

Young lawyer, said Paula. You don't know him.

What do you want to go out with a young lawyer for? I said.

He's a very intelligent boy, said Paula.

That's not important, I said.

I know it, said Paula.

Tell him you're sick, I said, and come to town and have dinner with me.

Can't, said Paula.

What the hell you talking about? I said.

We're going to be married, said Paula. Just like in the movies.

You're kidding, I said.

Look in next Sunday's *Examiner*, said Paula. My picture, his name.

Jesus Christ, I said.

I'm in love with him, said Paula.

Sure, I said. You sound *madly* in love. You're crazy.

We're going to the Hawaiian Islands, said Paula.

Listen, Paula, I said. I want to see you tonight. Go ahead and get married. I don't care about that. But I want to see you tonight. What time will you be through with the young lawyer?

You can't, said Paula. When we come back from the Islands we're going to live in a big house in the hills, in Berkeley.

You're crazy, I said.

Maybe, and maybe not, said Paula. I'll know after a while.

Oh I see, I said.

I'd like to meet the lawyer, I said.

You can't, said Paula.

Oh, I said.

We didn't talk for a half a minute.

O.K., Paula, I said. I'll see you by accident in the street sometime.

Sure, said Paula. It's a small world. So long, Mike.

So long, Paula, I said.

I went back to the small table and Nick began bringing me drinks again. The more I drank the worse I felt. When I went outside it was raining. The rain was fine, and the air was clear and good. I walked through the wet melancholy streets to the Reno Club on Geary Street. I walked in and there was a seat open in a draw poker game. I sat down and bought ten dollars' worth of chips. I'm pretty lucky when I'm a little drunk. Apostolos, the Greek restaurant man, dealt the cards. I played two hours and came out four dollars ahead.

Then I went up to Fillmore Street to the Communist meeting, and began climbing the stairs.

I'm drunk, I said, and Paula's getting married to a lawyer, and Pete wants to save the world, and my grandmother is homesick for Armenia, and Nick's wife is going to have another baby, and listen, comrades, if I don't go easy climbing these stairs I'll fall down and bust my head, comrades. What good will it do when everybody has bread, comrades, what good will it do when everybody has cake, comrades, what good will do it when everybody has everything, comrades, everything isn't enough, comrades, and the living aren't alive, brothers, the living are dead, brothers, even the living are not alive, brothers, and you can't ever do anything about that.

JIM PEMBERTON
AND HIS BOY TRIGGER

PA came into Willy's Lunch Wagon on Peach Street where I was sitting at the counter talking to Ella the new waitress from Texas and eating a hamburger and drinking a cup of coffee, and he threw his hat on the marble machine and took off his coat and folded it and put it by his hat and he said, Trig, I'm going to knock your head off. You told Mrs. Sheridan I wasn't in the army.

I nearly choked on hamburger and coffee and Ella told me to hold up my left arm because that would stop me from coughing, and Pa said, Trigger, get up off of that stool.

Let me finish this hamburger anyway, Pa, I said.

All right, Pa said. You told Mrs. Sheridan I never killed anybody in my life and now she don't want to see me any more.

Well, let me finish this hamburger, Pa. I said. You never killed anybody and you know it.

How do you know? Pa said. Are you sure?

I ain't exactly sure, I said, but gosh, Pa, what would you go to work and kill anybody for?

Never mind that, Pa said. I ain't got time to explain about what for. Go ahead now and swallow that last bite of hamburger and stand up. I'm going to knock your head off.

He turned to Ella.

Hello Ella, he said politely. Fix me up a sirloin steak. Kind of rare.

Yes, Mr. Pemberton, Ella said. Are you going to fight Trigger again?

He can't go around telling lies about me, Pa said.

It ain't no lie, Pa, I said. Who'd you ever kill? Name one man.

One hell, Pa said. I could name fourteen men on the tips of my fingers.

You ain't got fourteen fingers, Pa. I said. You ain't even got ten. You've got eight. You lost them last two fingers of your left hand in Perry's Lumber Mill.

I lost them fingers in the War, Pa said. For my country.

Pa, I said, you know you never did go over to Europe. It's your imagination getting the best of you.

I'll show you what's getting the best of me, Pa said. Mrs. Sheridan claims I ain't no hero.

You ain't, Pa, I said.

All right, stand up then, Pa said. If that's the way you feel about it, I'm going to knock your head off.

You know I can whip you, Pa, I said. Don't make me do it again.

Again? Pa said. When did *you* ever whip *me?*

Why Mr. Pemberton, Ella said, Trigger whipped you yesterday right here in front of Willy's.

Fix me a side order of fried onions, Pa said. How've you been, Ella? Has my son been passing insolent remarks to you? I won't stand for it, you know. I'll knock his head off.

Why Mr. Pemberton, Ella said, Trigger's been as nice as nice can be. Trigger is the best-behaved and nicest-looking boy in Kingsburg.

I won't stand for anybody passing insolent remarks to an innocent girl like you, Ella, Pa said. If my son Trigger asks you out to the country, you just let me know and I'll knock his head off.

Why I'd love to go to the country with Trigger, Ella said.

Don't you do it, Pa said. Trigger would have you down in the tall grass in two minutes.

He wouldn't, either, Ella said.

He would too, Pa said. Wouldn't you, son?

I don't know, I said.

I looked at Ella and figured maybe Pa was right for once in his life. For once in his life Pa wasn't letting his wild imagination run away with him.

It looked like maybe Pa was going to forget to fight about Mrs. Sheridan and that made me feel pretty good. I didn't want to be spoiling the best years of Pa's life all the time pushing him around in what he thought were fighting contests.

Ella, Pa said, whatever you do, don't let Trigger carry you away with his fine talk and nice manners.

I been in town since day before yesterday, Ella said, and I ain't seen anybody I like half as much as I like Trigger.

She turned the steak over.

How's that look, Mr. Pemberton? she said.

Perfect, Pa said.

He sat down on the stool beside me.

Trigger, he said, would you mind waiting outside till I've had my supper? I can't put up any kind of a fight on an empty stomach.

I've got to go down to The Coliseum, Pa, I said.

You can wait five minutes, Pa said.

I've got an appointment to play Harry Wilke a little snooker, I said. What's on your mind, Pa?

I want you to drop over to Mrs. Sheridan's, Pa said, and tell her I killed seventeen Germans in the War. She's sitting on the front porch. I can't stand this kind of excellent weather without the affection and admiration of a handsome woman.

Gosh, Pa, I said, Mrs. Sheridan won't believe me.

Yes, she will, Pa said. She'll believe any crazy thing you say. Seventeen, now. Don't forget.

But you didn't really do it, did you, Pa? I said.

What difference does it make? Pa said.

Ella put the steak on a plate and set the plate on the counter between a tablespoon and a knife and fork. Pa cut off a big piece of steak. It was bloody red. He put it in his mouth and smiled at Ella.

You're a good innocent girl, Ella, he said. You'll be wanting to get married one of these days, so don't be going out to the country with Trigger.

Why I'd love to, Mr. Pemberton, Ella said.

All right then, Pa said. Go ahead and get yourself knocked up if you've got your heart set on it.

Pa turned to me.

Will you do that little thing for me, Trigger? he said.

Gosh, I felt proud of Pa. He was so big and crazy.

Sure Pa, I said. I'll tell Mrs. Sheridan you killed a whole troop of machine-gunners.

You go right on over to Mrs. Sheridan's, Pa said. You'll find her on the front porch, in the rocking chair. Tell her I'll be over just as soon as I've had my supper.

Sure Pa, I said.

Goodbye, Trigger, Ella said.

Goodbye, Ella, I said.

I went out to the curb and got on my Harley-Davidson and rode six blocks to Mrs. Sheridan's Rooming House on Elm Avenue.

Mrs. Sheridan was sitting on the front porch just like Pa said, only Ralph Aten was there with her. Mrs. Sheridan was sucking strawberry soda pop through a straw out of a bottle.

I leaned my motorcycle against the curb and walked up to the porch. Mrs. Sheridan looked comfortable and pretty, but Ralph Aten looked sore, especially about me. I never did like his daughter Effie, though. He just thought I did. He tried to make me marry her, but I asked him to prove it was me and not Gabe Fisher. He claimed it didn't look like Gabe Fisher, and I claimed it didn't look like me either. He got sore and said he would take the case to the Supreme Court, but he never did.

Good evening, Mrs. Sheridan, I said.

Good evening, Trigger, Mrs. Sheridan said. Come on up and sit down.

Good evening, Mr. Aten, I said, and Ralph Aten said, Son, what brings you here at this hour of the evening?

Come on up onto the porch and sit down, Mrs. Sheridan said. Me and Ralph want to talk to you.

I went up onto the porch and sat on the railing, facing Mrs. Sheridan and Mr. Aten.

Here I am, Mrs. Sheridan, I said. What do you want to talk to me about?

Well, said Mrs. Sheridan, about your son Homer out of Effie, Ralph's youngest daughter.

Homer ain't my son, I said.

You're wrong there, Ralph Aten said. Trigger, you're dead wrong in that opinion. Homer is the spitting image of you, and your father, and grandfather before him. Homer is a real Pemberton.

Mr. Aten, I said, I'm afraid you're letting your imagination get the best of you.

No, I ain't, Trigger, Mr. Aten said. Homer is your son. He's talking now, and he even talks like you.

Trigger, Mrs. Sheridan said, I think you ought to show a little more interest in your children.

Why Mrs. Sheridan, I said, how can you say a thing like that? What children? I ain't got no wife.

Wife or no wife, Mrs. Sheridan said, you've got over four children in these parts. You get around so easily on that motorcycle, Trigger. I don't suppose you realize how much time that machine saves you in reaching innocent girls and getting away from them in a hurry.

I use this machine to deliver the San Francisco papers to farmers who live in these parts, I said. That's what this motorcycle is for.

I ain't saying it ain't primarily for delivering papers, Trigger,

Mrs. Sheridan said, but you only deliver papers an hour or so early in the morning. Your children are the nicest-looking kids in Kings County, and I think it is very unkind of you to pay no attention to them.

Trigger, Mr. Aten said, why don't you marry my daughter Effie and settle down and make a name for yourself?

What kind of a name do you mean, Mr. Aten? I said.

A great name, Mr. Aten said. Why don't you settle down and be somebody?

Yes indeed, Trigger, Mrs. Sheridan said, I think with a little effort on your part you could develop into quite a personage.

I figured it was about time for me to begin working on Mrs. Sheridan, but I couldn't do it in front of a man like Mr. Aten, a man Pa never did like, so I figured I'd get him out of the way in a hurry.

Mr. Aten, I said, before I forget I want you to know I came here to tell you Charley Hagen wants to see you down at The Coliseum about a private matter. He said to hurry right down.

Mr. Aten jumped three feet out of his chair.

You mean Charley Hagen the banker, son? he said. You mean the richest man in Kings County, Trigger?

Yes sir, I said. Mr. Hagen claims he has something important to talk over with you.

Well, who would have guessed it? Mr. Aten said. Excuse me, Mrs. Sheridan?

Of course, Mrs. Sheridan said.

Mr. Aten scrambled down the steps of the porch, jumped across the front yard, and began running down Elm Avenue.

Mrs. Sheridan, I said, you may not believe it, but my Pa destroyed a whole regiment of crack German machine-gunners in the war. He crept up on them while they were asleep. That's how he did it.

Mrs. Sheridan put down the bottle of soda pop and straightened out her large front, wiggling with amazement.

Trigger, she said, what in hell are you talking about?

My Pa, I said. I'm talking about Jim Pemberton, The Lone Wolf of Kings County, The Terror of Thieves and Pickpockets, The Protector of Children and Innocent Girls, that's who.

What did you say your crazy Pa did in the War, Trigger? Mrs. Sheridan said.

I said he killed seventeen crack German machine-gunners single-handed, that's what.

I don't believe it, Mrs. Sheridan said.

All I can say is, I think you're letting your imagination get the best of you, Mrs. Sheridan, I said. It's the truth. Pa had papers to prove it, but he lost them. He had seven medals, but he had to sell them. Pa is a hero, Mrs. Sheridan.

Trigger, Mrs. Sheridan said, who sent you here with that crazy story? Yesterday you told me your Pa never went to Europe at all. Yesterday you told me your Pa wasn't even in the army.

Mrs. Sheridan, I said, was misinformed at the time. I was grossly misinformed.

Well, how did your Pa ever do such a brave thing? Mrs. Sheridan said. How in hell did he ever do it?

He crept up on them, I said. He killed eleven of them while they were asleep, hitting them over the head with the butt of his rifle. Then the other six woke up and started making trouble for Pa, but he turned one of their own machine-guns on them and mowed them down. He got seven medals for doing it, and two days later the War ended.

Mrs. Sheridan rocked back and forth very beautifully.

Well, what do you know about that? she said. Trigger, here's fifteen cents. Go down to Meyer's and get me a package of Chesterfields. This calls for some heavy cigarette smoking.

I ran half a block to Meyer's and bought Mrs. Sheridan a package of cigarettes. When I got back Pa was sitting on the porch, telling Mrs. Sheridan how he happened to do it. Pa was telling her in very tender and affectionate language.

Here, Trigger, Mrs. Sheridan said, give me them cigarettes.

I looked at Pa to see how he was making out while Mrs. Sheridan tore open the package of cigarettes, got one out and lighted it. Pa smiled and made a certain movement with his right hand that I knew meant everything was going along very nicely and many thanks. I made the movement back at Pa and Mrs. Sheridan inhaled deeply, looking exciting and lovely, so I knew my work was done.

Good night, Mrs. Sheridan, I said. It's been awful nice being in your company.

Not at all, Trigger, Mrs. Sheridan said. The pleasure's been mine.

Good night, Pa, I said.

Good night, Trigger, Pa said.

I went down to the curb and got my bike. Before I started the motor I heard Pa start talking in a low warm affectionate tone of voice and I knew he was all set for the rest of the night at least.

WAR

K ARL the Prussian is five, a splendid Teuton with a military manner of walking over the sidewalk in front of his house, and a natural discipline of speech that is both admirable and refreshing, as if the child understood the essential dignity of mortal articulation and could not bear to misuse the gift, opening his mouth only rarely and then only to utter a phrase of no more than three or four words, wholly to the point and amazingly pertinent. He lives in a house across the street and is the pride of his grandfather, an erect man of fifty with a good German moustache whose picture appeared in a newspaper several years ago in connection with a political campaign. This man began teaching Karl to walk as soon as the boy was able to stand on his legs, and he could be seen with the small blond boy in blue overalls, moving up and down a half block of sidewalk, holding the child's hands and showing him how to step forward precisely and a bit pompously, in the German royalist manner, knees stiff, each step resembling an arrested kick.

Every morning for several months the old man and the little boy practised walking, and it was a very pleasant routine to watch. Karl's progress was rapid but hardly hurried, and he seemed to understand the quiet sternness of his grandfather, and even from across the street it was easy to see that he believed in the importance of being able to walk in a dignified manner, and wished to learn to do it the way his grandfather was teaching him to do it. Fundamentally, the little boy and the old man were the same, the only difference being the inevitable difference of age and experience, and Karl showed no signs of wishing to rebel against the discipline imposed upon him by the old man.

After a while the little boy was walking up and down the stretch of sidewalk in front of his house, unassisted by the old man, who watched him quietly from the steps of his house, smoking a pipe and looking upon the boy with an expression of severity which was at the same time an expression of pride, and the little boy kicked himself forward very nicely. The walk was certainly old-fashioned and certainly a little undemocratic, but everyone in this neighborhood liked Karl and regarded him as a very fine little man. There was something about a small boy walking that way that was satisfying. True Teutons appreciate the importance of such relatively automatic functions as breathing, walking and talking, and they are able to bother about these simple actions in a manner that is both reasonable and dignified. To them, apparently, breathing and walking and talking are related closely to living in general, and the fuss they make about these actions isn't therefore the least ridiculous.

People living in the houses of this block have been breeding well during the past six or seven years, and the street has a fair population of children, all of them healthy and interesting, to me extremely interesting. Karl is only one of the group, and he is mentioned first because he is perhaps the only one who has been taught a conscious racial technique of living. The other children belong to a number of races, and while the basic traits of each race is apparent in each child, these traits have not been emphasized and strengthened as they have been emphasized and strengthened in Karl. In other words, each child is of his race naturally and instinctively, and it is likely that except for the instruction of his grandfather, Karl himself would now be more like the other children, more artless and unrepressed. He would not have the military manner of walking which is the chief difference between him and the other children, and the mannerism which sometimes get on the nerves of Josef, the Slovenian boy who lives in the flat downstairs.

Josef is almost a year older than Karl, and he is a lively boy whose every action suggests inward laughter. He has the bright and impish face of his father who is by trade a baker, and he is the sort of boy who talks a lot, who is interested in everything and everyone around him, and who is always asking questions. He wants to know the names of people, and his favorite question is *where have you been?* He asks this question in a way that suggests he is hoping you have just returned from some very strange and wonderful place, not like anything he has ever seen, and perhaps not like any place on earth, and I myself have always been embarrassed because I have had to tell him that I have come from a place no more wonderful than town, which he himself has seen at least a half dozen times.

Karl hardly ever runs, while Josef hardly ever walks, and is almost running or skipping or leaping, as if *going* from one place to another was a good deal more important to him than leaving one place and reaching another place, as if, I mean, the mere going was what pleased him, rather than any specific object in going. Josef plays, while Karl performs. The Slav is himself first and his race afterwards, while the Teuton is his race first and himself afterwards. I have been studying the children who live in this block for a number of years, and I hope no one will imagine that I am making up things about them in order to be able to write a little story, for I am not making up anything. The little episode of yesterday evening would be trivial and pointless if I had not watched the growth of these boys, and I only regret that I do not know more about Irving, the Jewish boy who cried so bitterly while Karl and Josef struck each other.

Irving came with his mother and father to this block last November, not quite four months ago, but I did not begin to see much of him until a month later when he began to appear in the street. He is a melancholy-looking boy, about Josef's age, and of the sort described generally as introspective, seeming to feel safer within himself. I suppose his parents are having him educated musically, for he has the appearance of someone who ought to develop into a pretty fine violinist or pianist, the large serious head, the slight body, and a delicate nervous system.

One evening, on the way to the grocer's I saw Irving sitting on the steps of his house, apparently dreaming the unspeakably beautiful dream of a child bewildered by the strangeness of being, and I hoped to speak to him quietly and try to find out, if possible, what was going on in his mind, but when he saw me coming toward him, he got up swiftly and scrambled up the steps and into the house, looking startled and very much afraid. I would give my phonograph to know what Irving had been dreaming that evening, for I believe it would somehow make explicable his weeping last night.

Karl is solid and very sure of his stance, extremely certain of himself because of the fact that discipline prohibits undue speculation regarding circumstances unrelated to himself, while Josef, on the other hand, though no less certain of himself, is a good deal less solid because of the fact that a lively curiosity about all things impels him to keep in motion, and to do things without thinking. The presence of Irving on this street is solid enough, but there is something about his presence that is both amusing and saddening, as if he himself cannot figure it out and as if, for all he knows, he were somewhere else. Irving is not at all certain of himself. He is neither dis-

ciplined nor undisciplined, he is simply melancholy. Eventually I
suppose, he will come to have the fullest understanding of himself
and his relation to all things, but at the moment he is much too
bewildered to have any definite viewpoint on the matter.

Not long ago there were riots in Paris, and shortly afterwards a
civil war developed in Austria. It is a well-known fact that Russia is
preparing to defend herself against Japan, and everyone is aware of
the fidgetiness which has come over all of Europe because of the
nationalistic program of the present dictator of Germany.

I mention these facts because they have a bearing on the story I
am telling. As Joyce would say, the earth haveth childers everywhere,
and the little episode of last night is to me as significant as the larger
episodes in Europe must be to the men who have grown up and
become no longer children. At least, seemingly.

The day began yesterday with thick fog, followed by a brief shower.
By three in the afternoon the sun was shining and the sky was clear
except for a number of white clouds, the kind of clouds that indicate
good weather, a clear moment, clean air, and so on. The weather
changes this way in San Francisco. In the morning the weather is
apt to be winter weather, and in the afternoon the winter weather is
apt to change suddenly to spring weather, any season of the year.
Hardly anyone is aware of seasons out here. We have all seasons all
the year round.

When I left my room in the morning, none of the children of this
street was outdoors, but when I returned in the evening, I saw Josef
and Irving standing together on my side of the street, in front of
Irving's house, talking. Karl was across the street, in front of his
house, walking in the military manner I have described, looking pompous in an amusing sort of way and seeming to be very proud of
himself. Farther down the street were five little girls, playing a
hopping game on the sidewalk: Josef's big sister, two Irish girls who
were sisters, and two Italian girls who were sisters.

After rain the air clears up and it is very pleasant to be abroad,
and these children were playing in the street, in the sunlight. It was
a very fine moment to be alive and to have love for all others alive
in one's time, and I mention this to show that the occasional ugliness
of the human heart is not necessarily the consequence of some similar
ugliness in nature. And we know that when the European countryside was loveliest this had no effect on the progress of the last war,
and that the rate of killing remained just as high as it had been during

the bad weather, and that the only thing that happened as a consequence of the lovely weather was some touching poetry by young
soldiers who wanted to create, who wanted wives and homes, and
who did not want to be killed.

Walking past Josef and Irving, I heard Josef say, speaking of Karl:
Look at him. Look at the way he's walking. Why does he walk that
way?

I had known for some time that Josef resented the pompous cer-
tainty of Karl's manner of walking, and therefore his remarks did not
surprise me. Besides, I have already said that he was naturally curious
about all things that came within the range of his consciousness, and
that he was always asking questions. It seemed to me that his interest
in Karl's way of walking was largely aesthetic, and I didn't seem to
detect any malice in his speech. I did not hear Irving make a reply,
and I came directly to my room. I had a letter to write and I went
to work on it, and when it was finished I stood at the window of my
room, studying the street. The small girls had disappeared, but Karl
was still across the street, and Josef and Irving were still together. It
was beginning to be dusk, and the street was very quiet.

I do not know how it happened, but when Josef and Irving began
crossing the street, going to Karl, I saw a whole nation moving the
line of its army to the borders of another nation, and the little boys
seemed so very innocent and likable, and whole nations seemed so
much like the little boys that I could not avoid laughing to myself.
Oh, I thought, there will probably be another war before long, and
the children will make a great fuss in the world, but it will probably
be very much like what is going to happen now. For I was certain
that Josef and Karl were going to express their hatred for each other,
the hatred that was stupid and wasteful and the result of ignorance
and immaturity, by striking one another, as whole nations, through
stupid hatred, seek to dominate or destroy one another.

It happened across the street, two small boys striking each other, a
third small boy crying about it, whole nations at war on the earth. I
did not hear what Josef said to Karl, or what Karl said to Josef, and
I am not sure just how the fight started, but I have an idea that it
started a long while before the two boys began to strike each other,
a year ago perhaps, perhaps a century ago. I saw Josef touch Karl,
each of them fine little boys, and I saw Karl shove Josef, and I saw
the little Jewish boy watching them, horrified and silent, almost
stunned. When the little Teuton and the little Slav began to strike

each other in earnest, the little Jew began to weep. It was lovely—
not the striking, but the weeping of the little Jew. The whole affair
lasted only a moment or two, but the implication was whole, and the
most enduring and refreshing part of it is this weeping I heard. Why
did he cry? He was not involved. He was only a witness, as I was a
witness. Why did he cry?

I wish I knew more about the little Jewish boy. I can only imagine
that he cried because the existence of hatred and ugliness in the heart
of man is a truth, and this is as far as I can go with the theory.

LOVE, HERE IS MY HAT

W HEN I woke up I didn't know what time it was, what day, or what city. I knew I was in a hotel room. It seemed to be either pretty late or a small town. I didn't know whether to get up or to go on lying on the bed in my clothes. It was dark.

I knew I was feeling the same.

Love is absurd, always has been, always will be. It's the only thing, but it's absurd. It's too good for anything but birds. It's too splendid for any form of life that's cluttered up with all the crazy things the human form of life is cluttered up with. It's too fine for creatures which wear clothes, which inhabit the world, who must work, who must earn money, who cannot live on air and water.

It's too good for animals that can talk.

I woke up and remembered where I was and why. I was in a room in the Riverside Hotel in Reno and I wasn't in Reno for divorce because I wasn't married. I was in Reno because she was in San Francisco.

I'm not a canary, oriole, dove, quail, robin, hummingbird, or any other kind of feathered creature that lives in or near trees, and exists only to love another canary, oriole, dove, quail, robin, or humming-bird, and sing about it. I'm an American. Fun is fun, but I know the difference between good wholesome fun and love, and love is too good for me or anybody like me. It's too wonderful. I can't fly and I can't sing and I need honest-to-God nourishment. I've got to have rare roast beef at least once a day and when I'm in love I can't eat.

I can't be that nice, either, and not feel ridiculous. It isn't my nature to be that nice. That may be all right for an oriole, but it's just a little absurd for me. I can be that nice when I don't mean it, but when I mean it, it's just too wonderful for words. Being that nice is all right for some good-looking dope in a movie, but it's just too won-derful in San Francisco.

I was in Reno because I wanted her to start eating regularly again and let me eat regularly too. I wanted her to get well, so I could get well too.

Look, I told her in San Francisco, I'm getting awfully hungry. Will you excuse me while I leave town?

Leave town? she said. If you go, I go.

Nothing would please me more, I said, but if you go with me, we won't be able to eat and what we need is food. We're both undernourished. Look at me. I'm scarcely a shadow of what I was three weeks ago.

You look wonderful, she said.

No, I don't, I said. I look hungry. I *am* hungry. You look hungry too.

I don't care if I do, she said. If you go away, I'm going with you. I can't live without you.

Yes, you can, I said. What you can't live without is roast beef.

I don't care if I ever eat again; she said.

Look, I said. You've got to get some food and sleep, and so do I.

I won't let you go, she said.

All right, I said. Then we'll die of starvation together. It's all right with me if it's all right with you.

It's all right with me, she said.

All right, I said. I won't go. What shall we do? I mean, first?

It was a little after eleven and we had just gotten home after a movie and an attempt to eat sandwiches that wouldn't go down, except dry. We ate the pickles and drank the coffee.

Let's stay here and listen to the phonograph, she said.

Or shall we go out and have a few drinks? I said.

Wouldn't you rather stay here and listen to the phonograph? she said.

I guess I would, I said.

So we went to bed.

It might have been a couple of orioles.

Three days later, though, we decided to let me go away. We laughed and she said she wouldn't try to find out where I had gone to and wouldn't follow me and I said I wouldn't write, wire, or telephone her.

I feel sick, she said.

Don't be silly, I said. Get in bed and go to sleep and when you wake up, have them bring you a big tray of food. Keep that up for a week.

All right, she said.

I rode to the airport in a cab and two hours later I was in Reno. Fifteen minutes later I was asleep in this room in the Riverside Hotel. I slept like a baby and when I woke up I didn't know what time it was, what day, or what city. Little by little I began to remember.

I got up and yawned. Then I went downstairs and ate a hearty but sad supper of rare roast beef. I don't think it did me much good. After supper I took a walk around town. It was bright and pleasant, but I didn't feel right. I wished I was back in San Francisco, so I got into a cab and rode out of town to The Tavern where I had eight or nine drinks. When I got back to the hotel it was a quarter after two. The desk clerk handed me the key to my room and eleven slips of paper asking me to telephone 783-J. That was a local number. I went to my room and telephoned 783-J.

Where are you? I said.

I'm in Reno, she said.

I know, I said. But where?

I'm at Leon & Eddy's, she said. That number's the number of the phone in the booth here. I'm drunk.

I'll come and get you, I said.

Are you all right? she said.

I'm fine, I said. Are you all right?

I want to cry, she said.

I'll come and get you, I said.

Did you eat? she said.

Yes, I said. Did you?

No, she said. I couldn't.

I'll be right down. How did you know I was in Reno?

The desk clerk told me, she said. I asked him if he knew where you had gone and he told me you had gone to Reno. He told the name of the hotel too. Did you tell him?

Yes, I said.

I didn't think you would, she said. Why did you do it?

I don't know, I said. I guess I thought maybe you might ask him. Why did you ask him?

I thought maybe you might tell him, she said.

I'll be right down, I said.

Leon & Eddy's was two blocks from the hotel, but I took a cab anyway.

When I saw her sitting at the small table, holding the tall glass and looking alone and lonely, I felt sick and happy again, only worse. It was goofy. It was the only thing, but it was crazy.

Come on, I said.

It was too good for me or anybody like me, but it seemed to be the will of the good Lord.

We walked to the hotel.

What we'll have to do, I said, is quarrel and hate one another. It's no use getting married.

I won't quarrel, she said.

We're bound to find something to quarrel about, I said. It may take another day or two, but we're bound to find something. If we don't, it'll be just too bad. This is terrible. I love you.

I love you too, she said.

We stayed in Reno eleven days. Then I told her what I knew she knew I was going to tell her.

Everything's fine, I said. I want it to stay that way.

All right, she said. But we didn't quarrel, did we?

No, I said. Would you prefer a small quarrel?

No, she said.

I'm glad we met, I said.

I took a train back to Frisco and was sick all the way. I knew I would get well, though, and I did.

It took me a long time, but after I got well, nothing was spoiled, and the next time I saw her, three months later, she was well too, so we had supper together.

It was the biggest and finest supper we ever had together, and we enjoyed everything.

Isn't it wonderful? she said.

It certainly is, I said.

THE GENIUS

U P at Izzy's one night a young genius in corduroy pants came up to me and said, I hear you're a writer. I've got a story that'll make a great movie, only I need somebody with experience to write it for me. I'd write it myself, only I've got to make a living working and when I get through working I'm too tired to write.

I was a little drunk, but I'm never too drunk and never too busy to listen to a fellow-artist, and I said, Go ahead, tell me the story. If it's good I'll write it and we'll get Metro-Goldwyn-Mayer to make a movie out of it. What happens?

If you've ever had a story printed in a national magazine and been around at all you've met all kinds of people with stories that will make great movies. The world is full of people with movie stories, all unwritten, but it seems the people who manufacture movies never meet these people, or if they do, never let them tell their stories, consequently the average movie manufactured is lousy, even in technicolor, even starring Clark Gable, John Barrymore, Norma Shearer, or anybody else. The people who manufacture movies just simply don't care to manufacture good movies.

Up at Izzy's as many as eighty-seven good movies are related in one night, but not one of them is ever filmed.

I told the boy to go ahead and tell me the story.

Shall I begin at the beginning? he said.

Not necessarily, I said. Begin anywhere. Begin at the end and work backward to the beginning. You might even sit down if you like.

Thanks, he said, I'd rather stand.

Take all the time you need, I said.

There ain't much to say, he said. The idea is this. Says, I'll do something. I won't be a clerk all my life. Ships out on a boat to Shanghai.

Who? I said.

The fellow, said the boy. Clark Gable.

Oh, I said. Clark Gable. Says he'll do something. Do what?

Coming up on deck he bumps into the girl.

The girl? I said.

Joan Crawford.

Ah, Joan, I said. What's it come to?

They fall in love.

So the boy does something?

Not right away. That's at the end.

I know, I said. Anything special?

He marries the girl.

How about the money? I said. Who's got the money?

She has. That's where the trouble comes in.

Oh, I said, the trouble.

Yeah, the boy ain't a gigolo, so he won't marry the girl when he finds out she's rich.

Why? I said.

He figures he can't marry a rich girl, even if he is in love with her, so they quarrel.

Just in fun, of course, I said. Nothing serious.

Plenty serious. The girl's got to marry somebody before the boat reaches Shanghai or she won't inherit the eighteen million dollars.

The how many million? I said.

Eighteen.

Do you think that's enough? I said. For all practical purposes? It's a tidy sum.

A trifle, I said. How does it turn out?

Well, the man who is engaged to the girl is a middle-aged banker. He ain't very good-looking. She don't want to marry him. That's where she gets a chance to do some acting.

Boy, I said.

After the boy and the girl fight, the girl says she's going to marry the banker, just to make the boy jealous.

That's another spot for some fancy acting, I said.

Yeah, so the Captain makes plans for a ship wedding. This is where it gets exciting. One thing after another happens, in quick succession. Chinese pirates take over the ship, and a Chinaman decides to marry the girl himself, without the formality of a wedding of course. The banker doesn't care, because he's scared, but the boy hates the Chinaman. He's a young educated Chinaman and speaks better English than anybody else on board the ship.

So? I said.

The Chinaman gets the girl in her cabin and starts chasing her around.

That's bad, I said.

The Chinaman is chasing the girl around the room, when the boy breaks the door down. The Chinaman and the boy have a fight. The Chinaman gets the boy flat on his back and gets out his dagger and is about to stick it in the boy.

Where? I said.

Right in the heart. The girl hits the Chinaman over the head with a chair.

That's love for you, I said.

In the meantime, a cablegram is received by the ship, asking the Captain to put the banker in chains for grand larceny and bigamy.

Just two little misdemeanors? I said.

And possible murder. The picture ends with the boy kissing the girl.

Boy, what an ending, I said.

How is it? he said.

It's fine, I said.

Is it exciting enough?

It's breath-taking, I said, especially where the Chinaman chases her.

I thought you'd like it, he said. First I think you ought to make a book out of it, and then sell it to the movies.

By God, I said, I'd do that little thing, only I gave up writing day before yesterday.

What for? he said.

I got bored, I said. Same old stuff over and over again.

This is different, he said. Think of the Chinaman. East against West.

Even so, I said. I gave up writing day before yesterday. *You* write it.

Do you think they'll print the book? he said.

They'd be fools not to, I said.

What style should I use? he said.

Oh, I said, don't worry about style. Just put it down on paper the way it comes to you after work and you'll find it'll be full of style. There'll be enough left over for two more movies.

My grammar ain't so hot, he said.

Neither is mine, I said. You don't need to worry about that. That'll be part of your style, part of your originality. Unless I'm badly mistaken, you're a genius.

No, he said. I just get these ideas for books and movies, that's all. I've forgotten enough ideas for books and movies to make a dozen books and movies.

Write them down, I said. Don't let them get away. You're losing money every minute.

Got a pencil? I said.

I'm afraid not, I said. I gave up writing day before yesterday.

What the hell for? he said.

My stuff's no good for movies, I said. I sell a story for thirty or forty dollars every now and then. I don't get movie ideas. I thought I would after a while, but I didn't, so I gave it up.

That's tough, he said. I get movie ideas left and right.

I know it, I said. All you got to do is get them down on paper and I know you'll be famous and rich in no time.

I'll tell you another idea I got for a movie, he said.

Joe, I said.

Joe came over to the table.

Joe, I said, here's a dime. Go get me a pencil.

Joe went over to Izzy and Izzy looked around and found a pencil. A little tiny one. Joe brought the pencil over to me. I handed it to the boy.

Listen, George, I said, you got no time to lose. Here's a pencil, all sharpened and everything. You take this pencil and go home and write them ideas down on paper. Any old kind of paper. Lincoln wrote his famous speech on the back of an envelope.

He took the pencil, but didn't start to go.

I thought I'd take it easy tonight and start writing tomorrow, he said.

No, I said, that ain't right. You go right home and go to work while the ideas are still fresh in your mind.

All right, he said.

He put the pencil in his inside coat pocket, pulled his hat down over his eyes, and went down the stairs.

Joe, I said, bring me three beers.

THE JOURNEY AND THE DREAM

NAGASAKI, Bull, Mr. Isaac, Dynamite, Hollywood Pete, and a kid in a leather coat who looked like a college student were playing stud when I walked into the joint with money burning holes in my pockets.

Well, said Bull. Where the hell have you been? Sit down and go broke.

Thanks, Bull, I said. I'll sit down, but I'll try not to go broke.

It was September, raining, and I had just come home from Europe and New York. Months ago when I got up from the game and left town, the players were sitting in the same seats they now occupied. Only Curley was out of sight.

Where's Curley? I said.

Nagasaki the Jap told me. Curley die, he said. Curley win big pot.

You're kidding, I said.

That's right, said Hollywood Pete. He tried to bluff out of that spot, but they called him.

Too bad, I said. Curley was O.K.

The best, said Bull. He broke me as many times as I tried to bluff him.

Waiter, I said. Perry the waiter came running over. Bring me some whiskey, I said. I want to drink to the memory of Curley.

Make it three, said Bull. And then everybody at the table except the kid in the leather coat decided to drink to the memory of the old gambler.

I sat down, and Flash, the Irish tenor who used to sing in burlesque, came over to find out how much worth of chips I wanted to buy.

Where you been? he said.

I just got back from Russia, I said.

I was born in Russia, said Dynamite. He was a smart Jew.

What city? I said.

Kiev, he said.

I stayed at the Karl Marx hotel in Kiev, I said.

God damn it, said Dynamite. You ain't kidding, are you?

No, I said.

I left Kiev when I was ten years old, he said. How's the river Dnieper?

Swell, I said.

Did you see Stalin? said Mr. Isaac. He was a little Jewish tailor.

No, I said. I went to see Russia. How's it going, Flash?

Bluffing the best way I know how, he said.

Bring me thirty dollars' worth, I said.

Fat Laramie was dealing and the first card he gave me was the Ace of Spades, which was swell. Perry came back with the drinks.

To Curley, I said.

To Curley, said the gamblers.

The kid in the leather coat was sitting on my left. Who's this guy Curley? he said.

He used to play here, I said. Usually he sat in the chair you're sitting in now. He was a great guy.

That calls for a drink, said the kid. Bring me the same.

How old a man was he? said the kid to the players.

He was a young man, said Bull, himself over sixty.

He was in his sixties, I said.

What the hell killed him? said the kid.

Bad heart, said Hollywood Pete.

Well, said the kid, I'm sitting in his chair. I don't suppose the game stops when a player dies.

No, said Nagasaki. Game go on all the time, night and day.

Neither night nor day nor storm nor war nor revolution interferes with this game, said Dynamite.

Where'd you get that? said Fat Laramie.

It's the truth, ain't it? said Dynamite.

Where'd you get it, though? said Fat Laramie.

I'm not as dumb as some of the players around here, said Dynamite. I know when to retreat. I got it out of a book.

I thought so, said Fat Laramie. I thought it didn't sound natural. What you mean is, this game goes on all the time.

It's a good game, said Nagasaki.

Yeah, said Bull. You haven't worked in two years. You've been in this game two years now. You never lose, do you, Nagasaki?

Sometimes lose very bad, said the Jap.

Yeah, said Fat Laramie, I know.

Somebody's got to lose, said the kid in the leather coat. I'm about twenty dollars in the hole right now.

One night, said Bull, I saw Curley lose eighty dollars in one pot to Crazy Gus who was drunk. Gus drew out on him. Curley had aces back to back and Gus had treys back to back. Curley bet everything in front of him on the fourth card. He wanted the poor fool to know he had the best, but Gus was too drunk to know anything; or maybe drunk *enough* to know everything. Anyway, he called and made two pair.

That was tough, said the kid.

Wait a minute, said Bull. Curley fished into his pocket and brought out a quarter and a dime. He bought seven white chips. Two hours later Crazy Gus got up from the table broke, and Curley had all his chips.

That's *luck* for you, said the kid.

Luck nothing, said Bull. Curley knew how to play. They can draw out on you once in a while, but not all the time.

Mr. Isaac said something, then Nagasaki said something, and then Hollywood Pete, and one after another each of the players said something while the game moved along into the night and the year. It was great and I knew I was home again. Somebody went broke and got up and went away and somebody else sat down in his chair, and I began to forget everything. It was fine. It was perfect because I wanted to forget everything. I played the way the cards demanded that I play and the cards were full of kindness. They didn't race after me, and they didn't trick me.

It was a little after midnight, and I was home again from Europe. The streets of all the cities I visited, and the people of these streets, and the words of the foreign languages, began to return to the wakeful dream, and I began to return to each place I had visited for a day, or an afternoon, or an hour, and I began to see again each face I had seen, each street, each configuration of city and village.

I knew I'd be playing poker till the journey ended. All winter, most likely.

I drank whiskey all night and left the game sober and hushed early in the morning. I went into the cafeteria on the corner and ordered buckwheat cakes with bacon and hot coffee. Then I walked three miles to my room through rain. I took off my wet clothes and got into bed. I slept and dreamed the journey, almost wakening now and then to listen more consciously to the sound of the train rushing from Paris to Vienna, through the Swiss and Austrian Alps. To look more clearly upon the green fields of Europe. To breathe more deeply the clear cold air of dawn in Austria. And when I got up at three in the afternoon, I felt stronger and wiser and more melancholy than ever before in my life.

I was beginning to forget everything, and the only way you can do that is to remember everything in the conscious dream and return everything to the living void of memory.

Then you'll be born again. Then you'll waken from the sleep of unbirth to the wakeful sleep of mortality.

The game lasted a long time, longer than the reckoning of days on the calendar, longer than time pulsing to inhale and exhale of breath, and the come and go of sea-tide, every moment wakeful and dreamed, inhabiting present and past, absorbing all movement over sea and continent, bringing the world together into one swiftly perceived reality and truth, and one morning when I got up from the game I knew the journey was ended and when I walked into the street I was laughing because it was so good to be in the world, so excellent to be a part of the chaos and unrest and agony and magnificence of this place of man, the world so comic and tragic to be alive during a moment of its change, the sea, and the sea's sky, and London, and London's noise and fury, and the Cockney's lamentation, the King's Palace, the ballet at Covent Garden, and outside Covent Garden the real ballet, and France, and the fields of France, and Paris, and the streets of Paris, and the stations, and the trains, and the faces, and the eyes, and the grief, and Austria, and Poland, and Russia, and Finland, and Sweden, and Norway, and the world, man stumbling mournfully after God in the wilderness, the street musicians of Edinburgh crying out for God in the songs of America, dancing after Him down steep streets, the tragic dream stalking everywhere through day and night, so that when I walked into the street I was laughing and begging God to pity them, love them, protect them, the king and the beggar alike.

CORDUROY PANTS

Most people hardly ever, if ever at all, stop to consider how important pants are, and the average man, getting in and out of pants every morning and night, never pauses while doing so, or at any other time, even for the amusement in the speculation, to wonder how unfortunate it would be if he didn't have pants, how miserable he would be if he had to appear in the world without them, and how awkward his manners would become, how foolish his conversation, how utterly joyless his attitude toward life.

Nevertheless, when I was fourteen and a reader of Schopenhauer and Nietzsche and Spinoza, and an unbeliever, a scorner of God, an enemy of Jesus Christ and the Catholic Church, and something of a philosopher in my own right, my thoughts, profound and trivial alike, turned now and then to the theme of man in the world without pants, and much as you might suppose they were heavy melancholy thoughts no less than often they were gay and hilarious. That, I think, is the joy of being a philosopher: that knowing the one side as well as the other. On the one hand, a man in the world without pants *should* be a miserable creature, and probably would be, and then again, on the other hand, if this same man, *in* pants, and in the world, was usually a gay and easy-going sort of fellow, in all probability even without pants he would be a gay and easy-going sort of fellow, and might even find the situation an opportunity for all manner of delightful banter. Such a person in the world is not altogether incredible, and I used to believe that, in moving pictures at least, he would not be embarrassed, and on the contrary would know just what to do and how to do it in order to impress everyone with this simple truth: namely, that after all what is a pair of pants? and being without them is certainly not the end of the world, or the destruction of civilization. All the same, the idea that I myself might some day appear in the world without pants terrified me, inasmuch as I was sure I couldn't rise to the occasion and impress everybody with the triviality of the situation and make them know the world wasn't ending.

I had only one pair of pants, my uncle's, and they were very patched, very sewed, and not the style. My uncle had worn these pants five years before he had turned them over to me, and then I began putting them on every morning and taking them off every night. It was an honor to wear my uncle's pants. I would have been the last person in the world to suggest that it wasn't. I knew it was an honor, and I accepted the honor along with the pants, and I wore the pants, and I wore the honor, and the pants didn't fit.

They were too big around the waist and too narrow at the cuff. In my boyhood I was never regarded as well-dressed. If people turned to look at me twice, as they often do these days, it was only to wonder whose pants I was wearing. There were four pockets in my uncle's pants, but there wasn't one sound pocket in the lot. If it came to a matter of money, coins given and coins returned, I found that I had to put the coins in my mouth and remember not to swallow them.

Naturally, I was very unhappy. I took to reading Schopenhauer and despising people, and after people God, and after God, or before, or at the same time, the whole world, the whole universe, the whole impertinent scheme of life.

At the same time I knew that my uncle had honored me, of all his numerous nephews, by handing down his pants to me, and I *felt* honored, and to a certain extent clothed. My uncle's pants, I sometimes reasoned unhappily, were certainly better than no pants at all, and with this much of the idea developed my nimble and philosophical mind leapt quickly to the rest of the idea. Suppose a man appeared in the world without pants? Not that he wanted to. Not just for the fun of it. Not as a gesture of individuality and as a criticism of Western civilization, but simply because he had no pants, simply because he had no money with which to buy pants? Suppose he put on all his clothes excepting pants? His underwear, his stockings, his shoes, his shirt, and walked into the world and looked everybody straight in the eye? Suppose he did it? Ladies, I have no pants. Gentlemen, I have no money. So what? I have no pants, I have no money. I am an inhabitant of this world. I intend to remain an inhabitant of this world until I die or until the world ends. I intend to go on moving about in the world, even though I have no pants.

What could they do? Could they put him in jail? If so, for how long? And why? What sort of a crime could it be to appear in the world, among one's brothers, without pants?

Perhaps they would feel sorry, I used to think, and want to give me an old pair of pants, and this possibility would drive me almost crazy. Never mind giving me your old pants, I used to shout at them. Don't try to be kind to me. I don't want your old pants, and I don't want your new pants. I want my own pants, straight from the store, brand new, size, name, label, and guarantee. I want my own God damn pants, and nobody else's. I'm in the world, and I want my own pants.

I used to get pretty angry about people perhaps wanting to be kind to me, because I couldn't see it that way. I couldn't see people *giving* me something, or *anything*. I wanted to get my stuff the usual way. How much are these pants? They are three dollars. All right, I'll take them. Just like that. No hemming or hawing. How much? Three dollars. O.K., wrap them up.

The day I first put on my uncle's pants my uncle walked away several paces for a better view and said, They fit you perfectly.

Yes, sir, I said.

Plenty of room at the top, he said.

Yes, sir, I said.

And nice and snug at the bottom, he said.

Yes, sir, I said.

Then, for some crazy reason, as if perhaps the tradition of pants had been handed down from one generation to another, my uncle was deeply moved and shook my hand, turning pale with joy and admiration, and being utterly incapable of saying a word. He left the house as a man leaves something so touching he cannot bear to be near it, and I began to try to determine if I might be able, with care, to get myself from one point to another in the pants.

It was so, and I could walk in the pants. I felt more or less en-cumbered, yet it was *possible* to move. I did not feel secure, but I knew I was covered. and I knew I could move, and with practice I believed I would be able to move swiftly. It was purely a matter of adaption. There would be months of unfamiliarity, but I believed in time I would be able to move about in the world gingerly, and with sharp effect.

I wore my uncle's pants for many months, and these were the un-happiest months of my life. Why? Because *corduroy pants* were the style. At first *ordinary* corduroy pants were the style, and then a year later there was a Spanish renaissance in California, and *Spanish corduroy pants* became the style. These were bell-bottomed, with a touch of red down there, and in many cases five-inch waists, and in several cases small decorations around the waist. Boys of fourteen in corduroy pants of this variety were boys who not only felt secure and snug, but knew they were in style, and consequently could do any number of gay and lighthearted things, such as running after girls, talking with them, and all the rest of it. I couldn't. It was only natural, I suppose, for me to turn, somewhat mournfully, to Schopenhauer and to begin despising women, and later on men, children, oxen, cattle, beasts of the jungle, and fish. What is life? I used to ask. Who do they think they are, just because they have Spanish bell-bottomed corduroy pants? Have they read Schopenhauer? No. Do they knew there is no God? No. Do they so much as suspect that love is the most boring experience in the world? No. They are ignorant. They are wearing the fine corduroy pants, but they are blind with ignorance. They do not know that it is all a hollow mockery and that they are the victims of a horrible jest.

I used to laugh at them bitterly.

Now and then, however, I forgot what I knew, what I had learned about everything from Schopenhauer, and in all innocence, without any profound philosophical thought one way or another, I ran after girls, feeling altogether gay and lighthearted, only to discover that I was being laughed at. It was my uncle's pants. They were not pants in which to run after a girl. They were unhappy, tragic, melancholy pants, and being in them, and running after a girl in them, was a very comic thing to see, and a very tragic thing to do.

I began saving up every penny and nickle and dime I could get hold of, and I began biding my time. Some day I would go down to the store and tell them I would like to buy a pair of the Spanish bell-bottomed pants, price no consideration.

A mournful year went by. A year of philosophy and hatred of man.

I was saving the pennies and nickles and dimes, and in time I would have my own pair of Spanish style corduroy pants. I would have covering and security and at the same time a garment in which a man could be nothing if not gay and lighthearted.

Well, I saved up enough money all right, and I went down to the store all right, and I bought a pair of the Spanish bell-bottomed corduroy pants all rights, but a month later when school opened and I went to school I was the only boy at school in this particular style of corduroy pants. It seems the Spanish renaissance had ended. The new style corduroy pants were very conservative, no bell-bottoms, no five-inch waists, no decorations. Just simple ordinary corduroy pants.

How could I feel gay and lighthearted? I didn't *look* gay and lighthearted. And that made everything worse, because my pants *did* look gay and lighthearted. My own pants. Which I had bought. *They* looked gay and lighthearted. It meant simply, I reasoned, that I would have to be, in everything I did, as gay and lighthearted as my pants. Otherwise, naturally, there could never be any order in the world. I could not go to school in such pants and not be gay and lighthearted, so I decided to *be* gay and lighthearted. I was very witty at every opportunity and had my ears boxed, and I laughed very often and discovered that invariably when I laughed nobody else did.

This was agony of the worst kind, so I quit school. I am sure I should not now be the philosopher I am if it were not for the trouble I had with Spanish bell-bottomed corduroy pants.

MY NAME IS ARAM

The Pomegranate Trees

My uncle Melik was just about the worst farmer that ever lived. He was too imaginative and poetic for his own good. What he wanted was beauty. He wanted to plant it and see it grow. I myself planted over one hundred pomegranate trees for my uncle one year back there in the good old days of poetry and youth in the world. I drove a John Deere tractor too, and so did my uncle. It was all pure esthetics, not agriculture. My uncle just liked the idea of planting trees and watching them grow.

Only they wouldn't grow. It was on account of the soil. The soil was desert soil. It was dry. My uncle waved at the six hundred and eighty acres of desert he had bought and he said in the most poetic Armenian anybody ever heard, Here in this awful desolation a garden shall flower, fountains of cold water shall bubble out of the earth, and all things of beauty shall come into being.

Yes, sir, I said.

I was the first and only relative to see the land he had bought. He knew I was a poet at heart, and he believed I would understand the magnificent impulse that was driving him to glorious ruin. I did. I knew as well as he that what he had purchased was worthless desert land. It was away over to hell and gone, at the foot of the Sierra Nevada Mountains. It was full of every kind of desert plant that ever sprang out of dry hot earth. It was overrun with prairie dogs, squirrels, horned toads, snakes, and a variety of smaller forms of life. The space over this land knew only the presence of hawks, eagles, and buzzards. It was a region of loneliness, emptiness, truth, and dignity. It was nature at its proudest, dryest, loneliest, and loveliest.

My uncle and I got out of the Ford roadster in the middle of his land and began to walk over the dry earth.

This land, he said, is my land.

He walked slowly, kicking into the dry soil. A horned toad scrambled over the earth at my uncle's feet. My uncle clutched my shoulder and came to a pious halt.

What is that animal? he said.

That little tiny lizard? I said.

That mouse with horns, my uncle said. What is it?

I don't know for sure, I said. We call them horny toads.

The horned toad came to a halt about three feet away and turned its head.

My uncle looked down at the small animal.

Is it poison? he said.

To eat? I said. Or if it bites you?

Either way, my uncle said.

I don't think it's good to eat, I said. I think it's harmless. I've caught many of them. They grow sad in captivity, but never bite. Shall I catch this one?

Please do, my uncle said.

I sneaked up on the horned toad, then sprang on it while my uncle looked on.

Careful, he said. Are you sure it isn't poison?

I've caught many of them, I said.

I took the horned toad to my uncle. He tried not to seem afraid. A lovely little thing, isn't it? he said. His voice was unsteady.

Would you like to hold it? I said.

No, my uncle said. You hold it. I have never before been so close to such a thing as this. I see it has eyes. I suppose it can see us.

I suppose it can, I said. It's looking up at you now.

My uncle looked the horned toad straight in the eye. The horned toad looked my uncle straight in the eye. For fully half a minute they looked one another straight in the eye and then the horned toad turned its head aside and looked down at the ground. My uncle sighed with relief.

A thousand of them, he said, could kill a man, I suppose.

They never travel in great numbers, I said. You hardly ever see more than one at a time.

A big one, my uncle said, could probably bite a man to death.

They don't grow big, I said. This is as big as they grow.

They seem to have an awful eye for such small creatures, my uncle said. Are you sure they don't mind being picked up?

I suppose they forget all about it the minute you put them down, I said.

Do you really think so? my uncle said.

I don't think they have very good memories, I said.

My uncle straightened up, breathing deeply.

Put the little creature down, he said. Let us not be cruel to the innocent creations of Almighty God. If it is not poison and grows no larger than a mouse and does not travel in great numbers and has no memory to speak of, let the timid little thing return to the earth. Let us be gentle toward these small things which live on the earth with us.

Yes, sir, I said.

I placed the horned toad on the ground.

Gently now, my uncle said. Let no harm come to this strange dweller on my land.

The horned toad scrambled away.

These little things, I said, have been living on soil of this kind for centuries.

Centuries? my uncle said. Are you sure?

I'm not sure, I said, but I imagine they have. They're still here, anyway.

My uncle looked around at his land, at the cactus and brush growing out of it, at the sky overhead.

What have they been eating all this time? he shouted.

I don't know, I said.

What would you say they've been eating? he said.

Insects, I guess.

Insects? my uncle shouted. What sort of insects?

Little bugs, most likely, I said. I don't know their names. I can find out tomorrow at school.

We continued to walk over the dry land. When we came to some holes in the earth my uncle stood over them and said, What lives down there?

Prairie dogs, I said.

What are *they*? he said.

Well, I said, they're something like rats. They belong to the rodent family.

What are all these things doing on my land? my uncle said.

They don't know it's your land, I said. They've been living here a long while.

I don't suppose that horny toad ever looked a man in the eye before, my uncle said.

I don't think so, I said.

Do you think I scared it or anything? my uncle said.

I don't know for sure, I said.

If I did, my uncle said, I didn't mean to. I'm going to build a house here some day.

I didn't know that, I said.

Of course, my uncle said. I'm going to build a magnificent house.

It's pretty far away, I said.

It's only an hour from town, my uncle said.

If you go fifty miles an hour, I said.

It's not fifty miles to town, my uncle said. It's thirty-seven.

Well, you've got to take a little time out for rough roads, I said.

I'll build me the finest house in the world, my uncle said. What else lives on this land?

Well, I said, there are three or four kinds of snakes.

Poison or non-poison? my uncle said.

Mostly non-poison, I said. The rattlesnake is poison, though.

Do you mean to tell me there are *rattlesnakes* on this land? my uncle said.

This is the kind of land rattlesnakes usually live on, I said.

How many? my uncle said.

Per acre? I said. Or on the whole six hundred and eighty acres?

Per acre, my uncle said.

Well, I said, I'd say there are about three per acre, conservatively.

Three per acre? my uncle shouted. Conservatively?

Maybe only two, I said.

How many is that to the whole place? my uncle said.

Well, let's see, I said. Two per acre. Six hundred and eighty acres. About fifteen hundred of them.

Fifteen hundred of them? my uncle said.

An acre is pretty big, I said. Two rattlesnakes per acre isn't many. You don't often see them.

What else have we got around here that's poison? my uncle said.

I don't know of anything else, I said. All the other things are harmless. The rattlesnakes are pretty harmless too, unless you step on them.

All right, my uncle said. You walk ahead and watch where you're going. If you see a rattlesnake, don't step on it. I don't want you to die at the age of eleven.

Yes, sir, I said. I'll watch carefully.

We turned around and walked back to the Ford. I didn't see any rattlesnakes on the way back. We got into the car and my uncle lighted a cigarette.

I'm going to make a garden of this awful desolation, he said.

Yes, sir, I said.

I know what my problems are, my uncle said, and I know how to solve them.

How? I said.

Do you mean the horny toads or the rattlesnakes? my uncle said.

I mean the problems, I said.

Well, my uncle said, the first thing I'm going to do is hire some Mexicans and put them to work.

Doing what? I said.

Clearing the land, my uncle said. Then I'm going to have them dig for water.

Dig where? I said.

Straight down, my uncle said. After we get water, I'm going to have them plow the land and then I'm going to plant.

What are you going to plant? I said. Wheat?

Wheat? my uncle shouted. What do I want with wheat? Bread is five cents a loaf. I'm going to plant pomegranate trees.

How much are pomegranates? I said.

Pomegranates, my uncle said, are practically unknown in this country.

Is that all you're going to plant? I said.

I have in mind, my uncle said, planting several other kinds of trees.

Peach trees? I said.

About ten acres, my uncle said.

How about apricots? I said.

By all means, my uncle said. The apricot is a lovely fruit. Lovely in shape, with a glorious flavor and a most delightful pit. I shall plant about twenty acres of apricot trees.

I hope the Mexicans don't have any trouble finding water, I said. Is there water under this land?

Of course, my uncle said. The important thing is to get started. I shall instruct the men to watch out for rattlesnakes. Pomegranates, he said. Peaches. Apricots. What else?

Figs? I said.

Thirty acres of figs, my uncle said.

How about mulberries? I said. The mulberry tree is a very nice-looking tree.

Mulberries, my uncle said. He moved his tongue around in his mouth. A nice tree, he said. A tree I knew well in the old country. How many acres would you suggest?

About ten, I said.

All right, he said. What else?

Olive trees are nice, I said.

Yes, they are, my uncle said. One of the nicest. About ten acres of olive trees. What else?

Well, I said, I don't suppose apple trees would grow on this kind of land.

I suppose not, my uncle said. I don't like apples anyway.

He started the car and we drove off the dry land on to the dry road. The car bounced about slowly until we reached the road and then we began to travel at a higher rate of speed.

One thing, my uncle said. When we get home I would rather you didn't mention this *farm* to the folks.

Yes, sir, I said. (*Farm?* I thought. *What farm?*)

I want to surprise them, my uncle said. You know how your grandmother is. I'll go ahead with my plans and when everything is in order I'll take the whole family out to the farm and surprise them.

Yes, sir, I said.

Not a word to a living soul, my uncle said.

Yes, sir, I said.

Well, the Mexicans went to work and cleared the land. They cleared about ten acres of it in about two months. There were seven of them. They worked with shovels and hoes. They didn't understand anything about anything. It all seemed very strange, but they never complained. They were being paid and that was the thing that counted. They were two brothers and their sons. One day the older brother, Diego, very politely asked my uncle what it was they were supposed to be doing.

Señor, he said, please forgive me. Why are we cutting down the cactus?

I'm going to farm this land, my uncle said.

The other Mexicans asked Diego in Mexican what my uncle had said and Diego told them.

They didn't believe it was worth the trouble to tell my uncle he couldn't do it. They just went on cutting down the cactus.

The cactus, however, stayed down only for a short while. The land which had been first cleared was already rich again with fresh cactus

and brush. My uncle made this observation with considerable amazement.

It takes deep plowing to get rid of cactus, I said. You've got to plow
it out.

My uncle talked the matter over with Ryan, who had a farm-implement business. Ryan told him not to fool with horses. The modern
thing to do was to turn a good tractor loose on the land and do a
year's work in a day.

So my uncle bought a John Deere tractor. It was beautiful. A
mechanic from Ryan's taught Diego how to operate the tractor, and
the next day when my uncle and I reached the land we could see the
tractor away out in the desolation and we could hear it booming in
the awful emptiness of the desert. It sounded pretty awful. It *was*
awful. My uncle thought it was wonderful.

Progress, he said. There's the modern age for you. Ten thousand
years ago, he said, it would have taken a hundred men a week to do
what the tractor's done today.

Ten thousand years ago? I said. You mean yesterday.

Anyway, my uncle said, there's nothing like these modern con-
veniences.

The tractor isn't a convenience, I said.

What is it, then? my uncle said. Doesn't the driver sit?

He couldn't very well stand, I said.

Any time they let you sit, my uncle said, it's a convenience. Can
you whistle?

Yes, sir, I said. What sort of a song would you like to hear?

Song? my uncle said. I don't want to hear any song. I want you to
whistle at that Mexican on the tractor.

What for? I said.

Never mind what for, my uncle said. Just whistle. I want him to
know we are here and that we are pleased with his work. He's probably
plowed twenty acres.

Yes, sir, I said.

I put the second and third fingers of each hand into my mouth and
blew with all my might. It was good and loud. Nevertheless, it didn't
seem as if Diego had heard me. He was pretty far away. We were
walking toward him anyway, so I couldn't figure out why my uncle
wanted me to whistle at him.

Once again, he said.

I whistled once again, but Diego didn't hear.

Louder, my uncle said.

This next time I gave it all I had, and my uncle put his hands over his ears. My face got very red, too. The Mexican on the tractor heard the whistle this time. He slowed the tractor down, turned it around, and began plowing straight across the field toward us.

Do you want him to do that? I said.

It doesn't matter, my uncle said.

In less than a minute and a half the tractor and the Mexican arrived. The Mexican seemed very delighted. He wiped dirt and perspiration off his face and got down from the tractor.

Señor, he said, this is wonderful.

I'm glad you like it, my uncle said.

Would you like a ride? the Mexican asked my uncle.

My uncle didn't know for sure. He looked at me.

Go ahead, he said. Hop on. Have a little ride.

Diego got on the tractor and helped me on. He sat on the metal seat and I stood behind him, holding him. The tractor began to shake, then jumped, and then began to move. It moved swiftly and made a good deal of noise. The Mexican drove around in a big circle and brought the tractor back to my uncle. I jumped off.

All right, my uncle said to the Mexican. Go back to your work.

The Mexican drove the tractor back to where he was plowing.

My uncle didn't get water out of the land until many months later. He had wells dug all over the place, but no water came out of the wells. Of course he had motor pumps too, but even then no water came out. A water specialist named Roy came out from Texas with his two younger brothers and they began investigating the land. They told my uncle they'd get water for him. It took them three months and the water was muddy and there wasn't much of it. There was a trickle of muddy water. The specialist told my uncle matters would improve with time and went back to Texas.

Now half the land was cleared and plowed and there was water, so the time had come to plant.

We planted pomegranate trees. They were of the finest quality and very expensive. We planted about seven hundred of them. I myself planted a hundred. My uncle planted quite a few. We had a twenty-acre orchard of pomegranate trees away over to hell and gone in the strangest desolation anybody ever saw. It was the loveliest-looking absurdity imaginable and my uncle was crazy about it. The only trouble was, his money was giving out. Instead of going ahead and trying to make a garden of the whole six hundred and eighty acres, he decided to devote all his time and energy and money to the pomegranate trees.

Only for the time being, he said. Until we begin to market the pomegranates and get our money back.

Yes, sir, I said.

I didn't know for sure, but I figured we wouldn't be getting any pomegranates to speak of off those little trees for two or three years at least, but I didn't say anthing. My uncle got rid of the Mexican workers and he and I took over the farm. We had the tractor and a lot of land, so every now and then we drove out to the farm and drove the tractor around, plowing up cactus and turning over the soil between the pomegranate trees. This went on for three years.

One of these days, my uncle said, you'll see the loveliest garden in the world in this desert.

The water situation didn't improve with time, either. Every once in a while there would be a sudden generous spurt of water containing only a few pebbles and my uncle would be greatly pleased, but the next day it would be muddy again and there would be only a little trickle. The pomegranate trees fought bravely for life, but they never did get enough water to come out with any fruit.

There were blossoms after the fourth year. This was a great triumph for my uncle. He went out of his head with joy when he saw them.

Nothing much ever came of the blossoms, though. They were very beautiful, but that was about all. Purple and lonely.

That year my uncle harvested three small pomegranates.

I ate one, he ate one, and we kept the other one up in his office.

The following year I was fifteen. A lot of wonderful things had happened to me. I mean, I had read a number of good writers and I'd grown as tall as my uncle. The farm was still our secret. It had cost my uncle a lot of money, but he was always under the impression that very soon he was going to start marketing his pomegranates and get his money back and go on with his plan to make a garden in the desert.

The trees didn't fare very well. They grew a little, but it was hardly noticeable. Quite a few of them withered and died.

That's average, my uncle said. Twenty trees to an acre is only average. We won't plant new trees just now. We'll do that later.

He was still paying for the land, too.

The following year he harvested about two hundred pomegranates. He and I did the harvesting. They were pretty sad-looking pomegranates. We packed them in nice-looking boxes and my uncle shipped them to a wholesale produce house in Chicago. There were eleven boxes.

We didn't hear from the wholesale produce house for a month, so one night my uncle made a long-distance phone call. The produce man, D'Agostino, told my uncle nobody wanted pomegranates.

How much are you asking per box? my uncle shouted over the phone.

One dollar, D'Agostino shouted back.

That's not enough, my uncle shouted. I won't take a nickel less than five dollars a box.

They don't want them at one dollar a box, D'Agostino shouted.

Why not? my uncle shouted.

They don't know what they are, D'Agostino shouted.

What kind of a business man are you anyway? my uncle shouted. They're pomegranates. I want five dollars a box.

I can't sell them, the produce man shouted. I ate one myself and I don't see anything so wonderful about them.

You're crazy, my uncle shouted. There is no other fruit in the world like the pomegranate. Five dollars a box isn't half enough.

What shall I do with them? D'Agostino shouted. I can't sell them. I don't want them.

I see, my uncle whispered. Ship them back. Ship them back express collect.

The phone call cost my uncle about seventeen dollars.

So the eleven boxes came back.

My uncle and I ate most of the pomegranates.

The following year my uncle couldn't make any more payments on the land. He gave the papers back to the man who had sold him the land. I was in the office at the time.

Mr. Griffith, my uncle said, I've got to give you back your property, but I would like to ask a little favor. I've planted twenty acres of pomegranate trees out there on that land and I'd appreciate it very much if you'd let me take care of those trees.

Take care of them? Mr. Griffith said. What in the world for?

My uncle tried to explain, but couldn't. It was too much to try to explain to a man who wasn't sympathetic.

So my uncle lost the land, and the trees, too.

About three years later he and I drove out to the land and walked out to the pomegranate orchard. The trees were all dead. The soil was heavy again with cactus and desert brush. Except for the small dead pomegranate trees the place was exactly the way it had been all the years of the world.

We walked around in the orchard for a while and then went back to the car.

We got into the car and drove back to town.

We didn't say anything because there was such an awful lot to say, and no language to say it in.

Locomotive 38, the Ojibway

One day a man came to town on a donkey and began loafing around in the public library where I used to spend most of my time in those days. He was a tall young Indian of the Ojibway tribe. He told me his name was Locomotive 38. Everybody in town believed he had escaped from an asylum.

Six days after he arrived in town his animal was struck by the Tulare Street trolley and seriously injured. The following day the animal passed away, most likely of internal injuries, on the corner of Mariposa and Fulton streets. The animal sank to the pavement, fell on the Indian's leg, groaned and died. When the Indian got his leg free he got up and limped into the drug store on the corner and made a long distance telephone call. He telephoned his brother in Oklahoma. The call cost him a lot of money, which he dropped into the slot as requested by the operator as if he were in the habit of making such calls every day.

I was in the drug store at the time, eating a Royal Banana Special, with crushed walnuts.

When he came out of the telephone booth he saw me sitting at the soda fountain eating this fancy dish.

Hello, Willie, he said.

He knew my name wasn't Willie—he just liked to call me that.

He limped to the front of the store where the gum was, and

bought three packages of Juicy Fruit. Then he limped back to me and said, What's that you're eating, Willie? It looks good.

This is what they call a Royal Banana Special, I said.

The Indian got up on the stool next to me.

Give me the same, he said to the soda fountain girl.

That's too bad about your animal, I said.

There's no place for an animal in this world, he said. What kind of an automobile should I buy?

Are you going to buy an automobile? I said.

I've been thinking about it for several minutes now, he said.

I didn't think you had any money, I said. I thought you were poor.

That's the impression people get, he said. Another impression they get is that I'm crazy.

I didn't get the impression that you were crazy, I said, but I didn't get the impression that you were rich, either.

Well, I am, the Indian said.

I wish I was rich, I said.

What for? he said.

Well, I said, I've been wanting to go fishing at Mendota for three years in a row now. I need some equipment and some kind of an automobile to get out there in.

Can you drive an automobile? The Indian said.

I can drive anything, I said.

Have you ever driven an automobile? he said.

Not yet, I said. So far I haven't had any automobile to drive, and it's against my family religion to steal an automobile.

Do you mean to tell me you believe you could get into an automobile and start driving? he said.

That's right, I said.

Remember what I was telling you on the steps of the public library the other evening? he said.

You mean about the machine age? I said.

Yes, he said.

I remember, I said.

All right, he said. Indians are born with an instinct for riding, rowing, hunting, fishing, and swimming. Americans are born with an instinct for fooling around with machines.

I'm no American, I said.

I know, the Indian said. You're an Armenian. I remember. I asked you and you told me. You're an Armenian born in America. You're fourteen years old and already you know you'll be able to drive an automobile the minute you get into one. You're a typical American, although your complexion, like my own, is dark.

Driving a car is no trick, I said. There's nothing to it. It's easier than riding a donkey.

All right, the Indian said. Just as you say. If I go up the street and buy an automobile, will you drive for me?

Of course, I said.

How much in wages would you want? he said.

You mean you want to give me wages for driving an automobile? I said.

Of course, the Ojibway said.

Well, I said, that's very nice of you, but I don't want any money for driving an automobile.

Some of the journeys may be long ones, he said.

The longer the better, I said.

Are you restless? he said.

I was born in this little old town, I said.

Don't you like it? he said.

I like mountains and streams and mountain lakes, I said.

Have you ever been in the mountains? he said.

Not yet, I said, but I'm going to reach them some day.

I see, he said. What kind of an automobile do you think I ought to buy?

How about a Ford roadster? I said.

Is that the best automobile? he said.

Do you want the *best*? I said.

Shouldn't I have the best? he said.

I don't know, I said. The best costs a lot of money.

What is the best? he said.

Well, I said, some people think the Cadillac is the best. Others like the Packard. They're both pretty good. I wouldn't know which is best. The Packard is beautiful to see going down the highway, but so is the Cadillac. I've watched a lot of them fine cars going down the highway.

How much is a Packard? he said.

Around three thousand dollars, I said. Maybe a little more.

Can we get one right away? he said.

I got down off the stool. He sounded crazy, but I knew he wasn't.

Listen, Mr. Locomotive, I said, do you really want to buy a Packard right away?

You know my animal passed away a few minutes ago, he said.

I saw it happen, I said. They'll probably be arresting you any minute now for leaving the animal in the street.

They won't arrest me, he said.

They will if there's a law against leaving a dead donkey in the street, I said.

No, they won't, he said.

Why not? I said.

Well, he said, they won't after I show them a few papers I carry around with me all the time. The people of this country have a lot of respect for money, and I've got a lot of money.

I guess he is crazy after all, I thought.

Where'd you get all this money? I said.

I own some land in Oklahoma, he said. About fifty thousand acres.

Is it worth money? I said.

No, he said. All but about twenty acres of it is worthless. I've got some oil wells on them twenty acres. My brother and I.

How did you Ojibways ever get down to Oklahoma? I said. I always thought the Ojibways lived up north, up around the Great Lakes.

That's right, the Indian said. We used to live up around the Great Lakes, but my grandfather was a pioneer. He moved west when everybody else did.

Oh, I said. Well, I guess they won't bother you about the dead donkey at that.

They won't bother me about anything, he said. It won't be because I've got money. It'll be because they think I'm crazy. Nobody in this town but you knows I've got money. Do you know where we can get one of them automobiles right away?

The Packard agency is up on Broadway, two blocks beyond the public library, I said.

All right, he said. If you're sure you won't mind driving for me, let's go get one of them. Something bright in color, he said. Red, if they've got red. Where would you like to drive to first?

Would you care to go fishing at Mendota? I said.

I'll take the ride, he said. I'll watch you fish. Where can we get some equipment for you?

Right around the corner at Homan's, I said.

We went around the corner to Homan's and the Indian bought twenty-seven dollars' worth of fishing equipment for me. Then we went up to the Packard agency on Broadway. They didn't have a red Packard, but there was a beautiful green one. It was light green, the color of new grass. This was back there in 1922. The car was a beautiful sports touring model.

Do you think you could drive this great big car? the Indian said.

I *know* I can drive it, I said.

The police found us in the Packard agency and wanted to arrest the Indian for leaving the dead donkey in the street. He showed them the papers he had told me about and the police apologized and went away. They said they'd removed the animal and were sorry they'd troubled him about it.

It's no trouble at all, he said.

He turned to the manager of the Packard agency, Jim Lewis, who used to run for Mayor every time election time came around.

I'll take this car, he said.

I'll draw up the papers immediately, Jim said.

What papers? the Indian said. I'm going to pay for it now.

You mean you want to pay three thousand two hundred seventeen dollars and sixty-five cents *cash?* Jim said.

Yes, the Indian said. It's ready to drive, isn't it?

Of course, Jim said. I'll have the boys go over it with a cloth to take off any dust on it. I'll have them check the motor too, and fill the gasoline tank. It won't take more than ten minutes. If you'll step into the office I'll close the transaction immediately.

Jim and the Indian stepped into Jim's office.

About three minutes later Jim came over to me, a man shaken to the roots.

Aram, he said, who is this guy? I thought he was a nut. I had Johnny telephone the Pacific-Southwest and they said his bank account is being transferred from somewhere in Oklahoma. They said his account is something over a million dollars. I thought he was a nut. Do you know him?

He told me his name is Locomotive 38, I said. That's no name.

That's a translation of his Indian name, Jim said. We've got his full name on the contract. Do you know him?

I've talked to him every day since he came to town on that donkey that died this morning, I said, but I never thought he had any money.

He says you're going to drive for him, Jim said. Are you sure you're the man to drive a great big car like this, son?

Wait a minute now, Mr. Lewis, I said. Don't try to push me out of this chance of a lifetime. I can drive this big Packard as well as anybody else in town.

I'm not trying to push you out of anything, Jim said. I just don't want you to drive out of here and run over six or seven innocent people and maybe smash the car. Get into the car and I'll give you a few pointers. Do you know anything about the gear shift?

I don't know anything about anything yet, I said, but I'll soon find out.

All right, Jim said. Just let me help you.

I got into the car and sat down behind the wheel. Jim got in beside me.

From now on, son, he said, I want you to regard me as a friend who will give you the shirt off his back. I want to thank you for bringing me this fine Indian gentleman.

He told me he wanted the best car on the market, I said. You know I've always been crazy about driving a Packard. Now how do I do it?

Well, Jim said, let's see.

He looked down at my feet.

My God, son, he said, your feet don't reach the pedals.

Never mind that, I said. You just explain the gear shift.

Jim explained everything while the boys wiped the dust off the car and went over the motor and filled the gasoline tank. When the Indian came out and got into the car, in the back where I insisted he should sit, I had the motor going.

He says he knows how to drive, the Indian said to Jim Lewis. By instinct, he said. I believe him, too.

You needn't worry about Aram here, Jim said. He can drive all right. Clear the way there, boys, he shouted. Let him have all the room necessary.

I turned the big car around slowly, shifted, and shot out of the agency at about fifty miles an hour, with Jim Lewis running after the car and shouting, Take it easy, son. Don't open up until you get out on the highway. The speed limit in town is twenty-five miles an hour.

The Indian wasn't at all excited, even though I was throwing him around a good deal.

I wasn't doing it on purpose, though. It was simply that I wasn't very familiar with the manner in which the automobile worked.

You're an excellent driver, Willie, he said. It's like I said. You're an American and you were born with an instinct for mechanical contraptions like this.

We'll be in Mendota in an hour, I said. You'll see some great fishing out there.

How far is Mendota? the Indian said.

About ninety miles, I said.

Ninety miles is too far to go in an hour, the Indian said. Take two hours. We're passing a lot of interesting scenery I'd like to look at a little more closely.

All right, I said, but I sure am anxious to get out there and fish.

Well, all right then, the Indian said. Go as fast as you like this time, but some time I'll expect you to drive a little more slowly, so I can see some of the scenery. I'm missing everything. I don't even get a chance to read the signs.

I'll travel slowly *now* if you want me to, I said.

No, he insisted. Let her go. Let her go as fast as she'll go.

Well, we got out to Mendota in an hour and seventeen minutes. I would have made better time except for the long stretch of dirt road.

I drove the car right up to the river bank. The Indian asked if I knew how to get the top down, so he could sit in the open and watch me fish. I didn't know how to get the top down, but I got it down. It took me twenty minutes to do it.

I fished for about three hours, fell into the river twice, and finally landed a small one.

You don't know the first thing about fishing, the Indian said.

What am I doing wrong? I said.

Everything, he said. Have you ever fished before?

No, I said.

I didn't think so, he said.

What am I doing wrong? I said.

Well, he said, nothing in particular, only you're fishing at about the same rate of speed that you drive an automobile.

Is that wrong? I said.

It's not exactly wrong, he said, except that it'll keep you from getting anything to speak of, and you'll go on falling into the river.

I'm not falling, I said. They're pulling me in. They've got an

awful pull. This grass is mighty slippery, too. There ain't nothing
around here to grab hold of.

I reeled in one more little one and then I asked if he'd like to go
home. He said he would if I wanted to, too, so I put away the
fishing equipment and the two fish and got in the car and started
driving back to town.

I drove that big Packard for this Ojibway Indian, Locomotive 38,
as long as he stayed in town, which was all summer. He stayed at the
hotel all the time. I tried to get him to learn to drive, but he said
it was out of the question. I drove that Packard all over the San
Joaquín Valley that summer, with the Indian in the back, chewing
eight or nine sticks of gum. He told me to drive anywhere I cared
to go, so it was either to some place where I could fish, or some
place where I could hunt. He claimed I didn't know anything about
fishing or hunting, but he was glad to see me trying. As long as I
knew him he never laughed, except once. That was the time I shot
at a jack-rabbit with a 12-gauge shotgun that had a terrible kick,
and killed a crow. He tried to tell me all the time that that was my
average. To shoot at a jack-rabbit and kill a crow. You're an American, he said. Look at the way you took to this big automobile.

One day in November that year his brother came to town from
Oklahoma, and the next day when I went down to the hotel to get
him, they told me he'd gone back to Oklahoma with his brother.

Where's the Packard? I said.

They took the Packard, the hotel clerk said.

Who drove? I said.

The Indian, the clerk said.

They're both Indians, I said. Which of the brothers drove the
car?

The one who lived at this hotel, the clerk said.

Are you sure? I said.

Well, I only saw him get into the car out front and drive away,
the clerk said. That's all.

Do you mean to tell me he knew how to shift gears? I said.

It *looked* as if he did, the clerk said. He looked like an expert
driver to me.

Thanks, I said.

On the way home I figured he'd just wanted me to *believe* he
couldn't drive, so I could drive all the time and feel good. He was
just a young man who'd come to town on a donkey, bored to death

or something, who'd taken advantage of the chance to be entertained by a small town kid who was bored to death, too. That's the only way I could figure it out without accepting the general theory that he was crazy.

The Poor and Burning Arab

My uncle Khosrove, himself a man of furious energy and uncommon sadness, had for a friend one year a small man from the old country who was as still as a rock inwardly, whose sadness was expressed by brushing a speck of dust from his knee and never speaking.

This man was an Arab named Khalil. He was no bigger than a boy of eight, but, like my uncle Khosrove, had a very big mustache. He was probably in his early sixties. In spite of his mustache, however, he impressed one as being closer to a child in heart than to a man. His eyes were the eyes of a child, but seemed to be full of years of remembrance—years and years of being separated from things deeply loved, as perhaps his native land, his father, his mother, his brother, his horse, or something else. The hair on his head was soft and thick and as black as black ever was, and parted on the left side, the way small boys who had just reached America from the old country were taught by their parents to part their hair. His head was, in fact, the head of a schoolboy, except for the mustache, and so was his body, except for the broad shoulders. He could speak no English, only a little Turkish, a few words of Kurdish, and only a few of Armenian, but he hardly ever spoke anyway. When he did, he spoke in a voice that seemed to come not so much from himself as from the old country. He spoke, also, as if he regretted the necessity to do so, as if it were pathetic for one to try to express what could never be expressed, as if anything he might say would only add to the sorrow already existing in himself.

How he won the regard of my uncle Khosrove, a man who *had* to say *something* at least, is a thing none of us ever learned. Little enough was learned from people who are always talking, let alone from people who hardly ever talk, except, as in the case of my uncle Khosrove, to swear or demand that someone else stop talking. My uncle Khosrove probably met the Arab at the Arax Coffee House.

My uncle Khosrove picked his friends and enemies from the way they played *tavli*, which in this country is known as backgammon. Games of any sort are tests of human behavior under stress, and, even though my uncle Khosrove himself was probably the worst loser in the world, he despised any other man who lost without grace.

What are you grieving about? he would shout at such a loser. It's a game, isn't it? Do you lose your life with it?

He himself lost *his* life when he lost a game, but it was inconceivable to him that anyone else might regard the symbols of the game as profoundly as he did. To the others the game was *only* a game, as far as he was concerned. To himself, however, the game was destiny—over a board on a table, with an insignificant man across the table rattling the dice, talking to them in Turkish, coaxing them, whispering, shouting, and in many other ways humiliating himself.

My uncle Khosrove, on the other hand, despised the dice, regarded them as his personal enemies, and never spoke to them. He threw them out of the window or across the room, and pushed the board off the table.

The dogs! he would shout.

And then, pointing furiously at his opponent, he would shout, And you! My own countryman! You are not ashamed. You debase yourself before them. You pray to them. I am ashamed for you. I spit on the dogs.

Naturally, no one ever played a game of *tavli* with my uncle Khosrove twice.

This Coffee House was a place of great fame and importance in its day. In this day it is the same, although many have died who went there twenty years ago.

For the most part the place was frequented by Armenians, but others came, too. All who remembered the old country. All who loved it. All who had played *tavli* and the card game *scrambile* in the old country. All who enjoyed the food of the old country, the wine, the *rakhi*, and the small cups of coffee in the afternoons. All who loved the songs, and the stories. And all who liked to be in a place with a familiar smell, thousands of miles from home.

Most of the time my uncle Khosrove reached this place around three in the afternoon. He would stand a moment looking over the men, and then sit down in a corner, alone. He usually sat an hour, without moving, and then would go away, terribly angry, although no one had said a word to him.

Poor little ones, he would say. Poor little orphans. Or, literally, Poor and burning orphans.

Poor and burning—it's impossible to translate this one. Nothing, however, is more sorrowful than the *poor and burning* in life and in the world.

Most likely, sitting in this Coffee House one day, my uncle Khosrove noticed the little Arab, and knew him to be a man of worth. Perhaps the man had been seated, playing *tavli*, his broad shoulders over the board, his child's head somber and full of understanding and regret, and perhaps after the game my uncle Khosrove had seen him get up and stand, no bigger than a child.

It may even be that the man came to the Coffee House and, not knowing my uncle Khosrove, played a game of *tavli* wth him and *lost*, and did not complain and, in fact, understood *who* my uncle Khosrove was—without being told. It may even be that the Arab did not pray to the dice.

Whatever the source of their friendship, whatever the understanding between the two, and whatever the communion they shared, they were at any rate together occasionally in our parlor, and welcome.

The first time my uncle Khosrove brought the Arab to our house, he neglected to introduce him. My mother assumed that the Arab was a countryman of ours, perhaps a distant cousin, although he was a little darker than most of the members of our tribe, and smaller. Which, of course, was no matter; nothing more than the charm of a people; the variety; the quality which made them human and worthy of further extension in time.

The Arab sat down that first day only after my mother had asked him a half-dozen times to be at home.

Was he deaf? she thought.

No, it was obvious that he could hear; he listened so intently.

Perhaps he didn't understand our dialect. My mother asked what city was he from. He did not reply, except to brush dust from the sleeve of his coat. Then in Turkish my mother said, Are you an Armenian? This the Arab understood; he replied in Turkish that he was an Arab.

A poor and burning little orphan, my uncle Khosrove whispered.

For a moment my mother imagined that the Arab might wish to

speak, but it was soon obvious that, like my uncle Khosrove, nothing grieved him more than to do so. He could, if necessary, speak, but there was simply nothing, in all truth, to say.

My mother took the two men tobacco, and coffee, and motioned to me to leave.

They want to talk, she said.

Talk? I said.

They want to be alone, she said.

I sat at the table in the dining room and began turning the pages of a year-old copy of the *Saturday Evening Post* that I knew by heart—especially the pictures: Jello, very architectural; automobiles, with high-toned people standing around; flashlights flashing into dark places; tables set with bowls of soup steaming; young men in fancy ready-made suits and coats; and all sorts of other pictures.

I must have turned the pages a little too quickly, however.

My uncle Khosrove shouted, Quiet, boy, quiet.

I looked into the parlor just in time to see the Arab brushing dust from his knee.

The two men sat in the parlor an hour, and then the Arab breathed very deeply through his nose and without a word left the house.

I went into the parlor and sat where he had sat.

Quiet, my uncle Khosrove said.

Well, what is his name? I said.

My uncle Khosrove was so irritated he didn't know what to do. He called out to my mother, as if he were being murdered.

Mariam! he shouted. Mariam!

My mother hurried into the parlor.

What is it? she said.

Send him away—please, my uncle Khosrove said.

What is the matter?

He wants to know the Arab's name.

Well, all right, my mother said. He's a child. He's curious. Tell him.

I see, my uncle Khosrove groaned. You, too. My own sister. My own poor and burning little sister.

Well, what is the Arab's name? my mother said.

I won't tell, my uncle Khosrove said. That's all. I won't tell.

He got up and left the house.

He doesn't know the man's name, my mother explained. And you've got no business irritating him.

Three days later when my uncle Khosrove and the Arab came to our house I was in the parlor.

My uncle Khosrove came straight to me and said, His name is Khalil. Now go away.

I left the house and waited in the yard for one of my cousins to arrive. After ten minutes, nobody arrived, so I went to my cousin Mourad's house and spent an hour arguing with him about which of us would be the stronger in five years. We wrestled three times and I lost three times, but once I *almost* won.

When I got home the two men were gone. I ran straight to the parlor from the back of the house, but they weren't there. The only thing in the room was their smell and the smell of tobacco smoke.

What did they talk about? I asked my mother.

I didn't listen, my mother said.

Did they talk at all? I said.

I don't know, my mother said.

They didn't, I said.

Some people talk when they have something to say, my mother said, and some people don't.

How can you talk if you don't say anything? I said.

You talk without words. We are always talking without words.

Well, what good are words, then?

Not very good, most of the time. Most of the time they're only good to keep back what you really want to say, or something you don't want known.

Well, do *they* talk? I said.

I think they do, my mother said. They just sit and sip coffee and smoke cigarettes. They never open their mouths, but they're talking all the time. They understand one another and don't need to open their mouths. They have nothing to keep back.

Do they really know what they're talking about? I said.

Of course, my mother said.

Well, what is it? I said.

I can't tell you, my mother said, because it isn't in words; but they know.

For a year my uncle Khosrove and the Arab came to our house every now and then and sat in the parlor. Sometimes they sat an hour, sometimes two.

Once my uncle Khosrove suddenly shouted at the Arab, *Pay no attention to it, I tell you,* although the Arab had said nothing.

But most of the time nothing at all was said until it was time for them to go. Then my uncle Khosrove would say quietly, The poor and burning orphans, and the Arab would brush dust from his knee.

One day when my uncle Khosrove came to our house alone, I realized that the Arab had not visited our house in several months.

Where is the Arab? I said.

What Arab? my uncle Khosrove said.

That poor and burning little Arab that used to come here with you, I said. Where is he?

Mariam! my uncle Khosrove shouted. He was standing, terrified.

Oh-oh, I thought. What's wrong now? What have I done now?

Mariam! he shouted. Mariam!

My mother came into the parlor.

What is it? she said.

If you please, my uncle Khosrove said. He is your son. You are my little sister. Please send him away. I love him with all my heart. He is an American. He was born here. He will be a great man some day. I have no doubt about it. Please send him away.

Why, what is it? my mother said.

What is it? *What is it?* He talks. He asks questions. I love him.

Aram, my mother said.

I was standing too, and if my uncle Khosrove was angry at me, I was angrier at him.

Where is the Arab? I said.

My uncle Khosrove pointed me out to my mother—with despair. There you are, his gesture said. Your son. My nephew. My own flesh and blood. You see? We are all poor and burning orhpans. All except *him.*

Aram, my mother said.

Well, if you don't talk, I said, I can't understand. *Where is the Arab?*

My uncle Khosrove left the house without a word.

The Arab is dead, my mother said.

When did he tell you? I said.

He didn't tell me, my mother said.

Well, how did you find out? I said.

I don't know how, my mother said, but he is dead.

My uncle Khosrove didn't visit our house again for many days.
For a while I thought he would *never* come back. When he came
at last he stood in the parlor with his hat on his head and said, The
Arab is dead. He died an orphan in an alien world, six thousand
miles from home. He wanted to go home and die. He wanted to see
his sons again. He wanted to talk to them again. He wanted to smell
them. He wanted to hear them breathing. He had no money. He
used to think about them all the time. Now he is dead. Now go
away. I love you.

I wanted to ask some more questions, especially about the Arab's
sons, how many there were, how long he had been away from them,
and so on, but I decided I would rather visit my cousin Mourad
and see if I couldn't hold him down *now*, so I went away without
saying a word—which most likely pleased my uncle Khosrove very
much, and made him feel maybe there was some hope for me,
after all.

THE LAUGHING MATTER

THEY sat down to breakfast. The eyes of the children filled with gladness at the ceremony of the table, at the presence of their mother and father, at the ease and charity in each of them for the other, and for their children. They talked pleasantly, and the eyes of the children filled with wonder. Even the eyes of the man and woman filled with it, and almost with tears, too, for they knew, each of them knew, how wrong it was to insist upon a moment of decent peace in themselves for the children to see, since the peace was false. Each of them knew how wrong it was to be *forced* by disaster into an essay at decency. They worked hard at it, gladly even, and neither of them, in speaking to the children, said anything that was hurtful to the other. They were trying. For whatever might be in it for the children, for themselves, they were trying. It made failure seem almost impossible.

The harmony achieved was real, in spite of the reason for its achievement. They *were* a family together. They did love one another. There was *hope* for them. Nothing could touch or hurt them. It was astonishing and painful to know, but it was true. They were still precisely who they were, who they had been, but they were also together, belonged together, and nothing else mattered. It was almost unbelievable that out of disaster a family could become more truly a family, out of disgrace and pain *could* become more proudly and irresistibly a family.

After breakfast the woman went off to bathe and dress the girl, and the man filled the tub in Dade's bathroom for the boy. While the boy bathed, Evan Nazarenus sorted out the currency Dade had handed him the night before. There were a good many hundreds and fifties, and with the exception of six or seven tens, the rest were twenties, but there were a great many of them. He didn't count the money. He stacked it carefully, opened the drawer of Dade's bureau, saw the three pistols there, placed the biggest pistol on top of the money, stacked in two piles, and pushed the drawer shut. He then opened his wallet and counted the money in it. There was a twenty, a ten, two fives, and three ones.

The boy was soon back in his own room, getting into his best suit, a grey flannel. When they went out into the parlor the woman was there with the girl, waiting. The girl had on a yellow dress with small blue flowers done into it with thread. She was thrilled with the dress, and the whole adventure of going to church.

Everybody's clothes were new, so that when they walked there was a Sunday formality to it, but the boy watched the grass, and the girl grew tired and was picked up by the man. The woman moved and spoke as a young girl does, and the man would not permit any thought or memory to come between him and the ritual of their being together. He spoke with gladness in his voice, speaking to each of them.

They reached Clovis in time to have a look at each of the three churches, to pick and choose, to discuss which would be the one they would enter. They decided on the Presbyterian because, while it was not as big and handsome as the Catholic, or as lonely-looking and appealing as the Methodist, it had large stained-glass windows that Red and Eva wanted to see from the inside, and seemed to all of them in appearance most nearly what a church ought to be. It was built of wood, painted white, had a nice steeple, and when they reached it the bell was ringing.

They went in and sat on a bench in the first row, on the right, because Red and Eva wanted to get as near as possible. The place was about a third full when they walked down the center aisle. A woman was playing something on the organ. The windows were beautiful pictures, one mainly in blue, one mainly in red, one mainly in green, and one mainly in yellow. The light that filled the place had all of these colors in it. The place was both dazzling and peaceful.

The adventure started with a man coming out of a door and standing behind a pulpit with a book on it. He said a few things, then everybody got up, opened a book, and began to sing. Red was astonished at this and looked around to see who was doing it. Everybody was. He heard his father sing, then began to sing, too, just making the sounds, not being able to sing the words until after a while. Eva's mother began to sing, too, and Eva sang with her. Eva looked at Red once, giggled, and put her hand over her mouth. Red's eyes got angry at her, she straightened out immediately, but only a moment later she giggled again, and again put her hand over her mouth. Her mother giggled, too, and put *her* hand over her mouth. Red's eyes got angry at both of them.

After the song they sat down, the preacher said some more things, the people opened another book, the preacher said something, the people spoke together and said something back to him. The preacher sounded like a fine man, and the people speaking together sounded fine, too.

A man sang a solo. Eight women and eight men standing behind him sang part of the song with him.

The preacher prayed and said a lot of different things.

After that four men wearing white gloves came to where four wooden plates were stacked in a pile, picked them up, and handed them to people. Evan Nazarenus took a plate, put a half dollar in it, and handed it to Red beside him. Red put a quarter in it and handed it to Eva, who put a quarter in it and handed it to Swan, who put a half dollar in it and held it until a man came to get it. Red turned and watched the way they did it.

Then the preacher got up and talked. He talked a long time, but it was all right because there were always the windows to look at, and the people, too. Eva fell asleep. Her mother rested Eva's head on her lap.

After a while it was all over. They got up and watched the people leave the church. They went out, too, and began to walk home.

The walk home from church was fun, too, but it was hot by then. It was so hot that Red asked to take off his coat, his shoes and socks, and Eva had to be carried almost the whole way. They were each given a bowl of cold cereal and milk for a quick lunch, then each of them went off for a nap.

When they were both asleep, the man said to the woman, "Thanks for what you did."

"I can do it every day," the woman said.

"I've got to telephone a friend in San Francisco for Cody Bone's boy, and then I want to lie down on the sofa in the parlor and take a nap myself."

"I'll take a nap, too," the woman said.

He went to the telephone, called his friend, then called Bart, and told him the story. His friend, a man named Harold Trabing, would call Evan sometime tomorrow afternoon, and Evan would call Bart.

"God," the boy said, "I'm going to be awful nervous until you call tomorrow afternoon."

"I'll call the minute Trabing calls," Evan said.

"Did he sound as if I might have a chance?"

"Yes," Evan said. "I think you'll be making the voyage all right, but forget the whole thing until tomorrow afternoon."

"O.K.," the boy said. "I'll get in my car and drive all day and all night." He stopped suddenly. "Listen," he said, "let me bring the car over and leave it in the driveway. Why not take the family for a Sunday drive? Take them to the dam at Friant, or to the river at Piedra. I don't need the car. I'll walk to Clovis, and take in a movie."

Evan went to the parlor and stretched out on the sofa. He was almost asleep when the telephone bell rang. It was Dade.

"They just surrendered," he said. "The game's over."

"You mean you haven't had any sleep *yet?*"

"I'm going to bed now."

"What are you going to do when you wake up?"

"Go back to sleep."

"When you're through sleeping fly here, will you?"

"Yes."

"We had breakfast together, then went to church. I'm driving them to Piedra for a picnic later on."

"Is my car back?"

"Not yet," Evan said. "Cody's boy is lending me his car. When will you get here?"

"I need a lot of sleep," Dade said. "I mean, I *want* a lot. Tomorrow night at the earliest, maybe the night after."

"I've put the money in the top drawer of your bureau," Evan said.

"That's yours," Dade said. "That was nothing. Just put it away in your satchel. I'll phone you from the airport in Fresno." In their own language he said, "Tell me."

"I'm *trying,*" Evan said in the language.

"It is right," Dade said in the language, and then in English, "Sometime during the day teach Red to say, 'My name is Rex Nazarenus.' Teach him something new every day."

"O.K.," Evan said.

He went back to the sofa, stretched out, and was soon deep in sleep, but not so deep that he was free. He begged his sleep to annoy him no more, let him rest, let him forget, so that he might in time learn what to do, in the time of another night, another day, another night and day, know what to do, know how to do it, know how for the rest of his life.

When he woke up he went out onto the front porch and saw Bart's car in the driveway. He went to Swan and found her fast asleep. He found Red awake, and spoke to him about the picnic. Red jumped out of bed, and then the whole house was alive with the idea, Swan making sandwiches and Red and Eva urging her to hurry up, so they could go.

"*I'm* going, too," Eva said. "Papa's taking *me*, too."

The man took Red aside and said, "I want you to sit in the back with Mama because I hurt Eva when I didn't take her with us last night. I want her to sit alone up front with me. I know you understand."

When they were ready to go the man said, "Now let's see. Mama and Red in the back, and Papa and Eva in the front." He watched the girl's face. She was so pleased and surprised she became speechless. She scrambled into her place, sat there, folded her hands, turned several times to look at her mother and her brother. At last she said, "I'm in the front with Papa."

They wore light clothing. The windows of the car were open. The air they breathed was good. The man followed country roads as far as possible, driving slowly, stopping now and then to look at a vineyard, a tree, or an abandoned house. He got out of the car once to take some ripe nectarines off a tree, and Red got out with him. The nectarines were a little hot, but they were juicy and sweet. He counted out three for each of them. When they came to the river at Piedra he drove along the riverside road until they found a green place, a cluster of three willows. There they sat on a blanket.

"It would be heaven to live here," the woman said.

"This is the best time of the year," the man said. "Everything's ripe now. The air's full of the smell of it. I'll tell you what I want to do. I want to use this fine rock for a pillow, stretch out and breathe the good air." He set the boulder down, just beyond the edge of the blanket, stretched out, and rested his head on it.

"Look at Papa," the girl said. "He's made a pillow out of a rock."

"I want to get in the water," Red said.

"So do I," Eva said.

"All right," the man said. "Take off your clothes and get in. The rocks are slippery, so try not to fall."

"They're wearing suits across the river," Red said. "Have we got suits?"

"Wear your shorts," the man said.

They got out of their clothes and waded into the water, where for ten or fifteen feet it was only a foot or two deep, with clean water moving swiftly over boulders, most of them big ones, some of them as big as the one his head rested on. He listened to them gasping because the water was cold, shouting and laughing, and he saw Red slip, get up, and say, "God damn that rock!"

After they had been in the water five minutes they waded out and sat on the hot white sand just beyond the shade of the trees, burying their feet in the sand, working it into piles with their hands. Every now and then they looked over at their father and mother under the shade of the trees. The woman was sitting close to the man with her legs crossed under her, the way she always sat when there wasn't a chair.

"Evan?" the woman said softly.

"I don't want to talk about it, Swan. I don't even want to *think* about it. One good day can make a lot of difference for them. This is their day. I want it to be *altogether* their day."

"I do too, Evan. Can I say just one thing?"

"Let it be *altogether* their day, Swan."

"I just want to say—"

"Don't say it, Swan."

"You don't know what I want to say."

"Whatever it is, don't say it. Not for a while. I just want to breathe the good air my kids are breathing."

"I love you," she said. "That's all I want to say."

"I know, Swan," he said. "Don't say anything more. Let it be their day. We'll eat the sandwiches when they're hungry."

"I brought a bottle of wine for you," she said.

She fished around in the basket, brought out the bottle. He sat up to get the cork out, then drank from the bottle.

"Thanks for remembering," he said. He handed her the bottle. The woman drank from the bottle, too, then pressed the cork back into it. She stretched out, not close to him, but close enough, so that no matter how softly he spoke or she spoke they could hear one another.

"God, what fools we are," she said.

"Yes, Swan."

"I think everybody must be crazy, and I can't understand why."

"I'm not going to try to understand just now. I want to listen to Red and Eva, that's all.

The woman listened with him. They didn't hear the words, they heard the voices. They listened to the voices of their children a long time, their own voices stilled by the sound of the voices of their children. The man lifted his head to notice their bodies. After a moment he let his head return to the rock, then closed his eyes, hearing their voices, the summer voices of his son and his daughter. He didn't open his eyes a long time, not sleeping, but not being altogether awake, either.

"What are you doing, Red?" Eva said.

"Looking at this sand," Red said.

"Let me see."

"Look at it. One piece."

"Where is it?"

"In my hand. Can't you see it?"

"Where?"

"Here," he said, putting a finger near it.

"I see it," the girl said. "What are you looking at it for?"

"It's a piece of sand."

"Let me see." She looked again. "It's very small."

"You can *see* it, though, can't you?"

"I see it," Eva said. "I see it right there." She looked at her own hands and saw that they were covered with sand. She brushed the sand off her hands, but saw that quite a few pieces hadn't gone. She looked at these carefully. "Look at mine," she said. "How many have I got?"

"Let me see," Red said. He looked at the sand stuck to the palm of her hand. "Well," he said, "you've got a lot of them."

"How many?"

"One, two, three," Red said. "Four, five, six, seven, eight, nine, ten, eleven, twelve, and many more."

Eva brushed more sand from her hand, then said, "How many now?"

He looked again, counted to himself, and said, "Nine."

She brushed still more sand from her hand, then said, "Now how many?"

"Three."

"How many *are* there?"

"Where?"

"In the whole world."

"Well," Red said, "there are hundreds of places like this, I suppose, with millions of pieces of sand in each place."

"What are they doing there?"

"Nothing."

"How many pieces of sky are there?"

"Sky isn't sand, Eva."

"What is it?"

"Something else."

"How many pieces of water are there?"

"Water isn't sand, either."

"Water's rain," Eva said. She looked at her hand again and noticed that it was again covered with sand. "How many pieces of people are there?"

"You think everything is sand," Red said.

"No, I don't," Eva said. "Look at the sand on my hand *now*. Every piece is a people. This one's a man, this one's a woman, this one's a boy, this one's a girl. And this one—What's this one, Red?"

"Another man?"

"No, a dog," Eva said. "And this one—What's this one?" She pointed to a large black grain of sand. "This one's my father," she said.

"Let me see," Red said. He looked at the grain of sand in her hand, then looked at his father lying on the blanket, his head resting on the rock. The girl looked at him, too. "Yes," Red said. He pointed to a very bright grain of sand in her hand. "Who's that?"

"My mother," Eva said. "This one's my father. This one's my mother. Right here in my hand. And there they are over there, under the trees. My father told me to sit in front beside him in the car, didn't he, Red?"

"Yes," Red said.

"My father's a good man," Eva said. "My father's a sad man."

"Sad?" Red said.

"Oh, yes," Eva said. "I know. When he carries me I look at his face. It's a sad face." She got an idea suddenly, and Red saw her face darken. "What is *sad*, Red? What is that?"

"Well," Red said. "You know what glad is. Well, sad is *not* glad."

"Why is my father sad?"

"He's not *always* sad."

"He's sad now," Eva said. "Look at him."

They both looked and Red said, "No. He's justing resting, that's all."

"I'm tired of sitting," the girl said. "Let's go back into the water."

They got up and went back into the water.

When the man sat up for another drink of wine he saw the woman with her dress tied above her knees holding their hands and wading with them about thirty yards down the river.

She was *trying*. She *was* beautiful when she tried. He had never seen her flesh so luminous. He took a long drink of the cold wine and watched her with her children, her own son and her own daughter, out of her own flesh. They were beautiful, the three of them were as beautiful as any mother and son and daughter had ever been, or could ever be. Their bodies were beautiful. He had never seen bodies so sweetly alive and so delightfully, so painfully beautiful. It's not them alone I love, he thought. I love her, too. I still love her.

When they came back he dried the girl while Swan dried the boy. They helped the children back into their clothes, then sat together and ate the sandwiches. She'd brought along a bottle of soda pop for each of them, which they loved on picnics, and they drank out of their bottles as he drank out of the bottle of wine. The sandwiches were thin and easy to eat. After the food Eva stretched out in front of the man. He put his arm around her, and held her hand. After a moment Red stretched out in front of his mother, and she held his hand. Soon both of the children were asleep, and the woman said again, speaking softer than ever this time, "Evan?"

"No, Swan," he said. "Listen to them breathing. That's all we've got to do now."

THE RETURN TO THE
POMEGRANATE TREES

THERE are journeys you take again and again, like books you read or music you listen to, faces you see or people you speak to, and each time something is changed and something is the same.

There are places I heard about when I was a kid, and never saw, like the town Goshen, near Fresno. Ever since, I've planned to go to Goshen, but so far I haven't, although I've been to all the other towns anywhere near Fresno. It may be that Goshen isn't a town at all, or if it is, it's one of those towns you never know is a town, a crossroads and a store with a hound on the porch and a rooster badgering two hens alongside.

Oleander's another place like Goshen, but even though I've been to Oleander I can't remember where it is or what it's like.

Fresno is in the center of the great valley that is named San Joaquin, which is pronounced Wahkeen, about which my pal Fat Khashkhash's brother Leo sang to a student body at Longfellow Junior High in 1919 or 1920:

> San Joaquin, valley green,
> You're the nicest place I've seen.
> Orange blossoms scent the air.
> The sun is shining everywhere.

In order to get from Fresno to the central and north coast of California, and the cities there, you've got to get through the Coast Ranges, either by way of Pacheco Pass, which begins at Los Banos and ends at Hollister and Gilroy, or by way of the cut-through after Tracy, which ends around Livermore just before you get to the outskirts of Oakland.

But there are other ways, too, and I took one of them in August once. You go to Kerman, on to Mendota, and then you are on a dirt road in low hills with nothing around except hawks and now and then a flock of sheep and a Basque shepherd with his dog.

Pretty soon, though, and for miles, for an hour at least—traveling twenty-five or thirty miles an hour because you don't want to drive any faster and oughtn't to anyhow since the road is unmarked and unfamiliar—there is nothing, and except for the car you're driving you might be in Spain, Italy, Greece, or Asia Minor, and you almost believe you are.

The one thought that occurs to you is, "They sure could put a lot of fine people in here and make this whole place over into orchards and vineyards and towns, couldn't they?"

Well, if they could, they haven't, and in any case it isn't easy. It takes doing, and the people might prefer to stay in New York, anyway.

The road I followed has a number and a name, but I know neither: it has history, too, which I also don't know. It's a fine drive, though, and I expect to make it again.

The drives from Fresno to San Francisco or Los Angeles, around two hundred miles each, or from San Francisco to Los Angeles to Fresno are commonplace, but exciting every time I take them. I guess it has to do with leaving one place and heading for another.

The drives around Fresno, to the familiar places, are always pleasant, and I make them again and again, but the drive I want to remember is this one:

The first short story I wrote in the collection that became the book called *My Name Is Aram* was called "The Pomegranate Trees."

When I wrote the story I was in San Francisco. The year was 1935 and I had been away from Fresno on and off since 1926, about nine years. The story itself concerned a still earlier time, when I was fifteen, so that I was writing about stuff that seemed at the time far away.

I didn't know "The Pomegranate Trees" was to become the first of a series of stories. I thought it was only another story. I sent it to *The Atlantic Monthly*, after it had been rejected by a dozen or more editors. *The Atlantic* took it, and Edward Weeks, the editor, suggested that I write more stories of that kind. As a matter of fact, I *had* written more of them by that time, but his letter put me to work in earnest.

The story concerned 640 acres of barren land that my mother's youngest sister's husband Dikran had bought and planned to transform into a garden.

On a portion of this land Dikran planted pomegranate trees— twenty acres of them.

I worked on the land, and I planted the trees, working with a man named Nazaret Torossian who had been a wrestler at one time.

The project failed, the land reverted to its original owners, the pomegranate trees were abandoned, and Dikran moved along to other projects.

But while Nazaret and I were planting the trees (we worked for weeks, tending the trees after they had been planted) I couldn't help thinking I would some day return to the orchard and see the wonderful trees loaded with the wonderful fruit.

Years went by and whenever I happened to be in Fresno I remembered the pomegranate trees and where Nazaret and I had planted them, but I never drove out there.

The drive was out Ventura Avenue to where a right turn takes you to Sanger, but you make a left turn there and follow the road eight or nine miles, and then somewhere in that area is the land of the pomegranate trees.

One year, at last, I made the drive again.

With me was my son, at that time aged five, named Aram after the boy in *My Name Is Aram*.

The drive began with no destination in mind. It was just a drive in the summertime along the roads, among the vineyards and orchards around Fresno. I stopped many times, so the boy could get out and pick grapes or peaches and eat them.

After a while, though, I began to drive and not stop, and pretty soon I was at the place on Ventura Avenue where if you turn right you go to Sanger.

My father's younger brother Levon and his four sons had vineyards near Sanger, and I suppose I had had in mind visiting them, but I turned left and began to speed down the road.

"Where we going?" Aram said.

"I planted some pomegranate trees down here about twenty-five years ago."

At the proper place I stopped the car, and my son and I got out and began to walk over the dry land, as I had walked over it a quarter of a century ago.

"Where's the trees?"

"Well, we planted them somewhere around here, but they're not here any more."

"Where are they?"

"Nowhere. They died."

The whole place was taken over again by the little burrowing animals, the horned toads, and the jack rabbits. It didn't seem wrong, either.

I believed I might find one tree hanging on, but I didn't.

My son and I went back to the car and drove off.

"What are they?" he said.

"The little animals?"

"No, what you planted."

"Pomegranates."

"I want to see one."

I drove him to my father's brother's place in Sanger, and in the family orchard adjoining the house I showed him an old pomegranate tree, and the pomegranates on it. They weren't ready yet, but I took one off the tree and handed it to him.

My father's brother came out of the house and took us in, and we visited him for an hour or more.

When we got back to the hotel in Fresno and up to the room we were sharing I saw my son bring the pomegranate out of his pocket. He looked at it a moment, then placed it on the bureau.

The following morning we drove back to San Francisco by way of Pacheco Pass.

When we got home he put his stuff away, and I saw him place the pomegranate on his bureau.

It stayed there a long time. After more than a month it got to looking pretty sad. His mother wanted to know if she ought to throw it out.

"No," he said, "I want it."

Several days later the whole family drove to Fresno and the boy said, "Let's drive out there again."

"Where?"

"Where you planted the trees."

So once again, twice in forty days or so, I drove to a place I hadn't driven to in twenty-five years.

When my son and I had walked a hundred yards or more into the dry land and I had stopped to light a cigarette, I saw him bring the pomegranate out of his pocket. He glanced at it, glanced around at the whole place, and then very carefully set it down on the earth.

I waited for him to say something, but since he didn't I didn't either, and after a moment we went back to the car and drove back to Fresno.

He never said anything about the pomegranate again.

I haven't tried to figure it out, because they are always doing things like that, and there's no telling why.

THE TIME OF YOUR LIFE

Presented by The Theatre Guild in association with Eddie Dowling at the Booth Theatre, New York City, October 25, 1939, with the following cast:

NEWSBOY	*Ross Bagdasarian*
DRUNK	*John Farrell*
WILLIE	*Will Lee*
JOE	*Eddie Dowling*
NICK	*Charles De Sheim*
TOM	*Edward Andrews*
KITTY DUVAL	*Julie Haydon*
DUDLEY	*Curt Conway*
HARRY	*Gene Kelly*
WESLEY	*Reginald Beane*
LORENE	*Nene Vibber*
BLICK	*Grover Burgess*
ARAB	*Houseley Stevens, Sr.*
MARY L	*Celeste Holm*
KRUPP	*William Bendix*
MC CARTHY	*Tom Tully*
KIT CARSON	*Len Doyle*
NICK'S MA	*Michelette Burani*
SAILOR	*Randolph Wade*
ELSIE	*Cathie Bailey*
A KILLER	*Evelyn Geller*
HER SIDE KICK	*Mary Cheffey*
A SOCIETY LADY	*Eva Leonard Boyne*
A SOCIETY GENTLEMAN	*Ainsworth Arnold*
FIRST COP	*Randolph Wade*
SECOND COP	*John Farrell*

SCENE

ACT   I   Nick's Pacific Street saloon, restaurant and entertainment palace at the foot of the Embacadero, San Francisco.

SCENE

ACT II   Scenes 1 and 3, same as Act I. Scene 2—Room in the New
York Hotel, San Francisco.

ACT III   Same as Act I.

TIME: Afternoon and night of a day in October, 1939.

ACT ONE

In the time of your life, live—so that in that good time there shall
be no ugliness or death for yourself or for any life your life touches.
Seek goodness everywhere, and when it is found, bring it out of its
hiding-place and let it be free and unashamed. Place in matter and in
flesh the least of the values, for these are the things that hold death
and must pass away. Discover in all things that which shines and is
beyond corruption. Encourage virtue in whatever heart it may have
been driven into secrecy and sorrow by the shame and terror of the
world. Ignore the obvious, for it is unworthy of the clear eye and
the kindly heart. Be the inferior of no man, nor of any man be the
superior. Remember that every man is a variation of yourself. No
man's guilt is not yours, nor is any man's innocence a thing apart.
Despise evil and ungodliness, but not men of ungodliness or evil.
These, understand. Have no shame in being kindly and gentle, but
if the time comes in the time of your life to kill, kill and have no
regret. In the time of your life, live—so that in that wondrous time
you shall not add to the misery and sorrow of the world, but shall
smile to the infinite delight and mystery of it.

*Nick's is an American place: a San Francisco waterfront honky-
tonk. At a table,* JOE: *always calm, always quiet, always thinking,*

always eager, always bored, always superior. His expensive clothes are casually and youthfully worn and give him an almost boyish appearance. He is thinking. Behind the bar, NICK: *a big red-headed young Italian-American with an enormous naked woman tattooed in red on the inside of his right arm. He is studying The Racing Form. The* ARAB, *at his place at the end of the bar. He is a lean old man with a rather ferocious old-country mustache, with the ends twisted up. Between the thumb and forefinger of his left hand is the Mohammedan tattoo indicating that he has been to Mecca. He is sipping a glass of beer. It is about eleven-thirty in the morning.* SAM *is sweeping out. We see only his back. He disappears into the kitchen. The* SAILOR *at the bar finishes his drink and leaves, moving thoughtfully, as though he were trying very hard to discover how to live. The* NEWSBOY *comes in.*

NEWSBOY *(cheerfully).* Good morning, everybody. *(No answer. To* NICK.*)* Paper, Mister? *(*NICK *shakes his head, no. The* NEWSBOY *goes to* JOE.*)* Paper, Mister?

*(*JOE *shakes his head, no. The* NEWSBOY *walks away, counting papers.)*

JOE *(noticing him).* How many you got?
NEWSBOY. Five.

*(*JOE *gives him a quarter, takes all the papers, glances at the headlines with irritation, throws them away.)*

(The NEWSBOY *watches carefully, then goes.)*

ARAB *(picks up paper, looks at headlines, shakes head as if rejecting everything else a man might say about the world).* No foundation. All the way down the line.

(The DRUNK *comes in. Walks to the telephone, looks for a nickel in the chute, sits down at* JOE'S *table.)*

*(*NICK *takes the* DRUNK *out. The* DRUNK *returns.)*

DRUNK *(champion of the Bill of Rights).* This is a free country, ain't it?

*(*WILLIE, *the marble-game maniac, explodes through the swinging doors and lifts the forefinger of his right hand comically, indicating one beer. He is a very young man, not more than twenty. He is wearing*

heavy shoes, a pair of old and dirty corduroys, a light green turtle-neck jersey with a large letter "F" on the chest, an oversize two-button tweed coat, and a green hat, with the brim up. NICK *sets out a glass of beer for him, he drinks it, straightens up vigorously, saying Aaah, makes a solemn face, gives* NICK *a one-finger salute of adieu, and begins to leave, refreshed and restored in spirit. He walks by the marble game, halts suddenly, turns, studies the contraption, gestures as if to say, Oh, no. Turns to go, stops, returns to the machine, studies it, takes a handful of small coins out of his pants pocket, lifts a nickel, indicates with a gesture, One game, no more. Puts the nickel in the slot, pushes in the slide, making an interesting noise.)*

NICK. You can't beat that machine.

WILLIE. Oh, yeah?

(The marbles fall, roll, and take their place. He pushes down the lever, placing one marble in position. Takes a very deep breath, walks in a small circle, excited at the beginning of great drama. Stands straight and pious before the contest. Himself vs. the machine. Willie vs. Destiny. His skill and daring vs. the cunning and trickery of the novelty industry of America, and the whole challenging world. He is the last of the American pioneers, with nothing more to fight but the machine, with no other reward than lights going on and off, and six nickels for one. Before him is the last champion, the machine. He is the last challenger, the young man with nothing to do in the world. WILLIE *grips the knob delicately, studies the situation carefully, draws the knob back, holds it a moment, and then releases it. The first marble rolls out among the hazards, and the contest is on. At the very beginning of the play "The Missouri Waltz" is coming from the phonograph. The music ends here.)*

(This is the signal for the beginning of the play.)

*(*JOE *suddenly comes out of his reverie. He whistles the way people do who are calling a cab that's about a block away, only he does it quietly.* WILLIE *turns around, but* JOE *gestures for him to return to his work.* NICK *looks up from The Racing Form.)*

JOE *(calling).* Tom. *(To himself.)* Where the hell is he, every time I need him? *(He looks around calmly: the nickel-in-the-slot phonograph in the corner; the open public telephone; the stage; the marble game; the bar; and so on. He calls again, this time very loud.)* Hey, Tom.

NICK (*with morning irritation*). What do you want?

JOE (*without thinking*). I want the boy to get me a watermelon, that's what I want. What do *you* want? Money, or love, or fame, or what? You won't get them studying The Racing Form.

NICK. I like to keep abreast of the times.

(TOM *comes hurrying in. He is a great big man of about thirty or so who appears to be much younger because of the child-like expression of his face: handsome, dumb, innocent, troubled, and a little bewildered by everything. He is obviously adult in years, but it seems as if by all rights he should still be a boy. He is defensive as clumsy, self-conscious, overgrown boys are. He is wearing a flashy cheap suit.* JOE *leans back and studies him with casual disapproval.* TOM *slackens his pace and becomes clumsy and embarrassed, waiting for the bawling-out he's pretty sure he's going to get.*)

JOE (*objectively, severely, but a little amused*). Who saved your life?

TOM (*sincerely*). You did, Joe. Thanks.

JOE (*interested*). How'd I do it?

TOM (*confused*). What?

JOE (*even more interested*). How'd I do it?

TOM. Joe, you know how you did it.

JOE (*softly*). I want you to answer me. How'd I save your life? I've forgotten.

TOM (*remembering, with a big sorrowful smile*). You made me eat all that chicken soup three years ago when I was sick and hungry.

JOE (*fascinated*). Chicken soup?

TOM (*eagerly*). Yeah.

JOE. Three years? Is it that long?

TOM (*delighted to have the information*). Yeah, sure. 1937. 1938. 1939. This is 1939, Joe.

JOE (*amused*). Never mind what year it is. Tell me the whole story.

TOM. You took me to the doctor. You gave me money for food and clothes, and paid my room rent. Aw, Joe, you know all the different things you did.

(JOE *nods, turning away from* TOM *after each question.*)

JOE. You in good health now?

TOM. Yeah, Joe.

JOE. You got clothes?

TOM. Yeah, Joe.

JOE. You eat three times a day. Sometimes four?

TOM. Yeah, Joe. Sometimes five.

JOE. You got a place to sleep?

TOM. Yeah, Joe.

(JOE *nods. Pauses. Studies* TOM *carefully.*)

JOE. Then, where the hell have you been?

TOM (*humbly*). Joe, I was out in the street listening to the boys. They're talking about the trouble down here on the waterfront.

JOE (*sharply*). I want you to be around when I need you.

TOM (*pleased that the bawling-out is over*). I won't do it again. Joe, one guy out there says there's got to be a revolution before anything will ever be all right.

JOE (*impatient*). I know all about it. Now, here. Take this money. Go up to the Emporium. You know where the Emporium is?

TOM. Yeah, sure, Joe.

JOE. All right. Take the elevator and go up to the fourth floor. Walk around to the back, to the toy department. Buy me a couple of dollars worth of toys and bring them here.

TOM (*amazed*). Toys? What *kind* of toys, Joe?

JOE. Any kind of toys. Little ones that I can put on this table.

TOM. What do you want toys for, Joe?

JOE (*mildly angry*). What?

TOM. All right, all right. You don't have to get sore at *everything*. What'll people think, big guy like me buying toys?

JOE. What *people?*

TOM. Aw, Joe, you're always making me do crazy things for you, and I'm the guy that gets embarrassed. You just sit in this place and make me do all the dirty work.

JOE (*looking away*). Do what I tell you.

TOM. O.K., but I wish I knew *why*. (*He makes to go.*)

JOE. Wait a minute. Here's a nickel. Put it in the phonograph. Number seven. I want to hear that waltz again.

TOM. Boy, I'm glad *I* don't have to stay and listen to it. Joe, what do you hear in that song anyway? We listen to that song ten times a day. Why can't we hear number six, or two, or nine? There are a lot of other numbers.

JOE (*emphatically*). Put the nickel in the phonograph. (*Pause*). Sit down and wait till the music's over. Then go get me some toys.

TOM. O.K. O.K.

JOE (*loudly*). Never mind being a martyr about it either. The cause isn't worth it.

(TOM *puts the nickel into the machine, with a ritual of impatient and efficient movement which plainly shows his lack of sympathy or enthusiasm. His manner also reveals, however, that his lack of sympathy is spurious and exaggerated. Actually, he is fascinated by the music, but is so confused by it that he pretends he dislikes it.*)

(*The music begins. It is another variation of "The Missouri Waltz," played dreamily and softly, with perfect orchestral form, and with a theme of weeping in the horns repeated a number of times.*)

(*At first* TOM *listens with something close to irritation, since he can't understand what is so attractive in the music to* JOE, *and what is so painful and confusing in it to himself. Very soon, however, he is carried away by the melancholy story of grief and nostalgia of the song.*)

(*He stands, troubled by the poetry and confusion in himself.*)

(JOE, *on the other hand, listens as if he were not listening, indifferent and unmoved. What he's interested in is* TOM. *He turns and glances at* TOM.)

(KITTY DUVAL, *who lives in a room in The New York Hotel, around the corner, comes beyond the swinging doors, quietly, and walks slowly to the bar, her reality and rhythm a perfect accompaniment to the sorrowful American music, which is her music, as it is Tom's. Which the world drove out of her, putting in its place brokenness and all manner of spiritually crippled forms. She seems to understand this, and is angry. Angry with herself, full of hate for the poor world, and full of pity and contempt for its tragic, unbelievable, confounded people. She is a small powerful girl, with that kind of delicate and rugged beauty which no circumstance of evil or ugly reality can destroy. This beauty is that element of the immortal which is in the seed of good and common people, and which is kept alive in some of the female of our kind, no matter how accidently or pointlessly they may have entered the world.* KITTY DUVAL *is somebody. There is an angry purity, and a fierce pride, in her.*)

(In her stance, and way of walking, there is grace and arrogance.
JOE *recognizes her as a good person immediately. She goes to the bar.)*

KITTY. Beer.

(NICK places a glass of beer before her mechanically.)

(She swallows half the drink, and listens to the music again.)

(TOM turns and sees her. He becomes dead to everything in the world
but her. He stands like a lump, fascinated and undone by his almost
religious adoration for her. JOE *notices* TOM.*)*

JOE *(gently).* Tom. *(*TOM *begins to move toward the bar, where*
  KITTY *is standing. Loudly.)* Tom. *(*TOM *halts, then turns, and*
  JOE *motions to him to come over to the table.* TOM *goes over.*
  Quietly.) Have you got everything straight?
TOM *(out of the world).* What?
JOE. What do you mean, what? I just gave you some instructions.
TOM *(pathetically).* What do you want, Joe?
JOE. I want you to come to your senses.

(He stands up quietly and knocks Tom's hat off. TOM *picks up his*
hat quickly.)

TOM. I got it, Joe. I got it. The Emporium. Fourth floor. In the
  back. The toy department. Two dollars' worth of toys. That you
  can put on a table.
KITTY *(to herself).* Who the hell is he to push a big man like that
  around?
JOE. I'll expect you back in a half hour. Don't get side-tracked anywhere. Just do what I tell you.
TOM *(pleading).* Joe? Can't I bet four bits on a horse race? There's
  a long shot—Precious Time—that's going to win by ten lengths.
  I got to have money.

*(*JOE *points to the street.* TOM *goes out.* NICK *is combing his hair,*
looking in the mirror.)

NICK. I thought you wanted him to get you a watermelon.
JOE. I forgot. *(He watches* KITTY *a moment. To* KITTY, *clearly, slowly,*
  with great compassion.) What's the dream?
KITTY *(moving to* JOE, *coming to).* What?
JOE *(holding the dream for her).* What's the dream, now?

KITTY (*coming still closer*). What dream?

JOE. What dream! The dream you're dreaming.

NICK. Suppose he did bring you a watermelon? What the hell would you do with it?

JOE (*irritated*). I'd put it on this table. I'd look at it. Then I'd eat it. What do you *think* I'd do with it, sell it for a profit?

NICK. How should I know what *you'd* do with *anything*? What I'd like to know is, where do you get your money from? What work do you do?

JOE (*looking at* KITTY). Bring us a bottle of champagne.

KITTY. Champagne?

JOE (*simply*). Would you rather have something else?

KITTY. What's the big idea?

JOE. I thought you might like some champagne. I myself am very fond of it.

KITTY. Yeah, but what's the big idea? You can't push *me* around.

JOE (*gently but severely*). It's not in my nature to be unkind to another human being, I have only contempt for wit. Otherwise I might say something obvious therefore cruel, and perhaps untrue.

KITTY. You be careful what you think about me.

JOE (*slowly, not looking at her*). I have only the noblest thoughts for both your person, and your spirit.

NICK (*having listened carefully and not being able to make it out*). What are you talking about?

KITTY. You shut up. You—

JOE. He owns this place. He's an important man. All kinds of people come to him looking for work. Comedians. Singers. Dancers.

KITTY. I don't care. He can't call me names.

NICK. All right, sister. I know how it is with a two-dollar whore in the morning.

KITTY (*furiously*). Don't you dare call me names. I used to be in burlesque.

NICK. If you were ever in burlesque, I used to be Charlie Chaplin.

KITTY (*angry and a little pathetic*). I *was* in burlesque. I played the burlesque circuit from coast to coast. I've had flowers sent to me by European royalty. I've had dinner with young men of wealth and social position.

NICK. You're dreaming.

KITTY (*to* JOE). I *was in burlesque*. Kitty Duval. That was my name.

Life-sized photographs of me in costume in front of burlesque theaters all over the country.

JOE *(gently, coaxingly).* I believe you. Have some champagne.

NICK *(going to table, with champagne bottle and glasses).* There he
goes again.

JOE. Miss Duval?

KITTY *(sincerely, going over).* That's not my *real* name. That's my
stage name.

JOE. I'll call you by your stage name.

NICK *(pouring).* All right, sister, make up your mind. Are you going
to have champagne with him, or not?

JOE. Pour the lady some wine.

NICK. O.K., Professor. Why you come to this joint instead of one of
the high-class dumps uptown is more than I can understand.
Why don't you have champagne at the St. Francis? Why don't
you drink with a lady?

KITTY *(furiously).* Don't you call me names—you dentist.

JOE. Dentist?

NICK *(amazed, loudly).* What kind of cussing is that? *(Pause. Looking at* KITTY, *then at* JOE, *bewildered.)* This guy doesn't belong
here. The only reason I've got champagne is because *he* keeps
ordering it all the time. *(To* KITTY.*)* Don't think you're the only
one he drinks champagne with. He drinks with *all* of them.
(Pause.) He's crazy. Or something.

JOE *(confidentially).* Nick, I think you're going to be all right in a
couple of centuries.

NICK. I'm sorry, I don't understand your English.

*(*JOE *lifts his glass.)*

*(*KITTY *slowly lifts hers, not quite sure of what's going on.)*

JOE *(sincerely).* To the spirit, Kitty Duval.

KITTY *(beginning to understand, and very grateful, looking at him).*
Thank you.

(They drink.)

JOE *(calling).* Nick.

NICK. Yeah?

JOE. Would you mind putting a nickel in the machine again?
Number—

NICK. Seven. I know. I know. I don't mind at all, Your Highness, although, personally, I'm not a lover of music. *(Going to the machine.)* As a matter of fact I think Tchaikowsky was a dope.

JOE. Tchaikowsky? Where'd you ever hear of Tchaikowsky?

NICK. He was a dope.

JOE. Yeah. Why?

NICK. They talked about him on the radio one Sunday morning. He was a sucker. He let a woman drive him crazy.

JOE. I see.

NICK. I stood behind that bar listening to the God damn stuff and cried like a baby. *None but the lonely heart!* He was a dope.

JOE. What made you cry?

NICK. What?

JOE *(sternly)*. What made you cry, Nick?

NICK *(angry with himself)*. I don't know.

JOE. I've been underestimating you, Nick. Play number seven.

NICK. They get everybody worked up. They give everybody stuff they shouldn't have.

(NICK puts the nickel into the machine and the Waltz begins again. He listens to the music. Then studies The Racing Form.)

KITTY *(to herself, dreaming)*. I like champagne, and everything that goes with it. Big houses with big porches, and big rooms with big windows, and big lawns, and big trees, and flowers growing everywhere, and big shepherd dogs sleeping in the shade.

NICK. I'm going next door to Frankie's to make a bet. I'll be right back.

JOE. Make one for me.

NICK *(going to JOE)*. Who do you like?

JOE *(giving him money)*. Precious Time.

NICK. *Ten dollars?* Across the board?

JOE. No. On the nose.

NICK. O.K. *(He goes.)*

(DUDLEY R. BOSTWICK, as he calls himself, breaks through the swinging doors, and practically flings himself upon the open telephone beside the phonograph.)

(DUDLEY is a young man of about twenty-four or twenty-five, ordinary and yet extraordinary. He is smallish, as the saying is, neatly dressed in bargain clothes, over-worked and irritated by the routine and dullness and monotony of his life, apparently nobody and nothing, but in

*reality a great personality. The swindled young man. Educated, but
without the least real understanding. A brave, dumb, salmon-spirit
struggling for life in weary, stupefied flesh, dueling ferociously with a
banal mind which has been only irritated by what it has been taught.
He is a great personality because, against all these handicaps, what he
wants is simple and basic: a woman. This urgent and violent need,
common yet miraculous enough in itself, considering the unhappy environment of the animal, is the force which elevates him from nothing-
ness to greatness. A ridiculous greatness, but in the nature of things
beautiful to behold. All that he has been taught, and everything he
believes, is phony, and yet he himself is real, almost super-real, because of this indestructible force in himself. His face is ridiculous. His
personal rhythm is tense and jittery. His speech is shrill and violent.
His gestures are wild. His ego is disjointed and epileptic. And yet
deeply he possesses the same wholeness of spirit, and directness of
energy, that is in all species of animals. There is little innate or cul-
tivated spirit in him, but there is no absence of innocent animal force.
He is a young man who has been taught that he has a chance, as a
person, and believe it. As a matter of fact, he hasn't a chance in the
world, and should have been told by somebody, or should not have
had his natural and valuable ignorance spoiled by education, ruining
an otherwise perfectly good and charming member of the human race.)*

*(At the telephone he immediately begins to dial furiously, hesitates,
changes his mind, stops dialing, hangs up furiously, and suddenly begins again.)*

(Not more than half a minute after the firecracker arrival of DUDLEY
R. BOSTWICK, *occurs the polka-and-waltz arrival of* HARRY.)

*(*HARRY *is another story.)*

*(He comes in timidly, turning about uncertainly, awkward, out of
place everywhere, embarrassed and encumbered by the contemporary
costume, sick at heart, but determined to fit in somewhere. His arrival
constitutes a dance.)*

*(His clothes don't fit. The pants are a little too large. The coat, which
doesn't match, is also a little too large, and loose.)*

*(He is a dumb young fellow, but he has ideas. A philosophy, in fact.
His philosophy is simple and beautiful. The world is sorrowful. The*

world needs laughter. HARRY *is funny. The world needs* HARRY. HARRY *will make the world laugh.)*

(He has probably had a year or two of high school. He has also listened to the boys at the pool room.)

(He's looking for NICK. *He goes to the* ARAB, *and says, Are you Nick? The* ARAB *shakes his head. He stands at the bar, waiting. He waits very busily.)*

HARRY *(as* NICK *returns).* You Nick?
NICK *(very loudly). I am Nick.*
HARRY *(acting).* Can you use a great comedian?
NICK *(behind the bar).* Who, for instance?
HARRY *(almost angry).* Me.
NICK. You? What's funny about you?

*(*DUDLEY *at the telephone, is dialing. Because of some defect in the apparatus the dialing is very loud.)*

DUDLEY. Hello. Sunset 7349? May I speak to Miss Elsie Mandelspiegel?

(Pause.)

HARRY *(with spirit and noise, dancing).* I dance and do gags and stuff.
NICK. In costume? Or are you wearing your costume?
DUDLEY. All I need is a cigar.
KITTY *(continuing the dream of grace).* I'd walk out of the house, and stand on the porch, and look at the trees, and smell the flowers, and run across the lawn, and lie down under a tree, and read a book. *(Pause.)* A book of poems, maybe.
DUDLEY *(very, very clearly).* Elsie Mandelspiegel. *(Impatiently.)* She has a room on the fourth floor. She's a nurse at the Southern Pacific Hospital. Elsie Mandelspiegel. She works at night. Elsie. Yes. *(He begins waiting again.)*

*(*WESLEY, *a colored boy, comes to the bar and stands near* HARRY, *waiting.)*

NICK. Beer?
WESLEY. No, sir. I'd like to talk to you.
NICK *(to* HARRY). All right. Get funny.
HARRY *(getting funny, an altogether different person, an actor with great energy, both in power of voice, and in force and speed of*

physical gesture). Now, I'm standing on the corner of Third and
Market. I'm looking around. I'm figuring it out. There it is. Right
in front of me. The whole city. The whole world. People going
by. They're going somewhere. I don't know where, but they're
going. I ain't going *anywhere.* Where the hell can you go? I'm
figuring it out. All right, I'm a citizen. A fat guy bumps his
stomach into the face of an old lady. They were in a hurry.
Fat and old. *They bumped.* Boom. I don't know. It may mean
war. *War.* Germany. England. Russia. I don't know for sure.
*(Loudly, dramatically, he salutes, about faces, presents arms, aims,
and fires.)* WAAAAAR. *(He blows a call to arms.* NICK *gets sick of
this, indicates with a gesture that* HARRY *should hold it, and goes
to* WESLEY.)

NICK. What's on *your* mind?

WESLEY *(confused).* Well—

NICK. Come on. Speak up. Are you hungry, or what?

WESLEY. Honest to God, I ain't hungry. All I want is a job. I don't
want no charity.

NICK. Well, what can you do, and how good are you?

WESLEY. I can run errands, clean up, wash dishes, anything.

DUDLEY *(on the telephone, very eagerly).* Elsie? Elsie, this is Dudley.
Elsie, I'll jump in the bay if you don't marry me. Life isn't worth
living without you. I can't sleep. I can't think of anything but
you. All the time. Day and night and night and day. Elsie, I
love you. I love you. What? *(Burning up.)* Is this Sunset 7-3-4-9?
(Pause.) 7943? *(Calmly, while* WILLIE *begins making a small
racket.)* Well, what's *your* name? *Lorene?* Lorene Smith? I
thought you were Elsie Mandelspiegel. What? Dudley. Yeah.
Dudley R. Bostwick. Yeah. R. It stands for Raoul, but I never
spell it out. I'm pleased to meet *you,* too. What? There's a lot of
noise around here. *(WILLIE stops hitting the marblegame.)*
Where am I? At Nick's, on Pacific Street. I work at the S. P.
I told them I was sick and they gave me the afternoon off.
Wait a minute. I'll ask them. I'd like to meet *you,* too. Sure.
I'll ask them. *(Turns around to* NICK.) What's this address?

NICK. Number 3 Pacific Street, you cad.

DUDLEY. Cad? You don't know how I've been suffering on account
of Elsie. I take things too ceremoniously. I've got to be more
lackadaisical. *(Into telephone.)* Hello, Elenore? I mean, Lorene.
It's number 3 Pacific Street. Yeah. Sure. I'll wait for you. How'll

you know me? You'll *know* me. I'll recognize you. Good-bye, now. (*He hangs up.*)

HARRY (*continuing his monologue, with gestures, movements, and so on*). I'm standing there. I didn't do anything to anybody. Why should *I* be a soldier? (*Sincerely, insanely.*) BOOOOOOOOOOM. WAR! O.K. War *I* retreat. *I* hate war. I move to Sacramento.

NICK (*shouting*). All right, Comedian. Lay off a minute.

HARRY (*broken-hearted, going to* WILLIE). Nobody's got a sense of humor any more. The world's dying for comedy like never before, but nobody knows how to *laugh*.

NICK (*to* WESLEY). Do you belong to the union?

WESLEY. What union?

NICK. For the love of Mike, where've you been? Don't you know you can't come into a place and ask for a job and get one and go to work, just like that. You've got to belong to one of the unions.

WESLEY. I didn't know. I got to have a job. Real soon.

NICK. Well, you've got to belong to a union.

WESLEY. I don't want any favors. All I want is a chance to earn a living.

NICK. Go on into the kitchen and tell Sam to give you some lunch.

WESLEY. Honest, I ain't hungry.

DUDLEY (*shouting*). What I've gone through for Elsie.

HARRY. I've got all kinds of funny ideas in my head to help make the world happy again.

NICK (*holding* WESLEY). No, he isn't hungry.

(WESLEY *almost faints from hunger.* NICK *catches him just in time. The* ARAB *and* NICK *go off with* WESLEY *into the kitchen.*)

HARRY (*to* WILLIE). See if you think this is funny. It's my own idea. I created this dance myself. It comes after the monologue.

(HARRY *begins to dance.* WILLIE *watches a moment, and then goes back to the game. It's a goofy dance, which* HARRY *does with great sorrow, but much energy.*)

DUDLEY. Elsie. Aw, gee, Elsie. What the hell do I want to see Lorene Smith for? Some girl I don't know.

(JOE *and* KITTY *have been drinking in silence. There is no sound now except the soft shoe shuffling of* HARRY, *the Comedian.*)

JOE. What's the dream now, Kitty Duval?

KITTY (*dreaming the words and pictures*). I dream of home. Christ, I always dream of home. I've no *home*. I've no place. But I always dream of all of us together again. We had a farm in Ohio. There was nothing good about it. It was always sad. There was always trouble. But I always dream about it as if I could go back and Papa would be there and Mamma and Louie and my little brother Stephen and my sister Mary. I'm Polish. Duval! My name isn't Duval, it's Koranovsky. Katerina Koranovsky. We lost everything. The house, the farm, the trees, the horses, the cows, the chickens. Papa died. He was old. He was thirteen years older than Mamma. We moved to Chicago. We tried to work. We tried to stay together. Louie got into trouble. The fellows he was with killed him for something. I don't know what. Stephen ran away from home. Seventeen years old. I don't know where he is. Then Mamma died. (*Pause.*) What's the dream? I dream of home.

(NICK *comes out of the kitchen with* WESLEY.)

NICK. Here. Sit down here and rest. That'll hold you for a *while*. Why didn't you tell me you were hungry? You all right now?

WESLEY (*sitting down in the chair at the piano*). Yes, I am. Thank you. I didn't know I was *that* hungry.

NICK. Fine. (*To* HARRY *who is dancing.*) Hey. What the hell do you think you're doing?

HARRY (*stopping*). That's my own idea. I'm a natural-born dancer and comedian.

(WESLEY *begins slowly, one note, one chord at a time, to play the piano.*)

NICK. You're no good. Why don't you try some other kind of work? Why don't you get a job in a store, selling something? What do you want to be a comedian for?

HARRY. I've got something for the world and they haven't got sense enough to let me give it to them. Nobody knows me.

DUDLEY. Elsie. Now I'm waiting for some dame I've never seen before. Lorene Smith. Never saw her in my life. Just happened to get the wrong number. She turns on the personality, and I'm a cooked Indian. Give me a beer, please.

HARRY. Nick, you've got to see my act. It's the greatest thing of its kind in America. All I want is a chance. No salary to begin. Let me try it out tonight. If I don't wow 'em, O.K., I'll go home. If vaudeville wasn't dead, a guy like me would have a chance.

NICK. You're not funny. You're a sad young punk. What the hell do you want to try to be funny for? You'll break everybody's heart. What's there for you to be funny about? You've been poor all your life, haven't you?

HARRY. I've been poor all right, but don't forget that some things count more than some other things.

NICK. What counts more, for instance, than what else, for instance?

HARRY. Talent, for instance, counts more than money, for instance, that's what, and I've got talent. I get new ideas night and day. Everything comes natural to me. I've got style, but it'll take me a little time to round it out. That's all.

(By now WESLEY *is playing something of his own which is very good and out of the world. He plays about half a minute, after which* HARRY *begins to dance.)*

NICK *(watching).* I run the lousiest dive in Frisco, and a guy arrives and makes me stock up with champagne. The whores come in and holler at me that they're ladies. Talent comes in and begs me for a chance to show itself. Even society people come here once in a while. I don't know what for. Maybe it's liquor. Maybe it's the location. Maybe it's my personality. Maybe it's the crazy personality of the joint. The old honky-tonk. *(Pause.)* Maybe they can't feel at home anywhere else.

(By now WESLEY *is really playing, and* HARRY *is going through a new routine.* DUDLEY *grows sadder and sadder.)*

KITTY. Please dance with me.

JOE *(loudly).* I never learned to dance.

KITTY. Anybody can dance. Just hold me in your arms.

JOE. I'm very fond of you. I'm *sorry.* I *can't* dance. I wish to God I could.

KITTY. Oh, please.

JOE. Forgive me. I'd like to very much.

*(*KITTY *dances alone.* TOM *comes in with a package. He sees* KITTY *and goes ga-ga again. He comes out of the trance and puts the bundle on the table in front of* JOE.*)*

JOE *(taking the package).* What'd you get?

TOM. Two dollars' worth of toys. That's what you sent me for. The girl asked me what I wanted with toys. I didn't know what to tell her. (*He stares at* KITTY, *then back at* JOE.) I've got to have some money. After all you've done for me, I'll do anything in the world for you, but, Joe, you got to give me some money once in a while.

JOE. What do you want it for?

(TOM *turns and stares at* KITTY *dancing.*)

JOE (*noticing*). Sure. Here's five. (*Shouting.*) Can you dance?

TOM (*proudly*). I got second prize at the Palomar in Sacramento five years ago.

JOE (*loudly, opening package*). O.K., dance with her.

TOM. You mean *her*?

JOE (*loudly*). I mean Kitty Duval, the burlesque queen. I mean the queen of the world burlesque. Dance with her. She wants to dance.

TOM (*worshipping the name Kitty Duval, helplessly*). Joe, can I tell you something?

JOE (*he brings out a toy and winds it*). You don't have to. I know. You love her. You *really* love her. I'm not blind. I know. But take care of yourself. Don't get sick that way again.

NICK (*looking at and listening to* WESLEY *with amazement*). Comes in here and wants to be a dish-washer. Faints from hunger. And then sits down and plays better than Heifetz.

JOE. Heifetz plays the violin.

NICK. All right, don't get careful. He's good, ain't he?

TOM (*to* KITTY). Kitty.

JOE (*he lets the toy go, loudly*). Don't talk. Just *dance*.

(TOM *and* KITTY *dance.* NICK *is at the bar, watching everything.* HARRY *is dancing.* DUDLEY *is grieving into his beer.* LORENE SMITH, *about thirty-seven, very overbearing and funny-looking, comes to the bar.*)

NICK. What'll it be, lady?

LORENE (*looking about and scaring all the young men*). I'm looking for the young man I talked to on the telephone. Dudley R. Bostwick.

DUDLEY (*jumping, running to her, stopping, shocked*). Dudley R. (*Slowly.*) Bostwick? Oh, yeah. He left here ten minutes ago. You mean Dudley Bostwick, that poor man on crutches?

LORENE. Crutches?

DUDLEY. Yeah. Dudley Bostwick. That's what he *said* his name was. He said to tell you not to wait.

LORENE. Well. *(She begins to go, turns around.)* Are you sure *you're* not Dudley Bostwick?

DUDLEY. Who—me? *(Grandly.)* My name is Roger Tenefrancia. I'm a French-Canadian. I never saw the poor fellow before.

LORENE. It seems to me your voice is like the voice I heard over the telephone.

DUDLEY. A coincidence. An accident. A quirk of fate. One of those things. Dismiss the thought. That poor cripple hobbled out of here ten minutes ago.

LORENE. He said he was going to commit suicide. I only wanted to be of help. *(She goes.)*

DUDLEY. Be of help? What kind of help could she be, of? (DUDLEY *runs to the telephone in the corner.)* Gee whiz, Elsie. Gee whiz. I'll never leave you again. *(He turns the pages of a little address book.)* Why do I always forget the number? I've tried to get her on the phone a hundred times this week and I still forget the number. She won't come to the phone, but I keep trying anyway. She's out. She's not in. She's working. I get the wrong number. Everything goes haywire. I can't sleep. *(Defiantly.)* She'll come to the phone one of these days. If there's anything to true love at all, she'll come to the phone. Sunset 7349.

(He dials the number, as JOE *goes on studying the toys. They are one big mechanical toy, whistles, and a music box.* JOE *blows into the whistles, quickly, by way of getting casually acquainted with them.)*

*(*TOM *and* KITTY *stop dancing.* TOM *stares at her.)*

DUDLEY. Hello. Is this Sunset 7349? May I speak to Elsie? Yes. *(Emphatically, and bitterly.)* No, this is *not* Dudley Bostwick. This is Roger Tenefrancia of Montreal, Canada. I'm a childhood friend of Miss Mandelspiegel. We went to kindergarten together. *(Hand over phone.)* God damn it. *(Into phone.)* Yes. I'll wait, thank you.

TOM. I love you.

KITTY. You want to go to my room? (TOM *can't answer.)* Have you got two dollars?

TOM *(shaking his head with confusion).* I've got *five* dollars, but I *love* you.

KITTY *(looking at him).* You want to spend *all* that money?

(TOM embraces her. They go. JOE watches. Goes back to the toy.)

JOE. Where's that longshoreman, McCarthy?

NICK. He'll be around.

JOE. What do you think he'll have to say today?

NICK. Plenty, as usual. I'm going next door to see who won that third race at Laurel.

JOE. Precious Time won it.

NICK. That's what you think. *(He goes.)*

JOE *(to himself).* A horse named McCarthy is running in the sixth race today.

DUDLEY *(on the phone).* Hello. Hello, Elsie? Elsie? *(His voice weakens; also his limbs.)* My God. She's come to the phone. Elsie, I'm at Nick's on Pacific Street. You've got to come here and talk to me. Hello. Hello, Elsie? *(Amazed.)* Did she hang up? Or was I disconnected?

(He hangs up and goes to bar.)

(WESLEY is still playing the piano. HARRY is still dancing. JOE has wound up the big mechanical toy and is watching it work.)

(NICK returns.)

NICK *(watching the toy).* Say. That's some gadget.

JOE. How much did I win?

NICK. How do you know you *won?*

JOE. Don't be silly. He said Precious Time was going to win by ten lengths, didn't he? He's in love, isn't he?

NICK. O.K. I don't know why, but Precious Time won. You got eighty for ten. How do you do it?

JOE *(roaring).* Faith. Faith. How'd he win?

NICK. By a nose. Look him up in The Racing Form. The slowest, the cheapest, the worst horse in the race, and the worst jockey. What's the matter with my luck?

JOE. How much did you lose?

NICK. Fifty cents.

JOE. You should never gamble.

NICK. Why not?

JOE. You always bet fifty cents. You've got no more faith than a flea, that's why.

HARRY (*shouting*). How do you like this, Nick? (*He is really busy now, all legs and arms.*)

NICK (*turning and watching*). Not bad. Hang around. You can wait table. (*To* WESLEY). Hey. Wesley. Can you play that again tonight?

WESLEY (*turning, but still playing the piano*). I don't know for sure, Mr. Nick. I can play *something*.

NICK. Good. You hang around, too. (*He goes behind the bar.*)

(*The atmosphere is now one of warm, natural, American ease; every man innocent and good; each doing what he believes he should do, or what he must do. There is deep American naïveté and faith in the behavior of each person. No one is competing with anyone else. No one hates anyone else. Every man is living, and letting live. Each man is following his destiny as he feels it should be followed; or is abandoning it as he feels it must, by now, be abandoned; or is forgetting it for the moment as he feels he should forget it. Although everyone is dead serious, there is unmistakable smiling and humor in the scene; a sense of the human body and spirit emerging from the world-imposed state of stress and fretfulness, fear and awkwardness, to the more natural state of casualness and grace. Each person belongs to the environment, in his own person, as himself:* WESLEY *is playing better than ever.* HARRY *is hoofing better than ever.* NICK *is behind the bar shining glasses.* JOE *is smiling at the toy and studying it.* DUDLEY, *although still troubled, is at least calm now and full of melancholy poise.* WILLIE, *at the marble-game, is happy. The* ARAB *is deep in his memories, where he wants to be.*)

(*Into this scene and atmosphere comes* BLICK.)

(BLICK *is the sort of human being you dislike at sight. He is no different from anybody else physically. His face is an ordinary face. There is nothing obviously wrong with him, and yet you know that it is impossible, even by the most generous expansion of understanding, to accept him as a human being. He is the strong man without strength —strong only among the weak—the weakling who uses force on the weaker.*)

(BLICK *enters casually, as if he were a customer, and immediately* HARRY *begins slowing down.*)

BLICK (*oily, and with mock-friendliness*). Hello, Nick.

NICK (*stopping his work and leaning across the bar*). What do you want to come here for? You're too big a man for a little honky-tonk.

BLICK (*flattered*). Now, Nick.

NICK. Important people never come here. *Here*. Have a drink. (*Whiskey bottle.*)

BLICK. Thanks, I don't drink.

NICK (*drinking the drink himself*). Well, why don't you?

BLICK. I have responsibilities.

NICK. You're head of the lousy Vice Squad. There's no vice here.

BLICK (*sharply*). Street-walkers are working out of this place.

NICK (*angry*). What do you want?

BLICK (*loudly*). I just want you to know that it's got to stop.

(*The music stops. The mechanical toy runs down. There is absolute silence, and a strange fearfulness and disharmony in the atmosphere now.* HARRY *doesn't know what to do with his hands or feet.* WESLEY'S *arms hang at his sides.* JOE *quietly pushes the toy to one side of the table eager to study what is happening.* WILLIE *stops playing the marble-game, turns around and begins to wait.* DUDLEY *straightens up very, very vigorously, as if to say: "Nothing can scare me. I know love is the only thing." The* ARAB *is the same as ever, but watchful.* NICK *is arrogantly aloof. There is a moment of this silence and tension, as though* BLICK *were waiting for everybody to acknowledge his presence. He is obviously flattered by the acknowledgment of Harry, Dudley, Wesley, and Willie, but a little irritated by Nick's aloofness and unfriendliness.*)

NICK. Don't look at me. I can't tell a street-walker from a lady. You married?

BLICK. You're not asking *me* questions. *I'm* telling *you*.

NICK (*interrupting*). You're a man of about forty-five or so. You *ought* to know better.

BLICK (*angry*). Street-walkers are working out of this place.

NICK (*beginning to shout*). Now, don't start any trouble with me. People come here to drink and loaf around. I don't care who they are.

BLICK. Well, I do.

NICK. The only way to find out if a lady is a street-walker is to walk

the streets with her, go to bed, and make sure. You wouldn't
want to do that. You'd *like* to, of course.

BLICK. Any more of it, and I'll have your joint closed.

NICK *(very casually, without ill-will)*. Listen. I've got no use for you,
or anybody like you. You're out to change the world from something bad to something worse. Something like yourself.

BLICK *(furious pause, and contempt)*. I'll be back tonight. *(He begins
to go.)*

KICK *(very angry but very calm)*. Do yourself a big favor and don't
come back tonight. Send somebody else. I don't like your personality.

BLICK *(casually, but with contempt)*. Don't break any laws. I don't
like yours, either.

(He looks the place over, and goes.)

(There is a moment of silence. Then WILLIE *turns and puts a new
nickel in the slot and starts a new game.* WESLEY *turns to the piano
and rather falteringly begins to play. His heart really isn't in it.* HARRY
walks about, unable to dance. DUDLEY *lapses into his customary
melancholy, at a table.* NICK *whistles a little: suddenly stops.* JOE
winds the toy.)

JOE *(comically)*. Nick. You going to kill that man?

NICK. I'm disgusted.

JOE. Yeah? Why?

NICK. Why should I get worked up over a guy like that? Why should
I hate *him*? He's nothing. He's nobody. He's a mouse. But every
time he comes into this place I get burned up. He doesn't want
to drink. He doesn't want to sit down. He doesn't want to take
things easy. Tell me one thing?

JOE. Do my best.

NICK. What's a punk like *that* want to go out and try to change the
world for?

JOE *(amazed)*. Does *he* want to change the world, too?

NICK *(irritated)*. You know what I mean. What's he want to bother
people for? He's *sick*.

JOE *(almost to himself, reflecting on the fact that* BLICK *too wants
to change the world)*. I guess he wants to change the world at
that.

NICK. So I go to work and hate him.

JOE. It's not him, Nick. It's everything.

NICK. Yeah, *I know*. But I've still got no use for him. He's no good. You know what I mean? He hurts little people. *(Confused.)* One of the girls tried to commit suicide on account of him. *(Furiously.)* I'll break his head if he hurts anybody around here. This is *my* joint. *(Afterthought.)* Or anybody's *feelings*, either.

JOE. He may not be so bad, deep down underneath.

NICK. I know all about him. He's no good.

(During this talk WESLEY *has really begun to play the piano, the toy is rattling again, and little by little* HARRY *has begun to dance.* NICK *has come around the bar, and now, very much like a child—forgetting all his anger—is watching the toy work. He begins to smile at everything: turns and listens to* WESLEY: *watches* HARRY: *nods at the* ARAB: *shakes his head at* DUDLEY: *and gestures amiably about* WILLIE. *It's his joint all right.)*

(It's a good, low-down, honky-tonk American place that lets people alone.)

NICK. I've got a good joint. There's nothing wrong here. Hey. Comedian. Stick to dancing tonight. I think you're O.K. Wesley? Do some more of that tonight. That's fine!

HARRY. Thanks, Nick. Gosh, I'm on my way at last. *(On telephone.)* Hello, Ma? Is that you, Ma? Harry. I got the job. *(He hangs up and walks around, smiling.)*

NICK *(watching the toy all the time)*. Say, that really is something. What is that, anyway?

*(*MARY L. *comes in.)*

JOE *(holding it toward* NICK, *and* MARY L.*)*. Nick, this is a toy. A contraption devised by the cunning of man to drive boredom, or grief, or anger out of children. A noble gadget. A gadget, I might say, infinitely nobler than any other I can think of at the moment.

(Everybody gathers around JOE's *table to look at the toy. The toy stops working.* JOE *winds the music box. Lifts a whistle: blows it, making a very strange, funny and sorrowful sound.)*

Delightful. Tragic, but delightful.

(WESLEY *plays the music-box theme on the piano.* MARY L. *takes a table.*)

NICK. Joe. That girl, Kitty. What's she mean, calling me a dentist? I wouldn't hurt anybody, let alone a tooth.

(NICK *goes to* MARY L.'s *table.* HARRY *imitates the toy. Dances. The piano music comes up, the light dims slowly, while the piano solo continues.*)

ACT TWO

An hour later. All the people who were at Nick's when the curtain came down are still there. JOE at his table, quietly shuffling and turning a deck of cards, and at the same time watching the face of the woman, and looking at the initials on her handbag, as though they were the symbols of the lost glory of the world. The WOMAN, in turn, very casually regards JOE occasionally. Or rather senses him; has sensed him in fact the whole hour. She is mildly tight on beer, and JOE himself is tight, but as always completely under control; simply sharper. The others are about, at tables, and so on.

JOE. Is it Madge—Laubowitz?
MARY. Is what *what?*
JOE. Is the name Mabel Lepescu?
MARY. What name?
JOE. The name the initials M. L. stand for. The initials on your bag.
MARY. No.
JOE (*after a long pause, thinking deeply what the name might be, turning a card, looking into the beautiful face of the woman*). Margie Longworthy?
MARY (*all this is very natural and sincere, no comedy on the part of the people involved: they are both solemn, being drunk*). No.
JOE (*his voice higher-pitched, as though he were growing alarmed*). Midge Laurie? (MARY *shakes her head.*) My initials are J. T.
MARY (*Pause*). John?
JOE. No. (*Pause.*) Martha Lancaster?
MARY. No. (*Slight pause.*) Joseph?

JOE. Well, not exactly. That's my first name, but everybody calls me
Joe. The last name is the tough one. I'll help you a little. I'm
Irish. (*Pause.*) Is it just plain Mary?

MARY. Yes, it is. I'm Irish, too. At least on my father's side. English
on my mother's side.

JOE. I'm Irish on both sides. Mary's one of my favorite names. I
guess that's why I didn't think of it. I met a girl in Mexico
City named Mary once. She was an American from Philadelphia.
She got married there. In Mexico City, I mean. While I was
there. We were in love, too. At least *I* was. You never know
about anyone else. They were engaged, you see, and her
mother was with her, so they went through with it. Must have
been six or seven years ago. She's probably got three or four
children by this time.

MARY. Are you still in love with her?

JOE. Well—no. To tell you the truth, I'm not sure. I guess I am. I
didn't even knew she was engaged until a couple of days before they got married. I thought *I* was going to marry her. I kept
thinking all the time about the kind of kids we would be likely
to have. My favorite was the third one. The first two were fine.
Handsome and fine and intelligent, but that third one was different. Dumb and goofy-looking. I liked *him* a lot. When she
told me she was going to be married, I didn't feel so bad about
the first two, it was that dumb one.

MARY (*after a pause of some few seconds*). What do you do?

JOE. Do? To tell you the truth, nothing.

MARY. Do you always drink a great deal?

JOE (*scientifically*). Not *always*. Only when I'm awake. I sleep seven
or eight hours every night, you know.

MARY. How nice. I mean to drink when you're awake.

JOE (*thoughtfully*). It's a privilege.

MARY. Do you really *like* to drink?

JOE (*positively*). As much as I like to *breathe*.

MARY (*beautifully*). Why?

JOE (*dramatically*). Why do I like to drink? (*Pause.*) Because I don't
like to be gypped. Because I don't like to be dead most of the
time and just a little alive every once in a long while. (*Pause.*)
If I don't drink, I become fascinated by unimportant things—
like everybody else. I get busy. Do things. All kinds of little
stupid things, for all kinds of little stupid reasons. Proud, selfish,

ordinary things. I've done them. Now I don't do anything. *I live all the time.* Then I go to sleep. *(Pause.)*

MARY. Do you sleep well?

JOE *(taking it for granted).* Of course.

MARY *(quietly, almost with tenderness).* What are your plans?

JOE *(loudly, but also tenderly).* Plans? I haven't got any. *I just get up.*

MARY *(beginning to understand everything).* Oh, yes. Yes, of course.

(DUDLEY *puts a nickel in the phonograph.*)

JOE *(thoughtfully).* Why do I drink? *(Pause, while he thinks about it. The thinking appears to be profound and complex, and has the effect of giving his face a very comical and naïve expression.)* That question calls for a pretty complicated answer. *(He smiles abstractly.)*

MARY. Oh, I didn't mean—

JOE *(swiftly, gallantly).* No. No. I *insist.* I *know* why. It's just a matter of finding words. Little ones.

MARY. It really doesn't matter.

JOE *(seriously).* Oh, yes, it does. *(Clinically.)* Now, why do I drink? *(Scientifically.)* No. Why does *anybody* drink? *(Working it out.)* Every day has twenty-four hours.

MARY *(sadly, but brightly).* Yes, that's true.

JOE. Twenty-four hours. Out of the twenty-four hours at *least* twenty-three and a half are—my God, I don't know why—dull, dead, boring, empty, and murderous. Minutes on the clock, *not time of living.* It doesn't make any difference who you are or what you do, twenty-three and a half hours of the twenty-four are spent *waiting.*

MARY. Waiting?

JOE *(gesturing, loudly).* And the more you wait, the less there is to wait for.

MARY *(attentively, beautifully his student).* Oh?

JOE *(continuing).* That goes on for days and days, and weeks and months and years, and years, and the first thing you know *all* the years are dead. All the minutes are dead. Yourself are dead. There's nothing to wait for any more. Nothing except *minutes* on the *clock.* No time of life. Nothing but minutes, and idiocy. Beautiful, bright, intelligent idiocy. *(Pause).* Does that answer your question?

MARY (*earnestly*). I'm afraid it does. Thank you. You shouldn't have gone to all the trouble.

JOE. No trouble at all. (*Pause.*) You have children?

MARY. Yes. Two. A son and a daughter.

JOE (*delighted*). How swell. Do they look like you?

MARY. Yes.

JOE. Then why are you sad?

MARY. I was always sad. It's just that after I was married I was allowed to drink.

JOE (*eagerly*). Who are you waiting for?

MARY. No one.

JOE (*smiling*). I'm not waiting for anybody, either.

MARY. My husband, of course.

JOE. Oh, sure.

MARY. He's a lawyer.

JOE (*standing, leaning on the table*). He's a great guy. I like him. I'm very fond of him.

MARY (*listening*). You have responsibilities?

JOE (*loudly*). *One*, and *thousands*. As a matter of fact, I feel responsible to everybody. At least to everybody I met. I've been trying for three years to find out if it's possible to live what I think is a civilized life. I mean a life that can't hurt any other life.

MARY. You're famous?

JOE. Very. Utterly unknown, but very famous. Would you like to dance?

MARY. All right.

JOE (*loudly*). I'm *sorry*. I don't dance. I didn't think you'd like to.

MARY. To tell you the truth, I don't like to dance at all.

JOE (*proudly. Commentator*). I can hardly walk.

MARY. You mean you're tight?

JOE (*smiling*). No. I mean *all* the time.

MARY (*looking at him closely*). Were you ever in Paris?

JOE. In 1929, and again in 1934.

MARY. What month of 1934?

JOE. Most of April, all of May, and a little of June.

MARY. I was there in November and December that year.

JOE. We were there almost at the same time. You were married?

MARY. Engaged. (*They are silent a moment, looking at one another. Quietly and with great charm.*) Are you *really* in love with me?

JOE. Yes.

MARY. Is it the champagne?

JOE. Yes. Partly, at least. (*He sits down.*)

MARY. If you don't see me again will you be very unhappy?

JOE. Very.

MARY (*getting up*). I'm so pleased. (JOE *is deeply grieved that she is going. In fact, he is almost panic-stricken about it, getting up in a way that is full of furious sorrow and regret.*) I must go now. Please don't get up. (JOE *is up, staring at her with amazement.*) Good-by.

JOE (*simply*). Good-by.

(*The* WOMAN *stands looking at him a moment, then turns and goes.* JOE *stands staring after her for a long time. Just as he is slowly sitting down again, the* NEWSBOY *enters, and goes to Joe's table.*)

NEWSBOY. Paper, Mister?

JOE. How many you got this time?

NEWSBOY. Eleven.

(JOE *buys them all, looks at the lousy headlines, throws them away.*)

(*The* NEWSBOY *looks at* JOE, *amazed. He walks over to* NICK *at the bar.*)

NEWSBOY (*troubled*). Hey, Mister, do you own this place?

NICK (*casually but emphatically*). I own this place.

NEWSBOY. Can you use a great lyric tenor?

NICK (*almost to himself*). Great lyric tenor? (*Loudly.*) Who?

NEWSBOY (*loud and the least bit angry*). Me. I'm getting too big to sell papers. I don't want to holler headlines all the time. I want to *sing.* You can use a great lyric tenor, can't you?

NICK. What's lyric about you?

NEWSBOY (*voice high-pitched, confused*). My voice.

NICK. Oh. (*Slight pause, giving in.*) All right, then—sing!

(*The* NEWSBOY *breaks into swift and beautiful song: "When Irish Eyes Are Smiling."* NICK *and* JOE *listen carefully:* NICK *with wonder,* JOE *with amazement and delight.*)

NEWSBOY (*singing*).

When Irish eyes are smiling,
Sure 'tis like a morn in Spring.
In the lilt of Irish laughter,
You can hear the angels sing.

When Irish hearts are happy,
All the world seems bright and gay.
But when Irish eyes are smiling—

NICK (*loudly, swiftly*). Are you Irish?

NEWSBOY (*speaking swiftly, loudly, a little impatient with the irrelevant question*). No. I'm Greek. (*He finishes the song, singing louder than ever.*)

Sure they steal your heart away.

(*He turns to* NICK *dramatically, like a vaudeville singer begging his audience for applause.* NICK *studies the boy eagerly.* JOE *gets to his feet and leans toward the* BOY *and* NICK.)

NICK. Not bad. Let me hear you again about a year from now.

NEWSBOY (*thrilled*). Honest?

NICK. Yeah. Along about November 7th, 1940.

NEWSBOY (*happier than ever before in his life, running over to* JOE). Did you hear it too, Mister?

JOE. Yes, and it's great. What part of Greece?

NEWSBOY. Salonica. Gosh, Mister. Thanks.

JOE. Don't wait a year. Come back with some papers a little later. You're a great singer.

NEWSBOY (*thrilled and excited*). Aw, thanks, Mister. So long. (*Running, to* NICK.) Thanks, Mister.

(*He runs out.* JOE *and* NICK *look at the swinging doors.* JOE *sits down,* NICK *laughs.*)

NICK. Joe, people are so wonderful. Look at that kid.

JOE. Of course they're wonderful. Every one of them is wonderful.

(MC CARTHY *and* KRUPP *come in, talking.*)

(MC CARTHY *is a big man in work clothes, whihc make him seem very young. He is wearing black jeans, and a blue workman's shirt. No tie. No hat. He has broad shoulders, a lean intelligent face, thick black hair. In his right back pocket is the longshoreman's hook. His arms are long and hairy. His sleeves are rolled up to just below his elbows. He is a casual man, easy-going in movement, sharp in perception, swift in appreciation of charm or innocence or comedy, and gentle in spirit. His speech is clear and full of warmth. His voice is powerful, but modulated. He enjoys the world, in spite of the mess it is, and he is fond of people, in spite of the mess they are.*)

(KRUPP *is not quite as tall or broadshouldered as* MC CARTHY. *He is physically encumbered by his uniform, club, pistol, belt, and cap. And he is plainly not at home in the role of policeman. His movement is stiff and unintentionally pompous. He is a naïve man, essentially good. His understanding is less than McCarthy's, but he is honest and he doesn't try to bluff.*)

KRUPP. You don't understand what I mean.
   Hi-ya, Joe.
JOE. Hello, Krupp.
MC CARTHY. Hi-ya, Joe.
JOE. Hello, McCarthy.
KRUPP. Two beers, Nick. (*To* MC CARTHY.) All I do is carry out orders, carry out orders. I don't know what the idea is behind the order. Who it's for, or who it's against, or why. All I do is carry it out.

(NICK *gives them beer.*)

MC CARTHY. You don't read enough.
KRUPP. I do read. I read *The Examiner* every morning. *The Call-Bulletin* every night.
MC CARTHY. And carry out orders. What are the orders now?
KRUPP. To keep the peace down here on the waterfront.
MC CARTHY. Keep it for who? (*To* JOE.)
Right?
JOE (*sorrowfully*). Right.
KRUPP. How do I know for who? The peace. Just keep it.
MC CARTHY. It's got to be kept for somebody. Who would you suspect it's kept for?
KRUPP. For citizens!
MC CARTHY. I'm a citizen!
KRUPP. All right, I'm keeping it for you.
MC CARTHY. By hitting me over the head with a club? (*To* JOE.) Right?
JOE (*melancholy, with remembrance*). I don't know.
KRUPP. Mac, you know I never hit you over the head with a club.
MC CARTHY. But you will if you're on duty at the time and happen to stand on the opposite side of myself, on duty.
KRUPP. We went to Mission High together. We were always good friends. The only time we ever fought was that time over Alma

Haggerty. Did you marry Alma Haggerty? (*To* JOE.) Right?

JOE. Everything's right.

MC CARTHY. No. Did you? (*To* JOE.) Joe, are you with me or against me?

JOE. I'm with everybody. One at a time.

KRUPP. No. And that's just what I mean.

MC CARTHY. You mean neither one of us is going to marry the thing we're fighting for?

KRUPP. *I don't even know what it is.*

MC CARTHY. You don't read enough, I tell you.

KRUPP. Mac, you don't know what you're fighting for, either.

MC CARTHY. It's so simple, it's fantastic.

KRUPP. All right, what are you fighting for?

MC CARTHY. For the rights of the inferior. Right?

JOE. Something like that.

KRUPP. The who?

MC CARTHY. The inferior. The world is full of Mahoneys who haven't got what it takes to make monkeys out of everybody else, near by. The men who were created equal. Remember?

KRUPP. Mac, you're not inferior.

MC CARTHY. I'm a longshoreman. And an idealist. I'm a man with too much brawn to be an intellectual, exclusively. I married a small, sensitive, cultured woman so that my kids would be sissies instead of suckers. A strong man with any sensibility has no choice in this world but to be a heel, or a *worker.* I haven't the heart to be a heel, so I'm a worker. I've got a son in high school who's already thinking of being a writer.

KRUPP. I wanted to be a writer once.

JOE. Wonderful. (*He puts down the paper, looks at* KRUPP *and* MC CARTHY.)

MC CARTHY. They *all* wanted to be writers. Every maniac in the world that ever brought about the murder of people through war started out in an attic or a basement writing poetry. It stank. So they got even by becoming important heels. And it's still going on.

KRUPP. Is it really, Joe?

JOE. Look at today's paper.

MC CARTHY. Right now on Telegraph Hill is some punk who is trying to be Shakespeare. Ten years from now he'll be a senator. Or a communist.

KRUPP. Somebody ought to do something about it.

MC CARTHY. *(mischievously, with laughter in his voice)*. The thing to do is to have more magazines. Hundreds of them. *Thousands.* Print everything they write, so they'll believe they're immortal. That way keep them from going haywire.

KRUPP. Mac, you ought to be a writer yourself.

MC CARTHY. I hate the tribe. They're mischief-makers. Right?

JOE *(swiftly)*. Everything's right. Right and wrong.

KRUPP. Then why do you read?

MC CARTHY *(laughing)*. It's relaxing. It's soothing. *(Pause.)* The lousiest people born into the world are writers. Language is all right. It's the people who use language that are lousy. *(The* ARAB *has moved a little closer, and is listening carefully.)* *(To the* ARAB.*)* What do you think, Brother?

ARAB *(after making many faces, thinking very deeply)*. No foundation. All the way down the line. What. What-not. Nothing. I go walk and look at sky. *(He goes.)*

KRUPP. What? What-not? *(To* JOE.*)* What's that mean?

JOE *(slowly, thinking, remembering)*. What? What-not? That means this side, that side. Inhale, exhale. What: birth. What-not: death. The inevitable, the astounding, the magnificent seed of growth and decay in all things. Beginning, and end. That man, in his own way, is a prophet. He is one who, with the help of *beer*, is able to reach that state of deep understanding in which what and what-not, the reasonable and the unreasonable, are one.

MC CARTHY. Right.

KRUPP. If you can understand that kind of talk, how can you be a longshoreman?

MC CARTHY. I come from a long line of McCarthys who never married or slept with anything but the most powerful and quarrelsome flesh. *(He drinks beer.)*

KRUPP. I could listen to you two guys for hours, but I'll be damned if I know what the hell you're talking about.

MC CARTHY. The consequence is that all the McCarthys are too great and too strong to be heroes. Only the weak and unsure perform the heroic. They've *got* to. The more heroes you have, the worse the history of the world becomes. Right?

JOE. Go outside and look at it.

KRUPP. You sure can philos—philosoph—Boy, you can talk.

MC CARTHY. I wouldn't talk this way to anyone but a man in uniform, and a man who couldn't understand a word of what I was saying. The party I'm speaking of, my friend, is YOU.

(The phone rings.)

(HARRY gets up from his table suddenly and begins a new dance.)

KRUPP *(noticing him, with great authority)*. Here, here. What do you think you're doing?

HARRY *(stopping)*. I just got an idea for a new dance. I'm trying it out. Nick. Nick, the phone's ringing.

KRUPP *(to MC CARTHY)*. Has he got a right to do that?

MC CARTHY. The living have danced from the beginning of time. I might even say, the dance and the life have moved along together, until now we have—*(To HARRY.)* Go into your dance, son, and show us what we have.

HARRY. I haven't got it worked out *completely* yet, but it starts out like this. *(He dances.)*

NICK *(on phone)*. Nick's Pacific Street Restaurant, Saloon, and Entertainment Palace. Good afternoon. Nick speaking. *(Listens.)* Who? *(Turns around.)* Is there a Dudley Bostwick in the joint?

(DUDLEY jumps to his feet and goes to phone.)

DUDLEY *(on phone)*. Hello. Elsie? *(Listens.)* You're coming down? *(Elated. To the saloon.)* She's coming down. *(Pause.)* No. I won't drink. Aw, gosh, Elsie.

(He hangs up, looks about him strangely, as if he were just born, walks around touching things, putting chairs in place, and so on.)

MC CARTHY *(to HARRY.)* Splendid. Splendid.

HARRY. Then I go into this little routine.

(He demonstrates.)

KRUPP. Is that good, Mac?

MC CARTHY. It's awful, but it's honest and ambitious, like everything else in this great country.

HARRY. Then I work along into this. *(He demonstrates.)* And *this* is where I *really* get going. *(He finishes the dance.)*

MC CARTHY. Excellent. A most satisfying demonstration of the present state of the American body and soul. Son, you're a genius.

HARRY (*delighted, shaking hands with* MC CARTHY). I go on in front of an audience for the first time in my life tonight.

MC CARTHY. They'll be delighted. Where'd you learn to dance?

HARRY. Never took a lesson in my life. I'm a natural-born dancer. And *comedian,* too.

MC CARTHY (*astounded*). You can make people *laugh?*

HARRY (*dumbly*). I can be funny, but they won't laugh.

MC CARTHY. That's odd. Why not?

HARRY. I don't know. They just won't laugh.

MC CARTHY. Would you care to be funny now?

HARRY. I'd like to try out a new monologue I've been thinking out.

MC CARTHY. Please do. I promise you if it's funny I shall *roar* with laughter.

HARRY. This is it. (*Goes into the act, with much energy.*) I'm up at Sharkey's on Turk Street. It's a quarter to nine, daylight saving. Wednesday, the eleventh. What I've got is a headache and a 1918 nickel. What I *want* is a cup of coffee. If I buy a cup of coffee with the nickel, I've got to walk home. I've got an eight-ball problem. George the Greek is shooting a game of snooker with Pedro the Filipino. *I'm in rags.* They're wearing thirty-five dollar suits, made to order. I haven't got a cigarette. They're smoking Bobby Burns panatelas. I'm thinking it over, like I always do. George the Greek is in a tough spot. If I buy a cup of coffee, I'll want another cup. What happens? My *ear* aches! My ear. George the Greek takes the cue. Chalks it. Studies the table. Touches the cue-ball delicately. Tick. What happens? He makes the three-ball! What do I do. I get confused. *I go out and buy a morning paper.* What the hell do I want with a morning paper? What I *want* is a cup of coffee, and a good used car. I go out and buy a morning paper. Thursday, the twelfth. Maybe the headline's about *me.* I take a quick look. No. *The headline is not about me.* It's about Hitler. Seven thousand miles away. I'm here. Who the hell is Hitler? Who's behind the eight-ball? I turn around. *Everybody's behind the eight-ball!*

(*Pause.* KRUPP *moves toward* HARRY *as if to make an important arrest.* HARRY *moves to the swinging doors.* MC CARTHY *stops* KRUPP.)

MC CARTHY (*to* HARRY). It's the funniest thing I've ever heard. Or *seen,* for that matter.

HARRY (*coming back to* MC CARTHY). Then, why don't you laugh?

MC CARTHY. I don't know, *yet.*

HARRY. I'm always getting funny ideas that nobody will laugh at.

MC CARTHY (*thoughtfully*). It may be that you've stumbled headlong into a new kind of comedy.

HARRY. Well, what good is it if it doesn't make anybody laugh?

MC CARTHY. There are *kinds* of laughter, son. I must say, in all truth, that I *am* laughing, although not *out loud.*

HARRY. I want to *hear* people laugh. *Out loud.* That's why I keep thinking of funny things to say.

MC CARTHY. Well. They may catch on in time. Let's go, Krupp. So long, Joe. (MC CARTHY *and* KRUPP *go.*)

JOE. So long. (*After a moment's pause.*) Hey, Nick.

NICK. Yeah.

JOE. Bet McCarthy in the last race.

NICK. You're crazy. That horse is a double-crossing, no-good—

JOE. Bet everything you've got on McCarthy.

NICK. I'm not betting a nickel on him. *You* bet everything you've got on McCarthy.

JOE. I don't need money.

NICK. What makes you think McCarthy's going to win?

JOE. McCarthy's name's McCarthy, isn't it?

NICK. Yeah. So what?

JOE. The *horse* named McCarthy is going to win, *that's all.* Today.

NICK. Why?

JOE. You do what I tell you, and everything will be all right.

NICK. McCarthy likes to talk, that's all. (*Pause.*) Where's Tom?

JOE. He'll be around. He'll be miserable, but he'll be around. Five or ten minutes more.

NICK. You don't believe that Kitty, do you? About being in burlesque?

JOE (*very clearly*). I believe dreams sooner than statistics.

NICK (*remembering*). She sure is somebody. Called me a dentist.

(TOM, *turning about, confused, troubled, comes in, and hurries to Joe's table.*)

JOE. What's the matter?

TOM. Here's your five, Joe. I'm in trouble again.

JOE. If it's not organic, it'll cure itself. If it is organic, science will cure it. What is it, organic or non-organic?

TOM. Joe, I don't know—(*He seems to be completely broken-down.*)

JOE. What's eating you? I want you to go on an errand for me.

TOM. It's Kitty.

JOE. What about her?

TOM. She's up in her room, crying.

JOE. Crying?

TOM. Yeah, she's ben crying for over an hour. I been talking to her all this time, but she won't stop.

JOE. What's she crying about?

TOM. I don't know. I couldn't understand anything. She kept crying and telling me about a big house and collie dogs all around and flowers and one of her brother's dead and the other one lost somewhere. Joe, I can't stand Kitty crying.

JOE. You want to marry the girl?

TOM (nodding). Yeah.

JOE (curious and sincere). Why?

TOM. I don't know why, exactly, Joe. (Pause.) Joe, I don't like to think of Kitty out in the streets. I guess I love her that's all.

JOE. She's a nice girl.

TOM. She's like an angel. She's not like those other street-walkers.

JOE (swiftly). Here. Take all this money and run next door to Frankie's and bet it on the nose of McCarthy.

TOM (swiftly). All this money, Joe? McCarthy?

JOE. Yeah. Hurry.

TOM (going). Ah, Joe. If McCarthy wins we'll be rich.

JOE. Get going, will you?

(TOM runs out and nearly knocks over the ARAB coming back in. NICK fills him a beer without a word.)

ARAB. No foundation, anywhere. Whole world. No foundation. All the way down the line.

NICK (angry). McCarthy! Just because you got a little lucky this morning, you have to go to work and throw away eight bucks.

JOE. He wants to marry her.

NICK. Suppose she doesn't want to marry him?

JOE (amazed). Oh, yeah (Thinking). Now, why wouldn't she want to marry a nice guy like Tom?

NICK. She's been in burlesque. She's had flowers sent to her by European royalty. She's dined with young men of quality and social position. She's above Tom.

(TOM comes running in.)

TOM (*disgusted*). They were running when I got there. Frankie wouldn't take the bet. McCarthy didn't get a call till the stretch. I thought we were going to save all this money. Then McCarthy won by two lengths.

JOE. What'd he pay, fifteen to one?

TOM. Better, but Frankie wouldn't take the bet.

NICK (*throwing a dish towel across the room*). Well, for the love of Mike.

JOE. Give me the money.

TOM (*giving back the money*). We would have had about a thousand five hundred dollars.

JOE (*bored, casually, inventing*). Go up to Schwabacher-Frey and get me the biggest Rand-McNally map of the nations of Europe they've got. On your way back stop at one of the pawn shops on Third Street, and buy me a good revolver and some cartridges.

TOM. She's up in her room crying, Joe.

JOE. Go get me those things.

NICK. What are you going to do, study the map, and then go out and shoot somebody?

JOE. I want to read the names of some European towns and rivers and valleys and mountains.

NICK. What do you want with the revolver?

JOE. I want to study it. I'm interested in things. Here's twenty dollars, Tom. Now go get them things.

TOM. A big map of Europe. And a revolver.

JOE. Get a good one. Tell the man you don't know anything about firearms and you're trusting him not to fool you. Don't pay more than ten dollars.

TOM. Joe, you got something on your mind. Don't go fool with a revolver.

JOE. Be sure it's a good one.

TOM. Joe.

JOE (*irritated*). What, Tom?

TOM. Joe, what do you send me out for crazy things for all the time?

JOE (*angry*). They're not crazy, Tom. Now, get going.

TOM. What about Kitty, Joe?

JOE. Let her cry. It'll do her good.

TOM. If she comes in here while I'm gone, talk to her, will you, Joe? Tell her about me.

JOE. O.K. Get going. Don't load that gun. Just buy it and bring it here.

TOM (*going*). You won't catch me loading any gun.

JOE. Wait a minute. Take these toys away.

TOM. Where'll I take them?

JOE. Give them to some kid. (*Pause.*) No. Take them up to Kitty. Toys stopped me from crying once. That's the reason I had you buy them. I wanted to see if I could find out *why* they stopped me from crying. I remember they seemed awfully stupid at the time.

TOM. Shall I, Joe? Take them up to Kitty? Do you think they'd stop *her* from crying?

JOE. They might. You get curious about the way they work and you forget whatever it is you're remembering that's making you cry. That's what they're for.

TOM. Yeah. Sure. The girl at the store asked me what I wanted with toys. I'll take them up to Kitty. (*Tragically.*) She's like a little girl. (*He goes.*)

WESLEY. Mr. Nick, can I play the piano again?

NICK. Sure. Practice all you like—until I tell you to stop.

WESLEY. You going to pay me for playing the piano?

NICK. Sure. I'll give you enough to get by on.

WESLEY (*amazed and delighted*). Get money for playing the piano?

(*He goes to the piano and begins to play quietly.* HARRY *goes up on the little stage and listens to the music. After a while he begins a soft shoe dance.*)

NICK. What were you crying about?

JOE. My mother.

NICK. What about her?

JOE. She was dead. I stopped crying when they gave me the toys.

(NICK'S MOTHER, *a little old woman of sixty or so, dressed plainly in black, her face shining, comes in briskly, chattering loudly in Italian, gesturing.* NICK *is delighted to see her.*)

NICK'S MOTHER (*in Italian*). Everything all right, Nickie?

NICK (*in Italian*). Sure, Mamma.

(NICK'S MOTHER *leaves as gaily and as noisily as she came, after half a minute of loud Italian family talk.*)

JOE. Who was that?

NICK *(to* JOE, *proudly and a little sadly).* My mother. *(Still looking at the swinging doors.)*

JOE. What'd she say?

NICK. Nothing. Just wanted to see me. *(Pause.)* What do you want with that gun?

JOE. I study things, Nick.

(An old man who looks as if he might have been Kit Carson at one time walks in importantly, moves about, and finally stands at Joe's table.)

KIT CARSON. Murphy's the name. Just an old trapper. Mind if I sit down?

JOE. Be delighted. What'll you drink?

KIT CARSON *(sitting down).* Beer. Same as I've been drinking. And thanks.

JOE *(to* NICK). Glass of beer, Nick.

*(*NICK *brings the beer to the table,* KIT CARSON *swallows it in one swig, wipes his big white mustache with the back of his right hand.)*

KIT CARSON *(moving in).* I don't suppose you ever fell in love with a midget weighing thirty-nine pounds?

JOE *(studying the man).* Can't say I have, but have another beer.

KIT CARSON *(intimately).* Thanks, thanks. Down in Gallup, twenty years ago. Fellow by the name of Rufus Jenkins came to town with six white horses and two black ones. Said he wanted a man to break the horses for him because his left leg was wood and he couldn't do it. Had a meeting at Parker's Mercantile Store and finally came to blows, me and Henry Walpal. Bashed his head with a brass cuspidor and ran away to Mexico, but he didn't die.

Couldn't speak a word. Took up with a cattle-breeder named Diego, educated in California. Spoke the language better than you and me. Said, Your job, Murph, is to feed them prize bulls. I said, Fine, what'll I feed them? He said, Hay, lettuce, salt, beer, and aspirin.

Came to blows two days later over an accordion he claimed I stole. I had *borrowed* it. During the fight I busted it over his head; ruined one of the finest accordions I ever saw. Grabbed a horse and rode back across the border. Texas. Got to talking with a fellow who looked honest. Turned out to be a Ranger who was looking for me.

JOE. Yeah. You were saying, a thirty-nine-pound midget.

KIT CARSON. Will I ever forget that lady? Will I ever get over that amazon of small proportions?

JOE. Will you?

KIT CARSON. If I live to be sixty.

JOE. Sixty? You look more than sixty now.

KIT CARSON. That's trouble showing in my face. Trouble and complications. I was fifty-eight three months ago.

JOE. That accounts for it, then. Go ahead, tell me more.

KIT CARSON. Told the Texas Ranger my name was Rothstein, mining engineer from Pennsylvania, looking for something worth while. Mentioned two places in Houston. Nearly lost an eye early one morning, going down the stairs. Ran into a six-footer with an iron-claw where his right hand was supposed to be. Said, You broke up my home. Told him I was a stranger in Houston. The girls gathered at the top of the stairs to see a fight. Seven of them. Six feet and an iron claw. That's bad on the nerves. Kicked him in the mouth when he swung for my head with the claw. Would have lost an eye except for quick thinking. He rolled into the gutter and pulled a gun. Fired seven times. I was back upstairs. Left the place an hour later, dressed in silk and feathers, with a hat swung around over my face. Saw him standing on the corner, waiting. Said, Care for a wiggle? Said he didn't. I went on down the street and left town. I don't suppose you ever had to put a dress on to save your skin, did you?

JOE. No, and I never fell in love with a midget weighing thirty-nine pounds. Have another beer?

KIT CARSON. Thanks. (*Swallows glass of beer.*) Ever try to herd cattle on a bicycle?

JOE. No, I never got around to that.

KIT CARSON. Left Houston with sixty cents in my pocket, gift of a girl named Lucinda. Walked fourteen miles in fourteen hours. Big house with barb-wire all around, and big dogs. One thing I never could get around. Walked past the gate, anyway, from hunger and thirst. Dogs jumped up and came for me. Walked right into them, growing older every second. Went up to the door and knocked. Big negress opened the door, closed it quick. Said, On your way, white trash.

Knocked again. Said, On Your way. Again. On your way. Again.
This time the old man himself opened the door, ninety, if he
was a day. Sawed-off shotgun, too.

Said, I ain't looking for trouble, Father. I'm hungry and thirsty,
name's Cavanaugh.

Took me in and made mint juleps for the two of us.

Said, Living here alone, Father?

Said, Drink and ask no questions. Maybe I am and maybe I ain't.
You saw the lady. Draw your own conclusions.

I'd heard of that, but didn't wink out of tact. If I told you that
old Southern gentleman was my grandfather, you wouldn't believe me, would you?

JOE. I might.

KIT CARSON. Well, it so happens he wasn't. Would have been romantic if he had been, though.

JOE. Where did you herd cattle on a bicycle?

KIT CARSON. Toledo, Ohio, 1918.

JOE. Toledo, Ohio? They don't herd cattle in Toledo.

KIT CARSON. They don't anymore. They did in 1918. One fellow did,
leastaways. Bookkeeper named Sam Gold. Straight from the
East Side, New York. Sombrero, lariats, Bull Durham, two
head of cattle and two bicycles. Called his place The Gold Bar
Ranch, two acres, just outside the city limits.

That was the year of the War, you'll remember.

JOE. Yeah, I remember, but how about herding two cows on a
bicycle? How'd you do it?

KIT CARSON. Easiest thing in the world. Rode no hands. Had to,
otherwise couldn't lasso the cows. Worked for Sam Gold till the
cows ran away. Bicycles scared them. They went into Toledo.
Never saw hide nor hair of them again. Advertised in every
paper, but never got them back. Broke his heart. Sold both bikes
and returned to New York.

Took four acres from a deck of red cards and walked to town.
Poker. Fellow in the game named Chuck Collins, liked to
gamble. Told him with a smile I didn't suppose he'd care to
bet a hundred dollars I wouldn't hold four aces the next hand.
Called it. My cards were red on the blank side. The other cards
were blue. Plumb forgot all about it. Showed him four aces.
Ace of spades, ace of clubs, ace of diamonds, ace of hearts. I'll

remember them four cards if I live to be sixty. Would have been killed on the spot except for the hurricane that year.

JOE. Hurricane?

KIT CARSON. You haven't forgotten the Toledo hurricane of 1918, have you?

JOE. No. There was no hurricane in Toledo in 1918, or any other year.

KIT CARSON. For the love of God, then what do you suppose that commotion was? And how come I came to in Chicago, dream-walking down State Street?

JOE. I guess they scared you.

KIT CARSON. No, that wasn't it. You go back to the papers of November 1918, and I think you'll find there was a hurricane in Toledo. I remember sitting on the roof of a two-story house, floating northwest.

JOE (seriously). Northwest?

KIT CARSON. Now, son, don't tell me *you* don't believe me, either?

JOE (pause. *Very seriously, energetically and sharply.*) Of course I believe you. Living is an art. It's not bookkeeping. It takes a lot of rehearsing for a man to get to be himself.

KIT CARSON (*thoughtfully, smiling, and amazed*). You're the first man I've ever met who believes me.

JOE (seriously). Have another beer.

(TOM *comes in with the Rand-McNally book, the revolver, and the box of cartridges.* KIT *goes to bar.*)

JOE (to TOM). Did you give her the toys?

TOM. Yeah, I gave them to her.

JOE. Did she stop crying?

TOM. No. She started crying harder than ever.

JOE. That's funny. I wonder why.

TOM. Joe, if I was a minute earlier, Frankie would have taken the bet and now we'd have about a thousand five hundred dollars. How much of it would you have given me, Joe?

JOE. If she'd marry you—*all* of it.

TOM. Would you, Joe?

JOE (*opening packages, examining book first, and revolver next*). Sure. In this realm there's only one subject, and you're it. It's my duty to see that my subject is happy.

TOM. Joe, do you think we'll ever have eighty dollars for a race sometime again when there's a fifteen-to-one shot that we like, weather good, track fast, they get off to a good start, our horse doesn't get a call till the stretch, we think we're going to lose all that money, and then it wins, by a nose?

JOE. I didn't quite get that.

TOM. You know what I mean.

JOE. You mean the impossible. No, Tom, we won't. We were just a little late, that's all.

TOM. We might, Joe.

JOE. It's not likely.

TOM. Then how am I ever going to make enough money to marry her?

JOE. I don't know, Tom. Maybe you aren't.

TOM. Joe, I got to marry Kitty. (*Shaking his head*). You ought to see the crazy room she lives in.

JOE. What kind of a room is it?

TOM. It's little. It crowds you in. It's bad, Joe. Kitty don't belong in a place like that.

JOE. You want to take her away from there?

TOM. Yeah. I want her to live in a house where there's room enough to live. Kitty ought to have a garden, or something.

JOE. You want to take care of her?

TOM. Yeah, sure, Joe. I ought to take care of somebody good that makes me feel like *I'm* somebody.

JOE. That means you'll have to get a job. What can you do?

TOM. I finished high school, but I don't know what I can do.

JOE. Sometimes when you think about it, what do you think you'd like to do?

TOM. Just sit around like you, Joe, and have somebody run errands for me and drink champagne and take things easy and never be broke and never worry about money.

JOE. That's a noble ambition.

NICK (*to* JOE). How do you do it?

JOE. I really don't know, but I think you've got to have the full co-operation of the Good Lord.

NICK. I can't understand the way you talk.

TOM. Joe, shall I go back and see if I can get her to stop crying?

JOE. Give me a hand and I'll go with you.

TOM (*amazed*). What! You're going to get up already?

JOE. She's crying, isn't she?

TOM. She's crying. Worse than ever now.

JOE. I thought the toys would stop her.

TOM. I've seen you sit in one place from four in the morning till two the next morning.

JOE. At my best, Tom, I don't travel by foot. That's all. Come on. Give me a hand. I'll find some way to stop her from crying.

TOM (*helping* JOE.) Joe, I never did tell you. You're a different kind of guy.

JOE (*swiftly, a little angry*). Don't be silly. I don't understand things. I'm trying to understand them.

(JOE *is a little drunk. They go out together. The lights go down slowly, while* WESLEY *plays the piano, and come up slowly on:*)

ACT THREE

A *cheap bed in Nick's to indicate room 21 of The New York Hotel, upstairs, around the corner from Nick's. The bed can be at the center of Nick's or up on the little stage. Everything in Nick's is the same, except that all the people are silent, immobile and in darkness, except* WESLEY *who is playing the piano softly and sadly.* KITTY DUVAL, *in a dress she has carried around with her from the early days in Ohio, is seated on the bed, tying a ribbon in her hair. She looks at herself in a hand mirror. She is deeply grieved at the change she sees in herself. She takes off the ribbon, angry and hurt. She lifts a book from the bed and tries to read. She begins to sob again. She picks up an old picture of herself and looks at it. Sobs harder than ever, falling on the bed and burying her face. There is a knock, as if at the door.*

KITTY (*sobbing*). Who is it?

TOM'S VOICE. Kitty, it's me. Tom. Me and Joe.

(JOE, *followed by* TOM, *comes to the bed quietly.* JOE *is holding a rather large toy carousel.* JOE *studies* KITTY *a moment.*)

(*He sets the toy carousel on the floor, at the foot of Kitty's bed.*)

TOM (*standing over* KITTY *and bending down close to her*). Don't cry any more, Kitty.

KITTY (*not looking, sobbing*). I don't like this life.

(JOE *starts the carousel which makes a strange, sorrowful, tinkling music. The music begins slowly, becomes swift, gradually slows down, and ends.* JOE *himself is interested in the toy, watches and listens to it carefully.*)

TOM (*eagerly*). Kitty. Joe got up from his chair at Nick's just to get you a toy and come here. This one makes music. We rode all over town in a cab to get it. Listen.

(KITTY *sits up slowly, listening, while* TOM *watches her. Everything happens slowly and somberly.* KITTY *notices the photograph of herself when she was a little girl. Lifts it, and looks at it again.*)

TOM (*looking*). Who's that little girl, Kitty?

KITTY. That's me. When I was seven.

(KITTY *hands the photo to* TOM.)

TOM (*looking, smiling*). Gee, you're pretty, Kitty.

(JOE *reaches up for the photograph, which* TOM *hands to him.* TOM *returns to* KITTY *whom he finds as pretty now as she was at seven.* JOE *studies the photograph.* KITTY *looks up at* TOM. *There is no doubt that they really love one another.* JOE *looks up at them.*)

KITTY. Tom?

TOM (*eagerly*). Yeah, Kitty.

KITTY. Tom, when you were a little boy what did you want to be?

TOM. (*a little bewildered, but eager to please her*). What, Kitty?

KITTY. Do you remember when you were a little boy?

TOM (*thoughtfully*). Yeah, I remember sometimes, Kitty.

KITTY. What did you want to be?

TOM (*looks at* JOE. JOE *holds Tom's eyes a moment. Then* TOM *is able to speak*). Sometimes I wanted to be a locomotive engineer. Sometimes I wanted to be a policeman.

KITTY. I wanted to be a great actress. (*She looks up into Tom's face.*) Tom, didn't you ever want to be a doctor?

TOM (*looks at* JOE. JOE *holds Tom's eyes again, encouraging Tom by his serious expression to go on talking*). Yeah, now I remember. Sure, Kitty. I wanted to be a doctor—*once.*

KITTY (*smiling sadly*). I'm so glad. Because I wanted to be an actress and have a young doctor come to the theater and see me and fall in love with me and send me flowers.

(JOE *pantomimes to* TOM, *demanding that he go on talking.*)

TOM. I would do that, Kitty.

KITTY. I wouldn't know who it was, and then one day I'd see him in the street and fall in love with him. I wouldn't know *he* was the one who was in love with me. I'd think about him all the time. I'd dream about him. I'd dream of being near him the rest of my life. I'd dream of having children that looked like him. I wouldn't be an actress all the time. Only until I found him and fell in love with him. After that we'd take a train and go to beautiful cities and see the wonderful people everywhere and give money to the poor and whenever people were sick he'd go to them and make them well again.

(TOM *looks at* JOE, *bewildered, confused, and full of sorrow.* KITTY *is deep in memory, almost in a trance.*)

JOE (*gently*). Talk to her, Tom. Be the wonderful young doctor she dreamed about and never found. Go ahead. Correct the errors of the world.

TOM. Joe. (*Pathetically.*) I don't know what to say.

(*There is rowdy singing in the hall. A loud young* VOICE *sings:* "Sailing, sailing, over the bounding main.")

VOICE. Kitty. Oh Kitty! (KITTY *stirs, shocked, coming out of the trance.*) Where the hell are you? Oh, Kitty.

(TOM *jumps up, furiously.*)

WOMAN'S VOICE (*in the hall*). Who you looking for Sailor Boy?

VOICE. The most beautiful lay in the world.

WOMAN'S VOICE. Don't go any further.

VOICE (*with impersonal contempt*). You? No. Not you. Kitty. You stink.

WOMAN'S VOICE (*rasping, angry*). Don't you dare talk to me that way. You pickpocket.

VOICE (*still impersonal, but louder*). Oh, I see. Want to get tough, hey? Close the door. Go hide.

WOMAN'S VOICE. You pickpocket. All of you.

(*The door slams.*)

VOICE (*roaring with laughter which is very sad*). Oh—Kitty. Room 21. Where the hell is that room?

TOM (*to* JOE). Joe, I'll kill him.

KITTY (*fully herself again, terribly frightened*). Who is it?

(*She looks long and steadily at* TOM *and* JOE. TOM *is standing, excited and angry.* JOE *is completely at ease, his expression full of pity.* KITTY *buries her face in the bed.*)

JOE (*gently*). Tom. Just take him away.
VOICE. Here it is. Number 21. Three naturals. Heaven. My blue heaven. The west, a nest, and you. Just Molly and me.

(*Tragically.*) Ah, to hell with everything.

(*A young* SAILOR, *a good-looking boy of no more than twenty or so, who is only drunk and lonely, comes to the bed, singing sadly.*)

SAILOR. Hi-ya, Kitty. (*Pause.*) Oh. Visitors. Sorry. A thousand apologies. (*To* KITTY.) I'll come back later.
TOM (*taking him by the shoulders, furiously*). If you do, I'll kill you.

(JOE *holds* TOM. TOM *pushes the frightened boy away.*)

JOE (*somberly*). Tom. You stay here with Kitty. I'm going down to Union Square to hire an automobile. I'll be back in a few minutes. We'll ride out to the ocean and watch the sun go down. Then we'll ride down the Great Highway to Half Moon Bay. We'll have supper down there, and you and Kitty can dance.
TOM (*stupefied, unable to express his amazement and gratitude*). Joe, you mean you're going to go on an errand for me? You mean you're not going to send me?
JOE. That's right.

(*He gestures toward* KITTY, *indicating that* TOM *shall talk to her, protect the innocence in her which is in so much danger when* TOM *isn't near, which* TOM *loves so deeply.* JOE *leaves.* TOM *studies* KITTY, *his face becoming child-like and somber. He sets the carousel into motion, listens, watching* KITTY, *who lifts herself slowly, looking only at* TOM. TOM *lifts the turning carousel and moves it slowly toward* KITTY, *as though the toy were his heart. The piano music comes up loudly and the lights go down, while* HARRY *is heard dancing swiftly.*)

BLACKOUT

ACT FOUR

A *little later.*

WESLEY, *the colored boy, is at the piano.*

HARRY *is on the little stage, dancing.*

NICK *is behind the bar.*

The ARAB *is in his place.*

KIT CARSON *is asleep on his folded arms.*

The DRUNKARD *comes in. Goes to the telephone for the nickel that might be in the return-chute.* NICK *comes to take him out. He gestures for* NICK *to hold on a minute. Then produces a half dollar.* NICK *goes behind the bar to serve the* DRUNKARD *whiskey.*

THE DRUNKARD. To the old, God bless them.

(Another.) To the new, God love them.

(Another.) To—children and small animals, like little dogs that don't bite.

(Another. Loudly.) To *reforestation.*

(Searches for money. Finds some.) To—

President Taft. *(He goes out.)*

(The telephone rings.)

KIT CARSON *(jumping up, fighting).* Come on, *all* of you, if you're looking for trouble. I never asked for quarter and I always gave it.
NICK *(reproachfully).* Hey, Kit Carson.
DUDLEY *(on the phone).* Hello. Who? Nick? Yes. He's here. *(To* NICK.) It's for you. I think it's important.
NICK *(going to the phone).* Important! *What's* important?
DUDLEY. He sounded like big-shot.
NICK. Big *what?* *(To* WESLEY *and* HARRY.) Hey, you. Quiet. I want to hear this important stuff.

(WESLEY *stops playing the piano.* HARRY *stops dancing.* KIT CARSON *comes close to* NICK.)

KIT CARSON. If there's anything I can do, name it. I'll do it for you. I'm fifty-eight years old; been through three wars; married four times; the father of countless children whose *names* I don't even know. I've got no money. I live from hand to mouth. But if there's anything I can do, name it. I'll do it.

NICK (*patiently*). Listen, Pop. For a moment, please sit down and go back to sleep—*for me.*

KIT CARSON. I can do that, too.

(*He sits down, folds his arms, and puts his head into them. But not for long. As* NICK *begins to talk, he listens carefully, gets to his feet, and then begins to express in pantomime the moods of each of* Nick's *remarks.*)

NICK (*on phone*). Yeah? (*Pause.*) Who? Oh, I see (*Listens.*) Why don't you leave them alone? (*Listens.*) The church-people? Well, to hell with the church-people. I'm a Catholic myself. (*Listens.*) All right. I'll send them away. I'll tell them to lay low for a couple of days. Yeah, I know how it is. (*Nick's daughter* ANNA *comes in shyly, looking at her father, and stands unnoticed by the piano.*) What? (*Very angry.*) Listen. I don't like that Blick. He was here this morning, and I told him not to come back. I'll keep the girls out of here. You keep Blick out of here. (*Listens.*) I know his brother-in-law is important, but I don't want him to come down here. He looks for trouble everywhere, and he always finds it. I don't break any laws, I've got a dive in the lousiest part of town. Five years nobody's been robbed, murdered, or gypped. I leave people alone. Your swanky joints uptown make trouble for you every night. (NICK *gestures to* WESLEY *—keeps listening on the phone—puts his hand over the mouthpiece. To* WESLEY *and* HARRY.) Start playing again. My ears have got a headache. Go into your dance, son. (WESLEY *begins to play again.* HARRY *begins to dance.* NICK, *into mouthpiece.*) Yeah. I'll keep them out. Just see that Blick doesn't come around and start something. (*Pause.*) O.K. (*He hangs up.*)

KIT CARSON. Trouble coming?

NICK. That lousy Vice Squad again. It's that gorilla Blick.

KIT CARSON. Anybody at all. You can count on me. What kind of a gorilla is this gorilla Blick?

NICK. Very dignified. Toenails on his fingers.

ANNA *(to* KIT CARSON, *with great warm, beautiful pride, pointing at* NICK). That's my father.

KIT CARSON *(leaping with amazement at the beautiful voice, the wondrous face, the magnificent event).* Well, bless your heart, child. Bless your lovely heart. I had a little daughter point me out in a crowd once.

NICK *(surprised).* Anna. What the hell are you doing here? Get back home where you belong and help Grandma cook me some supper.

(ANNA *smiles at her father, understanding him, knowing that his words are words of love. She turns and goes, looking at him all the way out, as much as to say that she would cook for him the rest of her life.* NICK *stares at the swinging doors.* KIT CARSON *moves toward them, two or three steps.* ANNA *pushes open one of the doors and peeks in, to look at her father again. She waves to him. Turns and runs.* NICK *is very sad. He doesn't know what to do. He gets a glass and a bottle. Pours himself a drink. Swallows some. It isn't enough, so he pours more and swallows the whole drink.)*

(To himself.) My beautiful, beautiful baby. Anna, she is you again. *(He brings out a handkerchief, touches his eyes, and blows his nose.* KIT CARSON *moves close to* NICK, *watching Nick's face.* NICK *looks at him. Loudly, almost making* KIT CARSON *jump.)* You're broke, aren't you?

KIT CARSON. Always. Always.

NICK. All right. Go into the kitchen and give Sam a hand. Eat some food and when you come back you can have a couple of beers.

KIT CARSON *(studying* NICK). Anything at all. I know a good man when I see one.

(He goes.)

(ELSIE MANDELSPIEGEL *comes into Nick's. She is a beautiful, dark girl, with a sorrowful, wise, dreaming face, almost on the verge of tears, and full of pity. There is an aura of dream about her. She moves softly and gently, as if everything around her were unreal and pathetic.* DUDLEY *doesn't notice her for a moment or two. When he does finally see her, he is so amazed, he can barely move or speak. Her presence has the effect of changing him completely. He gets up from his chair, as if in a trance, and walks toward her, smiling sadly.)*

ELSIE *(looking at him).* Hello, Dudley.

DUDLEY *(brokenhearted).* Elsie.

ELSIE. I'm sorry. *(Explaining.)* So many people are sick. Last night a little boy died. I love you, but— *(She gestures, trying to indicate how hopeless love is. They sit down.)*

DUDLEY *(staring at her, stunned and quieted).* Elsie. You'll never know how glad I am to see you. Just to *see* you. *(Pathetically.)* I was afraid I'd never see you again. It was driving me crazy. I didn't want to live. Honest. *(He shakes his head mournfully, with dumb and beautiful affection.* TWO STREETWALKERS *come in, and pause near* DUDLEY, *at the bar.)* I know. You told me before, but I can't help it, Elsie. I love you.

ELSIE *(quietly, somberly, gently, with great compassion).* I know you love me, and I love you, but don't you see love is impossible in this world?

DUDLEY. Maybe it isn't, Elsie.

ELSIE. Love is for birds. They have wings to fly away on when it's time for flying. For tigers in the jungle because they don't know their end. We know *our* end. Every night I watch over poor, dying men. I hear them breathing, crying, talking in their sleep. Crying for air and water and love, for mother and field and sunlight. *We* can never know love or greatness. We *should* know both.

DUDLEY *(deeply moved by her words).* Elsie, I love you.

ELSIE. You want to live. *I* want to live, too, but where? Where can we escape our poor world?

DUDLEY. Elsie, we'll find a place.

ELSIE *(smiling at him).* All right. We'll try again. We'll go together to a room in a cheap hotel, and dream that the world is beautiful, and that living is full of love and greatness. But in the morning, can we forget debts, and duties, and the cost of ridiculous things?

DUDLEY *(with blind faith).* Sure, we can, Elsie.

ELSIE. All right, Dudley. Of course. Come on. The time for the new pathetic war has come. Let's hurry, before they dress you, stand you in line, hand you a gun, and have you kill and be killed.

(ELSIE looks at him gently, and takes his hand. DUDLEY *embraces her shyly, as if he might hurt her. They go, as if they were a couple of young animals. There is a moment of silence. One of the* STREET-WALKERS *bursts out laughing.)*

KILLER. Nick, what the hell kind of a joint are you running?

NICK. Well, it's not out of the world. It's on a street in a city, and people come and go. They bring whatever they've got with them and they say what they must say.

THE OTHER STREETWALKER. It's floozies like her that raise hell with our racket.

NICK (*remembering*). Oh, yeah. Finnegan telephoned.

KILLER. That mouse in elephant's body?

THE OTHER STREETWALKER. What the hell does *he* want?

NICK. Spend your time at the movies for the next couple of days.

KILLER. They're all lousy. (*Mocking.*) All about love.

NICK. Lousy or not lousy, for a couple of days the flat-foots are going to be romancing you, so stay out of here, and lay low.

KILLER. I always was a pushover for a man in uniform, with a badge, a club and a gun.

(KRUPP *comes into the place. The girls put down their drinks.*)

NICK. O.K., get going.

(*The* GIRLS *begin to leave and meet* KRUPP.)

THE OTHER STREETWALKER. We was just going.

KILLER. We was formerly models at Magnin's. (*They go.*)

KRUPP (*at the bar*). The strike isn't enough, so they've got to put us on the tails of the girls, too. I don't know. I wish to God I was back in the Sunset holding the hands of kids going home from school, where I belong. I don't like trouble. Give me a beer.

(NICK *gives him a beer. He drinks some.*)

KRUPP. Right now, McCarthy, my best friend, is with sixty strikers who want to stop the finks who are going to try to unload the *Mary Luckenbach* tonight. Why the hell McCarthy ever became a longshoreman instead of a professor of some kind is something I'll never know.

NICK. Cowboys and Indians, cops and robbers, longshoremen and finks.

KRUPP. They're all guys who are trying to be happy; trying to make a living; support a family; bring up children; enjoy sleep. Go to a movie; take a drive on Sunday. They're all good guys, so out of nowhere, comes trouble. All they want is a chance to get out of debt and relax in front of a radio while Amos and Andy go through their act. What the hell do they always want to make trouble for? I been thinking everything over, Nick, and you know what I think?

NICK. No. What?

KRUPP. I think we're all crazy. It came to me while I was on my way to Pier 27. All of a sudden it hit me like a ton of bricks. A thing like that never happened to me before. Here we are in this wonderful world, full of all the wonderful things—here we are—all of us, and look at us. Just look at us. We're crazy. We're nuts. We've got everything, but we always feel lousy and dissatisfied just the same.

NICK. Of course we're crazy. Even so, we've got to go on living together.

(He waves at the people in his joint.)

KRUPP. There's no hope. I don't suppose it's right for an officer of the law to feel the way I feel, but, by God, right or not right, that's how I feel. Why are we all so lousy? This is a good world. It's wonderful to get up in the morning and go out for a little walk and smell the trees and see the streets and the kids going to school and the clouds in the sky. It's wonderful just to be able to move around and whistle a song if you feel like it, or maybe try to sing one. This is a nice world. So why do they make all the trouble?

NICK. I don't know. Why?

KRUPP. We're crazy, that's why. We're no good any more. All the corruption everywhere. The poor kids selling themselves. A couple of years ago they were in grammar school. Everybody trying to get a lot of money in a hurry. Everybody betting the horses. Nobody going quietly for a little walk to the ocean. Nobody taking things easy and not wanting to make some kind of a killing. Nick, I'm going to quit being a cop. Let somebody else keep law and order. The stuff I hear about at headquarters. I'm thirty-seven years old, and I still can't get used to it. The only trouble is, the wife'll raise hell.

NICK. Ah, the wife.

KRUPP. She's a wonderful woman, Nick. We've got two of the swellest boys in the world. Twelve and seven years old. *(The ARAB gets up and moves closer to listen.)*

NICK. I didn't know that.

KRUPP. Sure. But what'll I do? I've wanted to quit for seven years. I wanted to quit the day they began putting me through the school. I didn't quit. What'll I do if I quit? Where's money going to be coming in from?

NICK. That's one of the reason's we're all crazy. We don't know where it's going to be coming in from, except from wherever it happens to be coming in from at the time, which we don't usually like.

KRUPP. Every once in a while I catch myself being mean, hating people just because they're down and out, broke and hungry, sick or drunk. And then when I'm with the stuffed shirts at headquarters, all of a sudden I'm nice to them, trying to make an impression. On who? People I don't like. And I feel disgusted. *(With finality.)* I'm going to quit. That's all. Quit. Out. I'm going to give them back the uniform and the gadgets that go with it. I don't want any part of it. This is a good world. What do they want to make all the trouble for all the time?

ARAB *(quietly, gently, with great understanding)*. No foundation. All the way down the line.

KRUPP. What?

ARAB. No foundation. No foundation.

KRUPP. I'll say there's no foundation.

ARAB. All the way down the line.

KRUPP *(to NICK)*. Is that all he ever says?

NICK. That's all he's been saying *this* week.

KRUPP. What is he, anyway?

NICK. He's an Arab, or something like that.

KRUPP. No, I mean what's he do for a living?

NICK *(to ARAB)*. What do you do for a living, brother?

ARAB. Work. Work all my life. All my life, work. From small boy to old man, work. In old country, work. In new country, work. In New York. Pittsburgh. Detroit. Chicago. Imperial Valley. San Francisco. Work. No beg. Work. For what? Nothing. Three boys in old country. Twenty years, not see. Lost. Dead. Who knows? What. What-not. No foundation. All the way down the line.

KRUPP. What'd he say last week?

NICK. Didn't say anything. Played the harmonica.

ARAB. Old country song, I play. *(He brings a harmonica from his back pocket.)*

KRUPP. Seems like a nice guy.

NICK. Nicest guy in the world.

KRUPP *(bitterly)*. But crazy. Just like all the rest of us. Stark raving mad.

(WESLEY and HARRY long ago stopped playing and dancing. They sat

at a table together and talked for a while; then began playing casino or rummy. When the ARAB *begins his solo on the harmonica, they stop their game to listen.*)

WESLEY. You hear that?

HARRY. That's *something.*

WESLEY. That's crying. That's crying.

HARRY. I want to make people laugh.

WESLEY. That's deep, deep crying. That's crying a long time ago. That's crying a thousand years ago. Some place five thousand miles away.

HARRY. Do you think you can play to that?

WESLEY. I want to *sing* to that, but I can't *sing.*

HARRY. You try and play to that. I'll try to dance.

(WESLEY *goes to the piano, and after closer listening, he begins to accompany the harmonica solo.* HARRY *goes to the little stage and after a few efforts begins to dance to the song. This keeps up quietly for some time.*)

(KRUPP *and* NICK *have been silent, and deeply moved.*)

KRUPP (*softly*). Well, anyhow, Nick.

NICK. Hmmmmmmmm?

KRUPP. What I said. Forget it.

NICK. Sure.

KRUPP. It gets me down once in a while.

NICK. No harm in talking.

KRUPP (*the* POLICEMAN *again, loudly*). Keep the girls out of here.

NICK (*loud and friendly*). Take it easy.

(*The music and dancing are now at their height.*)

CURTAIN

ACT FIVE

That evening. Fog-horns are heard throughout the scene. A man in evening clothes and a top hat, and his woman, also in evening clothes, are entering.

WILLIE *is still at the marble-game.* NICK *is behind the bar.* JOE *is*

at his table, looking at the book of maps of the countries of Europe.
The box containing the revolver and the box containing the cartridges
are on the table, beside his glass. He is at peace, his hat tilted back on
his head, a calm expression on his face. TOM *is leaning against the*
bar, dreaming of love and Kitty. The ARAB *is gone.* WESLEY *and*
HARRY *are gone.* KIT CARSON *is watching the boy at the marble-game.*

LADY. Oh, come on, please.

(The gentleman follows miserably.)

(The SOCIETY MAN *and* WIFE *take a table.* NICK *gives them a menu.)*

(Outside, in the street, the Salvation Army people are playing a song.
Big drum, tambourines, cornet and singing. They are singing "The
Blood of the Lamb." The music and words come into the place faintly
and comically. This is followed by an old sinner testifying. It is the
DRUNKARD. *His words are not intelligible, but his message is unmis-*
takable. He is saved. He wants to sin no more. And so on.)

DRUNKARD *(testifying, unmistakably drunk).* Brothers and sisters. I was
a sinner. I chewed tobacco and chased women. Oh, I sinned,
brothers and sisters. And then I was saved. Saved by the Salvation
Army. God forgive me.

JOE. Let's see now. Here's a city. Pribor. Czecho-slovakia. Little, lovely,
lonely Czecho-slovakia. I wonder what kind of a place Pribor was?
(Calling.) Pribor! *Pribor!* (TOM *leaps.)*

LADY. What's the matter with him?

MAN *(crossing his legs, as if he ought to go to the men's room).* Drunk.

TOM. Who you calling, Joe?

JOE. Pribor.

TOM. Who's Pribor?

JOE. He's a Czech. And a Slav. A Czechoslovakian.

LADY. How interesting.

MAN *(uncrosses legs.)* He's drunk.

JOE. Tom, Pribor's a city in Czecho-slovakia.

TOM. Oh. *(Pause.)* You sure were nice to her, Joe.

JOE. Kitty Duval? She's one of the finest people in the world.

TOM. It sure was nice of you to hire an automobile and take us for a
drive along the ocean-front and down to Half Moon Bay.

JOE. Those three hours were the most delightful, the most somber,
and the most beautiful I have ever known.

TOM. Why, Joe?

JOE. Why? I'm a student. (*Lifting his voice.*) Tom. (*Quietly.*) I'm a student. I study all things. All. All. And when my study reveals something of beauty in a place or in a person where by all rights only ugliness or death should be revealed, then I know how full of goodness this life is. And that's a good thing to know. That's a truth I shall always seek to verify.

LADY. Are you *sure* he's drunk?

MAN (*crossing his legs*). He's either drunk, or just naturally crazy.

TOM. Joe?

JOE. Yeah.

TOM. You won't get sore or anything?

JOE (*impatiently*). What is it, Tom?

TOM. Joe, where do you get all that money? You paid for the automobile. You paid for supper and the two bottles of champagne at the Half Moon Bay Restaurant. You moved Kitty out of the New York Hotel around the corner to the St. Francis Hotel on Powell Street. I saw you pay her rent. I saw you give her money for new clothes. Where do you get all that money, Joe? Three years now and I've never asked.

JOE (*looking at* TOM *sorrowfully, a little irritated, not so much with* TOM *as with the world and himself, his own superiority. He speaks clearly, slowly and solemnly*). Now don't be a fool, Tom. Listen carefully. If anybody's got any money—to hoard or to throw away—you can be sure he stole it from other people. Not from rich people who can spare it, but from poor people who can't. From their lives and from their dreams. I'm no exception. I *earned* the money I throw away. I stole it like everybody else does. I hurt people to get it. Loafing around this way, I *still* earn money. The money itself earns *more*. I *still* hurt people. I don't know who they are, or where they are. If I did, I'd feel worse than I do. I've got a Christian conscience in a world that's got no conscience at all. The world's trying to get some sort of a *social* conscience, but it's having a devil of a time trying to do *that*. I've got money. I'll always have money, as long as this world stays the way it is. I don't work. I don't make anything. (*He sips.*) I drink. I worked when I was a kid. I worked *hard*. I mean hard, Tom. People are supposed to enjoy living. I got tired. (*He lifts the gun and looks at it while he talks.*) I decided to get even on the world. Well, you can't enjoy living unless you work. Unless you do something. I don't do anything. I don't *want* to do anything any more.

There isn't anything I can do that won't make me feel embarrassed. Because I can't do simple, good things. I haven't the patience. And I'm too smart. Money is the guiltiest thing in the world. It stinks. Now, don't ever bother me about it again.

TOM. I didn't mean to make you feel bad, Joe.

JOE (*slowly*). Here. Take this gun out in the street and give it to some worthy hold-up man.

LADY. What's he saying?

MAN (*uncrosses legs*). You wanted to visit a honky-tonk. Well, *this* is a honky-tonk. (*To the world.*) Married twenty-eight years and she's still looking for adventure.

TOM. How should I know who's a hold-up man?

JOE. Take it away. Give it to somebody.

TOM (*bewildered*). Do I *have* to *give* it to somebody?

JOE. Of course.

TOM. Can't I take it back and get some of our money?

JOE. Don't talk like a business man. Look around and find somebody who appears to be in need of a gun and give it to him. It's a good gun, isn't it?

TOM. The man said it was, but how can I tell who needs a gun?

JOE. Tom, you've seen good people who needed guns, haven't you?

TOM. I don't remember. Joe, I might give it to the wrong kind of guy. He might do something crazy.

JOE. All right. I'll find somebody myself. (TOM *rises.*) Here's some money. Go get me this week's *Life, Liberty, Time,* and six or seven packages of chewing gum.

TOM (*swiftly, in order to remember each item*). Life, Liberty, Time, and six or seven packages of chewing gum?

JOE. That's right.

TOM. All that chewing gum? What kind?

JOE. Any kind. Mix 'em up. All kinds.

TOM. Licorice, too?

JOE. Licorice, by all means.

TOM. Juicy Fruit?

JOE. Juicy Fruit.

TOM. Tutti-frutti?

JOE. Is there such a gum?

TOM. I think so.

JOE. All right. Tutti-frutti, too. Get *all* the kinds. Get as many kinds as they're selling.

TOM. *Life, Liberty, Time,* and all the different kinds of gum. *(He begins to go.)*

JOE *(calling after him loudly).* Get some jelly beans too. All the different colors.

TOM. All right, Joe.

JOE. And the longest panatela cigar you can find. Six of them.

TOM. Panatela. I got it.

JOE. Give a news-kid a dollar.

TOM. O.K., Joe.

JOE. Give some old man a dollar.

TOM. O.K., Joe.

JOE. Give them Salvation Army people in the street a couple of dollars and ask them to sing that song that goes— *(He sings loudly.)* Let the lower lights be burning, send a gleam across the wave.

TOM *(swiftly).* Let the lower lights be burning, send a gleam across the wave.

JOE. That's it. *(He goes on with the song, very loudly and religiously.)* Some poor, dying, struggling seaman, you may rescue, you may save. *(Halts.)*

TOM. O.K., Joe. I got it. *Life, Liberty, Time,* all the kinds of gum they're selling, jelly beans, six panatela cigars, a dollar for a news-kid, a dollar for an old man, two dollars for the Salvation Army. *(Going.)* Let the lower lights be burning, send a gleam across the wave.

JOE. That's it.

LADY. He's absolutely insane.

MAN *(wearily crossing legs).* You asked me to take you to a honky-tonk, instead of to the Mark Hopkins. You're *here* in a honky-tonk. I can't help it if he's crazy. Do you want to go back to where people *aren't* crazy?

LADY. No, not just yet.

MAN. Well, all right then. Don't be telling me every minute that he's crazy.

LADY. You needn't be huffy about it.

(MAN refuses to answer, uncrosses legs.)

(When JOE began to sing, KIT CARSON turned away from the marble-game and listened. While the man and woman are arguing he comes over to Joe's table.)

KIT CARSON. Presbyterian?

JOE. I attended a Presbyterian Sunday School.

KIT CARSON. Fond of singing?

JOE. On occasion. Have a drink?

KIT CARSON. Thanks.

JOE. Get a glass and sit down.

(KIT CARSON *gets a glass from* NICK, *returns to the table, sits down,* JOE *pours him a drink, they touch glasses just as the Salvation Army people begin to fulfill the request. They sip some champagne, and at the proper moment begin to sing the song together, sipping champagne, raising hell with the tune, swinging it, and so on. The* SOCIETY LADY *joins them, and is stopped by her* HUSBAND.)

Always was fond of that song. Used to sing it at the top of my voice. Never saved a seaman in my life.

KIT CARSON (*flirting with the* SOCIETY LADY *who loves it*). I saved a seaman once. Well, he wasn't exactly a seaman. He was a darky named Wellington. Heavy-set sort of a fellow. Nice personality, but no friends to speak of. Not until I came along, at any rate. In New Orleans. In the summer of the year 1899. No. Ninety-eight. I was a lot younger of course, and had no mustache, but was regarded by many people as a man of means.

JOE. Know anything about guns?

KIT CARSON (*flirting*). All there is to know. Didn't fight the Ojibways for nothing. Up there in the Lake Takalooca Country, in Michi- gan. (*Remembering.*) Along about in 1881 or two. Fought 'em right up to the shore of the Lake. Made 'em swim for Canada. One fellow in particular, an Indian named Harry Daisy.

JOE (*opening the box containing the revolver*). What sort of a gun would you say this is? Any good?

KIT CARSON (*at sight of gun, leaping*). Yep. That looks like a pretty nice hunk of shooting iron. That's a six-shooter. Shot a man with a six-shooter once. Got him through the palm of his right hand. Lifted his arm to wave to a friend. Thought it was a bird. Fellow named, I believe, Carroway. Larrimore Carroway.

JOE. Know how to work one of these things? (*He offers* KIT CARSON *the revolver, which is old and enormous.*)

KIT CARSON (*laughing at the absurd question*). Know how to work it? Hand me that little gun, son, and I'll show you all about it. (JOE *hands* KIT *the revolver.*) (*Importantly.*) Let's see now. This is probably a new kind of six-shooter. After my time. Haven't nicked an Indian in years. I believe this here place is supposed to move out. (*He fools around and get the barrel out for loading.*) That's it. There it is.

JOE. Look all right?

KIT CARSON. It's a good gun. You've got a good gun there, son. I'll explain it to you. You see these holes? Well, that's where you put the cartridges.

JOE (*taking some cartridges out of the box*). Here. Show me how it's done.

KIT CARSON (*a little impatiently*). Well, son, you take 'em one by one and put 'em in the holes, like this. There's one. Two. Three. Four. Five. Six. Then you get the barrel back in place. Then cock it. Then all you got to do is aim and fire.

(*He points the gun at the* LADY *and* GENTLEMAN *who scream and stand up, scaring* KIT CARSON *into paralysis.*)

(*The gun is loaded, but uncocked.*)

JOE. It's all set?

KIT CARSON. Ready to kill.

JOE. Let me hold it.

(KIT *hands* JOE *the gun. The* LADY *and* GENTLEMAN *watch, in terror.*)

KIT CARSON. Careful, now, son. Don't cock it. Many a man's lost an eye fooling with a loaded gun. Fellow I used to know named Danny Donovan lost a nose. Ruined his whole life. Hold it firm. Squeeze the trigger. Don't snap it. Spoils your aim.

JOE. Thanks. Let's see if I can unload it.

(*He begins to unload it.*)

KIT CARSON. Of course you can.

(JOE *unloads the revolver, looks at it very closely, puts the cartridges back into the box.*)

JOE (*looking at gun*). I'm mighty grateful to you. Always wanted to see one of those things close up. Is it really a good one?

KIT CARSON. It's a beaut, son.

JOE (*aims the empty gun at a bottle on the bar*). Bang!

WILLIE (*at the marble-game, as the machine groans*). Oh, Boy (*Loudly, triumphantly.*) There you are, Nick. Thought I couldn't do it, hey? *Now*, watch. *(The machine begins to make a special kind of noise. Lights go on and off. Some red, some green. A bell rings loudly six times.)* One. Two. Three. Four, Five. Six. *(An American flag jumps up.* WILLIE *comes to attention. Salutes.)* Oh, boy, what a beautiful country. *(A loud music-box version of the song* "America." JOE, KIT, *and the* LADY *get to their feet.) (Singing.)* My country, 'tis of thee, sweet land of liberty, of thee I sing. *(Everything quiets down. The flag goes back into the machine.* WILLIE *is thrilled, amazed, delighted.* EVERYBODY *has watched the performance of the defeated machine from wherever he happened to be when the performance began.* WILLIE, *looking around at everybody, as if they had all been on the side of the machine.)* O.K. How's that? I knew I could do it. *(To* NICK.*)* Six nickels.

*(*NICK *hands him six nickels.* WILLIE *goes over to* JOE *and* KIT.*)* Took me a little while, but I finally did it. It's scientific, really. With a little skill a man can make a modest living beating the marble-games. Not that that's what I want to do. I just don't like the idea of anything getting the best of me. A machine or anything else. Myself, I'm the kind of guy who makes up his mind to do something, and then goes to work and does it. There's no other way a man can be a success at anything.

(Indicating the letter "F" on his sweater.)

See that letter? That don't stand for some little-bitty high school somewhere. That stands for *me*. Faroughli. Willie Faroughli. I'm an Assyrian. We've got a civilization six or seven centuries old, I think. Somewhere along in there. Ever hear of Osman? Harold Osman? He's an Assyrian, too. He's got an orchestra down in Fresno.

(He goes to the LADY *and* GENTLEMAN.*)*

I've never seen you before in my life, but I can tell from the clothes you wear and the company you keep *(Graciously indicating the* LADY*)* that you're a man who looks every problem in the eye, and then goes to work and *solves* it. I'm that way myself. Well. *(He smiles beautifully, takes* GENTLEMAN's *hand furiously.)* It's been wonderful talking to a nicer type of people for a change. Well. I'll be seeing you. So long. *(He turns, takes two steps, returns to the table. Very politely and seriously.)* Good-bye, lady. You've got a good man there. Take good care of him.

(WILLIE *goes, saluting* JOE *and the world.*)

KIT CARSON (*to* JOE). By God, for a while there I didn't think that young Assyrian was going to do it. That fellow's got something.

(TOM *comes back with the magazines and other stuff.*)

JOE. Get it all?

TOM. Yeah. I had a little trouble finding the jelly beans.

JOE. Let's take a look at them.

TOM. These are the jelly beans.

(JOE *puts his hand into the cellophane bag and takes out a handful of the jelly beans, looks at them, smiles, and tosses a couple into his mouth.*)

JOE. Same as ever. Have some. (*He offers the bag to* KIT.)

KIT CARSON (*flirting*). Thanks! I remember the first time I ever ate jelly beans. I was six, or at the most seven. Must have been in (*Slowly.*) eighteen—seventy-seven. Seven or eight. Baltimore.

JOE. Have some, Tom. (TOM *takes some.*)

TOM. Thanks, Joe.

JOE. Let's have some of that chewing gum.

(*He dumps all the packages of gum out of the bag onto the table.*)

KIT CARSON (*flirting*). He and a boy named Clark. Quinton Clark. Became a Senator.

JOE. Yeah. Tutti-frutti, all right. (*He opens a package and folds all five pieces into his mouth.*) Always wanted to see how many I could chew at one time. Tell you what, Tom. I'll bet I can chew more at one time than you can.

TOM (*delighted*). All right. (*They both begin to fold gum into their mouths.*)

KIT CARSON. I'll referee. Now, one at a time. How many you got?

JOE. Six.

KIT CARSON. All right. Let Tom catch up with you.

JOE (*while* TOM's *catching up*). Did you give a dollar to a news-kid?

TOM. Yeah, sure.

JOE. What'd he say?

TOM. Thanks.

JOE. What sort of a kid was he?

TOM. Little, dark kid. I guess he's Italian.

JOE. Did he seem pleased?

TOM. Yeah.

JOE. That's good. Did you give a dollar to an old man?

TOM. Yeah.

JOE. Was he pleased?

TOM. Yeah.

JOE. Good. How many you got in your mouth?

TOM. Six.

JOE. All right. I got six, too. (*Folds one more in his mouth.* TOM *folds one too.*)

KIT CARSON. Seven. Seven each. (*They each fold one more into their mouths, very solemnly, chewing them into the main hunk of gum.*) Eight. Nine. Ten.

JOE (*delighted*). Always wanted to do this. (*He picks up one of the magazines.*) Let's see what's going on in the world. (*He turns the pages and keeps folding gum into his mouth and chewing.*)

KIT CARSON. Eleven. Twelve. (KIT *continues to count while* JOE *and* TOM *continue the contest. In spite of what they are doing, each is very serious.*)

TOM. Joe, what'd you want to move Kitty into the St. Francis Hotel for?

JOE. She's a better woman than any of them tramp society dames that hang around that lobby.

TOM. Yeah, but do you think she'll feel at home up there?

JOE. Maybe not at first, but after a couple of days she'll be all right. A nice big room. A bed for sleeping in. Good clothes. Good food. She'll be all right, Tom.

TOM. I hope so. Don't you think she'll get lonely up there with nobody to talk to?

JOE (*looking at* TOM *sharply, almost with admiration, pleased but severe*). There's nobody *anywhere* for *her* to talk to—except *you.*

TOM (*amazed and delighted*). Me, Joe?

JOE (*while* TOM *and* KIT CARSON *listen carefully,* KIT *with great appreciation*). Yes, you. By the grace of God, you're the other half of that girl. Not the angry woman that swaggers into this waterfront dive and shouts because the world has kicked her around. *Anybody* can have *her.* You belong to the little kid in Ohio who once dreamed of living. Not with her carcass, for *money,* so she can have food and clothes, and pay rent. With *all* of her. I put her in that hotel, so she can have a chance to gather herself together again. She can't do that in the New York Hotel. You saw what happens there. There's nobody anywhere for her to talk to, except you. They all make her talk like a whore. After a while, she'll *believe* them. Then she won't be able to remember. She'll get lonely. Sure. People can get lonely for *misery*, even. I want her to go on being lonely for *you*, so she can come together again the way she was meant to be from the beginning. Loneliness is good for people. Right now it's the only thing for Kitty. Any more licorice?

TOM (*dazed*). What? Licorice? (*Looking around busily.*) I guess we've chewed all the licorice in. We still got Clove, Peppermint, Doublemint, Beechnut, Teaberry, and Juicy Fruit.

JOE. Licorice used to be my favorite. Don't worry about her, Tom, she'll be all right. You really want to marry her, don't you?

TOM (*nodding*). Honest to God, Joe. (*Pathetically.*) Only, I haven't got any money.

JOE. Couldn't you be a prize-fighter or something like that?

TOM. Naaaah. I couldn't hit a man if I wasn't sore at him. He'd have to do something that made me hate him.

JOE. You've got to figure out something to do that you won't mind doing very much.

TOM. I wish I could, Joe.

JOE (*thinking deeply, suddenly*). Tom, would you be embarrassed driving a truck?

TOM (*hit by a thunderbolt*). Joe, I never thought of that. I'd like that. Travel. Highways. Little towns. Coffee and hot cakes. Beautiful valleys and mountains and streams and trees and daybreak and sunset.

JOE. There *is* poetry in it, at that.

TOM. Joe, that's just the kind of work I *should* do. Just sit there and travel, and look, and smile, and bust out laughing. Could Kitty go with me, sometimes?

JOE. I don't know. Get me the phone book. Can you drive a truck?

TOM. Joe, you know I can drive a truck, or any kind of thing with a motor and wheels. (TOM *takes* JOE *the phone book.* JOE *turns the pages.*)

JOE (*looking*). Here! Here it is. Tuxedo 7900. Here's a nickel. Get me that number. (TOM *goes to telephone, dials the number.*)

TOM. Hello.

JOE. Ask for Mr. Keith.

TOM (*mouth and language full of gum*). I'd like to talk to Mr. Keith. (*Pause.*) Mr. Keith.

JOE. Take that gum out of your mouth for a minute. (TOM *removes the gum.*)

TOM. Mr. Keith. Yeah. That's right. Hello, Mr. Keith?

JOE. Tell him to hold the line.

TOM. Hold the line, please.

JOE. Give me a hand, Tom. (TOM *helps* JOE *to the telephone. At phone, wad of gum in fingers delicately.*) Keith? Joe. Yeah. Fine. Forget it. (*Pause.*) Have you got a place for a good driver? (*Pause.*) I don't think so. (*To* TOM.) You haven't got a driver's license, have you?

TOM (*worried*). No. But I can get one, Joe.

JOE (*at phone*). No, but he can get one easy enough. To hell with the union. He'll join later. All right, call him a Vice-President and say he drives for relaxation. Sure. What do you mean? Tonight? I don't know why not. San Diego? All right, let him start driving without a license. What the hell's the difference? Yeah. Sure. Look him over. Yeah. I'll send him right over. Right. (*He hangs up.*) Thanks. (*To telephone.*)

TOM. Am I going to get the job?

JOE. He wants to take a look at you.

TOM. Do I look all right, Joe?

JOE (*looking at him carefully*). Hold up your head. Stick out your chest. How do you feel? (TOM *does these things.*)

TOM. Fine.

JOE. You *look* fine, too.

(JOE *takes his wad of gum out of his mouth and wraps* Liberty *magazine around it.*)

JOE. You win, Tom. Now look. (*He bites off the tip of a very long panatela cigar, lights it, and hands one to* TOM, *and another to* KIT.) Have yourselves a pleasant smoke. Here. (*He hands two more to* TOM.) Give those slummers each one. (*He indicates the* SOCIETY LADY *and* GENTLEMAN.)

(TOM *goes over and without a word gives a cigar each to the* MAN *and the* LADY.)

(*The* MAN *is offended; he smells and tosses aside his cigar. The* WOMAN *looks at her cigar a moment, then puts the cigar in her mouth.*)

MAN. What do you think you're doing?

LADY. Really, dear. I'd like to.

MAN. Oh, this is too much.

LADY. I'd *really*, really like to, dear. (*She laughs, puts the cigar in her mouth. Turns to* KIT. *He spits out tip. She does the same.*)

MAN (*loudly*). The mother of five grown men, and she's still looking for *romance.* (*Shouts as* KIT *lights her cigar.*) No. I forbid it.

JOE (*shouting*). What's the matter with you? Why don't you leave her alone? What are you always pushing your women around for? (*Almost without a pause.*) Now, look, Tom. (*The* LADY *puts the lighted cigar in her mouth, and begins to smoke, feeling wonderful.*) Here's ten bucks.

TOM. Ten bucks?

JOE. He may want you to get into a truck and begin driving to San Diego tonight.

TOM. Joe, I got to tell Kitty.

JOE. I'll tell her.

TOM. Joe, take care of her.

JOE. She'll be all right. Stop worrying about her. She's at the St. Francis Hotel. Now, look. Take a cab to Townsend and Fourth. You'll see the big sign. Keith Motor Transport Company. He'll be waiting for you.

TOM. O.K., Joe. (*Trying hard.*) Thanks, Joe.

JOE. Don't be silly. Get going.

(TOM *goes.*)

(LADY *starts puffing on cigar.*)

(As TOM *goes,* WESLEY *and* HARRY *come in together.*)

NICK. Where the hell have you been? We've got to have some entertainment around here. Can't you see them fine people from uptown? (*He points at the* SOCIETY LADY *and* GENTLEMAN.)

WESLEY. You said to come back at ten for the second show.

NICK. Did I say that?

WESLEY. Yes, sir, Mr. Nick, that's exactly what you said.

HARRY. Was the first show all right?

NICK. That wasn't a show. There was no one here to see it. How can it be a show when no one sees it? People are afraid to come down to the waterfront.

HARRY. Yeah. We were just down to Pier 27. One of the longshoremen and a cop had a fight and the cop hit him over the head with a blackjack. We saw it happen, didn't we?

WESLEY. Yes, sir, we was standing there looking when it happened.

NICK (*a little worried*). Anything else happen?

WESLEY. They was all talking.

HARRY. A man in a big car came up and said there was going to be a meeting right away and they hoped to satisfy everybody and stop the strike.

WESLEY. Right away. *Tonight.*

NICK. Well, it's about time. Them poor cops are liable to get nervous and—shoot somebody. (*To* HARRY, *suddenly.*) Come back here. I want you to tend bar for a while. I'm going to take a walk over to the pier.

HARRY. Yes, sir.

NICK (*to the* SOCIETY LADY *and* GENTLEMAN). You society people made up your minds yet?

LADY. Have you champagne?

NICK (*indicating* JOE). What do you think he's pouring out of that bottle, water or something?

LADY. Have you a chilled bottle?

NICK. I've got a dozen of them chilled. He's been drinking champagne here all day and all night for a month now.

LADY. May we have a bottle?

NICK. It's six dollars.

LADY. I think we can manage.

MAN. I don't know. I *know* I don't know.

(NICK *takes off his coat and helps* HARRY *into it.* HARRY *takes a bottle of champagne and two glasses to the* LADY *and the* GENTLEMAN, *dancing, collects six dollars, and goes back behind the bar, dancing.* NICK *gets his coat and hat.*)

NICK (*to* WESLEY). Rattle the keys, a little, son. Rattle the keys.

WESLEY. Yes, sir, Mr. Nick. (NICK *is on his way out. The* ARAB *enters.*)

NICK. Hi-ya, Mahmed.

ARAB. No foundation.

NICK. All the way down the line. (*He goes.*)

(WESLEY *is at the piano, playing quietly. The* ARAB *swallows a glass of beer, takes out his harmonica, and begins to play.* WESLEY *fits his playing to the Arab's.*)

(KITTY DUVAL, *strangely beautiful, in new clothes, comes in. She walks*

*shyly, as if she were embarrassed by the fine clothes, as if she had no
right to wear them. The* LADY *and* GENTLEMAN *are very impressed.*
HARRY *looks at her with amazement.* JOE *is reading* Time *magazine.*
KITTY *goes to his table.* JOE *looks up from the magazine, without the
least amazement.)*

JOE. Hello, Kitty.

KITTY. Hello, Joe.

JOE. It's nice seeing you again.

KITTY. I came in a cab.

JOE. You been crying again? (KITTY *can't answer. To* HARRY.) Bring
a glass. (HARRY *comes over with a glass.* JOE *pours* KITTY *a drink.)*

KITTY. I've got to talk to you.

JOE. Have a drink.

KITTY. I've never been in burlesque. We were just poor.

JOE. Sit down, Kitty.

KITTY *(sits down).* I tried other things.

JOE. Here's to you, Katerina Koranovsky. Here's to you. And Tom.

KITTY *(sorrowfully).* Where *is* Tom?

JOE. He's getting a job tonight driving a truck. He'll be back in a
couple of days.

KITTY *(sadly).* I told him I'd marry him.

JOE. He wanted to see you and say good-by.

KITTY. He's too good for me. He's like a little boy. *(Wearily.)* I'm—
Too many things have happened to me.

JOE. Kitty Duval, you're one of the few truly innocent people I have
ever known. He'll be back in a couple of days. Go back to the
hotel and wait for him.

KITTY. That's what I mean. I can't stand being alone. I'm no good.
I tried very hard. I don't know what it is. I miss— *(She gestures.)*

JOE *(gently).* Do you really want to come back here, Kitty?

KITTY. I don't know. I'm not sure. Everything *smells* different. I don't
know how to feel, or what to think. *(Gesturing pathetically.)* I
know I don't belong there. It's what I've wanted all my life, but
it's too *late.* I try to be happy about it, but all I can do is remember and cry.

JOE. I don't know what to tell you, Kitty. I didn't mean to hurt you.

KITTY. You haven't hurt me. You're the only person who's ever been
good to me. I've never known anybody like you. I'm not sure
about love any more, but I know I love you, and I know I love
Tom.

JOE. I love you too, Kitty Duval.

KITTY. He'll want babies. I know he will. I know I will, too. Of course I will. I can't— *(She shakes her head.)*

JOE. Tom's a baby himself. You'll be very happy together. He wants you to ride with him in the truck. Tom's good for you. You're good for Tom.

KITTY *(like a child)*. Do you want me to go back and wait for him?

JOE. I can't *tell* you what to do. I think it would be a good idea, though.

KITTY. I wish I could tell you how it makes me feel to be alone. It's almost worse.

JOE. It might take a whole week, Kitty. *(He looks at her sharply, at the arrival of an idea.)* Didn't you speak of reading a book? A book of poems?

KITTY. I didn't know what I was saying.

JOE *(trying to get up)*. Of course you knew. I think you'll like poetry. Wait here a minute, Kitty. I'll go see if I can find some books.

KITTY. All right, Joe. *(He walks out of the place, trying very hard not to wobble.)*

(Fog-horn. Music. The NEWSBOY *comes in. Looks for* JOE. *Is broken-hearted because* JOE *is gone.)*

NEWSBOY *(to* SOCIETY GENTLEMAN*)*. Paper?

MAN *(angry)*. No.

(The NEWSBOY *goes to the* ARAB.*)*

NEWSBOY. Paper, Mister?

ARAB *(irritated)*. No foundation.

NEWSBOY. What?

ARAB *(very angry)*. No foundation. *(The* NEWSBOY *starts out, turns, looks at the* ARAB, *shakes head.)*

NEWSBOY. No foundation? How do you figure?

*(*BLICK *and* TWO COPS *enter.)*

NEWSBOY *(to* BLICK*)*. Paper, mister?

*(*BLICK *pushes him aside. The* NEWSBOY *goes.)*

BLICK *(walking authoritatively about the place, to* HARRY*)*. Where's Nick?

HARRY. He went for a walk.

BLICK. Who are you?

HARRY. Harry.

BLICK (*to the* ARAB *and* WESLEY). Hey, you. Shut up. (*The* ARAB *stops playing the harmonica,* WESLEY *the piano.*)

BLICK (*studies* KITTY). What's your name, sister?

KITTY (*looking at him*). Kitty Duval. What's it to you?

(KITTY'S *voice is now like it was at the beginning of the play: tough, independent, bitter and hard.*)

BLICK (*angry*). Don't give me any of your gutter lip. Just answer my questions.

KITTY. You go to hell, you.

BLICK (*coming over, enraged*). Where do you live?

KITTY. The New York Hotel. Room 21.

BLICK. Where do you work?

KITTY. I'm not working just now. I'm looking for work.

BLICK. What kind of work? (KITTY *can't answer.*) What kind of work? (KITTY *can't answer.*) (*Furiously.*) WHAT KIND OF WORK? (KIT CARSON *comes over.*)

KIT CARSON. You can't talk to a lady that way in *my* presence. (BLICK *turns and stares at* KIT. *The* COPS *begin to move from the bar.*)

BLICK (*to the* COPS). It's all right, boys. I'll take care of this. (*To* KIT.) What'd you say?

KIT CARSON. You got no right to hurt people. Who are *you?*

(BLICK, *without a word, takes* KIT *to the street. Sounds of a blow and a groan.* BLICK *returns, breathing hard.*)

BLICK (*to the* COPS). O.K., boys. You can go now. Take care of him. Put him on his feet and tell him to behave himself from now on. (*To* KITTY *again.*) Now answer my question. What kind of work?

KITTY (*quietly*). I'm a whore, you son of a bitch. You know what kind of work I do. And I know what kind you do.

MAN (*shocked and really hurt*). Excuse me, officer, but it seems to me that your attitude—

BLICK. Shut up.

MAN (*quietly*).—is making the poor child say things that are not true.

BLICK. Shut up, I said.

LADY. Well. (*To the* MAN.) Are you going to stand for such insolence?

BLICK (*to* MAN, *who is standing*). Are you?

MAN (*taking the* WOMAN'S *arm*). I'll get a divorce. I'll start life all over again. (*Pushing the* WOMAN). Come on. Get the hell out of here!

(*The* MAN *hurries his* WOMAN *out of the place,* BLICK *watching them go.*)

BLICK (*to* KITTY). Now. Let's begin again, and see that you tell the truth. What's your name?

KITTY. Kitty Duval.

BLICK. Where do you live?

KITTY. Until this evening I lived at the New York Hotel. Room 21. This evening I moved to the St. Francis Hotel.

BLICK. Oh. To the St. Francis Hotel. Nice place. Where do you work?

KITTY. I'm looking for work.

BLICK. What kind of work do you do?

KITTY. I'm an actress.

BLICK. I see. What movies have I seen you in?

KITTY. I've worked in burlesque.

BLICK. You're a liar.

(WESLEY *stands, worried and full of dumb resentment.*)

KITTY (*pathetically, as at the beginning of the play*). It's the truth.

BLICK. What are you doing here?

KITTY. I came to see if I could get a job here.

BLICK. Doing what?

KITTY. Singing—and—dancing.

BLICK. You can't sing or dance. What are you lying for?

KITTY. I can. I sang and danced in burlesque all over the country.

BLICK. You're a liar.

KITTY. I said lines, too.

BLICK. So you danced in burlesque?

KITTY. Yes.

BLICK. All right. Let's see what you did.

KITTY. I can't. There's no music, and I haven't got the right clothes.

BLICK. There's music. (*To* WESLEY). Put a nickel in that phonograph. (WESLEY *can't move.*) Come on. Put a nickel in that phonograph. (WESLEY *does so. To* KITTY). All right. Get up on that stage and do a hot little burlesque number.

(KITTY *stands. Walks slowly to the stage, but is unable to move.* JOE *comes in, holding three boooks.*) Get going, now. Let's see you dance the way you did in burlesque, all over the country. (KITTY *tries to do a burlesque dance. It is beautiful in a tragic way.*)

BLICK. All right, start taking them off!

(KITTY *removes her hat and starts to remove her jacket.* JOE *moves closer to the stage, amazed.*)

JOE (*hurrying to* KITTY). Get down from there. (*He takes* KITTY *into his arms. She is crying. To* BLICK.) What the hell do you think you're doing!

WESLEY (*like a little boy, very angry*). It's that man, BLICK. He made her take off her clothes. He beat up the old man, too.

(BLICK *pushes* WESLEY *off, as* TOM *enters.* BLICK *begins beating up* WESLEY.)

TOM. What's the matter, Joe? What's happened?

JOE. Is the truck out there?

TOM. Yeah, but what's happened? Kitty's crying again!

JOE. You driving to San Diego?

TOM. Yeah, Joe. But what's he doing to that poor colored boy?

JOE. Get going. Here's some money. Everything's O.K. (*To* KITTY.) Dress in the truck. Take these books.

WESLEY'S VOICE. You can't hurt me. You'll get yours. You wait and see.

TOM. Joe, he's hurting that boy. I'll kill him!

JOE (*pushing* TOM). Get out of here! Get married in San Diego. I'll see you when you get back. (TOM *and* KITTY *go.* NICK *enters and stands at the lower end of the bar.* JOE *takes the revolver out of his pocket. Looks at it.*) I've always wanted to kill somebody, but I never knew who it should be. (*He cocks the revolver, stands real straight, holds it in front of him firmly and walks to the door. He stands a moment watching* BLICK, *aims very carefully, and pulls trigger. There is no shot.*)

(NICK *runs over and grabs the gun, and takes* JOE *aside.*)

NICK. What the hell do you think you're doing?

JOE (*casually, but angry*). That dumb Tom. Buys a six-shooter that won't even shoot once.

(JOE *sits down, dead to the world.*)

(BLICK *comes out, panting for breath.*)

(NICK *looks at him. He speaks slowly.*)

NICK. Blick! I told you to stay out of here! Now get out of here. (*He takes* BLICK *by the collar, tightening his grip as he speaks, and pushing him out.*) If you come back again, I'm going to take you in that room where you've been beating up that colored boy, and I'm going to murder you—slowly—with my hands. Beat it! (*He pushes* BLICK *out. To* HARRY.) Go take care of the colored boy. (HARRY *runs out.*) (WILLIE *returns and doesn't sense that anything is changed.* WILLIE *puts another nickel into the machine, but he does so very violently. The consequence of this violence is that the flag comes up again.* WILLIE, *amazed, stands at attention and salutes. The flag goes down. He shakes his head.*)

WILLIE (*thoughtfully*). As far as I'm concerned, this is the *only* country in the world. If you ask me, *nuts* to Europe! (*He is about to push the slide in again when the flag comes up again. Furiously, to* NICK, *while he salutes and stands at attention, pleadingly.*) Hey, Nick. This machine is out of order.

NICK (*somberly*). Give it a whack on the side.

(WILLIE *does so. A hell of a whack. The result is the flag comes up and down, and* WILLIE *keeps saluting.*)

WILLIE (*saluting*). Hey, Nick. Something's wrong.

(*The machine quiets down abruptly,* WILLIE *very stealthily slides a new nickel in, and starts a new game.*)

(*From a distance two pistol shots are heard, each carefully timed.*)

(NICK *runs out.*)

(*The* NEWSBOY *enters, crosses to Joe's table, senses something is wrong.*)

NEWSBOY (*softly*). Paper, Mister?

(JOE *can't hear him.*)

(*The* NEWSBOY *backs away, studies* JOE, *wishes he could cheer* JOE *up. Notices the phonograph, goes to it, and puts a coin in it, hoping music will make* JOE *happier.*)

(*The* NEWSBOY *sits down. Watches* JOE. *The music begins.* "The Missouri Waltz.")

(*The* DRUNKARD *comes in and walks around. Then sits down.* NICK *comes back.*)

NICK (*delighted*). Joe, Blick's dead! Somebody just shot him, and none of the cops are trying to find out who. (JOE *doesn't hear.* NICK *steps back, studying* JOE.)

NICK (*shouting*). Joe.

JOE (*looking up*). What?

NICK. Blick's dead.

JOE. Blick? Dead? Good! That God damn gun wouldn't go off. I *told* Tom to get a good one.

NICK (*picking up gun and looking at it*). Joe, you wanted to kill that guy! (HARRY *returns.* JOE *puts the gun in his coat pocket.*) I'm going to buy you a bottle of champagne.

(NICK *goes to bar.* JOE *rises, takes hat from rack, puts coat on. The* NEWSBOY *jumps up, helps* JOE *with coat.*)

NICK. What's the matter, Joe?

JOE. Nothing. Nothing.

NICK. How about the champagne?

JOE. Thanks. (*Going.*)

NICK. It's not eleven yet. Where you going, Joe?

JOE. I don't know. Nowhere.

NICK. Will I see you tomorrow?

JOE. I don't know. I don't think so.

(KIT CARSON *enters, walks to* JOE. JOE *and* KIT *look at one another knowingly.*)

JOE. Somebody just shot a man. How are you feeling?

KIT. Never felt better in my life. (*Loudly, bragging, but somber.*) I shot a man once. In San Francisco. Shot him two times. In 1939, I think it was. In October. Fellow named Blick or Glick or something like that. Couldn't stand the way he talked to ladies. Went up to my room and got my old pearl-handled revolver and waited for him on Pacific Street. Saw him walking, and let him have it, two times. Had to throw the beautiful revolver into the Bay.

(HARRY, NICK, *the* ARAB *and the* DRUNKARD *close in around him.*)

(JOE *searches his pockets, brings out the revolver, puts it in Kit's hand, looks at him with great admiration and affection.* JOE *walks slowly to the stairs leading to the street, turns and waves.* KIT, *and then one by one everybody else, waves, and the marble-game goes into its beautiful American routine again: flag, lights, and music. The play ends.*)

CURTAIN

THE ARMENIAN WRITERS

THERE are several kinds of Armenians who write in English for a living, or as a way of life, as the saying is: and I am deeply devoted to each kind in a fraternal and familiar manner, first because they are Armenians, and second because they are writers, although generally bad ones.

The truth of the matter is that I don't really care about Armenian writers, as such, any more than I do about American writers, as such: it is just that I have never been able to get over being, myself, an Armenian: which in turn impels me to marvel at anybody else I meet who also happens to be an Armenian, although I frequently wish he might have been an Uz or a Bek or one or another of the other peoples hidden away in the great, faraway mountains of the world.

Why should I have to meet him, with his well-combed hair and his systematic method of translating thought into language, as when he says, "Look here, now we are of the same family, we understand one another, now isn't that so?"

And, of course, it isn't at all, but what can I say, being half courteous most of the time?

"Yes," I say, "that's quite true," when as a matter of fact nothing could be more sharply and deeply untrue, for at best his name is Chuchulingirian, whereas mine is Zavzak: his family has its roots somewhat loosely in a place called Alavart, while time has its roots quite firmly in a place called Vosp.

Frequently his first name is Aspadour, whereas mine has always been Avak, or in full Avak Zavzak, as a good many literate people know.

My style as a writer, and for that matter as an Armenian, or even as an American, born in Detroit and brought up in Delano, is direct and simple, while his style is heavy and confused and considerably involved in such exclamations as *Ahkh and Dohkh*.

But Aspadour Chuchulingirian isn't the only Armenian writer I am apt to meet at an Armenian parlor, and with whom I am apt to exchange a few routine words in our own delightful language, beginning, of course, with the question, In Armenian, "Do you speak Armenian?"

Now, if it happens that I have been the one to ask the question, he generally replies, in Armenian, of course, "A little," and then in English, but with an accent, "After all, I am an American. My work is with Americans. I have little occasion to speak Armenian. I can, of course, if I must."

A moment later, however, he speaks for fifteen minutes in Armenian, and quite well, too, using any number of words I have never before heard, which nevertheless sound authentic and, for all I know, mean something.

But if it happens that he asks me if I speak Armenian, I say without the slightest hesitation, "Yes," or as we say, "*Eye-yo*."

And then to demonstrate how I speak it I say, "*Eench ga, chi-ga?*" Or, "What is, what isn't?" Or, "What's doing?" Or, "No fancy talk around here, please."

Whereupon old Chuchulingirian says, "*Votch-eench*," or perhaps, "*Haytch*," which, of course, we know is only a routine and courteous answer to a surprising or meaningless question, rather than what the words really mean, which in both cases is "nothing"—but this particular nothing also means that one has not had a bad time lately, and hence all is quite well, thank you.

As I say, from time to time, year in and year out, I chance upon one or another of the Armenians who write in English, and as compatriots and as fellow writers we chat in our own language as well as in English, and at the same time keep a good deal to ourselves.

For instance, the first thing I want to say to Aspadour Chuchulingirian when I have been informed that that is in fact who he is, is, "Now, it seems to me I should tell you before I say anything else that I wish you would go to the trouble sometime of trying to write something that is interesting in itself rather than these preposterously unhappy stories about impossible old men and old women that you have been publishing in the Armenian-American papers."

But how could I say such a thing? To begin with, it's too long. By the time I am half finished with the remark I have forgotten the first part and am not sure about the second.

At the same time, why should I be the one to hurt his feelings? Isn't he having troubles enough, the same as anybody else?

Of course he is, so of course I have got to keep a great many things to myself, as he does, too.

As we chat I notice how he keeps things to himself, and I daresay he notices the same thing about me. How else would we be able to account for our sudden bursts of laughter, and our frequent use of the term "*Bot-meh, bot-meh,*" Tell it, tell it, or "*Khoss-sire,*" Talk.

Alas, there is so much to be said, and so little. We are Armenians. We are writers. (And then, each of us keeps this part to himself: So what?) Again we burst into laughter, light cigarettes, inhale, and think something or other, such as, "If only Charentz were an American, if only he were here, or Raffi, or Mamigonian—instead of *him.* Wouldn't it be better?"

Of course it would, but those fellows are all dead.

"Do you know," Aspadour says suddenly, "this is quite an event for me? I have always wanted to meet Zavzak, our own Zavzak, and here you are at last, not at all as I thought you would be, but at the same time I think I understand your writing much better now that I have met you. The strange humor, I mean. I am sure there is more humor in your work than most people suspect. Am I right?"

"Yes and no," I reply because I haven't the faintest idea what he's talking about. "And I may say this is quite an event for *me,* too. The name Chuchulingirian has always seemed to me to signify something quite—how shall I put it? special? I mean, a man with a name like that must be very good at spelling. A name like that is proud of itself, and has a right to be. I often wonder how Ara Solp has been able to write one word with a name like that, but there he is, the author of all sorts of things—stories, essays, patriotic and religious poems, memoirs, accounts of travel, and now and then another of those astonishing Solp novels. Ara is a whirlwind. I am absolutely proud to be a countryman of his."

Now, Chuchulingirian quickly agrees with every sentiment I have expressed, but at the same time there is a troubled shadow halfway across his face and I know he doesn't care very much for Solp's writing. Still, we are men of courtesy, and besides, Solp happens to be an Armenian, just as we are, and it isn't permissible for us to attack his work. Not yet, at any rate. Plenty of time to attack Solp. Right now what we want to do is feel good about having met at last, and to give one another the impression that we are not only countrymen but writers who are great enough to speak warmly and charitably of a rather undistinguished contemporary.

Drink, and feel good.

"Solp!" Chuchulingirian says with what appears to be authentic affection. "What a wild man—now at prayer, now at drinking. Tomorrow, what? Perhaps tomorrow he will be telling lies about his dangerous adventures somewhere or other?"

"No doubt. Didn't he go to Syria recently?"

"That was Raspoontz."

"Ashod? Did Ashod go to Syria?"

"Greece and Egypt as well."

"Greece, Egypt, and Syria. I'm sure we'll be hearing about the terrible dangers he faced everywhere."

"I wonder," Chuchulingirian says. "I mean, I wonder if we will. He's a very slow writer. When we met in Philadelphia seven years ago he remarked with great earnestness that he was catching up with his life from the very beginning and that after twenty years of hard work he had only reached the age of eleven. Well, at that rate, now that he is a man of almost fifty, when can we expect to hear about his recent adventures in Egypt?"

"Raspoontz almost fifty? I had no idea. I keep thinking of him as a very young man."

"In spirit, yes—but not only is he almost fifty, he's aged quite noticeably. Three drinks and he's singing *Pompvorodan*, and he's got no voice at all. He bangs the table with a clenched fist every time, too, and tears come into his eyes. There we are again."

"Where? *Where* we are?"

"Angry," Chuchulingirian says. "Angry and deeply hurt because so many things have turned out so poorly."

"What has turned out so poorly?"

"Well, to begin with," Aspadour says, "what happened to the theater the wealthy Armenians of New York were going to put up on the corner of Twenty-third Street and Lexington Avenue?" Chuchulingirian pauses a moment, inhales deeply, and then says, "Nothing. As usual. The wealthy Armenians gathered together at the Waldorf, they ate supper, they made speeches, they looked at one another, and then they went home. The theater was never put up."

"Oh, the theater," I say. "I thought perhaps you were thinking about—well, geography."

"What geography?"

"The map of Armenia."

"Well, of course," Aspadour says quickly. "I certainly am think-

ing of that, too. *Always,* but at the same time here we are American
citizens, our homeland far away—what's the harm of a theater at the
corner of Twenty-third and Lexington in the meantime?"

"In *what* meantime?"

"While we are waiting for the geography to be properly restored.
We have actors. We have acting companies. Why shouldn't they
have a theater in which to present their plays?"

"They should," I say. "They *should.* Why did the rich Armenians
fail to put up the theater?"

"Why? Why?" Chuchulingirian says with bitter anger. "Rich
men are rich in the first place because they know how to put their
money into things that will bring them *more* money, that's why.
I sometimes think that rich men belong to another nationality entirely, no matter what their actual nationality happens to be. The
nationality of the rich. If they are Armenians, they are Armenians,
too, but before they are Armenians they are rich, and that means
that they know a thing or two about hanging on to their money."

"Well," I say, "a theater—after all, that's a pretty risky proposi-
tion. At the same time is it possible that the Armenians of America
don't need an Armenian theater? After all, there is a great deal of
drama in every Armenian home every day. Enough's enough, isn't
it? Why should they pay fifty cents to sit in a theater for three
hours and see some actors pretending to be hard-working people who
are fighting among themselves about who's who, and why, and who's
entitled to the fullest use of the kitchen?"

"No," Chuchulingirian says, "say what you will, on this one point
I must disagree with you. We *need* a theater. Our acting companies
are breaking up. The great stars of our theater are taking common
employment here and there."

"What kind of work are they doing?"

"It is painful even to think of it," Aspadour says. "They are *selling*
things. It is disgraceful. The last I heard of Muzhdentz, he was selling Nashes."

"Nashes?"

"Had it been Cadillacs I might not have felt so badly about it.
But who wants to hear that Muzhdentz is selling Nashes?"

"I don't. Perhaps it's temporary. At any rate, let's hope so."

"Of course it's temporary. Do you think there's one Armenian in
America who'll buy a Nash?"

"I suppose not."

"Muzhdentz should act in our own Armenian theater," Aspadour says with conviction. "I will never forget the majesty of his Pooto."

"Pooto?"

"Surely you've heard of Pooto?"

"What did *he* do?"

"What *didn't* he do would be more like it. My God, he out-witted kings, that's all."

"Well, it was probably some time ago. Perhaps it's just as well that Muzhdentz is not acting the part of Pooto any more. There will be other characters for other players to perform as time goes on. Perhaps Pooto has had his day, as Muzhdentz has. But tell me, Aspadour —I hope I may call you by your first name—what are you writing? What are you writing these days?"

"Ah," he says, "I wish I knew. A novel of some kind, I suppose."

"A novel. Good. And how is it going?"

"Badly, of course. And I know why, too. Let's face it. A writer just can't earn a living, that's all."

"Well, how do you manage, then?"

"I am with Drell."

"Drell? Is it possible I know who Drell is?"

"Dreloumanjian," he says.

"Dreloumanjian? Sumpad? Isn't he the cheerful dentist? The one who believes that if he fixes your teeth you must forever after be healthy, happy, and prosperous?"

"None other."

"And is it so—healthy, happy, and prosperous?"

"It seems unlikely enough, I suppose, but do you know there *is* something to his theory? I mean, his hearty manner is quite con-tagious, and almost everybody who visits his office feels better."

"But what do you do for Drell?"

"Well, as you know, I had several years at M.I.T."

"No, as a matter of fact, I didn't."

"Engineering, of course, but at that time I was fishing. I really had no idea what I wanted to do—for a living, I mean. I suppose I went to M.I.T. because it was there."

"Yes, that's often how such a thing happens, but what do you do for Drell?"

"Well," Aspadour Chuchulingirian says, "let me see if I can sum it up." He stops to think, and then he says, "No, I can't. To begin with I open his office at eight in the morning. I look after his mail.

I keep his books, I sit behind a desk, I keep him to his work schedule. I receive his patients, I write his advertisements which he sends to Armenians everywhere by mail, I run errands, and sometimes when he needs a strong arm to hold a frightened old man in the chair I help him in that kind of work, too."

Now, only five minutes have gone by since I met Chuchulingirian, and yet in that short space of time we have covered quite a lot of territory. We have talked in two languages, we have asked and answered questions, we have discussed contemporaries, economics, politics, geography, drama, and many other things, but we haven't so much as begun to do the big talking we both know we are going to do before we say goodnight and wish one another good luck. We have accepted from our good host two straight shots of *rahki* apiece, we have glanced at some of our host's other eminent guests—being a rich man he entertains only the eminent—and we have breathed deeply of the scent of food cooking in the kitchen—all kinds of food. There is plenty of time to talk.

"Before I forget," Aspadour says as he takes a third shot of *rahki* off the tray, "I want to drink a toast to the Armenian writers of America."

This is something I must drink to also, and for good reasons, too. First, because the least one Armenian writer can do for another is to drink to him now and then: second, because the work of Chuchulingirian does for Sumpad Dreloumanjian, or Drell, as he prefers to be called, has depressed me a little: third, because across the room I have noticed the quiet but nevertheless excited arrival of still another contemporary, Ara Solp himself, and I feel that if my talk with Aspadour Chuchulingirian begins to go flat, I can bring Ara Solp into the discussion and thereby postpone its collapse for an hour or two: fourth, because the mingling scents of the half dozen Armenian foods being cooked in the kitchen have made me quite pleased about having once again taken a chance on a rich man's invitation to dinner and I want to have six or seven shots because a little drinking makes me hungry: and finally, I remove a small glass of *rahki* off the tray and hold it out to my fellow writer because that is what you always do on such occasions. Not to mention that I am curious to know what Aspadour is going to say about the Armenian writers of America.

We touch glasses and he says, "Let us drink, my countryman, my friend, my fellow writer—" And then he stops suddenly to give the matter a little additional thought, but when he speaks again he speaks Armenian. "What shall I say?" he asks. "Let us drink to—"

"It's early," I suggest. "Plenty of time to think of something worthy to say. In the meantime, suppose we just drink."

And so saying I gulp down the third shot. Our host, a man who has earned a fortune of almost a quarter of a million dollars in thirty years of very hard work, a man who considers writers remarkable fellows, who enjoys watching them eat the fine food he spreads before them, who makes the same speech at each of his parties, a speech in which he lavishes warm, sentimental, fierce, and atrocious praise on what he calls his America, speaking in English, and saying, "My America—all dese good tings my America give me," so that one can only hope a little of America is left over for the rest of us—our host, sensing a momentous toast, has remained beside us, with, of course, the solid-silver tray on which the shots of *rahki* rest, and as I have gulped down the third he has very kindly nodded encouragement and invited me to grasp and gulp down the fourth, which I am quite prepared to do.

Chuchulingirian gulps down his third shot also, and seizes his fourth, and now our host waits to hear the toast. Aspadour extends his small glass again, and again I touch it.

"Let us drink," he says, and now he looks our host straight in the eye, and they exchange solemn nods, "let us drink to America, to the America of our good host, *his* America," and this seems to me reasonable enough, since he *has* furnished the Armenian parlor and the Armenian drink, and so we drink, breaking into joyous laughter and swift speech—happiness, happiness, and much success—more and more success.

Our host is deeply moved by this spontaneous expression of admiration for him—as well as for his fortune—for these two are not businessmen, they are not clever fellows in matters of money, they are writers, and when they drink a toast to you it is an honor. Proud and grateful tears come to his eyes as he says with deep earnestness, "My boys, I am proud of you—I am proud of you." A little overcome, he turns and moves across the room to Ara Solp, who is, after all, a writer, too, and who may, given time and enough shots of *rahki*, drink a toast to him, too. Poor fellows when it comes to money, but gentlemen and—above all—Armenians, true Armenians.

"I had had in mind," Chuchulingirian says with a tone of guilt, "a different toast, perhaps a better one, but do you know, I'm not sure there *is* a better one. He *is* a fathead, no doubt about that, but he *has* worked hard and he has made a fortune, and he is kind— he never forgets us. I am sure the food I shall eat here tonight will be the finest I have eaten in many months, perhaps in many years. It was impossible not to drink to him."

"Or to his money."

"He and his money are the same thing, but you and I know he is a good fellow, too."

"He is. I'm quite fond of him."

"As I am," Aspadour says, "but I wish drinking to him hadn't reminded me so early in the evening what a lonely and silly thing it is to be an Armenian writer in America."

"It's probably just as lonely and silly to be any other kind of writer in America, except perhaps that the American writers in America don't get invitations to dinner from good fellows like our host, so let's drink to him all night."

"Good enough. It's certainly not his fault we're not rich."

"And if we were, I doubt if we'd ever invite *him* to dinner, so let's forget the whole thing and just enjoy this wonderful Armenian parlor. Shall we join Ara Solp and find out what *he's* got to say?"

"By all means," Aspadour Chuchulingirian says, and so we move across the crowded parlor, laughing and talking as we go, while Ara Solp waits with great expectancy for our arrival, nodding his head and cheering us on with, "Come, come, Armenian writers, let us talk."

THE BICYCLE RIDER
IN BEVERLY HILLS

I HAVE driven my Cadillac more than 100,000 miles. The cross-country drives were great, from the Pacific to the Atlantic, or the other way around. But I have never driven to evening without loneliness, despair, regret, and all the other things that are of the end. For one end evokes the others, and the end of day evokes the end of life, especially for the traveler. The end of life evokes the errors of it, and a fellow wishes he had known better.

I almost always drove alone. That is the privilege of the traveler who goes by car. Certain drives are like an affair, and they have got to be private. A man is in love with a great many things strewn about haphazardly all over the country. He gets in his car and drives out to them, to have another look at them, and he doesn't want anybody to be sitting beside him. A man can be in love with streets, towns, and cities: railroad tracks, telegraph poles, houses, porches, lawns. He can go out in search of a fresh assorting and arranging of these things, and of the people of them.

A man's car can thus become a pew on wheels—in the church of the world. That it is why I have always been angry when my car has failed to work as I have expected it to work, for this has been a failure of my own soul in search of truth. I could have searched in any case, but the automobile gave breadth and depth to the search. The truth is not in the landscape, but neither is it out of it. My car is not like any other car in the world. It is my car and it is like myself.

Before I was sixteen I had many bicycles. I have no idea what became of them. I remember, though, that I rode them so hard they were always breaking down. The spokes of the wheels were always getting loose so that the wheels became crooked. The chains were always breaking. I bore down on the handlebars with so much force in sprinting, in speeding, in making quick getaways, that the handlebars were always getting loose and I was always tightening them. But the thing about my bicycles that I want to remember is the way I rode them, what I thought while I rode them, and the music that came to me.

First of all, my bikes were always rebuilt second-hand bikes. They were lean, hard, tough, swift, and designed for usage. I rode them with speed and style. I found out a great deal about style from riding them. Style in writing, I mean. Style in everything. I did not ride for pleasure. I rode to get somewhere, and I don't mean from the house on San Benito Avenue in Fresno to the Public Library there. I mean I rode to get somewhere *myself*. I did not loaf on my bike. I sometimes rested on it after a hard day's riding, on my way home to supper and sleep, sliding off the seat a little to the left, pedaling with the left leg, resting the other on the saddle, and letting the bike weave right and left easily as I moved forward. The style I learned was this: I learned to go and make it fast. I learned to know at one and the same time how my bike was going, how it was holding up, where I was, where I would soon be, and where in all probability I would finally be.

In the end I always went home to supper and sleep.

A man learns style from everything, but I learned mine from things on which I moved, and as writing is a thing which moves I think I was lucky to learn as I did.

A bike can be an important appurtenance of an important ritual. Moving the legs evenly and steadily soon brings home to the bike-rider a valuable knowledge of pace and rhythm, and a sensible respect for timing and the meeting of a schedule.

Out of rhythm come many things, perhaps all things. The physical action compels action of another order—action of mind, memory, imagination, dream, hope, order, and so on. The physical action also establishes a deep respect for grace, seemliness, effectiveness, power with ease, naturalness, and so on. The action of the imagination brings home to the bicycle-rider the limitlessness of the potential in all things. He finds out that there are many excellent ways in which to ride a bike effectively, and this acquaintanceship with the ways and the comparing of them gives him an awareness of a parallel potential in all other actions. Out of the imagination comes also music and memory.

In the early days of the search I heard many great symphonies which no composer ever put to paper and no orchestra ever performed. This is understandable, I hope. As the saying is, they came to me. I was born restless and was forever eager to be going. There never seemed to be enough of going for me. I wanted to get out to more and more. This might have worn me out, but what it actually did was refresh and strengthen me. Wanting to go and not being able to do so might have given me another order of strength, but the order that I received was to *want* to go and to go. To want to search and to do so.

On the way I found out all the things without which I could never be the writer I am. I was not yet sixteen when I understood a great deal, from having ridden bicycles for so long, about style, speed, grace, purpose, value, form, integrity, health, humor, music, breathing, and finally and perhaps best of all the relationship between the beginning and the end.

My eyes (by which I lived even more than by bread, by which, that is, living had reason, purpose, and a hope of meaning) were continuously assaulted by the elements, especialy during the three years I rode a bicycle for a living. Unless I was able to see clearly my entire efficiency as a bicycle-rider was nullified, and I found myself at the side of the road, the bike halted but still propped up under me while I tried to restore vision to my eyes.

The wind carried many things into my eyes, and these things did everything from blur my vision to stop it entirely. The things were dust, dirt, pieces of fine gravel, insects, soot, cinders, and many other things. These things were lifted off the ground or driven out of the air into my eyes. I was forever in trouble with the wind. Insects stang in my eyes, filling them with the water which meant to cleanse them. After they were cleansed it would be some time before the eyes were restored to clear vision. Dirt—anything—in my eyes always brought me to an instantaneous halt, and I didn't like to halt. I once bought a pair of inexpensive goggles and wore them, but they were no good at all. The goggles bothered my eyes. I put them away, and thereafter the way it worked was this: I hoped not to have the wind blow anything into my eyes. But I doubt if there ever was a whole day in which nothing was blown into them.

I loved the wind, but it was often a great nuisance to me, a maker of bitter mischief. More than anything else I needed to see clearly. That was what it came to. In order to go—which was my work—I had to be able to see where I was going. Not to see where I was going meant that I had to stop. And to stop was to fail. And did not enjoy failing. I have always been angered by failure. I am still angered by it. My success as a telegraph messenger depended on my eyes.

Consequently, *all* hope of effectiveness depended on them. My effectiveness as a messenger became inseparable from my hope to be effective as a writer.

There were times when blindness, despair, and anger were so great that I believed I would throw it all over, turn in my messenger's coat and cap, put aside my bike, keep myself and my eyes out of the wind, sit down in the Public Library, and devote my time exclusively to the book, my eyes entirely secure now from the wind. But that was not to be.

First I needed the money the job brought me. That is, the Saroyan family needed it.

Second, I needed the action of myself in the world. That is, the writer needed it.

Third, I needed to go, to continue to go, to continue my study of rhythm, pace, speed, and effectiveness. I needed all this in order to understand who I was, who I could be, and how.

Watching the wind work far off on eucalptus trees was a great joy. Listening to it among the leaves of them when I reached the trees was sweet music. But best of all was when the wind had great power, when it was erratic and did swift and sudden things, stopped suddenly, picked up suddenly, ran in a circle, sprinted straight ahead, stopped, turned, came back.

Now and then when the wind was very strong I found it difficult to make my way through it on my bike, but I don't believe it was ever able to stop me entirely, except through trickery, by blinding me with dirt. Many times it almost unseated me, but I always managed to hang on.

The wind with the rain made other difficulties. Getting wet meant little or nothing, but rain driven into the eyes by the wind can also blur the vision. The difficulty of blurred vision is great, almost greater than blindness itself, for the eye with blurred vision, likes to believe it still has enough vision on which to keep going. I soon learned, however, that to keep going when vision is poor is folly. Even so, I was often tempted to take a chance. If I had no work to do the wind and the rain would have been a joy to behold. The weather fascinated me, especially storms, but it is one thing to watch a storm and another to fight it.

A second difficulty for the bike-rider in the rain is the slipperiness of the streets and the muddiness of the roads. I have had to get off my bike on muddy roads and push through on foot to where I was to deliver a telegram. Many times I slipped and spilled on the wet streets, for having misjudged the pace I could maintain efficiently.

I also had to be concerned about the vision of others in the streets, the drivers of automobiles especially, for it was not enough for me to see and know where I was going, it was necessary to see where a motorist was going, and be able to predict where he would soon be.

The heat of the summer softened the tar of the outlying streets of Fresno, so that getting the bike over them meant rising up off the saddle and bringing the entire weight of the body to bear upon the pedals—or sprinting, although the amount of speed I was able to achieve may scarcely be associated with the implication of the word sprint. More often than not I was barely able to keep the bike from stopping, but that was the idea—to *move* myself upon my bike to where I was going.

The heat and the riding in it all day made me very thirsty. This thirst was almost unquenchable during July, August, and September. I had a lot of respect for money, consequently I was not given to throwing it around on treats for myself, but after a great deal of thought I saw the wisdom of one transaction that I made at least once a day in the summer, occasionally twice a day. There was a place named The Danish Dairy on Fresno Avenue, across the street from the Hippodrome Theater, where for five cents anybody could stand and pour cold buttermilk out of a pitcher into a tall glass and drink as much as he liked. This was the perfect drink for the messenger in the summer. Around two or half past two in the afternoon when I stepped into The Danish Dairy I would drink a great deal of buttermilk for five cents. I never drank fewer than four large glasses of it, and frequently, taking my time on the last two or three glasses, I drank seven or eight. The liquid was especially thirst-quenching, cooling, and deeply satisfying. It was also food. The girls and women who took care of the buttermilk-drinkers knew me well and did not ever suggest by any act of expression that I was going too far. If anything they seemed pleased to see me and glad when I drank a very great deal of buttermilk. The little specks of butter floating on top or swimming throughout the liquid were a delight when they were filtered in the mouth and tasted. The big salt-shaker was there on the white marble counter—half a dozen of them—and the taste of the salt was a real joy. The place smelled clean and wonderful, it was cool, and the faces and bodies of the girls and women were fresh and sweet-smelling. The drinking of the buttermilk every afternoon was something I looked forward to all day, and the actual drinking of it was something that made me feel absolutely lordly in my aliveness.

The work was hard, but The Danish Dairy was there, and for a nickel I could drink all the cold buttermilk I liked. And I did. That was one of the great pleasures of the summer, almost as good as the eating of cold watermelon at home after work. I frequently ate an entire watermelon, and not a small one. The summer brought deep thirst to me, and there were good things by which to quench it.

My ears (by which, with my eyes, I lived and learned) had excellent hearing until I was seventeen or eighteen, so that I heard the sounds made by very small creatures, all manner of insects, mice at night, hummingbirds, leaves stirring or letting go and falling, soft whistlings, hummings, moanings.

When I was surely not much more than six, though, I began to hear with the inner ear, too, and although my memory is inaccurate about some of this I know that one of the important inner sounds I heard was what I must call the sound of wings.

This was probably the result of nothing more than an actual apparatus of the interior ear adjusting itself, restoring itself, fighting off illness or partial deafness, or the action of blood itself in my head at a moment of partial blockade somewhere, in some small but important vein in some small but important area. Or it was something else, something I have no way of naming. Whatever it was, from time to time, and not always at night before I fell asleep, I would hear (and feel) a plunging, shifting, charging action in my head which seemed to me to have a quality of seift flight, as if an enormous wing had brushed my soul. When this action was first noticed by me it stopped me cold on my tracks and frightened me, for I felt that the wing was death. A small boy is apt to give an experience of this order such a value. Later on, much later on, the action having become familiar was considered nothing, certainly nothing stranger than the continuous accumulation of phlegm in my nasal passages and throat.

I heard other things with the inner ear. I have already mentioned the music I heard. I had better remark further on this. As I rode my bike, music began to *happen* to me. Insofar as I am able to describe it it was orchestral music. The piano was often involved, but on the whole the music was that of a large orchestra which had become a single instrument. The music had magnificent form, great accumulative power, and passion of a high order—the passion, that is, of control, restraint, and denial—the human conditions out of which we know collective passion is most apt to reach an individual body and soul. Even though I alone knew about this music, I cherished it deeply and took great pride in it.

I both listened to the music and made it, or at any rate so it seemed. It was certainly happening to me, and it was happening as I performed other, less magnificent, work—as I delivered or picked up telegrams. The adventure of the music was always great, but in a quiet way. While the music was happening I kept wondering how it would fulfill itself, how it would round out its form and be finished. The music, I think it is quite understandable, tended to end when a bike ride ended, but this was not always so. Frequently one work, in one key of music or one dimension of memory or inner experience, would endure an entire work day and then carry itself over into evening, night, and sleep. In the morning, though, it would be gone and forgotten. It would be forgotten, that is, in its details, but not in its quality. If I took to the music actively and began to whistle as well as listen to it, this did not stop the orchestra. But when the bike ride ended and it was time for me to go among people to deliver or pick up a telegram, the orchestral portion of the music would fall away from inner hearing, no doubt because now the external hearing was involved with other sounds, but the whistling would continue while I was among the people, in a business office, or in a grape packing house, or in the telegraph office itself. This whistling bothered some people. The wife of the manager of the telegraph office once complaind about it to her husband who took me aside and with some awkwardness asked me not to whistle while I was in the telegraph office. I was astonished by this request for two reasons: first, because I hadn't been aware of the whistling, and second, because I couldn't imagine anybody resenting it. But genius is often deeply resented by small souls, so that if the world were a reasonable place all geniuses would be despised outcasts and eccentrics.

I was not always lucky in what I heard. It was not always an orchestra at work on a grand symphony. It was frequently a song, and quite strangely it would be a song which was not whole, which never in fact became whole. It would be a fragment of a song, certainly insofar as the words were concerned. And here perhaps lies the clue to the failure of this form to fulfill itself—its involvement in words.

For words are inadequate instruments of communication, or of the making of wholeness. Sounds and rhythms and measures must apparently see themselves through to ends, but words must be *driven* to their ends, and that is the difficulty and majesty of writing. All the same I was lucky enough. At a time when the air of the world still had purity I heard great music which no one else heard.

I was thirteen when I bought a phonograph and one record and carried it home under my arm on my bicycle to the house on San Benito Avenue. My mother was fiercely angry at me for spending twelve dollars on a piece of junk. She cursed the machine and me and was unable not to come at me with such violence that I had to run out of the house. She followed me in a kind of insane but nevertheless comic chase around the house. The phonograph was resting on the table in the parlor. I ran quickly up the front porch steps, into the parlor to the phonograph. I quickly wound it, put needle to disc, and ran out of the house again just as my mother came into the parlor. She was on her way after me when she began to hear the music of the phonograph record. I was something called *Sonia*, performed by Paul Whiteman's band. I expected my mother to continue the chase, but she didn't. I myself stopped in the backyard to listen to the music. After about a minute I went back into the house. My mother was standing over the machine, listening to the music. Her anger was gone and in place of it I saw in her face the deep sorrow of her nature, her family, her race. A moment of jazz-band orchestration had done this.

When the record ended she turned to me and said, "All right. I had no idea. It is all right. Take good care of the machine. You have this one record only?"

I told her there was another song on the reverse side of the record. She sat down and said, "Please let me hear it."

On the reverse side was something called "*Hi-li, Hi-lo*," I believe.

That was the beginning of external music in my own life, in my own family, and in my own house. My sisters and my brothers were thrilled by the phonograph, and the one record. My mother established the rule that I alone might buy one new record a week, which I did. She waited eagerly for the arrival of this record and she listened to it again and again. This music must have been very strange to her, certainly music altogether unlike anything she had ever heard in Armenia, unlike the hymns she'd heard and sung at church. And yet she loved the music.

After a time I sent two dollars to a mail order house and received twelve records. This was a great bargain. The quality of the music was poor, but having twelve records for the price of three was exciting, and it satisfied the family necessity to be economical in all things.

But I had been listening to my own bike-riding music long before the arrival of the phonograph.

Now, it is important to understand two things: first, that after the phonograph became an important part of the family life I continued to hear my own music, and second, as I listened more and more to the music of the phonograph I heard my own music less and less.

If the external ear is surfeited with music, the internal ear tends to become deaf. If the body is satisfied, the soul tends to become unwilling or unable to seek satisfaction.

On the last day of August in the year 1908 in the city of Fresno I came into the world, sick to death with astonishment, anger and gladness. My father Armenak Saroyan was thirty-four years of age, my mother Takoohi Saroyan twenty-six.

In less than three years my father was dead. My mother survived him by thirty-nine years.

My father had been educated at the American Presbyterian School in Bitlis. He was a preacher by profession. He kept a journal in English and in Armenian, he wrote philosophical essays, poems, accounts of his travels. He was a good extemporaneous speaker.

My mother received no formal education, but learned to read and write Armenian. She also learned to read English and could sign her name. Her reading in English was poor, however, so that she glanced only at newspapers now and then.

Her mother, Lucy, could read and write no language, but spoke eloquently in Armenian, Kurdish and Turkish.

My father's father's name was Petrus, who was the son of Sarkis, who was a Saroyan by adoption, hence while both sides of my family bear the same name they are not related. My mother's father's name was Minas, but I have forgotten his father's name. Family memory was confined to the city of Bitlis. I heard no family lore involving any other city. The city (and its name) has always meant a great deal to me.

My father reached New York alone in 1905. After two years he was reunited there with his wife, his daughters Cosetts and Zabel, which appears to be a variant of Isabelle. He saw for the first time his son Henry, born in Erzeroum, enroute to America.

This journey from Bitlis to New York took almost two years, for it was necessary for my grandmother Lucy who was in charge of the journey to halt several times while she and her daughters Takoohi and Verkine and her son Aram worked to earn money for further passage.

They spent three or four months in Erzeroum, a month or two in Marseille, and almost six months in Havre. My uncle Aram, then eleven or so, learned French and acted as interpreter for many Armenians on their way to America. The women knitted stockings which Aram sold to small shopkeepers.

My father preached to an Armenian congregation in Paterson, New Jersey, for a time. He also wrote articles for *The Christian Herald*, or at any rate was connected in some capacity with that publication. His best friend in America was a Presbyterian minister called Dr. William Stonehill who died a few months before I was born. I was named William after this man. Had he not died I have heard that it was my father's intention to name me Petrus after his father.

Dr. Stonehill was the center of a religious circle of young ministers educated by the Presbyterians in Armenia, Greece, Bulgaria, Serbia, Egypt and a number of other Near Eastern countries. There was always in my life a photograph of these young men standing around Dr. Stonehill and his wife. Most of them wore large black moustaches, and all of them seemed enormously earnest. For a number of years I knew the names of everybody in the photograph, but I no longer remember them.

In 1928 when I first went to New York from California I went to Brooklyn and pressed the doorbell of Mrs. William Stonehill's house. She herself came to the door, looked at me a moment, and then said quietly, "You are Armenak Saroyan's son. Please come in."

I had not written to her, telling of my intention to visit her because I felt that I might not do so at the last minute. I had no idea why I wanted to see where she lived, for it was a new house, not a house my father had ever entered. I recognized her instantly as the lady in the photograph. She was very kind and told me about my father and my mother when she had known them. My father liked to go about in good clothes and to dress for the pulpit, she said, but my mother resisted the clothes of America. She had had considerable difficulty with my mother about clothing. My mother confirmed that this had been true. She remarked that she preferred her own clothes, from Bitlis, because they *were* her own, because she was comfortable in them, and because she did not like to wear other people's clothing.

I was just twenty when I visited Mrs. Stonehill. In reply to her questions I told her how my family had fared in California, and I remarked that I had come to New York because I had always wanted to, and because I was a writer. She then revealed that she too was a writer, and handed me two booklets she had had published at her own expense. In the booklets were poems she had written. On the subway back to New York I read through each of the booklets, and again in my furnished room in the New York Hotel, near Washington Market, for which I paid three dollars a week, a room which stank. The poems were terribly lovely, lonely, meaningless, artificial and absurd. They broke my heart and brought tears to my eyes. She had invited me to a church social and was discreetly astonished when I remarked as politely as possible that I never went to such affairs because I never felt at ease at them, and also because my spare time was spent in the streets of New York or at the Public Library on Fifth Avenue. She remarked that my father had always taken active part in church affairs. I replied that I was determined to become a good writer.

My father wasn't home the night I was born. My uncle Mousheg Saroyan's mother was midwife. The birth was swift, relatively painless, and unrecorded. A few minutes before I was born my mother was on her feet, holding a door for support, which appears to have been a family custom. My father was at the vineyard home of his cousins the Mouradians, near Sanger, eleven miles east of Fresno. He was working on their vineyard. He had been promised the Armenian church in Yettem, not far from Fresno, but the congregation there was Turkish-speaking and my father spoke Turkish poorly. He had therefore found himself out of work and had taken any work that had been available.

When I was two he moved his family to San Bruno, twenty-five miles south of San Francisco. Then he moved to San Francisco where he was connected for a time with the Salvation Army, and finally he moved to Campbell, a small town near San Jose, California, where he died in July of 1911.

In Campbell, much like Sherwood Anderson's father somewhere in the Midwest, he raised chickens and sold eggs, but this venture was not successful, either. The chicks died in enormous lots, the hens caught all sorts of diseases, they laid poorly, and finally the market for eggs was bad the whole time he was in the business.

Near the home in Campbell lived a very old Portuguese lady whose children had all married and wandered away. My mother called her Papchah, which was probably the way my mother heard the old lady's name. This woman was a frequent visitor at our house, chatting with my mother in Portuguese while my mother replied in Armenian. The old lady always went home with me after a visit, for she missed her children. My mother said that whenever she went to Papchah's to fetch me home she found me sitting on a box watching the old lady and listening to her, a thick slice of buttered bread in my hand, three or four flies walking around on the butter.

My mother also remembered an Assyrian woman on the boat from Havre to New York, in steerage. This woman helped my mother take care of her children, keep them fed and clean and comfortable in an area of the boat that was crowded, filthy, and painfully depressing. The woman had watched my mother the first few hours out of Havre, and then she had gone to my mother and after saying a few words in Assyrian which my mother had not understood she had gone to work helping her and delivering her from the anxiety and fear that was plainly showing in her face. My mother told me a few years before she died that she would never forget this woman and that she would always thank God for her.

Another friend on the boat was a blond Norwegian sailor who took shy pleasure in bringing food to my mother, in smiling at her, and in hugging my sisters and my brother. My mother said that if she had ever loved a man she had loved this one. He said a few words in Norwegian each time he visited her and my mother said a few in Armenian, and after a moment he disappeared, but every day of the voyage he came with food and love.

Who are these people? Papchah, the Assyrian woman, the young Norwegian seaman? They are my family. They are the people of love.

A man must think well of his family. It is the basic requirement by which he may achieve authentic personal identity, or the illusion of it, which is either the same thing or just as good. It is accurate for a man to think well of his family, no matter what kind of people they may appear to have been, or be, for if a man notices only that the

members of his faimly are nothing much, it is he himself that is
nothing much, it is he himself who lacks intelligence, understanding,
imagination and most important of all love. If a man considers any
family with intelligence, understanding, imagination and love, that
family must be seen to be great in something or other—in the
capacity to survive, for instance, if in nothing else, which is enough.
Merely to survive is to keep the hope of greatness, accuracy, and
grace alive. The hope of these things is as important as the things
themselves, for if a family hasn't them, they may get them, and if a
family has them, they may lose them.

I decided very early to love my family, and to see in each of its
members something rare and good as well as the miserable and
painful things that were obvious. I do not think that in writing of
them I ever lied, I merely chose to notice in them the things I
cherished and preferred, and to refer to the things I didn't cherish
with humor and charity. The writer in the end creates his family, his
nation, his culture and worth, and I believe that I have more effectively than any other member of the Saroyan family created that
family, which appears all through my writing but especially in the
small book called *My Name Is Aram*.

The last two letters of the name William are the same as the
last two letters of the name Aram. Had I been invited to choose a
name for myself I believe I would have chosen Aram. The early
life and young manhood of my mother's brother Aram appealed to
me deeply, I admired his speed and humor, and I liked the name
itself with the name Saroyan. The two seemed to go well together.
The name Aram had long been a favorite of the Armenians. I had
seen heroic drawings of a number of famous Armenians named Aram
in various Armenian newspapers, magazines and books, and I
liked the whole inaccurate lore that I came to associate with the
name. I gave Aram of the book *My Name Is Aram* the last name
of Garoghlanian because that was my grandmother Lucy's name before she married Minas Saroyan when she was eleven and he was
twenty-one or twenty-two. I gave my son the Aram because I had
come to think of the name as my true name, and since it was too
late for me to have it, I wanted him to have it.

There were times, however, in my life when I found my family and
the name Saroyan unbearable.

I thought of running away from home. I thought of changing my
name. And I thought of finding a wife as soon as possible and

starting a family of my own with a name of its own. I began to have these troubled longings when I was not much more than eight or nine, and they continued to be valid until I was nineteen or twenty, but as the years went by they became less and less valid, so that after I was thirteen or fourteen I knew they were nonsense.

It was clear to me that a change of scene and name would not change *me*. The scene would change, the name would be different, but I would still be who I was, and the challenge of seeking to become who I wished to be would be the same. I never in my life thought of denying my nationality. If my family happened to annoy me I sometimes found that I wanted to be rid of them once and for all, but this feeling was never of duration.

My cousin Haig Saroyan, Byzant's son, when we sold *The Fresno Evening Herald* together, told George Riekas that he, Haig, was an American. I told Haig we were all Americans, but what Riekas wanted to know was the nationality of Haig's family, which was Armenian. Haig said, "No, my nationality is not Armenian. I had a fight with my father last night, and I quit." A few days later, though, he told me that his nationality was Armenian again, as he and his father had made up.

Now and then the name Saroyan seemed silly to me, as any word is apt to seem if one thinks about it long enough. And of course it was not the name that was ever silly, it was myself, it was the frustration I felt of my desire to become effective in my life. The name simply didn't stand for anything. It didn't mean anything. I might as well have been named Mud, as I once wrote.

In the midst of this annoyance with my family there was always a great affection for them, and a good deal of hopefulness about my intention to give the name importance. The name William was sometimes all right and sometimes not, but little by little both names began to be all right. They were the sounds and images which somewhat accurately signified myself.

Once in the third grade at Emerson School a substitute teacher looking over the class before taking the roll nodded to me, half-smiled and said, "You are, I take it, William Saroyan."

I was absolutely delighted, and went entirely out of my way not to annoy her, and not to permit anybody else to do so. She had been informed by the Principal that I would be the problem of her assignment, and she had taken a chance on guessing which face would fit the name. Had she asked someone else I am sure I would have driven her from the room in tears in a good deal under an hour. I considered her quite pretty and rather intelligent. Actually, D. D. Davis may have told her that my hair would be uncombed and he may have given her a brief description of myself and my nature. Even so, the fact that she knew who I was made a fool of me. I was so well-behaved I was ashamed of myself.

A good deal of this naive pride in recognition by strangers still exists, so that if a rake-man in a gambling house calls out to me, "Hiya, Bill!" I must gamble at his table, chat with him, and permit others to know that I am known by a rake-man, have traveled, and am somebody. I am pleased when I am greeted by name by a stranger. I have been friendly with half-drunken school teachers who have come to my table in a restaurant or a nightclub and reported to me that they have read my book. Many people who greet a writer tell him they have read his book, making it difficult for the writer to know which book they are talking about. Once, after a few minutes, it turned out that the book was *The Grapes of Wrath* by John Steinbeck. I remember that I remarked, "I am sorry. I didn't write that book. William Faulkner wrote it."

A man goes to a great deal of trouble to create his name, only to discover that the name is now creating him. He finds that he must live up to a lore which has come to be associated with his name. This living up to the lore soon becomes natural.

When I visited George Bernard Shaw in 1944 I sensed immediately that such had been the case with him, for he was a gentle, delicate, kind, little man who had established a pose, and then lived it so steadily and effectively that the pose had become real. Like myself, his nature had been obviously a deeply troubled one in the beginning. He had been a man who had seen the futility, meaninglessness and sorrow of life, but had permitted himself to thrust aside these feelings and to perform another George Bernard Shaw, which is art and proper.

The young heart knows a sickness of family. A man's involvement in a family is not all love and gladness. Every man wonders at one time or another why he is a member of his own family instead of a member of another one. If one's own family is unimportant, insignificant, undistinguished, commonplace, ineffective, or merely unknown, it is understandable that a young member of the family may now and then wish he'd had better luck in the matter of his birth.

I was once astonished by a man who remarked unhappily that he wished he had been born to a poor family because he had always wanted to be a writer. His family was socially prominent in the city of San Francisco and enormously wealthy. He said that it had been impossible for him under those circumstances to become a writer. After a moment I stopped being astonished and began to see the validity of his remarks.

Displeasure with one's family must be very nearly universal. Members of all families must know it in one degree or another. And in the end it is quite unlikely that there has ever lived a man who did not find the human race itself distasteful to him.

But the fact remains that if a man is to go on enduring time, it is in order for him to accept his own family, and to cherish the whole human family. A man cannot live his life effectively hating what he is. Illness and hatred go together and they are involved in death. While a man lives it is better for him to avoid purposeful involvement in death, for the inevitable involvement is always more than enough for him to put up with or to put to use in the style with which he lives and works.

A man longs to belong to a family which is noble, honorable, intelligent, graceful, handsome, useful, courageous, spiritually, wealthy, kind, loving, healthy, and amusing, but he invariably finds that he belongs to no such family. If he notices nobility in his family, he also notices far greater absence of it. And the same is true of the other things. There is always more of the poor things than of the good things. Somebody in the family is feeble-minded. Somebody else is dishonest. Somebody else is ugly in body, face, and nature. Somebody else is pathetic. Somebody else has no more courage than a mouse. And so on. It is not easy for a man to adjust himself to the truth that the human race is such an inferior order of animal life, or that his own family is not much better than the human race in general.

It is natural for newcomers to expect a great deal of the family to which they belong.

In the end I decided I must consider *myself* my family entirely. I saw that I could not do much about the other members of the family. I decided I must do as much as possible about myself.

When I stopped expecting anything important of anybody except-

ing myself I began to find many things of worth in everybody else
that I had never before noticed, and I began to look upon the
worthless things I saw with amusement and affection.

This is an important achievement in the growth of a soul, for it
is true that one is one's self the human race insofar as the achievement of excellence is concerned. It is not permissible or proper to
make demands of anyone but one's self. Nothing can come of it.
One cannot demand of a father or a mother, of a brother or a sister,
of a wife or a son or a daughter. One can demand only of one's own
self, and to all others give understanding or love or both.

But the achievement of excellence is forever no more than a matter
of essay and trial. Failure is constant and inevitable so that by noticing
failure in others with amusement, understanding, and affection, one's
own failure becomes less and less annoying.

My family had in its lore many absurd people, few wonderful
ones. The wonderful ones were dead and gone but they were not
forgotten. I heard about the miserable ones with shame and regret,
the wonderful ones with thankfulness and pleasure. But even the
wonderful ones weren't much. Their fame was local and meaningless.

As for the current members of the family, they simply weren't
much. For the most part they were stupid or uselessly clever, physically junky and unattractive, unconscious, unaware, indifferent,
apathetic, or devoid of any special quality by which I could feel there
was any point in their being alive at all.

They seemed to be part of the horde of unborn souls which come
and go, which no one notices have come or have gone.

Among these people, who were my own family, I was a stranger.
There was no one I could speak to meaningfully. The talk was in-
cessantly about things that were not only boring but infuriating.
Everybody was devoid of ideas. There was no turning out after truth,
honor, grace. There was eating, sleeping, working, earning money,
saving money, dreaming of money, fretting about money.

The true religion of my family was always personal.

We weren't irreligious, but we had long preferred to keep our religion to ourselves. It is true that one of our boys had made the pil-
grimage to Jerusalem in 1801, but the family has it that he was in-
sincere, for he transacted considerable profitable business enroute,
and spent a rather long time in Constantinople on the way back—

a city at that time even more involved in matters of pleasure than it is now. Still, from the time of his return to the end of his life he was appropriately honored for having made the trip.

The family had God, but the attitude was that He was one of the early members of the family. The pose of Christ, his intelligence, manners and wit were carefully examined and found wanting.

If we had any Saints at all, they were members of the family about whom over the years a vast lore of lies had been invented, which in time came to considered amusing gospel.

One of these Saints was a boy named Kissak who died at the age of eleven. He was the handsomest, wisest, most shining man who had ever lived. This world and life were too coarse for him to put up with, that's all.

Two others were the twins, Ara and Araxi Saroukhan, as the name was said at that time and still is by several branches of the family. Ara had dark skin, eyes, and hair, Araxi fair skin, blue eyes, red hair. These two were lied into Sainthood on the basis of handsomeness, beauty, wit, mimicry, arrogance, and contempt for law and reality. Araxi married a Kurd when she was twelve, bore him three sons and three daughters, thereby bringing the entire Kurdish nation into the fold of the family. Ara, when he was twenty-seven, fell off his father's house while drunk, got up, walked away, and is said to have gone to India.

These were lies. Everybody in the family knew they were, and yet variations of them, as well as an assortment of new ones, are still being told, disbelieved, and finally believed, for as time goes by any man reconsidering any fable he may have heard before he was ten, however unlikely, is apt to believe it *might* be true, for he knows he heard his own father tell him the fable, and he knows the *telling* of it—if nothing else about it—actually happened.

And between the reality of the fable itself and the reality of the telling of it, he does not feel there is enough difference to warrant the destruction of an old church and the founding of a new one.

The family *was* the church, and part of the religion was to tell lies because it was intelligent and imaginative to do so, and because it tended to improve the nature of the family.

The lies were told in Bitlis, in the fortress city high in the mountains, in the long snow of winter, in the long hot quietude of summer.

In Bitlis there was no formal Saint.

In Fresno there was one. But even *he* did not wear the title.

In the rented house on San Benito Avenue, on the piano in the parlor, was a white-chalk slab about the size of a sheet of typing paper on which the head of an old man had been carved in bas-relief and then painted brown. Whoever this man was, he is the nearest thing to a formal Saint I am willing to believe ever entered into my life. I saw the bas-relief from the time I was eight, I still have it, and it still means something to me.

At first I saw it there on the piano and scarcely looked at it. It was a slab, almost square-shaped, that someone had given a place of honor in the house, and that was enough for me. I suppose I felt at first that anything clearly defined, such as the slab, was an object of beauty and therefore deserved to be placed somewhere where it would be seen and where it would exert an influence. The slab certainly succeeded in exerting an influence on me. I believed it to be important.

One day I happened to notice that it was more than a shape. I got up on the piano stool and examined it. What it was was the head of an old man with a long square beard in what I think is called three-quarter profile. This also seemed proper—that is, that the shape should contain the image of the head of an old man. It also seemed proper that the old man appeared to be deeply earnest and sorrowful. I could readily understand that he *might* be. I believed he must be a member of the family.

Thereafter when I felt angry or confused I found that I wanted to look at the old man, and I would go to the piano, get up on the stool, and look at him until I no longer felt angry or confused. Just looking at the carved outline of his head and beard brought peace to my soul and resignation to my heart and mind about my personal ignorance and insignificance. For a long time I did not need to know anything more about the man, but one day I spoke to my grandmother Lucy about him.

"Who is he?" I said.

"Krikor Illuminator," she replied in Armenian, which would be, "Krikor Loosavoreach," as my grandmother pronounced the language. Loosavoreach, however it may be pronounced or spelled in English, means The Illuminator, or more literally The Light-Thrower. My grandmother did not call him *Saint* Krikor Loosavoreach, but I have seen him referred to in English as St. Gregory the Illuminator. One way or the other he is the same man. The bas-relief of his head found

its way into the house in which I lived, my eyes found their way to
the shape of the slab, to the image of the head of the man himself,
and finally my imagination, ignorance, insignificance, longing and
many other things gave the carving reality: he was myself, he was
the way I felt about this life and world at the age of eight,
nine, and ten, and he would be the way I would feel at eighty, most
likely.

Here memory fails me and I may as well confess it. I do not remember if my grandmother told me that he invented the Armenian alphabet, or that he took the spoken language and put it
into print, or that he translated the Bible into the Armenian language—into of course *Krabar*, or The Written Word, which is
classical Armenian, as against *Ahshkharabar*, which is The World's
Word. My own family's language is the World's Word. At any
rate, I found out that his name was Krikor, and the name became
in some of my earliest stories the name of my brother. Again and
again I wrote, *My brother Krikor.*

Krikor's probable involvement in language, in the alphabet, in
The Word, in the matter of Light, of Enlightenment, of the holy
hope of banishing ignorance from the human heart, head, body and
soul seemed precisely right to me, and I was deeply influenced by
this intelligence, or mistaken intelligence, for as I've said I'm not
sure about any of this. Krikor Illuminator may have been so named
for other reasons than the alphabet, The Word, language, paper,
print, books. It doesn't matter. Whoever he was, I *believed* he was
involved in these things, for by then I was involved in them, and
Krikor and I were the same man.

My grandmother had purchased the slab for twenty-five cents.
What impelled her to squander the money I can't imagine, but I
am sure it must have been something deeply religious in a very
personal way.

The wish to change the world, or to rid it of insects, must be
a basic one in the early lives of writers, for I haven't met a writer yet,
unknown or famous, who wasn't in his childhood annoyed by ants,
bugs, insects, or parents.

Still, the world goes right on making debris, insects come forth
delicately out of rot and ferment, and parents fight it out with children.

The streets are the hope of both: angry fathers turn to them for peace, and impatient sons run to them for the beginning they believe will get them somewhere.

The streets of Oakland were much involved in sleep, as all streets, are in the end. I saw them, dreamed them, saw them again, and still they were not out of sleep. I walked in them more asleep than awake, woke up in them only to feel I had awakened into deeper sleep, for the streets are sleep itself, not one man's sleep, but the sleep of the dead. It is in the streets that the dead live on. It is there that the life of man is immortal, for there is no man dead who isn't in the streets again, going his way.

Fred Finch was a number of buildings, a few acres in which there was a vegetable garden, a barn, a storage building, and something like a meadow, after which came woods, but the best woods were past the boundaries of the place.

Peralta Street was in the hills which were not big. I walked that street from the time immediately after I was three to the time immediately after I was seven. From Peralta a curved road climbed to the Administration Building, then went down to Peralta again.

I was walking down that road one day when a boy on a bicycle knocked me down. My head struck one of the jagged stones bordering the road, and I got up with a cut over my left eye. I wasn't hurt but I *was* surprised and annoyed and I began to bawl, although I knew I didn't need to. No one believed I didn't need to, though. My face was covered with blood. I might have gone on bawling, but I couldn't imagine what the good of that would be, so I stopped. I was bored.

John Wesley Hagan took me by horse and wagon to a doctor who sewed the cut together. It was no trouble for the doctor to do this simple surgical work. The man sewed the flesh back together, and I stood and waited while he did it. He said nothing, John Wesley Hagan said nothing, and I said nothing.

After that John Wesley Hagan and I were friends, and a theory that I was a brave fellow got around in the orphanage. It was a false theory as far as I was concerned because I hadn't saved anybody from drowning in the sea or from burning to death in a small locked room somewhere. I didn't go to any trouble to dispute the theory, though, mainly I think because I didn't know how.

John Wesley Hagan was the Superintendent of Fred Finch. He was Scotch, fifty or so, slim and quiet, and he seemed to have an earnest nature and a sense of humor at the same time. Now and then when it was time for him to take the horse and wagon to market, to fetch provisions he sought me out in the playground and told me I could go with him. We sat together on the seat of the uncovered wagon, and the horse took off, generally knowing where to go and when to stop. Hagan and I did not chat, as I remember it, but there was real communication between us. I remember being with him in a store and having him take a large spoon of chocolate and put it before my mouth. I opened my mouth and he dumped the chocolate in and I ate it. It was an hour or so before supper time and his own wife would have told him that he was spoiling me and spoiling my dinner, but he did it just the same—for she wasn't there —and I was glad that he did.

From the seat of the wagon the streets of Oakland were different. I was up, looking down. The streets were not the same from the seat of the wagon, nor was I, but it was Hagan more than the wagon that made the change in me. It was his having picked me out of the small boys to go with him. I didn't like him especially, because a small boy never likes a Superintendent, but I didn't hate him, either, as most boys did.

Later on, though, I *did* hate him, but it wasn't for long. I can't hate for long. It isn't worth it.

His wife was Lillian Pender. She was rather delicate and beautiful. She painted in oils, but bore him no children. She painted portraits of a number of the children at Fred Finch. One day I sat for her. I sat a few more times, I think, but I never saw the portrait. She never finished it, most likely. She finished the portrait of the boy who was killed in the automobile accident, though. The portrait was reproduced in color on a postcard, and everybody old enough to do so was permitted to take a batch of these cards and go around ringing doorbells and selling them.

The money thus obtained was brought to Lillian Pender, for the orphanage, for the boy's mother, for a tombstone for him, I forget which. There was great rivalry among the older boys and girls in the matter of the number of cards sold and the amount of money brought to Lillian Pender. He was a blond boy of eight or so who wore light blue overalls and seemed awfully sad, almost as if he knew he would not live very long. Part of the lore of his death had to do with the opening up of new fields of adventure for the boys and girls who went out and sold the cards. Many of the boys kept some of the money for themselves or bought things they had al-

ways wanted: Pocket knives, mainly. Several boys proudly told of
stealing things in stores. The excitement got to be too much for the
smaller boys, so one day several of the boys who were in my ward,
the smallest boys at Fred Finch, Sammy Isaacs, Teddy Dolan and
myself, decided to get hold of some of the cards and go out into
the streets and sell them.

I went to Lillian Pender's office or studio and found hundreds of
the cards on her desk and nobody there to ask what I wanted. I
took a great many of the cards and left the office. I handed some to
Sammy Isaacs, some to Teddy Dolan, and kept some for myself. We
then took off to see how we would make out in this adventure.

I ran a block or so up Peralta, then down into another street, and
finally to the door of a house, to press the bell-button. A woman
came to the door. I told her the story of the boy's death. She went
inside a moment, came back with a number of coins, handed them
to me, and took a card. I remember that there were tears in her
eyes and that her voice was pity-laden.

She was sorry the poor little boy had been killed and glad I hadn't
and handed me the money.

This was rather strange.

It was good to ring a doorbell and have somebody unknown open
it, to speak to a stranger, and then to receive money from the
stranger, but it was something else, too. Money is good, children love
money for its own sake, as money, as coins, but this was funny
money. It was pity money. It was begged money. I took the money
and ran back to Sammy Isaacs and Teddy Dolan. We talked about
what happened to each of us. We knew it was not necessary to be
ten or eleven or twelve to ring a doorbell and get money for a postcard. Each of us had been given money by the person who had
come to the door. The money was not a nickel and a couple of pennies. It was real money. It was quarters and half-dollar pieces, and
a few nickels and dimes thrown in.

We went on with the work and soon each of us had a small
pocketful of coins. We then went to a store and spent some of the
money on candy and other things we wanted.

When it was dark we decided to call it a day and go back, but
when we reached the orphanage we found the whole place in an
uproar on the theory that we had got lost, had been kidnapped, or had
run away.

We turned in the money but were not thanked for it.

For awhile we believed we were to go without supper, since we had not been on time for it and everybody else had already had supper, but at last the cook fixed us a plate each and we sat down in the big dining room and ate in silence.

Years later I decided to write a play. I wrote it and called it *Subway Circus*. In this play a small boy is kept after school for dreaming. His teacher asks him questions of arithmetic.

"Now, if a boy has five apples and gives away two, how many apples remain?" she says.

"What kind of apples?" the boy says.

The teacher speaks to the Principal of the school about this. The Principal says to the teacher, "Let *him* ask you *questions*."

The boy then asks questions, and among them is this one: "What is a street?"

The year was 1935. I was in New York for the second time in my life. I was twenty-seven years old. I had had a book of short stories published. I was famous. I had been famous for two years. I had been famous before the publication of *The Daring Young Man on the Flying* Trapeze in Story Magazine, but not as a writer. I had been famous as myself. A few days after the story was published I was famous as a writer. How famous can you be? What is the good of it?

Still, I will not repudiate my fame. I got it, I earned it, I have it. My name is known to millians I do not know, and I wanted this to be so. I have met thousands of people I would not have met had I not become famous, and I wanted this to be so, too. My writing is careless, but all through it is something that is good, that is mine alone, that no other writer could ever achieve.

What is this thing?

It is love of streets. It is love of this world and this life, which in the end must become for each of us old and rotten, which each of us must regret, of which each of us must be ashamed.

Our comfort is the streets, the lanes we took, the time we took in them, the other walkers we saw in them, in the light of day, in the electric light of night, in wind, in rain, in snow—the hard, gray streets in which we lived or tried, in which we were blind or came to seeing.

One day on my way home from Sequoia School in Oakland where I was in the first grade I heard a small boy cry. The boy was my own age, and someone in his family had died, perhaps his mother or his father. The boy stood on a high porch. In front of the house was a hearse. I stood across the street, alone there, as the boy was alone on the porch. I heard the boy cry. I saw men carry a casket out of the house, across the porch, down the steps. I saw the boy follow them, dressed in his best clothes. I saw the men slide the casket into the hearse. In my own heart I wept for the stranger who was dead, as the boy wept.

What is a street? It is where the living weep, where the dead go off in silence to their peace.

Death made me sick. Death hurt me. Death annoyed me. Death and dirt kept me from thinking. Death in the streets made me want to know.

The weeping boy made me want to think of a way to get the dead one back for him. The sound of his weeping made me want to find out a way to do that. I believed something might be invented to bring back the dead. I went to work on this invention, brokenhearted by the boy's sorrow, thinking of his need of love.

I went to work on the invention in the playground at Fred Finch, working with discarded things. I searched among the stuff that would be carted away the following morning and found two empty tomato cans. I removed the labels on which I saw engravings of red tomatoes. I dug two holes in the earth. I placed a can in each of these holes, the open tops level with the earth. I filled one can with water, and sat all afternoon thinking about the can full of water and about the empty can beside it. I believed I was on my way to the answer for the boy.

If I could get the water out of the full can into the can which was empty, then no doubt the boy could get the dead back. He could get love back. I sat and thought. How could I get the water to transfer itself from the full can to the empty one? That was the problem. I concentrated on the problem, watching both cans intently, waiting for love to achieve this simple miracle. I believed love could do it. I waited, brooded, thought, remembered, concentrated. I packed the earth around the edges of the tops of each can, believing this might help. I dreamed about the joy of the boy seeing his father or mother walking up the street, not knowing how this thing had happened, not knowing I had done it.

The water remained where it was. The empty can remained empty.

I lifted the full can out of the earth and poured the water into the empty can and when it was full I lifted it out of the earth, too. I poured the water back and forth from one can to the other. I poured the water into one of the holes in the ground. I went back to the faucet and filled both cans with water and took them back to where I had been thinking. Now I had both cans filled with water, but I had invented nothing, and out of thought and love had not yet made anything impossible happen, which is what I wanted to do. I set the cans on the surface of the earth and watched them a long time, thinking steadily and remembering the boy and the anguish of the heart when it has lost something, when it has lost the source of love. Both cans were full of water in front of my eyes. I poured the water out of one can into the dry hole in the ground, and again saw the water disappear.

The problem was still simple and clear: to get the water in the full can to go by itself into the empty can.

This time the cans were not set into the earth, they were placed on the surface of it. There was a distance of eight or nine inches between them. The water did not lift itself out of one can into the other. The water did not disappear out of one can and re-appear in the other. One can remained full, the other empty. I brought the cans together, hoping this might do the trick.

I felt desperately that I must do this thing. I must witness it. I must make it come to pass. I kept hearing the boy cry. I kept seeing him follow the casket to the hearse.

But the thing would not happen.

I poured the water out of the full can and saw it steal away into the earth.

I kicked the can, and then I kicked the other can. By turns I kicked them both until I had gone all the way across the playground.

A number of boys I knew by face but not by name got into the game and the cans were kicked back and forth until they were out of shape and you could never get water into them again.

The invention failed. The dead did not come back. Death remained death. The end remained the end. When the bell rang I went into the dining room and ate supper. There was nothing else to do under the circumstances.

I am not taking the world street by street, for I never lived or walked or wrote in chronological order. In the beginning I lived in the end, I lived in the middle, I lived in the beginning, all at once and altogether, and it was so in the middle, and will be so in the end. I never had the time or the nature to live only in the beginning in the beginning, or to live only in the middle in the middle.

I walked every which way in the streets. I lived every which way in the time of them. I wrote every which way in my own time, which I knew was not my own time but anybody's, and the time of the dead as well. I longed for order and I longed for my own self. The order I found was the order of disorder. The self I came to, or the self that came to me, was not my own.

I was somebody more in the streets.

The first street of all was a road.

The horse was hitched to the wagon, the wagon was loaded with my father's belongings, my mother sat on the seat, my two sisters, my brother and myself sat in the back. My father got up onto the wagon and sat beside my mother. He took the reins and clicked at the horse. The horse and the wagon began to move down the country road. I looked back and saw a house surrounded by grape vines. We had lived there, but I did not remember that we had. The day smelled of heat, dust, grass and water. The wagon rocked. My father clicked at the horse again. I fell asleep.

After that, my father was dead. I saw him once and never haw him again. The road was near the town of Sanger, which is nine miles east of Fresno. The wagon stopped in Fresno, and from there my father took his family by train to San Bruno, but I did not remember the arrival of the wagon in Fresno, the departure of the train, my father, or anything else.

From the beginning I slept and awoke by turns, but for a long time I didn't remember anything, and then for a long time I remembered one thing or another but didn't remember the greater part of anything.

Fresno, Sanger, San Jose, Campbell, San Bruno, San Francisco, Oakland—these are the places I knew when there was no true knowing, when it was all sleep and no memory.

The streets of Fresno followed the letters of the alphabet, and numbers, and they were named after saints, and others. Across the Southern Pacific tracks in 1908 was A Street, and still is, but Z Street was nowhere at all. H Street was just inside the S.P. tracks. Between Tulare and Kern, on H Street was a house in 1908, in which I was born.

The name of the vineyard near Sanger I have forgotten, but it had a Spanish name. Was it La Paloma? I believe it was. I remember nothing. I go on hearsay.

I began in earnest at the Fred Finch Orphanage in Oakland, California. I said goodbye to my mother and began. I began to reason, to think, to wonder what it was all about. Until this goodbye there has been no reason to notice or remember. I had noticed and remembered by accident, but now I noticed and remembered because I wanted to know who I was, where I belonged, and what I was supposed to do. I was my father's son, but he was dead. I was my mother's son, but she was gone. I was Henry's brother. He was in another ward at the orphanage, the ward for boys who were six or over. I was Cosette's brother and Zabel's brother, and they were in the ward for girls. Still, the four of us were there in the orphanage together. I was called Willie. I didn't know much about the other name, although I had heard it. I do not remember having been sure it was my name. I did not know anything about nationality or religion.

In my ward this is what I knew: I was there with five or six other smal boys and our matron was a woman named Mrs. Winchester.

At night two or three of the boys in the ward rocked their cribs and wept, trying to hide from the others that they were doing so, for it had come to pass that it was shameful to rock a crib, cry, or wet the bed. In the dark of the ward the boys who were not rocking and crying talked to one another. They laughed at Mrs. Winchester and they laughed at the rockers and criers. Now and then somebody rocking and crying would stop to speak to the others, so that the others would perhaps believe he had not been rocking and crying. But then in a moment he would fall silent and soon he would be rocking and crying again. Finally, everybody would fall silent, and then asleep.

Who was I? I was one of the boys in the ward for small boys. Where did I belong? I didn't know, but I didn't believe I belonged where I was. What was I supposed to do? I was supposed to obey the rules, and I was supposed to learn to dress myself, tie my shoe laces, and to believe the story about God.

I saw my brother every day but he was in another part of the life at the place. I asked him where our mother was and he told me she was in San Francisco, working as a maid for a family. I asked him when we would see her again and he said he didn't know. I asked him if he liked this place and he said he hated it.

Everybody in the place hated it. It wasn't home, that's all.

One Sunday my mother came from San Francisco with a basket

full of sandwiches, and we had a picnic, sitting on the grass of a hill, my mother handing sandwiches around, all of us eating and talking. Her English was poor, but she could make herself understood. She spoke in Armenian to my oldest sister, Cosette, who was then twelve. I could not understand what they were saying.

Farewell to the boys and girls. Whoever he was I remember Melvin Athey. Whoever she was I remember Juanita Pollard. The white pitcher full of cold milk on warm afternoons I remember. The cook's meat pies with the golden crust. The Sunday breakfast eggs, brown and white. The martial walks to Sunday School. The witches in the hills. The hazelnuts in the trees. The ferns and the poison oak along the paths. The waterdogs, captured and brought home. The blue-bellied lizards which snapped off their tails in captivity. The climbing of the slim eucalyptus trees, making them bend to the earth again. The visiting tellers of tales. The German band on the steps of the Administration Building.

They invited me to spend a summer week with a family somewhere in Oakland and like a fool I let somebody come and take me by streetcar to this family. The place smelled, and I couldn't wait to get back. Every family has a smell. The smell in this family made me sick. I preferred the smell at Fred Finch which I no longer noticed.

I spent long days and years there, and the day I went away was a fine day. The locomotive came up with the train, and the four of us got aboard and sat down and the train began to go, and it went to Fresno, and I was seven, and I stayed in Fresno ten years.

I do not know what makes a writer, but it probably isn't happiness. A happy boy or man is not apt to need to write. But was there ever a happy boy? Is there ever a happy man?

In Oakland I woke up and began to notice and remember. In Fresno I went to work. The idea of going to work was my own. My brother Henry went to work selling *The Fresno Evening Herald*, so I went to work selling it, too. He was ten and a half and I was seven and a half. I went out into the streets and began to live in them. I had escaped from the orphanage at last. I had a home at last, the house at 2226 San Benito Avenue. I lived there with my mother, my sisters, and my brother. All through the city were branches of my father's family and branches of my mother's family. Each branch had its own house and its own members.

But the world was my home and I was glad to be in it.

Inside the world I found another world in the theatres of Fresno.

The Hippodrome had movies and vaudeville both, The Orpheum on Broadway had vaudeville only, The Liberty had movies only, and so it was with The Kinema and The Bijou. I got into all of these theatres free of charge through friendship with the ticket-takers or by sneaking in. I saw very nearly every movie that came to town, and very nearly every vaudeville show. This other world inside the real world was strange and wonderful. I found it necessary to inhabit this world, but I always attended to my work first, which was to sell papers.

My hope was to earn at least half a dollar every day. *The Herald* cost a nickel. Half was mine, half was the Herald's. If I sold two paper I had a profit of a nickel. If I sold twenty I had a profit of half a dollar. I had no regular customers. I sometimes sold twenty papers in a matter of minutes, and then sometimes I couldn't sell ten from half past three until half past eight or nine.

For a time it was permissible to turn in unsold papers, but this ruling was changed, so that if I took out twenty papers and sold only ten papers I had no profit for the day at all. The risk was great and now and then I sold only eight, losing a dime and taking home twelve papers.

Before I had been selling papers a month, though, I could get rid of twenty every afternoon and evening, so I took out twenty as a matter of course and hung on in the streets until I had sold them all, or had only three or four to go.

If it was very late I took one to a Greek candy store where I traded it for whatever the man there wanted to let me have, generally about a dime's worth of candy. I took another to the ticket-taker at the Liberty Theatre and went in and saw the show or part of it, and then I took one to the ticket-taker at the Hippodrome and went in there, too.

I sometimes didn't get home until after ten at night. When I was nine I sometimes didn't get home until the town was closed, or at any rate the theatres.

I loved the theatres, and even when I was hungry, I never spent money for food. The Greek's candy, and water, would be my food until I got home where I always knew there would be a pot on the stove full of something good to eat.

The streets made me, and the streets stink, but I love them, for I was born in them out of flesh and I was born in them out of spirit.

A WRITER'S DECLARATION

ON October 15, 1934, my first book, *The Daring Young Man on the Flying Trapeze and Other Stories,* was published. The year 1934 seems quite near, but the fact remains that it was twenty years ago, as I write. Many things happened in those twenty years, several of them to me.

I didn't earn one dollar by any means other than writing. I wrote short stories, plays, novels, essays, poems, book reviews, miscellaneous comment, letters to editors, private letters, and songs.

Nothing that I wrote was written to order, on assignment, or for money, although a good deal of what I wrote happened to earn money. If an editor liked a story as I had written it, he could buy it. If he wanted parts of it written over, I did not do that work. Nobody did it. One editor took liberties with a short piece about Christmas, and the writer of a cook book to which I had written a free Preface added a few lines by way of making me out a soldier-patriot. I protested to the editor and to the writer of the cook book, but of course the damage had been done. During the Second World War I wrote no propaganda of any kind, although I was invited several times to do so. The point is that for twenty years I have been an American writer who has been entirely free and independent.

I consider the past twenty years the first half of my life as a published writer, and the next twenty I consider the second half. At that time I shall be sixty-six years old, which can be very old, or not. I expect to be more creative in the next twenty years than I was in the first twenty, even though I start with a number of handicaps. To begin with, I owe so much in back taxes that it is very nearly impossible arithmetically to even the score by writing, and I have acquired other personal, moral, and financial responsibilities.

I have never been subsidized, I have never accepted money connected with a literary prize or award, I have never been endowed, and I have never received a grant or fellowship. A year or two after my first book was published I was urged by friends to file an application for a Guggenheim Fellowship. Against my better judgment I filed an application, which was necessarily if not deliberately haphazard. How should I know what I wanted to write, for instance? I couldn't possibly describe it. My application was turned down and I began to breathe freely again.

I am head over heels in debt. I expect to get out of debt by writing, or not at all. I have no savings account, no stocks or bonds, no real estate, no insurance, no cash, and no real property that is convertible into anything like a sum of money that might be useful. I simply have got to hustle for a living. I mention these matters impersonally, as facts, and not to arouse sympathy. I don't want any.

Had my nature been practical I might at this time know financial security, as it's called. There is nothing wrong with such security, I suppose, but I prefer another kind. I prefer to recognize the truth that I *must* work, and to believe that I *can*.

I squandered a great deal of money that I earned as a writer and I lost a lot of it gambling. It seems to have been my nature to squander and to gamble, that's all. I gave some away, perhaps a great deal. I am not unaware of the possible meaning of the discomfort I have felt when I have had money, and the compulsion I have had to get rid of it somehow or other. I think I have felt the need to be only a writer, a writing writer, and not a success of any kind.

The ability or compulsion to hoard money has always seemed to me a complicated if not offensive thing. And yet I have always had sympathy for those who have been experts at hoarding, at legal means by which not to pay taxes, at timely thrusts into new and profitable areas of money-making, such as investments, real estate, inventions, oil, uranium, government contracts, the backing of plays, manufacturing, and marketing. The noticeable shrewdness of such people has always amused me, even when I myself have been the party to be outwitted.

When I was in the Army, for instance, in the snow of Ohio, in the dead of winter, a very capable money-man who was quite rich and young and not in the Army flew from New York to Ohio to discuss with me changes he felt I ought to make in one of my plays on which he had paid me a thousand dollars in advance. I met him whenever the Army regulations permitted me to, and I heard him out, which took a great deal of time I would have preferred to keep to myself. The man talked around and around, and it suddenly occurred to me that what he was really trying to say but couldn't was that he didn't feel the play would be a hit, and that he was helpless not to do something about the thousand dollars. This did not astonish me. I took a check for a thousand dollars to his hotel and left it at the desk, along with a short note. I wanted to see if my hunch was right. It was. We were supposed to meet the following night. We didn't. He flew back to New York with the check, cashed it, and I never heard from him again. There was no legal, or even moral, reason for me to return the thousand dollars. I simply couldn't bear to see him so upset about the small sum of money, all the while pretending that he was concerned only about art.

At one of the biggest moving-picture factories in Hollywood, when I discovered that I had been hoodwinked into making a poor deal, I met the executives who had done the brilliant hoodwinking, I established that they *had* done it, and I got into my car and drove to San Francisco. I was informed several years later that I had left behind wages due me under the terms of the hoodwinking agreement that amounted to something between five and fifteen thousand dollars. I never investigated the matter. The factory and its chief beneficiaries were hoarding profits by the millions, working diligently and profitably with the government on shabby propaganda films, and yet six or seven of the executives found it absolutely necessary to act in unison and to outwit the writer of a story they wanted desperately, from which they acquired three or four more millions of dollars. I have no idea what they have done with their money, but I am sure it has been something cautious and useless.

Before my first book was published I was not a drinker, but soon after it came out I discovered the wisdom of drinking, and I think this is something worth looking into for a moment.

In 1935 I drank moderately, and traveled to Europe for the first time, but the following nine years, until I was drafted into the Army, I drank as much as I liked, and I frequently drank steadily for nine or ten hours at a time.

I was seldom drunk, however. I enjoyed the fun of drinking and talking loudly with friends—writers, painters, sculptors, newspapermen, and the girls and women we knew in San Francisco.

Drinking with good companions can be a good thing for a writer, but let a writer heed this humble and perhaps unnecessary warning: stop drinking when drinking tends to be an end in itself, for that is a useless end. I believe I have learned a lot while I have been drinking with friends, just as most of us may say we have learned a lot in sleep. There is, however, a recognizable limit to what may be learned by means of drinking.

In the writing that I have done during the past twenty years, what do I regret?

Nothing. Not one word.

Did I write enough?

No. No writer ever writes enough.

Might I have written differently? More intelligently, for instance? No.

First, I always tried my best, as I understand trying. Second, I believe I was quite intelligent all the time.

Then, what about the theory of certain critics and readers that my writing is unrealistic and sentimental?

Well, I think they are mistaken. In writing that is *effective* I don't think *anything* is unrealistic. As for my own writing, I think it has always been profoundly realistic if not ever superficially so. I don't think my writing is sentimental either, although it is a very sentimental thing to be a human being.

As I write, I am back in San Francisco, where I lived when my first book was published, where I have not lived in six or seven years, and the day is the thirteenth of October. I drove up from Malibu two days ago for a visit of ten or eleven days while my house on the beach is being painted inside and out. I did not drive to San Francisco in order to be here on the twentieth anniversary of the publication of my first book, but I shall be here on that day nevertheless.

Already I have walked in the various neighborhoods of San Francisco I have known, to notice again the various houses in which I have lived: 348 Carl Street, 1707 Divisadero, 2378 Sutter, 123 Natoma: and the various places in which I worked before I had had a story published in a national magazine: various branch offices of the Postal Telegraph Company—on Market Street in the Palace Hotel Building, on Powell Street at Market, on Taylor at Market in the Golden Gate Theatre Building, and at 405 Brannan, near Third.

I was a clerk and teletype operator in the first three offices, but I was the manager of the office on Brannan. I have always been a little proud of that, for I was the youngest manager of a Postal Telegraph branch office in America, nineteen years old and without a high school diploma.

Yesterday I walked through the Crystal Palace Market and visited the stand at which I once hustled potatoes and tomatoes, the *Fiore d'Italia.*

I went into the building at Market and Sixth where the offices of the Cypress Lawn Cemetery Company are located. I worked there, too.

The vice-president said, "Do you intend to make Cypress Lawn your lifetime career?"

I said, "Yes, sir."

I got the job.

I quit a month later, but working there was a valuable experience. I remember the arrival of Christmas week and the vice-president's bitter complaint that owing to the absence of an epidemic of influenza the company's volume of business for December over the previous year had fallen twenty-two per cent.

I remarked, "But everybody will catch up eventually, won't they?"

The vice-president lifted his glasses from the bridge of his nose to his forehead in order to have another look at me.

"I'm a writer," I said. "Unpublished."

He asked me to look at some slogans he had composed for the company: *Inter here. A lot for your money.*

I said he had a flair.

I walked along the Embarcadero to the Dodd Warehouse, across from Pier 17, for I worked there a month, too. The trouble with that job was the floating crap games of the longshoremen every lunch hour in empty boxcars or behind piles of lumber on the docks. My take-home pay every week was nothing, although I made a friend of the great Negro crapshooter and game manager who was called Dough-belly. The sunlight down there on the waterfront during those lunch-hour crap games was wonderful, and as I walked there yesterday I could almost see the huge old man calling the points of the game, and I had to remember that whenever he noticed I wasn't betting he correctly surmised that I was fresh out of funds and slipped me a silver dollar or two so that I might get back into the action.

Once, when I stayed away from the games for three days running in the hope of having a few dollars in my pocket for Saturday night, Doughbelly kept asking everybody, "Where's that Abyssinian boy?"

I was in the Dodd Warehouse eating sandwiches and reading Jack London, that's where I was.

It was at 348 Carl Street twenty years ago on this day, October 13, that I opened a package from Random House and saw a copy of my first book. That was a hell of a moment. I was so excited I couldn't roll a Bull Durham cigarette. After three tries I finally made it, and began to inhale and exhale a little madly as I examined the preposterous and very nearly unbelievable object of art and merchandise. What a book, what a cover, what a title page, what words, what a photograph—now just watch the women swarm around. For a young writer *does* write in order to expect pretty women to swarm around.

Alas, the swarmers aren't often pretty. This is a mystery that continues to baffle me. Pretty women swarm around fat little men who own and operate small businesses. They swarm around chiropractors who are full of talk about some of their interesting cases and achievements. They swarm around young men who wear black shirts and have five buttons on the sleeves of their sport coats, who have no visible means of support, who spend hours chatting amiably about last night's preposterous trivia as if it were history.

Pretty women swarm around everybody but writers.

Plain, intelligent women *somewhat* swarm around writers.

But it wasn't only to have pretty women swarm around that I hustled my first book into print. It wasn't that alone by a long shot.

I also meant to revolutionize American writing.

In the early thirties the word revolutionize enjoyed popularity and was altogether respectable, but a special poll invented by a special statistician would be the only means today by which to measure my success in revolutionizing American writing. To pretend that my writing hasn't had any effect at all on American writing, however, would be inaccurate. The trouble is that for the most part my writing influenced unpublished writers who remained unpublished, and to measure that kind of an influence calls for a lot of imagination and daring. The good writers that my writing influenced were already published, some of them long published, but the truth is that my writing *did* influence their writing, too, for I began to notice the improvement almost immediately. And I didn't notice it in short stories alone, I noticed it in novels and plays, and even in movies.

What did my writing have that might be useful to writing in general?

Freedom.

I think I demonstrated that if you have a writer, you have writing, and that the writer himself is of greater importance than his writing—until he quits, or is dead.

Thus, if you *are* a writer, you do not have to kill yourself every time you write a story, a play, or a novel.

But why did I want to revolutionize American writing?

I had to, because I didn't like it, and wanted to.

And why, as a writer, was I unwilling to act solemn? Didn't I know that unless I acted solemn the big critics would be afraid to write about my writing? I knew. I refused to act solemn because I didn't feel solemn. I didn't feel I *ought* to feel solemn, or even dignified, because I knew acting dignified was only a shadow removed from being pompous. Some writers are naturally solemn, dignified, or pompous, but that doesn't mean that they are also naturally great, or even effective.

There simply isn't any mysterious connection between solemnity and great writing. Some great writers had great solemnity, but most of them had almost none. They had something else.

What is this other thing?

I think it is an obsession to get to the probable truth about man, nature, and art, straight through everything to the very core of *one's own* being.

What is this probable truth?

It changes from day to day, certainly from year to year. You can measure the change from decade to decade, and the reason you can measure it is that there have been writers (and others) who have been obsessed about it, too.

To become free is the compulsion of our time—free of everything that is useless and false, however deeply established in man's fable. But this hope of freedom, this need of it, does not for a moment mean that man is to go berserk. Quite the contrary, since freedom, real freedom, true freedom, carries the life and fable of man nearer and nearer to order, beauty, grace, and meaning—all of which must always remain correctable in details—revised, improved, refined, enlarged, extended.

Intelligence *is* arriving into the fable of the life of man. It isn't necessarily welcome, though, certainly not in most quarters. In order to be a little less unwelcome it must be joined by humor, out of which the temporary best has always come. You simply cannot call the human race a dirty name unless you smile when you do so. The calling of the name may be necessary and the name itself may be temporarily accurate, but not to smile at the time is a blunder that nullifies usefulness, for without humor there is no hope, and man